A·N·N·U·A·L E·D·I·T·I·O·N·S

Human Development

99/00

Twenty-Seventh Edition

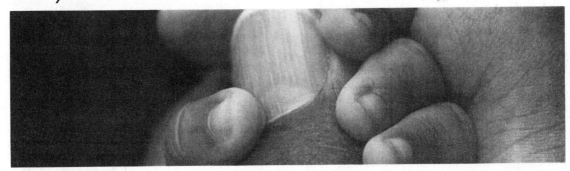

EDITOR

Karen L. Freiberg
University of Maryland, Baltimore County

Dr. Karen Freiberg has an interdisciplinary educational and employment background in nursing, education, and developmental psychology. She received her B.S. from the State University of New York at Plattsburgh, her M.S. from Cornell University, and her Ph.D. from Syracuse University. Freiberg has worked as a school nurse, a pediatric nurse, a public health nurse for the Navajo Indians, an associate project director for a child development clinic, a researcher in several areas of child development, and a university professor. She is the author of an award-winning textbook, *Human Development: A Life-Span Approach,* which is now in its fourth edition. Dr. Freiberg is currently on the faculty at the University of Maryland, Baltimore County.

Dushkin/McGraw-Hill
Sluice Dock, Guilford, Connecticut 06437

Visit us on the Internet
http://www.dushkin.com/annualeditions/

Credits

1. Genetic and Prenatal Influences on Development
Facing overview—Dushkin/McGraw-Hill illustration by Mike Eagle.
2. Development during Infancy and Early Childhood
Facing overview—© 1998 by Cleo Freelance Photography.
3. Development during Childhood: Cognition and Schooling
Facing overview—© 1998 by Cleo Freelance Photography.
4. Development during Childhood: Family and Culture
Facing overview—Dushkin/McGraw-Hill photo by Pamela Carley.
5. Development during Adolescence and Young Adulthood
Facing overview—© 1998 by Cleo Freelance Photography.
6. Development during Middle and Late Adulthood
Facing overview—© 1998 by PhotoDisc, Inc.

Copyright

Cataloging in Publication Data
Main entry under title: Annual Editions: Human development. 1999/2000.
1. Child study—Periodicals. 2. Socialization—Periodicals. 3. Old age—
Periodicals. I. Freiberg, Karen L., *comp.* II. Title: Human development.
ISBN 0-07-041365-7   155'.05   72-91973   HQ768.A44   ISSN 0278-4661

Twenty-Seventh Edition

Cover image © 1999 PhotoDisc, Inc.

Printed in the United States of America   1234567890BAHBAH54321098   Printed on Recycled Paper

iii

To the Reader

In publishing ANNUAL EDITIONS we recognize the enormous role played by the magazines, newspapers, and journals of the public press in providing current, first-rate educational information in a broad spectrum of interest areas. Many of these articles are appropriate for students, researchers, and professionals seeking accurate, current material to help bridge the gap between principles and theories and the real world. These articles, however, become more useful for study when those of lasting value are carefully collected, organized, indexed, and reproduced in a low-cost format, which provides easy and permanent access when the material is needed. That is the role played by ANNUAL EDITIONS.

New to ANNUAL EDITIONS is the inclusion of related World Wide Web sites. These sites have been selected by our editorial staff to represent some of the best resources found on the World Wide Web today. Through our carefully developed topic guide, we have linked these Web resources to the articles covered in this ANNUAL EDITIONS reader. We think that you will find this volume useful, and we hope that you will take a moment to visit us on the Web at *http://www.dushkin.com/* to tell us what you think.

Correction, vigilance, conscientiousness versus corruption, negligence, immorality: why do humans behave the way they do? Violence: we all see it (road rage, sports, videos, games, movies, TV, the news). Why do some people resist behaving aggressively while others explode? The world's economies: why do some cultures prosper while others are wiped out? What forces lead human development, for better or worse? Selecting a few representative articles of good quality is difficult due to the magnitude of the subject. I am grateful to all the members of my advisory board for helping me cull through the collection and select some of the best articles available for 99/00 to shed light on the above questions and on many others.

Annual Editions: Human Development 99/00 is organized according to the absolute time concept of chronos, chronological time, from conception through death. However, the reader should be aware of other relative time concepts: kairos (God's time); preterition (retrospective time), and futurity (prospective time); transientness (short duration) and diuturnity (long duration); and recurrent time. Human development is more akin to a continuous circle of life than to a line with a distinct beginning and end. Like stars whose light reaches us thousands of years after they expire, our ancestors influence our behaviors long after their deaths. Our hopes for our own futures and for our children's futures also predestine our development. With an eye to the circle of life, articles have been selected that bridge the gap left by clocked time and indiscreet ages and stages. Thus, prenatal articles may discuss adult development and late adulthood articles may focus on grandchildren.

As you explore this anthology, you will discover that many articles ask questions that have no answers. As a student, I felt frustrated by such writing. I wanted answers, right answers, right away. Part of the lessons in tolerance that are necessary to achieve maturity are lessons in accepting relativity and in acknowledging extenuating circumstances. Life frequently has no right or wrong answers but rather various alternatives with multiple consequences. Instead of right versus wrong, a more helpful consideration is "What will bring about the greater good for the greater number?" Controversies promote healthy mental exercise. Different viewpoints should be weighed against societal standards. Different cultural communities should be celebrated for what they offer in creativity and adaptability to changing circumstances. Many selections in this anthology reflect the cultural diversity and the cultural assimilation with which we live today.

The selections for *Annual Editions: Human Development 99/00* have attempted to reflect an ecological view of growth and change. Some articles deal with microsystems such as family, school, and employment. Some deal with exosystems such as television and community. Some writers discuss macrosystems such as economics and government. Most of the articles deal with mesosystems, those which link systems such as economics, health and nutrition, schools and culture, or heredity and environment. The unique individual's contribution to every system and every system linkage is always paramount.

We hope you will be energized and enriched by the readings in this compendium. Please complete and return the postage-paid article rating form on the last page to express your opinions. We value your input and will heed it in future revisions of *Annual Editions: Human Development*.

Karen Freiberg

Karen Freiberg, Ph.D.
Editor

Contents

A. GENETIC INFLUENCES

B. PRENATAL INFLUENCES

UNIT 1

Genetic and Prenatal Influences on Development

Eight selections discuss genetic influences on development, cloning, and the role of lifestyle, including the effects of substance abuse, on prenatal development.

The concepts in bold italics are developed in the article. For further expansion please refer to the Topic Guide and the Index.

v

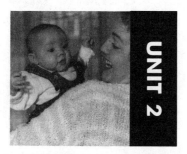

UNIT 2

Development during Infancy and Early Childhood

Six selections profile the impressive abilities of infants and young children, examine the ways in which children learn, and the development of empathy in early childhood.

The concepts in bold italics are developed in the article. For further expansion please refer to the Topic Guide and the Index.

UNIT 3

Development during Childhood: Cognition and Schooling

Seven selections examine human development during childhood, paying specific attention to social and emotional development, cognitive and language development, and development problems.

The concepts in bold italics are developed in the article. For further expansion please refer to the Topic Guide and the Index.

UNIT 4

Development during Childhood: Family and Culture

Seven selections discuss the impact
of home and culture on child rearing
and child development. The topics
include parenting styles, family
structure, and cultural influences.

The concepts in bold italics are developed in the article. For further expansion please refer to the Topic Guide and the Index.

UNIT 5

Development during Adolescence and Young Adulthood

Six selections explore a wide range of issues and topics concerning adolescence and early adulthood.

The concepts in bold italics are developed in the article. For further expansion please refer to the Topic Guide and the Index.

ix

UNIT 6

Development during Middle and Late Adulthood

Seven selections review a variety of biological and psychological aspects of aging, questioning the concept of set life stages.

The concepts in bold italics are developed in the article. For further expansion please refer to the Topic Guide and the Index.

B. LATE ADULTHOOD

The concepts in bold italics are developed in the article. For further expansion please refer to the Topic Guide and the Index.

Topic Guide

This topic guide suggests how the selections and World Wide Web sites found in the next section of this book relate to topics of traditional concern to human development students and professionals. It is useful for locating interrelated articles and Web sites for reading and research. The guide is arranged alphabetically according to topic.

The relevant Web sites, which are numbered and annotated on pages 4 and 5, are easily identified by the Web icon (⊚) under the topic articles. By linking the articles and the Web sites by topic, this ANNUAL EDITIONS reader becomes a powerful learning and research tool.

TOPIC AREA	TREATED IN	TOPIC AREA	TREATED IN
Adolescence	29. Growing Up Goes On and On 30. Adolescence: Whose Hell Is It? 31. What Is a Bad Kid? 32. Experts Scrambling on School Shootings ⊚ *1, 26, 27, 28, 29*		32. Experts Scrambling on School Shootings ⊚ *33, 21, 23, 26, 27, 28*
		Early Childhood	12. Your Child's Brain 13. Defining the Trait That Makes Us Human 14. Parents Speak ⊚ *6, 8, 9, 10, 11, 12, 14*
Aggression	20. Teaching Television 21. School Phobias 22. Fathers' Time 26. TV Violence: Myth and Reality 27. Biology of Soul Murder 31. What Is a Bad Kid? 32. Experts Scrambling on School Shootings ⊚ *2, 10, 13, 18, 21, 23, 27, 28*	**Education/ School**	13. Defining the Trait That Makes Us Human 18. Bell, Book, and Scandal 19. Death of Child Nature 20. Teaching Television 21. School Phobias 25. Effects of Poverty on Children 28. Cost of Children 31. What Is a Bad Kid? 37. Age Boom ⊚ *17, 19, 20*
Cognitive Development	7. Drug-Exposed Infants 9. Fertile Minds 11. Baby Talk 13. Defining the Trait That Makes Us Human 15. Genetics of Cognitive Abilities 16. Basing Teaching on Piaget's Constructivism 17. In Search of a Metatheory 25. Effects of Poverty on Children 30. Adolescence: Whose Hell Is It? 35. Man's World, Woman's World? 36. Memory 38. Studies Suggest Older Minds Are Stronger ⊚ *6, 9, 17, 18, 19, 20*	**Emotional Development/ Personality**	6. Maternal Emotions 7. Drug-Exposed Infants 9. Fertile Minds 10. Temperament and the Reactions to Unfamiliarity 12. Your Child's Brain 13. Defining the Trait That Makes Us Human 14. Parents Speak 22. Fathers' Time 23. Invincible Kids 24. Do Parents Really Matter? 25. Effects of Poverty on Children 29. Growing Up Goes On and On ⊚ *2, 5, 8, 13, 18, 23, 24, 25*
Creativity	19. Death of Child Nature ⊚ *15, 18, 19, 20*	**Ethics/Morality**	10. Temperament and the Reactions to Unfamiliarity 32. Experts Scrambling on School Shootings 39. Cure or Care? 40. DeathCare Business ⊚ *1, 2, 4*
Culture	6. Maternal Emotions 18. Bell, Book, and Scandal 19. Death of Child Nature 20. Teaching Television 27. Biology of Soul Murder 28. Cost of Children 37. Age Boom 39. Cure or Care? 40. DeathCare Business ⊚ *6, 9, 17, 18, 19, 20*	**Family/ Parenting**	13. Defining the Trait That Makes Us Human 14. Parents Speak 21. School Phobias 22. Fathers' Time 23. Invincible Kids 24. Do Parents Really Matter? 28. Cost of Children 30. Adolescence: Whose Hell Is It? 37. Age Boom ⊚ *22, 23, 24, 25*
Depression	29. Growing Up Goes On and On 30. Adolescence: Whose Hell Is It? ⊚ *26, 27, 28, 29*		
Divorce	33. Brain Sex and the Language of Love 34. Who Stole Fertility? ⊚ *22, 24, 25*	**Fertility**	3. Nature's Clones 34. Who Stole Fertility?
Drug Abuse	4. Role of Lifestyle 6. Maternal Emotions 7. Drug-Exposed Infants 8. Sperm under Siege 30. Adolescence: Whose Hell Is It? 31. What Is a Bad Kid?		

2

3

⊙ AE: Human Development

The following World Wide Web sites have been carefully researched and selected to support the articles found in this reader. If you are interested in learning more about specific topics found in this book, these Web sites are a good place to start. The sites are cross-referenced by number and appear in the topic guide on the previous two pages. Also, you can link to these Web sites through our DUSHKIN ONLINE support site at *http://www.dushkin.com/online/*.

The following sites were available at the time of publication. Visit our Web site—we update DUSHKIN ONLINE regularly to reflect any changes.

General Human Development Issues

1. Association for Moral Education
http://www.wittenberg.edu/ame/index.html
This association is dedicated to fostering communication, co-operation, training, curriculum development, and research that links moral theory to educational practices.

2. Behavior Analysis Resources
http://www.coedu.usf.edu/behavior/bares.htm
This site is dedicated to promoting the experimental, theoretical, and applied analysis of behavior. It encompasses contemporary scientific and social issues, theoretical advances, and the dissemination of professional and public information.

3. Healthfinder
http://www.healthfinder.org/default.htm
Healthfinder is a consumer health site that contains the latest health news, prevention and care choices, and information about every phase of human development.

4. Social Influence
http://www.public.asu.edu/~kelton/
This site focuses on persuasion, compliance, and propaganda and includes practical examples and applications.

Genetic and Prenatal Influences on Development

5. American Academy of Pediatrics
http://www.aap.org/
This organization provides data for optimal physical, mental, and social health for all children. The site links to professional educational sources and current research.

6. Basic Neural Processes
http://psych.hanover.edu/Krantz/neurotut.html
This highly interactive site provides an extensive tutorial on brain structures.

7. Evolutionary Psychology: A Primer
http://www.psych.ucsb.edu/research/cep/primer.htm
A complete paper on evolutionary psychology is at this site. A great deal of background information is included.

8. Human Genetics and Human Genome Project
http://www.kumc.edu/instruction/medicine/genetics/homepage.html
The University of Kansas Medical Center provides information on human genetics and the human genome project at this site. A number of links to research areas are available.

9. Serendip
http://serendip.brynmawr.edu/serendip/
Organized into five subject areas (brain and behavior, complex systems, genes and behavior, science and culture, and science education), this site contains interactive exhibits, articles, links to other resources, and a forum.

Development during Infancy and Early Childhood

10. Aggression and Cooperation: Helping Young Children Develop Constructive Strategies
http://ericps.crc.uiuc.edu/eece/pubs/digests/1992/jewett92.html
Jan Jewett wrote this ERIC Digest report on how to help children deal effectively with aggression. Helping children develop prosocial attitudes and behaviors is its goal.

11. Children's Nutrition Research Center (CNRC)
http://www.bcm.tmc.edu/cnrc/
CNRC, one of six USDA/ARS (Agricultural Research Service) facilities, is dedicated to defining the nutrient needs of healthy children, from conception through adolescence, and of pregnant and nursing mothers.

12. Early Childhood Care and Development
http://www.ecdgroup.com/
Child development theory, programming and parenting data, and research can be found at this site of the Consultative Group, which is dedicated to the improvement of conditions of young children at risk.

13. Society of Pediatric Psychology (SPP)
http://macserv.psy.miami.edu/SPP/
The homepage for the Society of Pediatric Psychology, which provides a forum for scientists and professionals who are interested in the health care of children, adolescents, and their families, links to publications and other sites.

14. Zero to Three: National Center for Infants, Toddlers, and Families
http://www.zerotothree.org/
This national organization is dedicated solely to infants, toddlers, and their families. It is headed by recognized experts in the field and provides technical assistance to communities, states, and the federal government.

Development during Childhood: Cognition and Schooling

15. Children Now
http://www.childrennow.org/
Children Now focuses on improving conditions for children who are poor or at risk. Articles include information on education, influence of media, health, and security.

16. Council for Exceptional Children
http://www.cec.sped.org/
This is the home page of the Council for Exceptional Children, which is dedicated to improving education for exceptional children and the gifted child.

17. Educational Resources Information Center (ERIC)
http://www.ed.gov/pubs/pubdb.html
This Web site is sponsored by the United States Department of Education and will lead to numerous documents related to elementary and early childhood education.

18. Federation of Behavioral, Psychological, and Cognitive Science

http://www.am.org/federation/

The Federation's mission is fulfilled through legislative and regulatory advocacy, education, and information dissemination to the scientific community. Hotlink to the National Institutes of Health's Project on the Decade of the Brain.

19. The National Association for the Education of Young Children (NAEYC)

http://www.naeyc.org/

The NAEYC is the nation's largest organization of professionals devoted to improving the quality of education programs for children from birth through the age of eight.

20. Project Zero

http://pzweb.harvard.edu/

Harvard's Project Zero has investigated the development of learning processes in children and adults for 30 years. Today, Project Zero is helping create communities of reflective, independent learners; to enhance deep understanding within disciplines; and to promote critical and creative thinking.

Development during Childhood: Family and Culture

21. Childhood Injury Prevention Interventions

http://weber.u.washington.edu/~hiprc/ childinjury//menu.html

This site offers systematic reviews of childhood injury prevention interventions on such diverse subjects as adolescent suicide, child abuse, accidental injuries, and youth violence.

22. Families and Work Institute

http://www.familiesandworkinst.org

The Families and Work Institute conducts policy research on issues related to the changing workforce and operates a national clearinghouse on work and family life.

23. National Committee to Prevent Child Abuse

http://www.childabuse.org/

This site is dedicated to the NCPCA's child abuse prevention efforts. It provides statistics, parenting tips, chapter data, and other resources.

24. The National Parent Information Network

http://ericps.crc.uiuc.edu/npin/

This NPIN site contains resources related to many of the controversial issues faced by parents raising children in contemporary society. Discussion groups are also available.

25. Parentsplace.com: Single Parenting

http://www.parentsplace.com/family/singleparent/

This resource focuses on issues concerning single parents and their children. The articles range from parenting children from infancy through adolescence.

Development during Adolescence and Young Adulthood

26. AMA - Adolescent Health On Line

http://www.ama-assn.org/adolhlth/adolhlth.htm

This AMA adolescent health initiative describes clinical preventive services that primary care physicians and other health professionals can provide to young people.

27. American Academy of Child and Adolescent Psychiatry

http://www.aacap.org/web/aacap/

This rich site provides up-to-date data on a host of topics: facts for families, public health, and clinical practice.

28. Ask NOAH About: Mental Health

http://www.noah.cuny.edu/illness/mentalhealth/ mental.html

An enormous resource, NOAH contains information about child and adolescent family problems, mental conditions and disorders, suicide prevention, and much more.

29. Biological Changes in Adolescence

http://www.personal.psu.edu/faculty/n/x/nxd10/ biologic2.htm

This site offers a discussion of puberty, sexuality, biological changes, cross-cultural differences, and nutrition for adolescents, including a look at obesity.

Development during Middle and Late Adulthood

30. The Alzheimer Page

http://www.biostat.wustl.edu/ALZHEIMER/

This site links to a wide range of sites devoted to Alzheimer's disease and dementia.

31. American Psychological Association's Division 20, Adult Development and Aging

http://www.iog.wayne.edu/APADIV20/lowdiv20.htm

Dedicated to studying the psychology of adult development and aging, this division provides links to research guides, laboratories, instructional resources, and other related areas.

32. Gero Web

http://www.iog.wayne.edu/GeroWebd/GeroWeb.html

This virtual library on aging contains information on gerontology, geriatrics, and the process of aging.

33. Goldenage.Net

http://elo.mediasrv.swt.edu/goldenage/intro.htm

Here is a great starting point for Internet research on aging topics such as housing and long term care, health, and nutrition. It links to home pages across the Web.

34. Grief Net

http://rivendell.org/

Produced by a nonprofit group, Rivendell Resources, this site provides many links to the Web on the bereavement process, resources for grievers, and support groups.

35. Huffington Center on Aging

http://www.hcoa.org/

The Huffington Center on Aging home page offers links to sites on aging and Alzheimer's disease.

We highly recommend that you review our Web site for expanded information and our other product lines. We are continually updating and adding links to our Web site in order to offer you the most usable and useful information that will support and expand the value of your Annual Editions. You can reach us at:
http://www.dushkin.com/annualeditions/.

www.dushkin.com/online/

Unit Selections

Genetic Influences

1. **The Struggle to Decipher Human Genes,** Nicholas Wade
2. **The World after Cloning,** Wray Herbert, Jeffrey L. Sheler, and Traci Watson
3. **Nature's Clones,** Jim Neimark

Parental Influences

4. **The Role of Lifestyle in Preventing Low Birth Weight,** Virginia Rall Chomitz, Lilian W. Y. Cheung, and Ellice Lieberman
5. **Behaviors of a Newborn Can Be Traced to the Fetus,** Beth Azar
6. **Maternal Emotions May Influence Fetal Behaviors,** Beth Azar
7. **Drug-Exposed Infants,** Lucy Salcido Carter and Carol S. Larson
8. **Sperm under Siege,** Anne Merewood

Key Points to Consider

❖ How much do we know about the human genome? Why do we want a complete genetic blueprint of humans?

❖ What controversies are emerging from cloning technology? How do you feel about the moral/ethical questions?

❖ Do studies of identical twins give answers to the age-old nature–nurture questions? What strategies can reduce the numbers of babies born with low birth weight and at risk of developmental disabilities?

❖ Why is prenatal tactile stimulation imperative to survival?

❖ How do women who are stressed or who smoke during pregnancy influence their baby's temperament?

❖ What is the status of drug abuse prevention and treatment programs for pregnant women?

❖ How do sperm contribute to prenatal development?

 **Links**   **www.dushkin.com/online/**

5. **American Academy of Pediatrics**
   http://www.aap.org/
6. **Basic Neural Processes**
   http://psych.hanover.edu/Krantz/neurotut.html
7. **Evolutionary Psychology: A Primer**
   http://www.psych.ucsb.edu/research/cep/primer.htm
8. **Human Genetics and Human Genome Project**
   http://www.kumc.edu/instruction/medicine/genetics/homepage.html
9. **Serendip**
   http://serendip.brynmawr.edu/serendip/

These sites are annotated on pages 4 and 5.

Genetic and Prenatal Influences on Development

In September 1998 a controversial book, *The Nurture Assumption*, was published. Readers were told that genes shape human development much more than other humans do. Personality, temperament, character, intelligence: these are the products of genes. Are they? For years people have assumed that parenting, education, nutrition, health care, peers, culture, and other nurturing human variables were more important than genes. Are they? The question may be hypothetical, but that does not mean it is not a heated topic for debate. Research in behavioral genetics, the field that studies the extent to which heredity shapes personality, has excited scientists with documentation of DNA pro- gramming for some human conduct. However, the unfolding of genetic potential still depends on prenatal nurture, and on all of the learning that takes place in the years of a person's life. Both nature and nurture are important. How they interact is yet to be resolved.

The human genome (23 pairs of chromosomes with their associated genes) is being mapped with great speed. As the arrangement of gene sites on chromosomes is uncovered, so too are genetic markers (DNA sequences associated with particular traits). This is of vast significance to students of human development. No longer are genes just thought of as important because some carry certain physical traits. Genes can be compared to an incredibly complicated computer program. They dictate every aspect of human development, including personality.

Human embryology (the study of the first through seventh weeks after conception) and human fetology (the study of the eighth week of pregnancy through birth) have given verification to the idea that behavior precedes birth. The developing embryo/fetus reacts to the internal and external environments provided by the mother and to substances that diffuse through the placental barrier from the mother's body. The embryo reacts to toxins (viruses, antigens) that pass through the umbilical cord. The fetus reacts to an enormous number of other stimuli. How the embryo/fetus reacts (e.g., weakly to strongly; positively to negatively) depends, in large part, on his or her genetic preprogramming. Genes and environment are so inextricably intertwined that the effect of each cannot be studied separately. Prenatal development always has strong genetic influences and vice versa.

The first article included in the genetic section of this unit is an overview of the work of the USA's National Human Genome Research Institute. It hopes to have the sequence of human genes mapped by 2005. Working in collaboration with geneticists worldwide, the American team is snipping and cloning and mapping and reducing and sequencing and reassembling strands of DNA. The article gives simple explanations of what these procedures mean.

The second article presents the most frequently asked questions about cloning today, such as "Could a human being be cloned?" and "Would a cloned person have its own soul?" Scientists, philosophers, and theologians, who are considered experts in these areas, have given perspicacious answers to each intriguing question. The exercise of reading the questions and answers will expand every reader's range of knowledge and, most probably, will stimulate many new questions.

The third genetic selection contemplates the phenomenon of twinning. Are identical twins nature's handmade clones? What behaviors, if any, of monozygotic twins are predetermined by their identical genes? Research studies are reviewed that both support and refute the twin evidence of biological behavior propensities.

The study of teratology (malformations of the embryo/fetus) and the study of normal prenatal development have historically focused on environmental factors. We know that the same environmental factors may influence uniquely developing fetuses in different ways due to their genes. Keeping individual differences in mind, certain teratogens are dangerous to all fetuses and certain nutrients are necessary for all fetuses.

The first article in the prenatal-influence section of this unit explores the role of the mother's lifestyle in protecting her baby from, or subjecting her baby to, an at-risk birth status. The authors discuss not only lifestyle choices but also demographic and stress risks, assessment of risk factors, barriers to change, and directions for prevention and intervention. It is an important paper that highlights the need for healthy mothers in order to have healthy babies.

The second and third prenatal-influence selections are excellent discussions of the impact of prenatal environments on the genetically predetermined potentialities for development. The second article focuses on sensory systems (smell, taste, touch, and balance) and on motoric responsivity. The activity of the fetus *in utero* is reflected in the behavior and activity of the baby *ex utero*. Knowledge of prenatal behavior can help researchers discover where and when physical development might go wrong. The third article focuses on emotional development ex utero and how it may be affected by maternal stress and maternal hormone levels in utero. Even small changes in a pregnant woman's moods are reflected in fetal emotional responsivity as measured by heart rate and movement.

The fourth article is an update on how pregnant women are being educated on the dangers that prenatal ingestion of drugs poses to unborn fetuses, and on how known substance-abusing pregnant women are being treated.

The fifth article in the prenatal section has been retained once again, despite its age, because of rave reviews from readers. The contributions of fathers to prenatal growth and change have long been overlooked. This article discusses how important it is for prospective fathers to practice health maintenance and to protect themselves from toxins (chemicals, alcohol, tobacco, drugs) for their sperm's sake. It is an eye-opening article for both males and females.

The Struggle to Decipher Human Genes

By NICHOLAS WADE

ST. LOUIS

I N a drab gray building in the industrial outskirts of St. Louis, a team of some 200 people is working 19 hours a day in pursuit of the ultimate self-knowledge. They are spearheading the effort to sequence the human genome by 2005.

The odds of success at this point are not overwhelming. At the end of this month, the project will be halfway through its planned 15-year course, yet only 3 percent of the genome has been completed. Of the nine American centers involved in the pursuit, just one, the Genome Sequencing Center here in St. Louis, is deciphering human DNA at a significant rate. Its only peer is the Sanger Center in Hinxton, England. Together the two centers have produced half of the 106 million letters of human DNA so far completed.

The goal of sequencing the entire three billion letters of human DNA is not just technically ambitious. The coiled double ribbon of DNA holds the genetic instructions to make and operate the human organism. It bears the record of how humans differ from apes, the saga of early human migrations and the program-

> **Translating the mysteries of the human spirit into biochemistry.**

ming variations that help make each individual unique. The genome is the basis for much of what scientists can hope to explain about the physical aspects of human life.

"For the first time, we humans are reducing ourselves down to DNA sequences," said Dr. Robert Weinberg, a leading cancer biologist at the Whitehead Institute in Boston. "We're not talking about how butterflies fly or trees grow: we are dealing here with the mystery of the human spirit. Analysis of these sequences will not define the essence of humanity, but aspects of human beings that have hitherto been as awe-inspiring will be reduced to rather banal biochemical explanations, and that's not altogether heartening—maybe the mystery is good."

As might be expected in so ambitious an undertaking, opinions differ as to whether the full human sequence can be completed on schedule. Dr. Francis S. Collins, the director of the National Human Genome Research Institute, said he was "quite optimistic this goal will be achieved, and without depending on a bolt-from-the-blue breakthrough." But the costs of sequencing are not coming down as fast as hoped, and the scientists involved in the effort are concerned that the necessary resources may not be available. One of them, Dr. Craig Venter of the Institute for Genomic Research in Rockville, Md., said that "every single group has fallen behind, even us."

The genome project has always seemed a stretch, and it still depends on an invent-as-you-go approach. For no other animal, not even the simplest, has the full genetic programming yet been decoded. Only recently have the first bacteria, with genomes of a mere one million or so letters of DNA, yielded to sequencing, the term for working out the order of the chemical units in DNA. The human genome is 3,000 times as large.

Sequencing the human genome is a tangible goal but only part of a much larger endeavor, that of understanding what the genetic instructions in the genome mean. Post-genomics, as this interpretive process is sometimes called, has already begun in earnest. A new discipline known as bioinformatics, or computational biology, has sprung up to handle and interpret the streams of DNA now entering computer data bases. GenBank, the DNA data base run by the National Center for Biotechnology Information, already holds more than a billion DNA bases from human and other species, and has grown so popular that some 8,000 biologists consult it daily.

Another spur to post-genomics has been a technique for fishing out small snippets of genes from the genome. The DNA sequence of these fragments can be programmed into a new device called a DNA chip, enabling the chip to tell which genes are expressed, or switched on, in particular tissues of the body. Biologists can now hope to understand many diseases at the level of the human cell by comparing gene expression in normal and diseased tissue.

"The fruits of the genome project will enormously speed our efforts to understand human diseases, both inherited and those that strike in lifetime," Dr. Weinberg said.

So vigorous is the thrust into post-genomics that those responsible for sequencing the DNA fear they may not get the support to complete their task on schedule. "You can't divert resources to other things without suffering on the sequencing," said Dr. Robert H. Waterston, director of the Genome Sequencing Center, which is part of the Washington University School of Medicine in St. Louis.

Dr. Waterston presides over a remarkable enterprise, which is part research laboratory and part industrial process. His colleagues, as arcane a group of specialists as one could find, are known as mappers, sequencers, finishers and annotators.

Biologists make their first serious foray into Big Science.

The mappers take fragments of human DNA and try to map them to the exact position on the chromosome from which they were derived. The 23 pairs of human chromosomes are the units in which the DNA is packaged, and the St. Louis center is currently focusing on chromosome No. 7, which is 170 million DNA letters, or base pairs, long.

The mapped fragments, each about 150,000 base pairs of DNA in length, are handed over to the four teams of sequencers, who break them down into shorter pieces some 1,500 bases long. These are fed into the center's 70 Applied Biosystems sequencing machines. In a clever process worked out by Frederick Sanger of Britain, the machines tag the DNA with four different dyes, one for each of the four letters in the DNA alphabet. The order in which the colors stream out of the machines represents the order of the bases in the DNA.

The finishers' job is to arrange the short sequences of DNA so that they overlap, allowing that of the parent fragments to be reconstructed. The problem is that in many cases the sequences do not overlap because the DNA has evaded one or another of the steps in the production process. The finishers have ways of bridging the gaps, some of which have been automated, but closing the gaps remains one of the major technical obstacles in the genome project.

The finishers rely heavily on two computer programs written by Philip Green of the University of Washington in Seattle. One program, named Phred, scans the output of the sequencing machines and calls the order of the bases along with the level of confidence that can be placed in each call.

The other, Phrap, tries to assemble the emerging sequences into overlapping sections. Much of the task is like the mental torture of doing a jigsaw puzzle in which all the pieces are virtually identical. The reason is that some 97 percent of human DNA consists of a variety of identical sequences repeated over and over. The repetitive sequences have no known function and used to be called junk DNA.

Perhaps foreseeing limits on Congress's interest in paying to sequence junk, biologists now refer to these DNA wastelands more delicately as "noncoding DNA," meaning DNA that does not code for genes. Only 3 percent of the human genome specifies working genes, of which there are thought to be between 60,000 and 100,000.

The world's biologists are so eager to get their hands on the data that new DNA sequences are posted every night on the center's Web site. But months more work may remain as the raw data are checked for accuracy, the present standard being no more than one error per 10,000 bases, and analyzed by the annotators.

The annotators' job, the culmination of the whole process, is to locate and identify genes. Picking out human genes from a DNA sequence is not easy: there is no punctuation, no known "start here" signal, just eyeglazing rows of A's, G's, T's and C's—the four letters of the DNA alphabet. The full genome, when and if ever printed out, would take up 200 volumes the size of telephone directories of 1,000 pages each. More probably it will just be recorded on a CD-ROM.

Analysis of the human genetic program is entrusted to computer programs as much as possible. The computer marks the sites of probable genes and, where possible, assigns the genes a function by comparing their DNA sequences with those of genes of known function from other species. Finally, large chunks of annotated DNA sequence are submitted to GenBank.

A foretaste of the fruits to be expected from sequencing the human genome is emerging from that of the C. elegans roundworm, whose genome is 100 million base pairs long, about the size of a single human chromosome. The worm's genome is being sequenced at a cost of $40 million at the Genome Sequencing Center and at the Sanger Center in Britain. The effort, which is almost complete, served as a test run for the techniques being used with the human genome. Early success with the worm helped Dr. Waterston and his English colleague, Dr. John E. Sulston, to persuade skeptical colleagues in 1993 that they were ready to move from the mapping to the sequencing phase of the human genome.

The worm's genome is of enormous interest to the biologists who are studying the organism, and their findings will help interpret the human genome, because the two organisms, despite their evolutionary distance, have genes of similar DNA sequence.

To help understand the C. elegans genome, the St. Louis center has been sequencing the genome of another species of roundworm, known as C. briggsae. The genes of the two worms turn out to be very similar, but the noncoding DNA between the genes is entirely different. The pattern demonstrates the power of natural selection, the motive force of evolution: the noncoding regions of DNA are evidently free to mutate without constraint, whereas the DNA that codes for genes must stay more or less constant so as to avoid generating a misshapen protein that will kill the organism.

Is the human genome project going well? To judge by all the postgenomic activity, and the enormous recent investment in genomics by the pharmaceutical industry, the project is already a startling success. But will it be finished on time?

At a meeting of the genome project's main participants last month in Bermuda, a chart was displayed comparing how much DNA each center had promised to sequence at last year's meeting and how much it had in fact done. "It was a useful reality check," Dr. Collins said, suggesting that some of the promises might have been efforts to impress financing agencies.

The human genome project is biologists' first serious foray into Big Science, an endeavor with which physicists have long been familiar in the form of constructing particle accelerators. One physicist, Dr. Steven E. Koonin, vice president of the California Institute of Technology, headed a group of physicists that criticized the human genome project recently for its lack of central coordination. "The managerial structure is much looser than in a physics project," he said.

Biologists, who take pride in the project's very lack of central control, do not respond to the physicists' opinions with conspicuous deference. But Dr. Koonin's concerns about the lack of good comparative cost data from the different sequencing centers are echoed by an internal critic. "I have been calling the group of scientists involved in human sequencing the Liars' Club," said Dr. Venter, a biologist of independent views who has his own institute. "They all have a different way of calculating their costs and the amount of sequencing they have actually accomplished."

Comparative cost is an issue the sequencers at the Bermuda meeting agreed should now be seriously addressed. Dr. Waterston said his center had brought its operating costs down to 40 cents per DNA base. But even at that price, completing the genome would cost $1.2 billion.

Sequencing the human genome would be cheap at almost any price, Dr. Venter noted, given that the search for the Huntington's disease gene alone cost more than $100 million. But he doubted if costs could fall much more because competition is driving up wages.

Dr. Venter also believes that the mapping problem has not yet been solved. "A billion was spent to map the genome, but out of all the upfront money spent for mapping, there are no sequence-ready clones," Dr. Venter said, referring to the essential first step of acquiring DNA fragments of known position on the chromosomes.

Dr. Collins, the National Institutes of Health's director for the genome project, said that there was "no major technical problem" in mapping the fragments and that Dr. Venter, who does not do his own mapping, was probably worried about keeping his sequencing machines busy.

Dr. Collins said that getting the human DNA sequence completed was a higher priority for his institute than the interpretive projects. "We are not going to take our eyes off the ball," he said in reference to Dr. Waterston's concerns about a diversion of effort.

The C. elegans genome, which served as the pilot project for that of the human genome, is nearing completion but the hardest parts of the sequence, like closing the remaining gaps, have been left until last.

"I doubt the worm will be finished this decade if they are held to the standard of closing all the gaps," Dr. Venter said.

Dr. Waterston, however, said that the worm's genome would be completed by the end of this year and that the remaining problems were manageable.

Dr. David Botstein, a leading biologist at Stanford University who has helped shape the human genome project, said that in his view the enterprise was reasonably well on track, despite having received about half the money originally envisioned.

The National Academy of Sciences committee that gave the project its imprimatur "assumed that virtually all the sequencing would be done during the last half of the project, so there's no cause for alarm at that end," Dr. Botstein said. The cost of sequencing has not fallen as much as hoped, he said, but he added that it "doesn't have to fall much further to be affordable and doable in the time required."

"It seems almost a miracle to me," Dr. James Watson, the co-discoverer of DNA, wrote recently, "that 50 years ago we could have been so ignorant of the genetic material and now can imagine that we will have the complete genetic blueprint of man." Dr. Watson said he was not disheartened by the state of progress reported at the Bermuda meeting, even though he had not foreseen that "everyone would regard the genome as gold," making it hard for the sequencers to prevent trained people from being hired away by pharmaceutical companies.

Sequencing efficiently is still difficult but "St. Louis does it beautifully, so it can be done," Dr. Watson said.

The world after cloning

A reader's guide to what Dolly hath wrought

By Wray Herbert, Jeffery L. Sheler, and Traci Watson

At first it was just plain startling. Word from Scotland last week that a scientist named Ian Wilmut had succeeded in cloning an adult mammal—a feat long thought impossible—caught the imagination of even the most jaded technophobe. The laboratory process that produced Dolly, an unremarkable-looking sheep, theoretically would work for humans as well. A world of clones and drones, of *The Boys From Brazil* and *Multiplicity,* was suddenly within reach. It was science fiction come to life. And scary science fiction at that.

In the wake of Wilmut's shocker, governments scurried to formulate guidelines for the unknown, a future filled with mind-boggling possibilities. The Vatican called for a worldwide ban on human cloning. President Clinton ordered a national commission to study the legal and ethical implications. Leaders in Europe, where most nations already prohibit human cloning, began examining the moral ramifications of cloning other species.

Like the splitting of the atom, the first space flight, and the discovery of "life" on Mars, Dolly's debut has generated a long list of difficult puzzles for scientists and politicians, philosophers and theologians. And at dinner tables and office coolers, in bars and on street corners, the development of wild scenarios spun from the birth of a simple sheep has only just begun. *U.S. News* sought answers from experts to the most intriguing and frequently asked questions.

Why would anyone want to clone a human being in the first place?

The human cloning scenarios that ethicists ponder most frequently fall into two broad categories: 1) parents who want to clone a child, either to provide transplants for a dying child or to replace that child, and 2) adults who for a variety of reasons might want to clone themselves.

Many ethicists, however, believe that after the initial period of uproar, there won't be much interest in cloning humans. Making copies, they say, pales next to the wonder of creating a unique human being the old-fashioned way.

Could a human being be cloned today? What about other animals?

It would take years of trial and error before cloning could be applied successfully to other mammals. For example, scientists will need to find out if the donor egg is best used when it is resting quietly or when it is growing.

Will it be possible to clone the dead?

Perhaps, if the body is fresh, says Randall Prather, a cloning expert at the University of Missouri-Columbia. The cloning method used by Wilmut's lab requires fusing an egg cell with the cell containing the donor's DNA. And that means the donor cell must have an intact membrane around its DNA. The membrane starts to fall apart after death, as does DNA. But, yes, in theory at least it might be possible.

Can I set up my own cloning lab?

Yes, but maybe you'd better think twice. All the necessary chemicals and equipment are easily available and relatively low-tech. But out-of-pocket costs would run $100,000 or more, and that doesn't cover the pay for a skilled developmental biologist. The lowest-priced of these scientists, straight out of graduate school, makes about $40,000 a year. If you tried to grow the cloned embryos to maturity, you'd encounter other difficulties. The Scottish team implanted 29 very young clones in 13 ewes, but only one grew into a live lamb. So if you plan to clone Fluffy, buy enough cat food for a host of surrogate mothers.

Would a cloned human be identical to the original?

Identical genes don't produce identical people, as anyone acquainted with identical twins can tell you. In fact, twins are more alike than clones would be, since they have at least shared the uterine environment, are usually raised in the same family, and so forth. Parents could clone a second child who eerily resembled their first in appearance, but all the evidence suggests the two would have very different personalities. Twins separated at birth do sometimes share quirks of personality, but such quirks in a cloned son or daughter would be haunting reminders of the child who was lost—and the failure to re-create that child.

Even biologically, a clone would not be identical to the "master copy." The clone's cells, for example, would have energy-processing machinery (mitochondria) that came from the egg donor, not from the nucleus donor. But most of the physical differences between originals and copies wouldn't be detectable without a molecular-biology lab. The one possible exception is fertility. Wilmut and his coworkers are not sure that Dolly will be able to have lambs. They will try to find out once she's old enough to breed.

Will a cloned animal die sooner or have other problems because its DNA is older?

Scientists don't know. For complex biological reasons, creating a clone from an older animal differs from breeding an older animal in the usual way. So clones of adults probably wouldn't risk the same birth defects as the offspring of older women, for example. But the age of the DNA used for the clone still might

From *U.S. News & World Report,* March 10, 1997, pp. 59-63. © 1997 by U.S. News & World Report. Reprinted by permission.

affect life span. The Scottish scientists will monitor how gracefully Dolly ages.

What if parents decided to clone a child in order to harvest organs?

Most experts agree that it would be psychologically harmful if a child sensed he had been brought into the world simply as a commodity. But some parents already conceive second children with nonfatal bone marrow transplants in mind, and many ethicists do not oppose this. Cloning would increase the chances for a biological match from 25 percent to nearly 100 percent.

If cloned animals could be used as organ donors, we wouldn't have to worry about cloning twins for transplants. Pigs, for example, have organs similar in size to humans'. But the human immune system attacks and destroys tissue from other species. To get around that, the Connecticut biotech company Alexion Pharmaceuticals Inc. is trying to alter the pig's genetic codes to prevent rejection. If Alexion succeeds, it may be more efficient to mass-produce porcine organ donors by cloning than by current methods, in which researchers inject pig embryos with human genes and hope the genes get incorporated into the embryo's DNA.

Wouldn't it be strange for a cloned twin to be several years younger than his or her sibling?

When the National Advisory Board on Ethics in Reproduction studied a different kind of cloning a few years ago, its members split on the issue of cloned twins separated in time. Some thought the children's individuality might be threatened, while others argued that identical twins manage to keep their individuality intact.

John Robertson of the University of Texas raises several other issues worth pondering: What about the cloned child's sense of free will and parental expectations? Since the parents chose to duplicate their first child, will the clone feel obliged to follow in the older sibling's footsteps? Will the older child feel he has been duplicated because he was inadequate or because he is special? Will the two have a unique form of sibling rivalry, or a special bond? These are, of course, just special versions of questions that come up whenever a new child is introduced into a family.

Could a megalomaniac decide to achieve immortality by cloning an "heir"?

Sure, and there are other situations where adults might be tempted to clone themselves. For example, a couple in which the man is infertile might opt to clone one of them rather than introduce an outsider's sperm. Or a single woman might choose to clone herself rather than involve a man in any way. In both cases, however, you would have adults raising children who are also their twins—a situation ethically indistinguishable from the megalomaniac cloning himself. On adult cloning, ethicists are more united in their discomfort. In fact, the same commission that was divided on the issue of twins was unanimous in its conclusion that cloning an adult's twin is "bizarre . . . narcissistic and ethically impoverished." What's more, the commission argued that the phenomenon would jeopardize our very sense of who's who in the world, especially in the family.

How would a human clone refer to the donor of its DNA?

"Mom" is not right, because the woman or women who supplied the egg and the womb would more appropriately be called Mother. "Dad" isn't right, either. A traditional father supplies only half the DNA in an offspring. Judith Martin, etiquette's "Miss Manners," suggests, "Most honored sir or madame." Why? "One should always respect one's ancestors," she says, "regardless of what they did to bring one into the world."

That still leaves some linguistic confusion. Michael Agnes, editorial director of *Webster's New World Dictionary,* says that "clonee" may sound like a good term, but it's too ambiguous. Instead, he prefers "original" and "copy." And above all else, advises Agnes, "Don't use 'Xerox.' "

A scientist joked last week that cloning could make men superfluous. Is it true?

Yes, theoretically. A woman who wanted to clone herself would not need a man. Besides her DNA, all she would require are an egg and a womb—her own or another woman's. A man who wanted to clone himself, on the other hand, would need to buy the egg and rent the womb—or find a very generous woman.

What are the other implications of cloning for society?

The gravest concern about the misuse of genetics isn't related to cloning directly, but to genetic engineering—the deliberate manipulation of genes to enhance human talents and create human beings according to certain specifications. But some ethicists also are concerned about the creation of a new (and stigmatized) social class: "the clones." Albert Jonsen of the University of Washington believes the confrontation could be comparable to what occurred in the 16th century, when Europeans where perplexed by the unfamiliar inhabitants of the New World and endlessly debated their status as humans.

Whose pockets will cloning enrich in the near future?

Not Ian Wilmut's. He's a government employee and owns no stock in PPL Therapeutics, the British company that holds the rights to the cloning technology. On the other hand, PPL stands to make a lot of money. Also likely to cash in are pharmaceutical and agricultural companies and maybe even farmers. The biotech company Genzyme has already bred goats that are genetically engineered to give milk laced with valuable drugs. Wilmut and other scientists say it would be much easier to produce such animals with cloning than with today's methods. Stock breeders could clone champion dairy cows or the meatiest pigs.

Could cloning be criminally misused?

If the technology to clone humans existed today, it would be almost impossible to prevent someone from cloning you without your knowledge or permission, says Philip Bereano, professor of technology and public policy at the University of Washington. Everyone gives off cells all the time—whenever we give a blood sample, for example, or visit the dentist—and those cells all contain one's full complement of DNA. What would be the goal of such "drive-by" cloning? Well, what if a woman were obsessed with having the child of an apathetic man? Or think of the commercial value of a dynasty-building athletic pedigree or a heavenly singing voice. Even though experience almost certainly shapes these talents as much as genetic gifts, the unscrupulous would be unlikely to be deterred.

Is organized religion opposed to cloning?

Many of the ethical issues being raised about cloning are based in theology. Concern for preserving human dignity and individual freedom, for example, is deeply rooted in religious and biblical principles. But until last week there had been surprisingly little theological discourse of the implications of cloning per se. The response so far from the religious community, while overwhelmingly negative, has been far from monolithic.

Roman Catholic, Protestant, and Jewish theologians all caution against applying the new technology to humans, but for varying reasons. Catholic opposition stems largely from the church's belief that "natural moral law" prohibits most kinds of tampering with human reproduction. A 1987 Vatican document, *Donum Vitae,* condemned cloning because it violates "the dignity both of human procreation and of the conjugal union."

Protestant theology, on the other hand, emphasizes the view that nature is "fallen" and subject to improvement. "Just because something occurs naturally doesn't mean it's automatically good," explains Max Stackhouse of Princeton Theological Seminary. But while they tend to support using technology to fix flaws in nature, Protestant theologians say cloning of humans crosses the line. It places too much power in the hands of sinful humans, who, says philosophy Prof. David Fletcher of Wheaton College in Wheaton, Ill., are subject to committing "horrific abuses."

Judaism also tends to favor using technology to improve on nature's shortcomings, says Rabbi Richard Address of the Union of American Hebrew Congregations. But cloning humans, he says, "is an area where we cannot go. It violates the mystery of what it means to be human."

Doesn't cloning encroach on the Judeo-Christian view of God as the creator of life? Would a clone be considered a creature of God or of science?

Many theologians worry about this. Cloning, at first glance, seems to be a usurpation of God's role as creator of humans "in his own image." The scientist, rather than God or chance, determines the outcome. "Like Adam and Eve, we want to be like God, to be in control," says philosophy Prof. Kevin Wildes of Georgetown University. "The question is, what are the limits?"

But some theologians argue that cloning is not the same as creating life from scratch. The ingredients used are alive or contain the elements of life, says Fletcher of Wheaton College. It is still only God, he says, who creates life.

Would a cloned person have its own soul?

Most theologians agree with scientists that a human clone and its DNA donor would be separate and distinct persons. That means each would have his or her own body, mind, and soul.

Would cloning upset religious views about death, immortality, and even resurrection?

Not really. Cloned or not, we all die. The clone that outlives its "parent"—or that is generated from the DNA of a dead person, if that were possible—would be a different person. It would not be a reincarnation or a resurrected version of the deceased. Cloning could be said to provide immortality, theologians say, only in the sense that, as in normal reproduction, one might be said to "live on" in the genetic traits passed to one's progeny.

Nature's Clones

Can genes explain our passions and prejudices, the mates we choose, that mystery we call the self? New research on twins upsets some of our most cherished notions about how we become who we are—and gives nature and nurture a whole new meaning. By JILL NEIMARK

Last April I went down to West 27th Street in Manhattan to sit in the audience of the *Maury Povich* show, and meet four sets of identical twins who had been separated at birth and adopted into different families. I wanted to see if the same soul stared out of those matched pairs of eyes, to contemplate the near miracle of DNA—double helix twisting around itself like twin umbilical cords—ticking out a perfect code for two copies of a human. One pair, a Polish nun and a Michigan housewife, had been filmed at the airport by CNN the week before, reunited for the first time in 51 years and weeping in each other's arms, marveling at their instinctive rapport. Yet how alike were they really, if one spent her days on rescue missions to places like Rwanda, while the other cleaned houses to supplement her husband's income?

Twins are nature's handmade clones, doppelgangers moving in synchrony through circumstances that are often eerily similar, as if they were unwitting dancers choreographed by genes or fate or God, thinking each other's thoughts, wearing each other's clothes, exhibiting the same quirks and odd habits. They leave us to wonder about our own uniqueness and loneliness, and whether it's possible to inhabit another person's being. Twins provoke questions about the moment our passions first ignite—for they have been seen on sonogram in the womb, kissing, punching, stroking each other. They are living fault lines in the ever shifting geography of the nature/nurture debate, and their peculiar puzzle ultimately impacts politics, crime and its punishment, education, and social policy. It isn't such a short leap from studies of behavioral genetics to books like the infamous *The Bell Curve* (by Richard Herrnstein and Charles Murray) and a kind of sotto-voce eugenics. And so everything from homosexuality to IQ, religious affiliation, alcoholism, temperament, mania, depression, height, weight, mortality, and schizophrenia has been studied in identical and fraternal twins and their relatives.

Yet the answers—which these days seem to confirm biology's power—raise unsettling questions. Twin research is flawed, provocative, and fascinating, and it topples some of our most cherished notions—the legacies of Freud and Skinner included—such as our beliefs that parenting style makes an irrevocable difference, that we can mold our children, that we are free agents piecing together our destinies.

Today, we've gone twin-mad. Ninety thousand people gather yearly at the International Twins Day Festival in Twinsburg, Ohio. We're facing a near epidemic of twins. One in 50 babies born this year will have a fraternal or identical double; the number of such births rose 33 percent in 1994 alone, peaking at over 97,000—largely due to women delaying childbirth (which skewers the odds in favor of twins) and to the fertility industry, which relies on drugs that superovulate would-be mothers. Recently, a stunning scientific feat enabled an ordinary sheep to give up a few cells and produce a delayed identical twin—a clone named Dolly, who was born with her donor's 6-year-old nucleus in every cell of her body. The international furor this Scottish lamb engendered has at its heart some of the same wonder and fear that every twin birth evokes. Twins are a break, a rift in the customary order, and they call into question our own sense of self. Just how special and unique are we?

The history of twins is rich with stories that seem to reveal them as two halves of the same self—twins adopted into different families falling down stairs at the same age, marrying and miscarrying in the same year, identical twins inventing secret languages, "telepathic" twins seemingly connected across thousands of miles, "evil" twins committing arson or murder together, conjoined twins sharing a single body, so that when one coughs the other reflexively raises a hand to cover the first one's mouth. And yet the lives of twins are full of just as many instances of discordance, differences, disaffection. Consider the 22-year-old Korean twins, Sunny and

MY TWIN MARRIAGE

A few years ago, I was playing the messages back on my answering machine just as my husband, Jeff, was coming into the apartment. He heard a familiar voice and ran for the answering machine.

"It's Phil!" he yelled, shrugging out of his coat. "Pick up the phone. Phil's calling."

Only it wasn't Phil. It was Phil's identical twin brother, Jeff.

"Oh, it's me," my husband said sheepishly. Sheepish in the sense of Dolly, the cloned sheep.

When I was first dating Jeff, the prospect of marrying an identical twin seemed magical. Jeff spoke of his brother as if he were talking about himself, almost as if he could bi-locate and live two contrasting yet mutually enriching lives. Jeff worked at a literary agency in Manhattan and loved boy fiction, thrillers, and horror novels, while Phil was overtly spiritual, editing a journal dedicated to the study of myth and tradition. When they were together they seemed to merge into one complex yet cohesive personality. They talked like hyper-bright little boys, each of them bringing equal heat and erudition to Stephen King and esoteric teachings, baseball, and the possibility of spiritual transformation. They argued—and still argue—like Trotsky and Lenin, desperate to define themselves as individuals, yet they define themselves against each other. Jeff and Phil love their wives and children, but they obey the orders they get from the mothership of their identical DNA.

My husband and his twin brother live by E. M. Forster's admonition, "Only connect." The pair e-mail each other at their respective offices two, four, even more times a day. A few weeks ago, Phil wrote Jeff that he was trying to decide his favorite 10 films of all time. He listed *Journey to the Center of the Earth, Star Wars,* seven other boy classics, and asked for Jeff's help thinking up a 10th.

"Phil and I decided that *Jurassic Park* is our favorite movie of all time," announced Jeff the other evening at dinner. In the course of dozens of soothing little dispatches Phil's movie list and Jeff's movie list had become one.

My marriage to Jeff has locked me into a triangle. The bond between these twins amazes and amuses me, yet it fills me with an unappeasable longing. After all, unlike Phil's wife, Carol, who is an only child, I was conditioned even before I was born to be with a twin. I am a fraternal twin, a girl born 10 minutes after a boy.

"What do you get out of being a twin?" I asked my husband the first day we had lunch. "What insight does it give you that's harder for single people to understand?"

"Trust," said my husband. "That pure physical trust that comes when you know someone loves and accepts you completely because they are just like you are."

I knew the primordial closeness he was talking about. As tiny premature babies, my brother Steve and I used to cuddle in the same crib holding hands. My earliest memory is of being lifted up high and feeling incredible joy as I gazed into my mother's vast, radiant face. I was put back down on a big bed. I remember sensing another baby lying next to me, my twin. His presence felt deeply familiar, and I know I had sensed him before we were born. For me, in the beginning there was the light but there was also the son. In addition to the vertical relationship I had with Mommy, I also had a lateral relationship, a constant pre-verbal reassurance that I had a peer. I was in it with somebody else. This feeling of extending in two directions, horizontal and vertical, made up the cross of my emotional life.

At the age of 3, I remember standing in the grass on a hot, bright day in El Paso, Texas, aware as never before that my brother was different from me, not just because he was smaller then and a boy, but because

Jeen Young Han of San Diego County; Jeen hired two teenagers to murder her sister, hoping to assume her identity.

So what is truly *other*, what is *self*? As the living embodiment of that question, twins are not just the mirrors of each other, they are a mirror for us all.

Separated at Birth But Joined at the Hip

The woman seated alone onstage at the opening of the *Maury Povich* show was already famous in the twin literature: Barbara Herbert, a plump 58-year-old with a broad, pretty face and short, silver hair, found her lost twin, Daphne Goodship, 18 years ago. Both had been adopted as babies into separate British families after their Finnish single mother killed herself.

The concordances in their lives send a shiver up the spine: both women grew up in towns outside of London, left school at 14, fell down stairs at 15 and weakened their ankles, went to work in local government, met their future husbands at age 16 at the Town Hall dance, miscarried in the same month, then gave birth to two boys and a girl. Both tinted their hair auburn when young, were squeamish about blood and heights, and drank their coffee cold. When they met, both were wearing cream-colored dresses and brown velvet jackets. Both had the same crooked little fingers, a habit of pushing up their nose with the palm of their hand—which both had nicknamed "squidging"—and a way of bursting into laughter that soon had people referring to them as the Giggle Twins. The two have been studied for years now at the University of Minnesota's Center for Twin and Adoption Research, founded by Thomas J. Bouchard, Ph.D. It is the largest, ongoing study of separated twins in the world, with nearly 100 pairs registered, and they are poked, probed, and prodded by psychologists, psychiatrists, cardiologists, dentists, ophthalmologists, pathologists, and geneticists, testing everything from blood pressure to dental caries.

At the center, it was discovered that the two women had the same heart murmurs, thyroid problems, and allergies, as well as IQ's a point apart. The two showed remarkably similar personalities on psychological tests. So do the other sets of twins in the study—in fact, the genetic influence is pervasive across most domains tested. Another set of twins had been reunited in a hotel room when they were young adults, and as they unpacked found that they used the same brand of shaving lotion (Canoe), hair tonic (Vitalis), and toothpaste (Vademecum). They both smoked Lucky Strikes, and after they met they returned to their separate cities and mailed each other identical birthday presents. Other pairs have discovered they like to read magazines from back to front, store rubber bands on their wrists, or enter the ocean backwards and only up to their knees. Candid photos of every pair of twins in the study show virtually all the identicals posed the same way; while fraternal twins positioned hands and arms differently.

Bouchard—a big, balding, dynamic Midwesterner who can't help but convey his irrepressible passion about this research—recalls the time he reunited a pair of twins in their mid-30s at the Minneapolis airport. "I was following them down the ramp to baggage claim and they started talking to each other. One would stop and a nanosecond later the other would start, and when she stopped a nanosecond later the other would start. They never once interrupted each other. I said to myself, 'This is incredible, I can't carry on a conversation like that with my wife and we've been married for 36 years. No psychologist would believe this is happening.' When we finally got to baggage claim they turned around and said, 'It's like we've known each other all our lives.' "

he was different inside. I loved him and felt protective towards him, as I would throughout my childhood, but I also felt the first stirrings of rebellion, of wanting to go vertical in my identity, to make it clear to my parents and everybody else that I was not the same as Steve.

I began to relish the idea of not being completely knowable. I developed a serious underground life. At 8, I twinned myself with an invisible black panther I called Striker. At 10, I became a spy. I made cryptic notes in a notebook. I had sinister passport photos taken. I had a plastic revolver I carried in a plastic attaché case. You may call me one of the twins, I thought to myself, but I come from a foreign country that has malevolent designs on your own.

No one ever calls me and Steve "the twins" anymore, except as an artifact of childhood. I tend to think of my birth twin, who is now a Porsche mechanic and a big, outdoorsy guy who lives with his wife and two kids in a small town outside of Boston, as the brother who was with me when I was born, who shared space with me in the womb. I feel close to him not because we are exactly the same, but because I still have bedrock sensation and empathy for his life.

Jeff claimed that his knowledge of trust from being an identical let him know that I was the person he wanted to marry. He felt twinship towards me right from the start he said, and I wasn't surprised. Accustomed to being twins, my husband and I fell right into acting like twins. We co-authored a book and both edit at *Publisher's Weekly*, yet we sometimes argue over who gets to use the little study in our apartment as if our identities were at stake. Lately, I've noticed that when I feel dominated by Jeff I tend to yearn for a "real" twin, a twin who mirrors me so lovingly and acceptingly that I can let go and be myself without fear or explanation. A single person might escape by daydreaming about a perfect lover, but my fantasies of romantic enmeshment have always incorporated the twin.

Years ago in Manhattan I was invited to attend a ceremony for the Santeria religion's god of thunder, Shango, because Shango loves twins. On the way, a revered old Cuban santera told me that twins were sacred in Santeria and in the African mother religion of Yoruba because they reflect the intersection of spirit and matter. Girl and boy twins were especially fascinating, according to the santera. Most girls were killed by the boy energy, they believed. A girl had to be very strong to survive.

The moment I heard that I realized that being a twin has heightened the drama of my life. Human beings are born double, pulled between the desire to merge with another yet emerge as an authentic self. Twins fascinate, I believe, because we are an externalized representation of an internal struggle everybody lives with all their lives. We cast the illusion of solving the unsolvable, though we're no closer than anyone else.—*Tracy Cochran*

Just Puppets Dancing To Music of the Genes?

I asked Bouchard if the results of his research puncture our myth that we consciously shape who we are.

"You're not a believer in free will, are you?" he laughed, a little too heartily. "What's free will, some magical process in the brain?"

Yet I am a believer (a mystical bent and fierce independence actually run in my family, as if my genes have remote controlled a beguiling but misbegotten sense of freedom and transcendence). I was mesmerized and disturbed by the specificity of the twins' concordances. David Teplica, M.D., a Chicago plastic surgeon who for the last 10 years has been photographing more than 100 pairs of twins, has found the same number of crow's feet at the corners of twins' eyes, the same skin cancer developing behind twins' ears in the same year. Says Teplica, "It's almost beyond comprehension that one egg and one sperm could predict that."

I could imagine, I told Bouchard, that since genes regulate hormones and neurochemicals, and thus impact sexual attraction and behavior, DNA might influence the shaving lotion twins liked or the hue they tinted their hair. But the same esoteric brand of toothpaste? Walking into the sea backwards? This implies an influence so far-reaching it's unnerving.

"Nobody has the vaguest idea how that happens," he admitted, unfazed. "We're studying a set of triplets now, two identical females and a brother, and all three have Tourette's syndrome. How can the genes get so specific? I was talking yesterday in Houston to a bunch of neuroscientists and I said, 'This is the kind of thing you guys have to figure out.' There is tons of stuff to work on here, it's all open territory."

He paused to marvel over the tremendous shift in our understanding of human behavior. "When we began studying twins at the university in 1979, there was great debate on the power of genetics. I remember arguing in one graduate school class that the major psychoses were largely genetic in origin. Everyone in the classroom just clobbered me. It was the era of the domination of behaviorism, and although there's nothing wrong with Skinner's work, it had been generalized to explain everything under the sun. Nothing explains everything. Even genetics influences us, on the average, about 50 percent."

Yet that 50 percent seems omnipresent. It impacts everything from extroversion to IQ to religious and social attitudes—and drops only in the influence on homosexuality and death. Though some researchers have criticized Minnesota's twin sample for being too small and perhaps self-selected (how many separated twins out there don't participate or don't even know they're twins?), it generally confirms the results of larger studies of twins reared together—studies that have taken place around the world.

BEYOND NATURE AND NURTURE: TWINS AND QUANTUM PHYSICS

I've been interested in identical twins ever since I was old enough to realize I am one. When my brother and I were young we were close but nonetheless epitomized the struggle of twins to achieve individual identities. Now in our 50s, we have both noticed a real convergence of our intellectual, spiritual and philosophical views.

Are the strikingly similar thoughts and behaviors of twins, even those reared apart, due to nature or nurture—or to a third factor? What if what I call the "nonlocal" nature of the mind is involved?

Nonlocal mind is a term I introduced in 1989 to account for some of the ways consciousness manifests, ways suggesting that it is not completely confined or localized to specific points in space or time. Nobel physicist Erwin Schrödinger believed that mind by its very nature is singular and one, that consciousness is not confined to separate, individual brains, that it is ultimately a unified field. David Chalmers, a mathematician and cognitive scientist from the University of California at Santa Cruz, has suggested that consciousness is fundamental in the universe, perhaps on a par with matter and energy, and that it is not derived from, nor reducible to, anything else. Nobel physicist Brian Josephson, of Cambridge University's Cavendish Laboratory, has proposed that nonlocal events at the subatomic level for example, the fact that there are correlations between the spin of subatomic particles, even after they are separated—can be amplified and may emerge in our everyday experience.

In other words, the macrocosm reflects the microcosm. Systems theorist Erwin Laszio has suggested that nonlocal mind may mediate events such as intercessory prayer, telepathy, precognition, and clairvoyance.

If consciousness is unbounded and unitary, strikingly similar thoughts and behaviors of identical twins, even separated twins, would not be surprising. Genes do determine how individual brains function, how we each process information, and nonlocal mind could be easier to access if two brains were almost identical in their functioning. Indeed, some people see analogies between the behavior of separated, identical twins and separated, identical subatomic particles.

According to the late Irish physicist John S. Bell, if two subatomic particles once in contact are separated to some arbitrary distance, a change in one is correlated with a change in the other—instantly and to the same degree. There is no travel time for any known form of energy to flow between them. Yet experiments have shown these changes do occur, instantaneously. Neither can these nonlocal effects be blocked or shielded—one of the hallmarks of nonlocality. Perhaps distant twins are mysteriously linked, like distant particles—or, to quote Ecclesiastes, "All things go in pairs, one the counterpart of the other."
—*Larry Dossey, M.D.*

Twin studies allow us to double blind our nature/nurture research in a unique way. Identical twins share 100 percent of their genes, while fraternals share 50 percent. But usually they grow up together, sharing a similar environment in the womb and the world. When separated, they give us a clue about the strength of genetic influence in the face of sometimes radically different environments. Soon Bouchard and his colleagues will study siblings in families that have adopted a twin, thus testing environmental influences when no genes are shared. Like a prism yielding different bands of light, twin studies are rich and multifaceted. Here are some of the major findings on nature and nurture thus far:

• **Political and social attitudes,** ranging from divorce to the death penalty, were found to have a strong genetic influence in one Australian study. A Swedish study found genes significantly influenced two of the so-called "big five" personality traits—"openness to experience" and "conscientiousness"—while environment had little impact. In contrast, environment influenced "agreeableness" more than genes did. (The two other traits are "neuroticism" and "extroversion.") Another study, at the University of Texas at Austin, found that personality in identicals correlated 50 percent, in fraternals about 25 percent.

• **Body fat is under genetic influence.** Identical twins reared together will have the same amount of body fat 75 percent of the time; for those reared apart it's 61 percent, showing a heavy genetic and mild environmental influence, according to a 1991 study.

• **Both optimism and pessimism** are heavily influenced by genes, but shared environment influences only optimism, not pessimism, according to a study of 522 pairs of middle-aged identical and fraternal twins. Thus family life and genes can be equal contributors to an optimistic outlook, which influences both mental and physical health. But pessimism seems largely controlled by genes.

• **Religiosity is influenced by genes.** Identical and fraternal twins, raised together and apart, demonstrate that 50 percent of religiosity (demonstrated by religious conviction and church attendance) can be attributed to genes.

• **Sexual orientation** is under genetic influence, though not solely, according to studies by Michael Bailey, Ph.D., associate professor of psychology at Northwestern University. In one study he found that if one identical twin is gay, the other is also gay 50 percent of the time. However, when Bailey analyzed a sample of 5,000 twins from the Australian twin registry, the genetic impact was less. In identical male twins, if one was gay the likelihood of his twin being gay was 20 percent; in fraternal twins the likelihood was almost zero. In women, there was little evidence of heritability for homosexuality.

• **When substance abuse** was studied in 295 identical and fraternal twin pairs, year of birth was the most powerful predictor of drug use. Younger twins were most likely to have abused drugs, reflecting widespread drug use in the culture at large. Alcoholism, however, has a significant genetic component, according to Andrew Heath, Ph.D., at the Virginia Institute for Psychiatric and Behavioral Genetics at Virginia Commonwealth University School of Medicine.

• **Attention deficit disorder** may be influenced by genes 70 percent of the time, according to Lindon Eaves, M.D., director of the Virginia Institute for Psychiatric and Behavioral Genetics. Eaves and colleagues studied 1,400 families of twins and found genetic influence on "all the juvenile behavior disorders," usually in the range of 30 to 50 percent.

• **Twins tend to start dating,** to marry, and to start having children at about the same time. David Lykken, Ph.D., and Matthew McGue, Ph.D., at the University of Minnesota, found that if an identical twin had divorced, there was a 45 percent chance the other had also. For fraternals, the chance was 30 percent. The researchers think this is due to inherited personality traits.

• **Schizophrenia** occurs more often in identical twins, and if one twin suffers from the disorder, the children of the healthy identical sibling are also at greater risk, according to psychiatrist Irving Gottesman, M.D., of the University of Virginia. The risk is about twice as high for the children of a twin whose identical counterpart is ill, as it is for the children of a twin whose fraternal counterpart is ill.

Hidden Differences Between Twins

A few fascinating kinks in the biology of twin research have recently turned up, weaving an even more complex pattern for us to study and learn from. It turns out that not all

identical twins are truly identical, or share all their genetic traits. In one tragic instance, one twin was healthy and a gymnast, while the other suffered from severe muscular dystrophy, a genetic disorder, and was dead by age 16. Yet the twins were identical.

> Some twins are bonded by a lifelong passion for each other that the rest of us experience only in the almost unbearably intense first flush of romantic love. England's notorious Gibbons twins were one such pair.

One way twins can differ is in the sex chromosomes that turn them into a male or female, and which contain other genes as well, such as those that code for muscular dystrophy or color blindness. All girls inherit two X chromosomes, one from each parent, while boys inherit an X and a Y. Girls automatically shut off one X in every cell—sometimes some of the mother's and some of the father's, in other cases all the mother's or all the father's. A girl may not shut off her extra set of X chromosomes in the same pattern as her identical twin does.

Identical twins may not be exposed to the same world in the womb, either. It depends on the time their mother's fertilized egg splits—and that timing may explain why some identical twins seem more eerily alike than others. At Lutheran University, researchers have looked at the placentas of some 10,000 twin births. They've found that an egg that separates in the first four days of pregnancy develops not only into separate twins, but results in separate placentas, chorionic casings, and amniotic sacs. These twins are like two singletons in the womb and have the best chance of survival. Twins who separate between the fifth and eighth days share a single placenta and chorion, but still have the benefit of two amniotic sacs. Here, one twin can have a distinct advantage over the other. The umbilical cord may be positioned centrally on one sac, while the other is on the margin, receiving fewer nutrients. Studies of these twins show that with a nurturing environment, the weaker twin will catch up in the first few years of life. However, it's possible that viruses may penetrate separate sacs at different rates or in different ways—perhaps increasing the risk for schizophrenia or other illnesses later in life.

Twins who split between the eighth and 12th days share their amniotic sac, and often their cords get entangled. One cord may be squeezed until no blood flows through it, and that twin dies. Finally, twins who split after the 12th day become conjoined—and even though they share organs and limbs, anecdotal evidence suggests that they often have distinctly different temperaments, habits, and food cravings.

In one hotly debated hypothesis, pediatrician and geneticist Judith Hall, of the University of British Columbia in Vancouver, speculates that twinning occurs because of genetic differences within an embryo. Perhaps mutations occur at a very early stage in some cells, which then are sensed as different, and expelled from the embryo. Those cells may survive and grow into a twin. Hall suggests this could account for the higher incidence of birth defects among twins.

While identical twins can be more distinct than we imagine, fraternal twins might come from the same egg, according to behavioral geneticist Charles Boklage, M.D., of the East Carolina University School of Medicine. Boklage proposes that occasionally an older egg may actually split before it is fertilized by two of the father's sperm. With advances in gene mapping and blood testing, he says, we may find that one-egg fraternal twins occur as often as do two-egg fraternals. We may be mistaking some same sex fraternal twins for identical twins.

Twins Who Vanish, Twins Who Merge

Whatever the cause of twinning, once it beings, mysterious and unsettling events can occur. Some twins disappear or even merge together into one person. Ultrasound equipment has revealed twin pregnancies that later turn into singletons. One of the twins is absorbed into the body, absorbed by the other twin, or shed and noticed by the mother only as some extra vaginal bleeding.

"Only one in 80 twin conceptions makes it to term as two living people," notes Boklage. "For every one that results in a twin birth, about 12 make it to term as a sole survivor. And those people never know they were twins." Because twins tend to be left-handed more often than singletons, Boklage speculates that many left-handers could be the survivors of a twin pregnancy. And a few of those twin pregnancies may lead to what Boklage terms a "chimera," based on the Greek monster with a tail of a serpent, body of a goat, and head of lion—a mosaic of separate beings. "We find people entirely by accident who have two different blood types or several different versions of a single gene. Those people look perfectly normal, but I believe they come from two different cell lines."

It's as if fantastical, primitive acts of love, death, merging, and emerging occur from the very moment life ignites, even as the first strands of DNA knit themselves into the human beings we will later become— carrying on those same acts in the world at large, acts that define us, and that we still are not certain we can call our own.

When Twins Die, Kill, Hate, and Burn

Though it doesn't happen often, occasionally in history a set of mythic twins seem to burst into our awareness, more wedded and bonded than any couple, even darkly so. Some twins live with a passion the rest of us experience only in the almost unbearably intense first flush of romantic love. England's Gibbons twins are one such pair.

Jennifer and June Gibbons were born 35 years ago, the youngest children of Aubrey Gibbons, a West Indian technician for the British Royal Air Force. The girls communicated with each other in a self-made dialect and were elective mutes with the rest of the world. By the time they were 11, they refused to sit in the same room with their parents or siblings. Their mother delivered their meals on a tray and slipped mail under the door. They taught themselves to read, and eventually locked themselves in their bedroom, writing literally millions of words in diaries.

Later they lost their virginity to the same boy within a week of each other, triggering jealous rage. Jennifer tried to strangle June with a cord, and June tried to drown Jennifer in a river. When publishers rejected their work, they went on a spree of arson and theft, and were committed to Broadmoor, England's most notorious institution for the criminally insane.

"Nobody suffers the way I do," June wrote in her diary. "This sister of mine, a dark shadow robbing me of sunlight, is my one and only torment." In another passage, Jennifer described June lying in the bunk bed above her: "Her perception was sharper than steel, it sliced through to my own perception... I read her mind, I knew all about her mood... My perception. Her perception... clashing, knowing, cunning, sly."

After more than a decade of confinement, they were set free. That same afternoon, Jennifer was rushed to the hospital with viral myocarditis, an inflammation of the heart, and that night she died. The pathologist who saw her heart seemed to be speaking poetically of their lethal passion when he described Jennifer's illness as "a fulminating, roaring inflammation with the heart muscle completely destroyed." June, the survivor, has said that she was "born in captivity, trapped in twinship." Eventually, June claims, they began to accept that one must die so the other could be free. Today, June lives in Wales.

Another set of twins, 22-year-old Jeen Young Han (nicknamed Gina) and her sister Sunny, have been dubbed the "evil" and "good" twins by the media, after one tried to murder the other. Although the twins were both valedictorians at their small country high school in San Diego County and got along well, after they graduated they began to battle one another. Both sisters were involved in petty crime, but when Gina stole Sunny's BMW and credit cards, Sunny had her jailed. She escaped, but in November 1996 Sunny and her roommate were attacked and Gina was arrested for conspiracy to commit murder. She'd planned to have Sunny killed at her Irvine condominium, and then assume her identity.

For twin researcher and obstetrician Louis Keith, M.D., of Northwestern University Medical School, the idea of killing a twin is practically unthinkable. "I'm an identical twin, and yesterday I attended the funeral of another identical twin. I kept trying to imagine what my life would be like without my twin. My brother and I have had telepathic experiences. I was in East Germany, being driven on a secluded highway with evening snow falling, and suddenly felt intense heat over the entire front of my body and knew it could only mean one thing, that my brother was sending intense signals to me to call him. When one of the Communist telephone operators agreed to put the call through, I found out that my aunt had died and my twin wanted me to come to the funeral. The twin bond is greater than the spousal bond, absolutely."

Raymond Brandt, publisher of *Twins World* magazine, agrees. "I'm 67, and my identical twin died when we were 20. I love my wife and sons in a very special way, but my twin was one half of me, he was my first love. Living without my twin for 47 years has been a hell of an existence."

These remarkable stories seem to indicate an extra dimension to the twin bond, as if they truly shared a common, noncorporeal soul. What little study has been done on paranormal phenomena and twins, however, indicates that—once again—genes may be responsible. A study by British parapsychologist Susan Blackmore found that when twins were separated in different rooms and asked to draw whatever came into their minds, they often drew the same things. When one was asked to draw an object and transmit that to the other twin, who then was asked to draw what she telepathically received, the results were disappointing. Blackmore concluded that when twins seem to be clairvoyant, it's simply because their thought patterns are so similar.

Is There No Nurture?

Over a century ago, in 1875, British anthropologist Francis Galton first compared a small group of identical and fraternal twins and concluded that "nature prevails enormously over nurture." Time and research seem to have proved him right. "It's no accident that we are what we are," contends Nancy Segal, Ph.D., professor of developmental psychology at California State University at Fullerton and director of the Twin Studies Center there. "We are born with biological propensities that steer us in one direction or another."

Yet critics of twin studies scoff. Richard Rose, Ph.D., professor of psychology and medical genetics at Indiana University in Bloomington, has studied personality in more than 7,000 pairs of identical twins and concluded that environment, both shared and unshared, has nearly twice the influence of genes.

However, both the nature and nurture camps may be looking at the same data and interpreting it differently. According to Lindon Eaves, unshared environment may actually be "chosen" by the genes, selected because of biological preferences. Scientists dub this the "nature of nurture." Genetically influenced personality traits in a child may cause parents to respond in specific ways. So how can we ever tease out the truth? Nature and nurture interact in a never-ending Mobius strip that can't be traced back to a single starting point.

Yet if genes are a powerful and a-priori given, they nonetheless have a range of activity that is calibrated in the womb by nutrition and later in life by the world. "Remember," says Eaves, "only 50 percent of who you are is influenced by genes. The other 50 percent includes the slings and arrows of outrageous fortune, accidents of development, sheer chaos, small and cumulative changes both within and without."

Environment, it turns out, may be most powerful when it limits—through trauma, deprivation, malnutrition. Studies by Sandra Scarr, Ph.D., professor of psychology at the University of Virginia, show that IQ scores for white twins at the bottom of the socioeconomic ladder, and for all black twins, are heavily influenced by environment. Social and economic deprivation keep scores artificially lower than twins' genetic potential.

Otherwise, Scarr postulates, genes bias you in a certain direction, causing you to select what you are already genetically programmed to enjoy. Children may be tiny gene powerhouses, shaping their parents' behavior as much as parents shape their children.

"Where does this leave us?" concludes Bouchard. "Your job as a parent is really to maximize the environment so that you and your children can manifest your full genetic potential."

Under the best of environmental circumstances, our genes might be free to play the entire symphony of self.

And yet what of Irina, the Michigan housewife, and her twin, Yanina, the Polish nun? I sat with them over lunch, newly united twins who couldn't stop smiling at each other, clasping each other's hands. Their luminous hazel eyes were virtual replicas, but the two women couldn't have appeared more different otherwise: Irina bejeweled and blonde, Yanina in a combat-green nun's habit, a few tufts of brown hair peeping out, skin weathered. She described rescuing bloodied children from the arms of mothers who'd been shot to death and rising at dawn in the convent to pray silently for hours; her American counterpart portrayed a life filled with errands, cleaning homes, and caring for family.

"Rushing, rushing, rushing to get everything done" was Irina's summary of her life. "Teaching love, the kind of love that will make you happy," was her sister's. Listening to them speak, one in slow, gentle Midwestern cadences, the other in the rolled drumbeat of a Slavic tongue enriched by laughter and hand gestures, it was hard to believe they carried the same genetic imprint.

To me, their differences are so striking they seem to defy the last 20 years of twin research. "Right now we understand a little bit about human behavior and its biological and cultural roots," says Eaves. "But our lived understanding is far richer than any of that. People are yielding the ground too easily to genetics."

As I mused over the intricate turnings of twin research, I could only conclude the findings were as complex as the self we hope to illuminate with these studies. Fascinating, tantalizing, yes, but twin research, like any great scientific endeavor, ultimately points us toward the ineffable, inexplicable.

As Charles Boklage notes: "The development of the self is chaotic, nonlinear, and dynamic. Very small variations in conditions can lead to huge changes. Different twin studies give different answers. And whenever the mind tries to understand something, it has to be bigger than the subject it compasses. You cannot bite your own teeth."

"In the end," says Eaves, "I don't give a damn whether you call it God or natural selection, we're trying to find words that instill reverence for the mysterious stuff from which we are made."

God, fate, genes, luck, a random event like a move to America or Poland, or perhaps something stubbornly individual and free about us all, something that can never be quantified but can only be lived... The play of self goes on, and whatever hand or eye has orchestrated us, who in the end, twin or not, can know the dancer from the dance?

The Role of Lifestyle in Preventing Low Birth Weight

Virginia Rall Chomitz
Lilian W. Y. Cheung
Ellice Lieberman

Abstract

Lifestyle behaviors such as cigarette smoking, weight gain during pregnancy, and use of other drugs play an important role in determining fetal growth. The relationship between lifestyle risk factors and low birth weight is complex and is affected by psychosocial, economic, and biological factors. Cigarette smoking is the largest known risk factor for low birth weight. Approximately 20% of all low birth weight could be avoided if women did not smoke during pregnancy. Reducing heavy use of alcohol and other drugs during pregnancy could also reduce the rate of low birth weight births. Pregnancy and the prospect of pregnancy provide an important window of opportunity to improve women's health and the health of children. The adoption before or during pregnancy of more healthful lifestyle behaviors, such as ceasing to smoke, eating an adequate diet and gaining enough weight during pregnancy, and ceasing heavy drug use, can positively affect the long-term health of women and the health of their infants. Detrimental lifestyles can be modified, but successful modification will require large-scale societal changes. In the United States, these societal changes should include a focus on preventive health, family-centered workplace policies, and changes in social norms.

Virginia Rall Chomitz, Ph.D., is project manager of the Eat Well and Keep Moving Project, Department of Nutrition, Harvard School of Public Health.

Lilian W. Y. Cheung, D.Sc., R.D., is a lecturer in the Department of Nutrition and director of the Harvard Nutrition and Fitness Project, Harvard School of Public Health, Department of Nutrition and Center for Health Communication.

Ellice Lieberman, M.D., Dr.PH., is assistant professor in the Department of Obstetrics, Gynecology, and Reproductive Biology, Harvard Medical School and in the Department of Maternal and Child Health, Harvard School of Public Health.

Many of the known risk factors associated with low birth weight, such as socioeconomic status, ethnicity, genetic makeup, and obstetric history, are not within a woman's immediate control. However, there are things that a woman can do to improve her chances of having a normal, healthy child. Lifestyle behaviors, such as cigarette smoking, use of other drugs, and nutrition, play an important role in determining fetal growth. Detrimental habits can be modified, but successful modification requires more than just a dose of individual "self control." Stopping lifelong addictive behaviors is very difficult, and a woman who suffers from them requires support and assistance not only from family members and individuals close to her, but also from the health care system and society.

The relationship between lifestyle risk factors and low birth weight is very complex and is affected by psychosocial, socioeconomic, and biological factors. While it is important to describe the independent effects of different behavioral and socioeconomic risk factors, we must bear in mind that these factors are not isolated events in women's lives, but are a part of many interrelated complex behaviors and environmental risks. Factors associated with the perinatal health of women and children include demographic factors, medical risks, and maternal behaviors. These risk factors may influence maternal and infant health directly (in terms of physiology) or indirectly (in terms of health behavior). In this article we focus primarily on lifestyle behavioral risk factors that are amenable to change and that, if modified before or during pregnancy, can improve the likelihood of the delivery of a full-term healthy infant of appropriate size.

There are things that a woman can do to improve her chances of having a normal, healthy child.

This paper is based on Healthy Mothers—Healthy Beginnings, *a paper written with a grant from the CIGNA Foundation and CIGNA Corporation, 1992.*

Demographic Factors

Socioeconomic status and race/ethnicity are indicators of complex linkages among environmental events, psychological states, and physiologic factors which may lead to low birth weight or preterm delivery. While we do not fully understand the specific biological pathways responsible, we do know that a woman's social and economic status will influence her general health and access to resources. (See the article by Hughes and Simpson in this journal issue for a detailed analysis of the effects of social factors on low birth weight.) In this section, we review the effects of some demographic indicators.

Socioeconomic Status

Low birth weight and infant mortality are closely related to socioeconomic disadvantage. Socioeconomic status, however, is difficult to measure accurately. Educational attainment, marital status, maternal age, and income are interrelated factors and are often used to approximate socioeconomic status, but no single factor truly measures its underlying influence.

Maternal education, maternal age, and marital status are all reflective of socioeconomic status and predictive of low birth weight. Twenty-four percent of the births in 1989 were to women with less than a high school education.[1] Low educational attainment is associated with higher rates of low birth weight.[2] For example, relative to college graduates, white women with less than a high school education were 50% more likely to have babies with very low birth weight (less than 1,500 grams, or 3 pounds, 5 ounces) and more than twice as likely to have babies with moderately low birth weight (between 1,500 grams and 2,500 grams, or 3 pounds, 5 ounces and 5 pounds, 8 ounces) than were women who graduated from college.[2] Teenage mothers are at greater risk of having a low birth weight baby than are mothers aged 25 to 34.[1] However, it is not clear if the risk of teenage childbearing is due to young maternal age or to the low socioeconomic status that often accompanies teenage pregnancy.

The marital status of the mother also appears to be independently associated with the rate of low birth weight,[2,3] although the relationship appears to vary by maternal age and race. The association of unmarried status with low birth weight is probably strongest for white women over 20 years of age.[2,4] Marital status may also serve as a marker for the "wantedness" of the child, the economic status of the mother, and the social support that the mother has—all of which are factors that may influence the health of the mother and infant.

It has been hypothesized that economic disadvantage may be a risk factor for low birth weight partly because of the high levels of stress and negative life events that are associated with being poor. Both physical stress and fatigue—particularly related to work during pregnancy—and psychological distress have been implicated.[5] In addition, stress and negative life events are associated with health behaviors such as smoking.[6] Social support may act as a moderator or as a buffer from the untoward effects of stressful life experiences and emotional dysfunction.[7]

Race/Ethnicity

The prevalence of low birth weight among white infants is less than half of that for African-American infants (6% and 13%, respectively). This difference reflects a two-fold increase of preterm and low birth weight births among African-American mothers.[1] African-American mothers are more likely to have less education, not to be married, and to be younger than white mothers.[1] However, at almost all educational levels and age categories, African-American women have about double the rates of low birth weight as white women.[8] This fact indicates that these demographic differences in education, marital status, and age do not account for the large disparity between African Americans and whites in the incidence of low birth weight.

Among infants of Hispanic origin, who represented approximately 15% of live births in 1989, the rate of low birth weight was relatively low (6.1% overall), particularly given that Hispanic women (except Cuban women) had limited educational attainment and were not as likely as non-Hispanic white women to receive prenatal care early in pregnancy.[1]

However, Hispanics are a very diverse group, and the low birth weight rates vary considerably by national origin. Low birth weight rates range from 9.4% among Puerto Rican mothers to 5.6% among Cuban mothers. Among Asian infants in 1989, the incidence of low birth weight ranged from 5.1% for Chinese births to 7.3% for Filipino births.[1]

It is not known why infants of African-American mothers are twice as likely as all other infants to be born with low birth weights. The etiology of racial disparities in infant mortality and low birth weight is probably multifactorial in nature and is not completely explained by differences in demographics, use of tobacco and other drugs, or medical illnesses.[9] During the primary childbearing years (ages 15 to 29), the general mortality of African-American women exceeds that of white women for virtually every cause of death.

African-American women have higher rates of hypertension, anemia, and low-level lead exposure than other groups,[10] suggesting that the general health status of African-American women may be suboptimal. Infants of African-American foreign-born mothers have lower risks of neonatal mortality than infants of African-American U.S.-born mothers, a relationship that is not seen between foreign- and U.S.-born white women.[11] In addition, racial or ethnic differences in familial structure and social networks may affect morbidity and mortality.[12] More research will be needed to clarify the reasons for these disparities.

Nutrition and Weight Gain

Concerns about nutrition during pregnancy fall into two basic areas, maternal weight gain and nutrient intake, both of which can potentially affect the health of the mother and infant. As with other lifestyle factors, a woman's nutrition and weight gain are closely linked to her socioeconomic status, cigarette smoking, and other health-related behaviors.

Maternal Weight Gain

Maternal weight gain during pregnancy results from a variety of factors, including maternal dietary intake, prepregnancy weight and height, length of gestation, and size of the fetus. The mother's prepregnancy weight and height are, in turn, a consequence of her genetic makeup, past nutritional status, and environmental factors. The relationship between a woman's caloric intake during pregnancy and her infant's birth weight is complex and is moderated through maternal weight gain and other mechanisms during pregnancy.[13,14]

Epidemiologic evidence has demonstrated a nearly linear association between maternal weight gain during pregnancy and birth weight,[15,16] and an inverse relationship to the rate of low birth weight.[16] It comes as no surprise that maternal weight gain during pregnancy is highly correlated with the birth weight of the infant because a large propor-

It is not known why infants of African-American mothers are twice as likely as all other infants to be born with low birth weights.

tion of the weight gain is due to the growth of the fetus itself. Women with total weight gains of 22 pounds (10 kilograms) or less were two to three times more likely to have growth-retarded full-term babies than were women with a gain of more than 22 pounds. Once corrected for the duration of pregnancy, the relationship between weight gain and preterm delivery is uncertain.[17,18]

On average, women gain about 30 pounds during pregnancy. Teenage mothers, older mothers, unmarried mothers, and mothers with less than a high school education are most likely to have low or inadequate weight gain during pregnancy. Even after accounting for gestational age and socioeconomic status, African-American mothers gain less weight than white mothers (28 versus 31 pounds).[19] It has been estimated that from 15% to 33% of women gain an inadequate amount of weight (less than 22 pounds) during pregnancy.[13,19] Low weight gain may in part be the result of outdated medical advice and personal beliefs. In one study, one-quarter of the pregnant women believed that they should not gain more than 20 pounds during pregnancy.[20] In addition, belief that a smaller baby is easier to deliver and thus that weight gain and fetal birth weight should be limited influences the amount of weight gained by some women.[21]

tionship between specific vitamins and minerals and low birth weight is unclear, and controversy exists over the association between maternal hematocrit levels (which is a marker for anemia) and preterm birth.[23–26]

A pregnant woman's current nutritional status is determined by her prepregnant nutritional status, her current intake of nutrients, and her individual physiological nutrient requirements. Members of the National Academy of Sciences recently reviewed the available literature on dietary intake of nutrients and minerals among pregnant women. They found that the energy intake (calories) for U.S. women was consistently below recommended levels and that the amount of important vitamins and minerals in their diet was also substantially lower than the recommended daily allowance. On average, intakes of protein, riboflavin, vitamin B-12, niacin, and vitamin C exceeded the recommended daily allowance.[27]

Women at particular risk of nutritional inadequacy during pregnancy may require nutritional counseling. Groups at risk include women voluntarily restricting caloric intake or dieting; pregnant adolescents; women with low income or limited food budgets; women with eating patterns or practices that require balancing food choices, such as strict

Approximately 20% to 25% of American women smoke cigarettes during pregnancy.[31,32] White, young, unmarried, and unemployed women, as well as women with fewer than 12 years of education and low socioeconomic status, are more likely to smoke during pregnancy, compared with nonwhite, older, married women with more than 12 years of education and higher socioeconomic status.[27,30,33,34] For example, 35% of mothers with less than a high school education smoke compared with 5% of college graduates.[35]

Smoking retards fetal growth. Birth weight is reduced by 150 to 320 grams (5.3 to 11.4 ounces) in infants born to smokers compared with those born to nonsmokers.[36] It has been consistently reported that, even after controlling other factors, women who smoke are about twice as likely to deliver a low birth weight baby as are women who do not smoke.[37] A dose-response relationship exists between the amount smoked and birth weight: the percent of low birth weight births increases with increasing number of cigarettes smoked during pregnancy. In addition, exposure to environmental cigarette smoke has also been associated with low birth weight.[38] Preterm birth is associated with smoking, but the association is weak compared with the association between low birth weight and smoking.[9,37] Cigarette smoking during pregnancy may account for up to 14% of preterm deliveries.[37]

Studies of women who quit cigarette smoking at almost any point during pregnancy show lower rates of low birth weight. Most fetal growth takes place in the last trimester, so that quitting early in pregnancy can decrease the negative effect of smoking on birth weight.[33] Quitting even as late as the seventh or eighth month has a positive impact on birth weight.[39]

Overall, about one-quarter of women who smoke prior to pregnancy quit upon learning of their pregnancies, and an additional one-third reduce the number of cigarettes they smoke.[33,40] Older women and more educated women are more likely to quit smoking during pregnancy.[41] Light smokers are more likely to quit smoking than heavier smokers. Heavier smokers are likely to reduce the amount they smoke, but are unlikely to quit.[42] Social support appears to be a critical factor in changing smoking behavior.[40]

Even among women who do quit smoking during pregnancy, about a third will relapse before childbirth.[43] In addition, nearly 80% of women who stop smoking during pregnancy relapse within one year after the delivery.[40] These high relapse rates reflect the physiological addictive nature of nicotine. While 57% of the pregnant smokers in one study were able to decrease their intake, 40% "tried and failed" to reduce.[44] Of women who both drank and smoked before pregnancy, fewer women were able to decrease

---

Smoking during pregnancy has been linked to 20% to 30% of low birth weight births.

While higher maternal weight gain is linked with healthier fetal weight gains, women and clinicians are concerned that women may retain weight after delivery and be at greater risk for obesity. Recent studies have shown that weight retention following delivery increased as weight gain increased, and African-American women retained more weight than white women with comparable weight gains during pregnancy (7.2 versus 1.6 pounds).[22] Thus, weight management programs would be appropriate for some women after delivery, but not during pregnancy.

Diet and Nutrient Intake

During pregnancy, the need for calories and nutrients, such as protein, iron, folate, and the other B vitamins, is increased to meet the demands of the fetus as well as the expansion of maternal tissues that support the fetus. As noted by Nathanielsz in this journal issue, the nutritional needs of the fetus are second only to the needs of the mother's brain. Thus, it is important for a pregnant woman to have a well-balanced, nutritious diet to meet the changing needs of her body and her fetus. Unfortunately, the direct rela-

vegetarians; women with emotional illness; smokers; women with poor knowledge of nutrition due to lack of education of illiteracy; and women with special difficulties in food resource management because of limited physical abilities and poor cooking or budgeting skills.[28]

Lifestyle Choices: Cigarette Smoking, Alcohol, Caffeine, and Illicit Drugs

Cigarette Smoking

Since the 1970s, the Surgeon General has reported that cigarette smoking during pregnancy is linked to fetal growth retardation and to infant mortality.[29] Smoking during pregnancy has been linked to 20% to 30% of low birth weight births and 10% of fetal and infant deaths.[30] Cigarette smoking is unequivocally the largest and most important known modifiable risk factor for low birth weight and infant death.

or quit smoking than drinking, despite feelings of social pressure to quit and feelings of guilt at continuing to smoke.[44] The high recidivism rate after childbirth also reflects diminished maternal contact with the health care system as health care provision shifts from obstetrics to pediatrics.[45]

The bulk of evidence shows a clear and consistent association between low birth weight (primarily due to growth retardation, not preterm birth) and infant mortality and smoking during pregnancy. Smoking also impacts on other aspects of the health status of women and infants. Smoking has been linked to long-term effects in infants such as physical, mental, and cognitive impairments.[46,47] The linkages between smoking and illnesses, such as cancer and cardiovascular and respiratory disease, are well known.[48] In addition, research on the effects of passive smoke indicates an increased frequency of respiratory and ear infections among infants and children exposed to this smoke.[33,49]

Alcohol Use

Alcohol use during pregnancy has long been associated with both short- and long-term negative health effects for infants. Alcohol abuse during pregnancy is clearly related to

Heavy alcohol consumption has been cited as the leading preventable cause of mental retardation worldwide.

a series of congenital malformations described as fetal alcohol syndrome. However, the effects of moderate drinking on the fetus are not well established. Alcohol use among women of childbearing age and, specifically, among pregnant women has apparently declined significantly in the past decades.[44] This decreasing trend has generally been confined to more educated and older women. However, there has been little or no change in drinking during pregnancy among smokers, younger women, and women with less than a high school education.[50]

Heavy Drinking During Pregnancy

Numerous studies report an association between chronic alcohol abuse and a series of fetal malformations. Fetal alcohol syndrome is characterized by a pattern of severe birth defects related to alcohol use during pregnancy which include prenatal and postnatal growth retardation, central nervous system

©1994 Custom Medical Stock Photo

disorders, and distinct abnormal craniofacial features.[51] Heavy alcohol consumption has been cited as the leading preventable cause of mental retardation worldwide.[52] It has been estimated that the prevalence of fetal alcohol syndrome is 1 to 3 per 1,000 live births with a significantly increased rate among alcoholics of 59 per 1,000 live births. Prenatally alcohol-exposed babies with birth defects who do not meet all required criteria for the syndrome are categorized as having fetal alcohol effects. The prevalence of fetal alcohol effects may be threefold that of fetal alcohol syndrome.[52]

The children of women who continued to drink an average of greater than one drink daily throughout their pregnancies are significantly smaller, shorter, and have smaller head circumferences than infants of control mothers who stop drinking.[53] The risk of low birth weight to women drinking three to five drinks per day was increased twofold over nondrinking mothers and almost threefold for those drinking six or more drinks daily when compared with women who did not drink.[54] A study of French women showed that those who consumed 35 drinks or more a week gave birth to infants that weighed 202 grams (about 7 ounces) less than the infants of women who consumed six or fewer drinks per week.[55]

Moderate Drinking During Pregnancy

While the effects of heavy daily drinking are well documented, the impact of moderate drinking is not as well established. Approximately 40% to 60% of pregnant women consume one drink or less a day. Alcohol use exceeding one drink daily ranges from 3% to 13%. Abstinence levels in pregnant women have been reported to range from 16% to 53%.[50,54,56] Women who consumed less than one alcoholic drink per day had only an 11% increased chance of delivering a growth-retarded infant.[54] Decrements in birth weight from 32 to 225 grams (1.1 to 8 ounces) have been reported for children born to women who drank one to three drinks daily.[55,57] Some studies with long-term follow-up have reported deleterious short-term effects and long-term effects, such as growth, mental, and motor delays, for infants of mothers who drink alcohol during pregnancy.[58,59] However, a number of studies demonstrate insignificant or no effects of "low to moderate" intake on growth at birth[60] and at four and five years of age.[58,61] The role of binge drinking is unknown.

Profile of the Pregnant Drinker

The profile of the pregnant drinker varies by the type of drinking. Any alcohol use during pregnancy is associated with older, white, professional, college-educated women with few previous children. Drinkers are also more likely to be unmarried and to smoke than are nondrinkers.[50] However, heavier alcohol use, in excess of two drinks daily, has been associated with African-American and Hispanic race/ethnicity, less than a high school education, and multiparity. Conversely, women who abstained during pregnancy were more likely to be younger, African-American, and/or of moderate income.[62]

During pregnancy, many women reduce their drinking[63] with decreases occurring in all types of drinkers.[64] In addition, as pregnancy advances, the proportion of women drinking decreases. In one study, 55% of women drank in the week prior to conception, 50% drank after 32 weeks, and only 20% drank in the last week of their pregnancies.[65]

Many of the studies investigating the relationship of maternal alcohol use to fetal effects suffer from methodologic problems common to substance use research. Most of the studies rely on self-reporting which, because of the stigma attached to alcohol use during pregnancy, may be inaccurate. Studies of drug use also often fail to consider other important factors, such as maternal nutrition, general health, or marijuana use. In addition, the usual dose, frequency of intake, and timing of drinking during pregnancy may result in different consequences, but this information is often lacking.

Caffeine Consumption

Caffeine is one of the most commonly used drugs. At least 52% of people in the United States drink coffee, 29% drink tea, and 58% consume soft drinks.[66] Caffeine is most commonly consumed in beverages such as coffee, tea, and soft drinks; eaten in the form of chocolate; and also taken as part of various prescription and nonprescription drugs. No consistent associations between caffeine and low birth weight or preterm birth have been observed.[67] Most studies have found no association between caffeine use and low birth weight, but some studies report positive yet inconsistent associations.[67] Several studies have found an interaction between caffeine and cigarette smoking, where the adverse effects of caffeine were observed only among smokers. The existence of such an interaction may help to explain the conflicting results.

Illicit Drug Use

In recent years, the rise in use of illegal drugs, particularly prenatal drug and cocaine, or "crack," use has received extensive coverage in the popular press and sparked many investigations. Prenatal cocaine and heroin abuse are clearly associated with adverse birth outcomes. Other factors in a drug addict's lifestyle, including malnutrition, sexually transmitted diseases, and polysubstance abuse, may contribute to an increased risk of adverse pregnancy outcome and often complicate the ability to examine the effects of individual drugs. The effect of marijuana use on the health of women and their infants is not as clear, nor are the effects of the occasional use of cocaine and other drugs.

Several methodologic problems hinder the interpretation and generalizability of much of the research on both the prevalence and effects of prenatal drug exposure. Studies are often based on small, nonrepresentative samples of mothers, and the bulk of the literature regarding illicit drug use relies on self-reporting. It is difficult to elicit valid information about illegal drug use, and a significant amount of underreporting probably takes place.[68] It is also unclear whether some of the effects of drug use are due to fetal drug exposure or to the generally poorer health and limited prenatal care of many addicted women. Finally, most research has been conducted with low-income urban women who are often in poorer health and under greater stress than their middle-class counterparts. The timing of drug use during the course of pregnancy and the dosage undoubtedly influences the consequences of the actions. However, most studies have been unable to characterize accurately the use of drugs in pregnancy. In addition, interactive effects of illicit drugs with alcohol, tobacco, or other drugs have not as yet been adequately examined.

Despite the limitations of the research, a number of studies have shown significant effects of individual illicit substances on women and infants. Elevated rates of fetal growth retardation, perinatal death, and pregnancy and delivery complications—such as abruptio placentae, high blood pressure, and preeclampsia—have been observed among drug-abusing women and their infants.[69–73]

Cocaine Use

Maternal cocaine use has been associated with low birth weight, preterm labor, abruptio placentae, and fetal distress.[68,74,75] Brain damage and genitourinary malformations of the neonate have been reported, as well as fetal hyperthermia, thyroid abnormalities, stroke, and acute cardiac events.[76] Neurobehavioral effects found in neonates born to cocaine-abusing mothers have also been reported. These effects include decreased interactive behavior and poor organizational response to environmental stimuli.[72,74]

Marijuana Use

The effects of prenatal marijuana use on pregnancy and infant outcomes are inconclusive. Children exposed to marijuana *in utero* may be smaller than nonexposed infants.[68] Other reports suggest that pregnant women who smoke marijuana are at higher risk of preterm labor, miscarriage, and stillbirth.[76] However, other studies find no difference between users of marijuana and nonusers in terms of rate of miscarriage, type of presentation at birth, Apgar status, and frequency of complications or major physical anomalies at birth.[77]

Very little is known about the number of women who use drugs while pregnant, their pattern of drug usage during pregnancy, or the intensity of use. The prevalence of illicit drug use among pregnant women has been estimated using state level and hospital-based studies. Based on anonymous urine toxicology analysis combined with self-reporting, the prevalence of drug use among pregnant women has been estimated at 7.5% to 15%.[78,79]

Cocaine use among pregnant women has been estimated at 2.3% to 3.4%.[79,80] Regional and hospital-based data report marijuana use during pregnancy in the range of 3% to 12%

Prenatal cocaine and heroin abuse are clearly associated with adverse birth outcomes.

---

and opiate (heroin) use in the range of 2% to 4%.[78,79] Regional data, such as New York City birth certificate data,[81] documented the dramatic increase in cocaine use relative to other drugs during the 1980s.

Figure 1 presents a profile of substance use among one sample of pregnant women.[62] Extrapolation of the data suggests that about half of all pregnant women may completely abstain from cigarette, alcohol, or drug use. However, approximately 14% of pregnant women engage in two or more high-risk behaviors during pregnancy, with about 2.5% of pregnant women, possibly about 100,000 nationwide, combining smoking, drinking, and recreational drug use.

Recent evidence suggests that, for pregnant women who receive treatment for drug abuse before their third trimester, the risks of low birth weight and preterm birth due to cocaine use may be minimized.[82] Little is known about which women quit or reduce drug use and why. In one study, college-educated, employed women were more likely to quit recreational drug use during pregnancy

Stress is widely cited in the popular literature as a serious risk to mothers and infants, but current research has not characterized its effects.

than were teenagers. The cessation rates were similar by racial/ethnic background and household income.[62] In another study, 14% of white women who used marijuana stopped using it upon starting prenatal care, as compared with 6% of African-American women.[83]

Stress, Physical Activity, Employment, Social Support, Violence, and Sexually Transmitted Diseases

As discussed in the previous section on demographic risk factors, physical and psychosocial stress may be associated with low birth weight. Stress is widely cited in the popular literature as a serious risk to mothers and infants, but current research has not characterized its effects. The scientific literature linking stress and anxiety to obstetric outcome has been equivocal, but there is some basis for the notion that maternal emotional distress may be linked to poor reproductive outcome.[84]

Stress

Stress is believed to influence maternal and infant health via changes in neuroendocrine functioning, immune system responses, and health behaviors. Thus, stress may influence pregnancy outcome directly (in terms of physiology) or indirectly (in terms of health behavior). Physiologically, stress has been associated with anxiety and depression.[85] It has been suggested that anxiety may increase metabolic expenditure and may lead to a lower gestational weight gain or to an anxiety-mediated change in catecholamine or hormonal balance which could provoke preterm labor.[37] Maternal psychological stress or emotional distress may interfere with the utilization of prenatal care of co-occur with particular health behaviors such as smoking and alcohol consumption.

However, the many methodological problems in much of the literature on stress and social support limit the extent to which studies can inform and guide policy and research. The studies are often based on small and ungeneralizable samples, and suffer from possible recall biases, poor reliability, and validity of study instruments and confounding. These difficulties arise from the multifactorial nature of stress and social support and from the problems inherent in trying to characterize these poorly understood elements of people's lives.

Physical Activity

Concerns about weight gain and health have resulted in a high level of consciousness about weight control. More than one-third of American women participate in some form of regular physical activity.[86] Moderate aerobic exercise during pregnancy appears to have little adverse effect on pregnancy outcomes, and the potential benefits of exercise appear to be considerable.[87] Moderate exercise may be particularly beneficial for women at risk of developing diabetes during pregnancy. Lower levels of blood sugar were observed among diabetic women who were randomly assigned to moderate exercise regimens.[88] Decreases in the discomforts of pregnancy, improved self-esteem, and reduced tensions were reported among women who had participated in moderate physical conditioning programs during pregnancy.[89]

Employment

The majority of American women are employed during pregnancy.[90] Women are employed in a wide range of occupations, which have varying degrees of physical and emotional demands, and varying levels of exposure to employment-related chemicals, radiation, or other toxic substances. Thus, defining a particular "exposure" that characterizes the potential risks of employment has been difficult. In addition, the interrelationship between employment and socioeconomic status is unavoidable. Employed mothers also may accrue positive effects of employment through increased socioeconomic status, better access to medical care, and improved overall lifestyle.[91]

In general, the results of studies evaluating the relationship between employment and low birth weight have been inconclusive.[92] Studies conducted outside the United States have found increased rates of low birth weight and preterm birth among employed women whose jobs required heavy physical labor. However, results of studies conducted in the United States are more mixed and have even demonstrated positive effects of employment. Further advances in this area will be hampered until we are able to better understand the complex relationship among socioeconomic status, employment, stress, and lifestyle.

Domestic Violence

Depending on the population surveyed and the questions asked, the prevalence of battering of pregnant women has been estimated to be 8% to 17%.[93,94] There is some evidence of low birth weight among women

Figure 1

Profile of Substance Use Among Pregnant Women

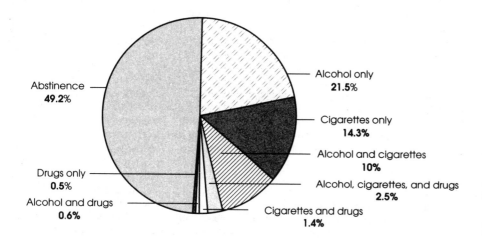

Abstinence 49.2%
Alcohol only 21.5%
Cigarettes only 14.3%
Alcohol and cigarettes 10%
Alcohol, cigarettes, and drugs 2.5%
Cigarettes and drugs 1.4%
Alcohol and drugs 0.6%
Drugs only 0.5%

Source: Adapted from Johnson, S. F., McCarter, R. J., and Ferencz, C. Changes in alcohol, cigarette, and recreational drug use during pregnancy: Implications for intervention. *American Journal of Epidemiology* (1987) 126,4:701. Reprinted with permission of the *American Journal of Epidemiology.*

who have been abused during pregnancy,[95] possibly due to a physical trauma that initiates abruption, infections, or uterine contractions leading to early onset of labor. In addition, victimization of women may lead to a neglect of chronic medical conditions or to later initiation of prenatal care.[94]

Sexually Transmitted Diseases

Whether or not a woman gets infected with a sexually transmitted disease is highly associated with her sexual behavior and the sexual behavior of her partners. The chance of being infected increases with the number of sexual partners. There is increasing evidence to indicate that various genital infections are associated with low birth weight and preterm delivery.[96] However, the large number of implicated organisms combined with the numerous genital tract sites that they might infect has made the investigation of sexually transmitted diseases and low birth weight very challenging. Aside from the devastating effects on the fetus of untreated syphilis or gonorrhea, few specific organisms or defined genital tract infections have conclusively been shown to be highly correlated with preterm birth or low birth weight.[96] Most of the evidence linking genital organisms or infections to birth outcomes has been inconsistent and has shown only a low to moderate association. Clinical trials of antibiotics aimed at removing the organisms or infections have not consistently improved pregnancy outcomes.[96]

Other maternal infections during pregnancy, such as cytomegalovirus, genitourinary infections, pyelonephritis, and HIV, as well as food- or environmentally-borne infections such as toxoplasmosis and listeriosis, may endanger the health of the mother and fetus.[5,97–99]

Assessing the Impact of Lifestyle Risk Factors on Maternal and Infant Health

In this section, we try to estimate the number of excess low birth weight or small-for-gestational-age babies born due to maternal lifestyle risk factors. As noted earlier, the risk factors for low birth weight described above do not occur as isolated events; rather, they are part of a complex web of social, environmental, and individual factors. To understand the importance of these individual risk factors, we must try to fit them into a framework that represents a realistic picture of what is occurring in women's lives. This task is made more difficult because of our limited knowledge of the many common risk factors and the many potential interactions between factors which would result in a compounding of adverse effects—such as alcohol abuse and heavy cigarette smoking—as well as the role of protective factors.

Figure 2

Prevalence of Low Weight Gain and Substance Use Among Pregnant Women

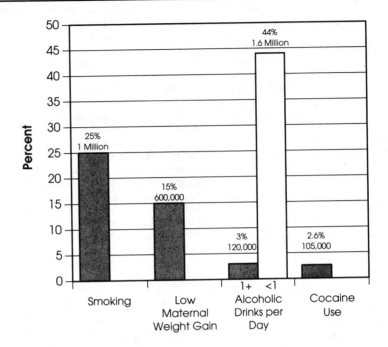

Source: Chomitz, V. R., Cheung, L., and Lieberman, E. *Healthy mothers—Healthy beginnings.* A white paper prepared by the Center for Health Communication, Harvard School of Public Health, Boston: President and Fellows of Harvard College, 1992.

The prevalence of battering of pregnant women has been estimated to be 8% to 17%.

We started by selecting the risk factors that have a consistent relationship with low birth weight and have been shown to be modifiable. These risk factors are cigarette smoking, alcohol abuse, cocaine abuse, and inadequate weight gain during pregnancy. The data on the prevalence of these factors and the risk incurred were derived from a variety of national and regional studies, and thus the estimates presented reflect the demographic and regional profile of the sample used. The estimates are not the result of a meta-analysis, but are based on published analyses that represent conservative and plausible risk.

We estimated the extra adverse birth outcomes attributed to high-risk lifestyle factors by applying the rate of low birth weight deliveries among cigarette smokers, women with inadequate weight gain, alcohol drinkers, and cocaine users, minus a baseline rate of low birth weight among low-risk women. The effects of reducing stress and exposure to infectious agents cannot be quantified at this time. The numbers we derived are very rough estimates and should be regarded only as order of magnitude estimates.

Prevalence of Lifestyle Risk Factors

From the literature, we extrapolated estimates of the prevalence of high-risk behaviors among pregnant women to the number of live births in the United States in 1989. Some 20% to 25% of pregnant women, or approximately one million, smoked during pregnancy.[32,33] (see Figure 2.) Approximately 15%, or about 600,000 nonobese women, may have an inadequate total weight gain of less than 22 pounds during their pregnancy. More than 40% of women may not completely abstain from alcohol but consume less than one drink per day during pregnancy; about 3%, or 120,000 women, may have one or more drinks per day.[54] Approximately 105,000, or 2.6% of women, may use cocaine around the time of delivery.[79]

Excess Adverse Birth Outcomes

In 1990, there were 4,158,212 births in the United States, and 6.97% (approximately 290,000) of these infants were born low birth weight.[100] It comes as no surprise that reducing cigarette smoking has the largest potential to reduce the incidence of low birth weight. Approximately 48,000 low birth weight births could have been prevented if women had not smoked during pregnancy.

Women who failed to gain adequate weight (less than 22 pounds) by term gave birth to approximately 22,000 extra low birth weight babies who were born at full term. Approximately 14,000 infants a year may be born small for their gestational age due to

maternal alcohol consumption, and 10,000 excess low birth weight births could be attributed to prenatal cocaine abuse.

The low birth weight births that are potentially preventable due to smoking, inadequate weight gain, and alcohol use would generally reduce the number of infants who were born too small due to growth retardation but would have little effect on the number of infants born preterm. The lack of a relationship between these risk factors and preterm birth indicates that little improvement in preterm birth rates could be expected with the elimination of these risk factors.

Our estimates of the number of low birth weight births are very rough and may be inaccurate, as these numbers are only as good as our current knowledge of the true relationships between these risk factors and birth outcomes. The number of low birth weight births estimated to be due to each of these factors cannot simply be added together to

derive the total number of births that might be prevented by lifestyle changes because these estimates do not take into consideration the interrelationships among the risk factors. For example, a woman who is a heavy smoker and drinker would be counted twice in these calculations.

Directions for Future Research: Identifying Barriers to Change

Women face systemic, psychosocial, biological, or knowledge and attitudinal barriers to lifestyle changes. Further research must identify successful strategies for influencing behaviors. Figure 3 illustrates the complexity and interrelationship of common barriers to improving prenatal care and nutritional status, and for modifying smoking, drinking, and drug use.

Figure 3

Barriers to Behavioral Change

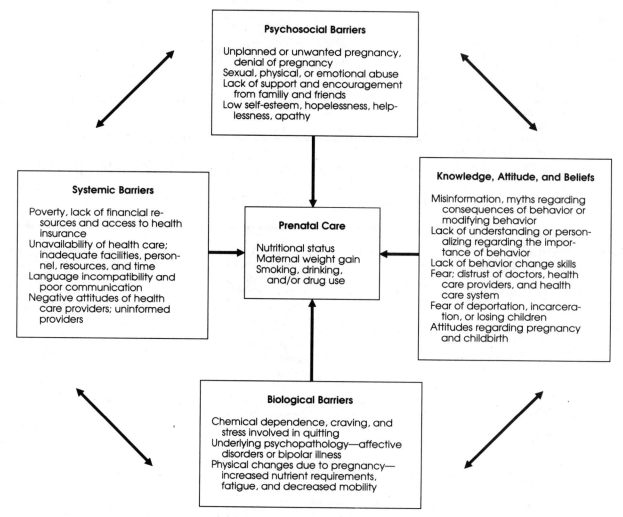

Source: Center for Health Communication, Harvard School of Public Health.

Although some individuals within an economically depressed or stressful situation may be involved in adverse lifestyle behaviors, most women are not. It is therefore important not only to conduct research with those individuals who have less healthy lifestyles, but also to profile and learn from those who, given similar environmental pressures, do not engage in high-risk behaviors or who have been able to change; that is, we must discover the protective strategies or resilience among individuals who are not engaged in adverse lifestyle behaviors, and apply the lessons learned to intervention programs.

must overcome. Expecting women simply to change or modify their behavior without support and attention from the health care system, society, and influential people in their lives is unrealistic and may help to foster the belief that women are solely to blame for undesirable behaviors.

Barriers to successful intervention will not be overcome in the short term and will require both system-level reform and indi-

Strategies that can reduce the burden of low birth weight do exist. The public and private sectors must work together to define, develop, and implement these strategies.

Pregnancy and the prospect of pregnancy provide a window of opportunity to improve a woman's health before pregnancy, during pregnancy, and after the birth of her child.

Directions for Prevention/Intervention

Pregnancy and the prospect of pregnancy provide a window of opportunity to improve a woman's health before pregnancy, during pregnancy, and after the birth of her child. Pregnancy provides an opportunity for increased contact with the health care system and is associated with a heightened concern regarding health. Moreover, healthier mothers are more likely to provide more healthful beginnings for their children.

The adoption of healthful lifestyle behaviors before or during pregnancy, such as ceasing to smoke cigarettes, eating foods that supply adequate nutrition and produce an appropriate pregnancy weight gain, ceasing or reducing alcohol consumption, and ceasing illicit drug use, can also positively affect the long-term health of women, future pregnancy outcomes, and the health of children.

The health of the family, in general, may also be improved through household dietary changes and the reduction of environmental risks such as secondhand smoke. However, it must be reiterated that behaviors should not be isolated from the environment (society, community, and family) that fosters and supports them, and thus a change in the elements within the environment will facilitate an individual's ability to change his or her behavior. Despite the importance of maternal behavior modification to the health of mothers, infants, and families, it is important to recognize that there are systemic, biological, psychosocial, and belief and attitudinal barriers to behavioral change which women also

vidual efforts. Many women who smoke, engage in high-risk behaviors, eat poorly, or lack access to health care also live surrounded by poverty and violence, and go without adequate housing or employment. Under such circumstances, living a healthful lifestyle may not be a priority compared with day-to-day survival.

Overcoming these social circumstances will require increased access and availability to quality health care, as well as other affiliated resources and facilities such as child care, social services, law enforcement services, affordable and quality food, transportation, and maternity provisions during employment.

Finding ways to improve maternal and infant health and decrease the low birth weight rate is difficult, at least in part because the known causes of low birth weight are multifactorial, and much of the etiology remains unknown. The independent effects of economic disadvantage and inadequate health care coverage on maternal and infant health are difficult to isolate. In addition, medical risk factors that are identified and managed either before or during pregnancy can positively influence the health of women and their infants. Thus, linking women to continuous health care early in pregnancy or, ideally, before conception is a high priority for intervention.

Health promotion efforts aimed at improving infant health must do so by improving women's health. Improving women's health before, during, and after pregnancy is the key to reducing the human and economic costs associated with infant mortality and morbidity. To improve both women's and infants' health, efforts must target long-term, societal elements that involve policy or legislative changes.

These efforts should include an emphasis on preventive health care services, family-oriented work site options, changes in social norms, and individual behavior modification.

Notes

1. National Center for Health Statistics. *Advance report of final natality statistics, 1991.* Monthly Vital Statistics Report, Vol. 42, No. 3, Suppl. Hyattsville, MD: Public Health Service, September 9, 1993.
2. Kleinman, J., and Kessel, S. Racial differences in low birthweight: Trends and risk factors. *New England Journal of Medicine* (1987) 317,12:749–53.
3. Ahmed, F. Unmarried mothers as a high-risk group for adverse pregnancy outcomes. *Journal of Community Health* (1990) 15,1:35–44.
4. Bennett, T. Marital status and infant health outcomes. *Social Science Medicine* (1992) 35,9:1179–87.
5. Institute of Medicine, Committee to Study the Prevention of Low Birthweight. *Preventing low birthweight.* Washington, DC: National Academy Press, 1985.
6. McCormick, M. C., Brooks-Gunn, J., Shorter, T., et al. Factors associated with smoking in low income pregnant women: Relationship to birthweight, stressful life events, social support, health behaviors, and mental distress. *Journal of Clinical Epidemiology* (1990) 43:441–48.
7. Brooks-Gunn, J. Support and stress during pregnancy: What do they tell us about low birthweight? In *Advances in the prevention of low birthweight: An international symposium.* H. Berendes, S. Kessel, and S. Yaffe, eds. Washington, DC: National Center for Education in Maternal and Child Health, 1991, pp. 39–60.
8. Collins, Jr., J. W., and David, R. J. The differential effect of traditional risk factors on infant birthweight among blacks and whites in Chicago. *American Journal of Public Health* (1990) 80,6:679.
9. Shiono, P., Klebanoff, M., and Rhoads, G. Smoking and drinking during pregnancy. *Journal of the American Medical Association* (1986) 255:82–84.
10. Geronimus, A. T., and Bound, J. Black/white differences in women's reproductive-related health status: Evidence from vital statistics. *Demography* (1990) 27,3:457–66.
11. Kleinman, J., Fingerhut, L. A., and Prager K. Differences in infant mortality by race, nativity status, and other maternal characteristics. *American Journal of Diseases of Children* (1991) 145:194–99.
12. Moss, N. Demographic and behavioral sciences five year research plan. Draft. Bethesda, MD: National Institute of Child Health and Human Development, 1991.
13. Scholl, T., Hediger, J., Khoo, C., et al. Maternal weight gain, diet and infant birth weight: Correlations during adolescent pregnancy. *Journal of Clinical Epidemiology* (1991) 44:423–28.
14. Susser, M. Maternal weight gain, infant birth weight, and diet: Causal sequences. *American Journal of Clinical Nutrition* (1991) 53,6:1384–96.
15. Kleinman, J. *Maternal weight gain during pregnancy: Determinants and consequences.*

Working Paper No. 33. Hyattsville, MD: National Center for Health Statistics, 1990.

16. Luke, B., Dickinson, C., and Petrie, R. H. Intrauterine growth: Correlations and maternal nutritional status and rate of gestational weight gain. *European Journal of Obstetrics, Gynecology, and Reproductive Biology* (1981) 12:113–21.

17. Kramer, M. S., McLean, F. H., Eason, E. L., and Usher, R. H. Maternal nutrition and spontaneous preterm birth. *American Journal of Epidemiology* (1992) 136:574–83.

18. Kramer, M. S., Coates, A. L., Michoud, M., and Hamilton, E. F. Maternal nutrition and idiopathic preterm labor. *Pediatric Research* (1994) 35,4:277A.

19. National Center for Health Statistics. *Advance report of maternal and infant health data from the birth certificate, 1990.* Monthly Vital Statistics Report, Vol. 42, No. 2, Suppl. Hyattsville, MD: Public Health Service, July 8, 1993.

20. Carruth, B. R., and Skinner, J. D. Practitioners beware: Regional differences in beliefs about nutrition during pregnancy. *Journal of American Dietetic Association* (1991) 91, 4:435–40.

21. Chez, R. Weight gain during pregnancy. *American Journal of Public Health* (1986) 76:1390–91.

22. Keppel, K. G., and Taffel, S. M. Pregnancy-related weight gain and retention: Implications of the 1990 Institute of Medicine Guidelines. *American Journal of Public Health* (1993) 83:1100–1103.

23. Klein, L. Premature birth and maternal prenatal anemia. *American Journal of Obstetrics and Gynecology* (1962) 83,5:588–90.

24. Klebanoff, M. A., Shiono, P. H., Selby, J. V., et al. Anemia and spontaneous preterm birth. *American Journal of Obstetrics and Gynecology* (1991) 164:59–63.

25. Lieberman, E., Ryan, K., Monson, R. R., and Schoenbaum, S. C. Association of maternal hematocrit with premature labor. *American Journal of Obstetrics and Gynecology* (1988) 159:107–14.

26. Klebanoff, J., and Shiono, P. H. Facts and artifacts about anemia and preterm birth. *Journal of the American Medical Association* (1989) 262:511–15.

27. Institute of Medicine, Subcommittee on Nutritional Status and Weight Gain During Pregnancy. *Nutrition during pregnancy.* Washington, DC: National Academy Press, 1990.

28. Dwyer, J. Impact of maternal nutrition on infant health. *Medical Times* (1983) 111:30–38.

29. U.S. Department of Health, Education, and Welfare. *The health consequences of smoking.* DHEW/HSM 73–8704. Washington, DC: DHEW, 1973.

30. Kleinman, J., and Madans, J. H. The effects of maternal smoking, physical stature, and educational attainment on the incidence of low birth weight. *American Journal of Epidemiology* (1985) 121:832–55.

31. National Center for Health Statistics. *Advance report of new data from the 1989 birth certificate, 1989: Final data from the National Center for Health Statistics.* Monthly Vital Statistics Report, Vol. 40, No. 12. Hyattsville, MD: Public Health Service, April 15, 1992.

32. National Center for Health Statistics. *Advance report of final mortality statistics, 1989: Final data from the National Center for Health Statistics.* Monthly Vital Statistics Report, Vol. 40, No. 8, Suppl. 2. Hyattsville, MD: Public Health Service, January 7, 1992.

33. U.S. Department of Health and Human Services. *The health benefits of smoking cessation: A report of the Surgeon General.* DHHS/CDC 90–8416. Washington, DC: DHHS, 1990.

34. Cardoza, L. D., Gibb, D. M. F., Studd, J. W. W., and Cooper, D. J. Social and obstetric features associated with smoking in pregnancy. *British Journal of Obstetrics and Gynecology* (1982) 89:622–27.

35. See note no. 32, National Center for Health Statistics, for mortality statistics in 1989.

36. Butler, N., Goldstein, H., and Ross, E. Cigarette smoking in pregnancy: Its influence on birth weight and perinatal mortality. *British Medical Journal* (1972) 2:127–30.

37. Kramer, M. S. Determinants of low birth weight: Methodological assessment and meta-analysis. *Bulletin of the World Health Organization* (1987) 65:663–737.

38. Martin, T., and Bracken, M. Association of low birth weight with passive smoke exposure in pregnancy. *American Journal of Epidemiology* (1986) 124:633–42.

39. Rush, D., and Cassano, P. Relationship of cigarette smoking and social class to birth weight and perinatal mortality among all births in Britain, 5–11 April 1970. *Journal of Epidemiology and Community Health* (1983) 37:249–55.

40. Wilner, S., Secker-Walker, R. H., Flynn, B. S., et al. How to help the pregnant woman stop smoking. In *Smoking and reproductive health.* M. J. Rosenberg, ed. Littleton, MA: PSG Publishing, 1987, pp. 215–22.

41. Fingerhut, L. A., Kleinman, J. C., and Kendrick, J. S. Smoking before, during, and after pregnancy. *American Journal of Public Health* (1990) 80:541–44.

42. Waterson, E. J., and Murray-Lyon, I. M. Drinking and smoking patterns amongst women attending an antenatal clinic—II. During pregnancy. *Alcohol and Alcoholism* (1989) 24,2:163–73.

43. Windsor, R. *The handbook to plan, implement and evaluate smoking cessation programs for pregnant women.* White Plains, NY: March of Dimes Birth Defects Foundation, 1990.

44. Condon, J. T., and Hilton, C. A. A comparison of smoking and drinking behaviors in pregnant women: Who abstains and why. *Medical Journal of Australia* (1988) 148:381–85.

45. Burns, D., and Pierce, J. P. *Tobacco use in California 1990–1991.* Sacramento: California Department of Health Services, 1992.

46. Brandt. E. N. Smoking and reproductive health. In *Smoking and reproductive health.* M. J. Rosenberg, ed. Littleton, MA: PSG Publishing, 1987, pp 1–3.

47. Weitzman, M., Gortmaker, S., Walker, D. K., and Sobol, A. Maternal smoking and childhood asthma. *Pediatrics* (1990) 85:505–11.

48. U.S. Department of Health and Human Services. *Reducing the health consequences of smoking: A report of the Surgeon General.* DHHS/CDC 89–8411. Rockville, MD: DHHS, 1989.

49. Samet, J. M., Lewit, E. M., and Warner, K. E. Involuntary smoking and children's health. *The Future of Children.* (Winter 1994) 4,3:94–114.

50. Serdula, M., Williamson, D., Kendrick, J., et al. Trends in alcohol consumption by pregnant women. *Journal of the American Medical Association* (1991) 265:876–79.

51. Ouellette, E. M., Rosett, H. L., Rosman, N. P., and Weiner, L. Adverse effects on offspring of maternal alcohol abuse during pregnancy. *New England Journal of Medicine* (1977) 297,10:528–30.

52. Abel, E. L., and Sokol, R. J. Incidence of fetal alcohol syndrome and economic impact of FAS-related anomalies. *Drug and Alcohol Dependence* (1987) 19:51–70.

53. Day, N. L., Jasperse, D., Richardson, G., et al. Prenatal exposure to alcohol: Effect on infant growth and morphologic characteristics. *Pediatrics* (1989) 84,3:536–41.

54. Mills, J. L., Graubard, B. I., Harley, E. E., et al. Maternal alcohol consumption and birth weight: How much drinking during pregnancy is safe? *Journal of the American Medical Association* (1984) 252,14:1875–79.

55. Larroque, B., Kaminski, M., Lelong, N., et al. Effects on birth weight of alcohol and caffeine consumption during pregnancy. *American Journal of Epidemiology* (1993) 137:941–50.

56. Halmesmaki, E., Raivio, K., and Ylikorkala, O. Patterns of alcohol consumption during pregnancy. *Obstetrics and Gynecology* (1987) 69:594–97.

57. Little, R., Asker, R. L., Sampson, P. D., and Renwick, J. H. Fetal growth and moderate drinking in early pregnancy. *American Journal of Epidemiology* (1986) 123,2:270–78.

58. Streissguth, A. P., Bookstein, F. L., Sampson, P. D., and Barr, H. M. Neurobehavioral effects of prenatal alcohol: Part III. PLS analyses of neuropsychologic tests. *Neurotoxicology and Teratology* (1989) 11,5:493–507.

59. Streissguth, A. P., Barr, H. M., and Sampson, P. D. Moderate prenatal alcohol exposure: Effects on child IQ and learning problems at age 7½ years. *Alcoholism, Clinical and Experimental Research* (1990) 14,5:662–69.

60. Walpole, I., Zubrick, S., and Pontre, J. Is there a fetal effect with low to moderate alcohol use before or during pregnancy? *Journal of Epidemiology and Community Health* (1990) 44,4:297–301.

61. Ernhart, C. B., Sokol. R. J., Ager, J. W., et al. Alcohol-related birth defects: Assessing the risk. *Annals of the New York Academy of Sciences* (1989) 562:159–72.

62. Johnson, S. F., McCarter, R. J., and Ferencz, C. Changes in alcohol, cigarette, and recreational drug use during pregnancy: Implications for intervention. *American Journal of Epidemiology* (1987) 126,4:695–702.

63. Little, R. Schultz, F., and Mandell, W. Alcohol consumption during pregnancy. *Journal of Studies on Alcohol* (1976) 37:375–79.

64. Russell, M. Drinking and pregnancy: A review of current research. *New York State Journal of Medicine* (1983) 8:1218–21.

65. See note no. 56, Halmesmaki, Raivio, and Ylikorkala, for more information about alcohol consumption patterns during pregnancy.

66. Lecos, C. Caffeine jitters: Some safety questions remain. *FDA Consumer* (December 1987/January 1988) 21:22.

67. Shiono, P. H., and Klebanoff, M. A. Invited commentary: Caffeine and birth outcomes. *American Journal of Epidemiology* (1993) 137:951–54.

68. Zuckerman, B., Frank, D. A., Hingson, R., et al. Effects of maternal marijuana and cocaine use on fetal growth. *New England Journal of Medicine* (1989) 320:762–68.

69. Zelson, C., Rubio, E., and Wasserman, E. Neonatal narcotic addiction: 10 year observation. *Pediatrics* (1971) 48,2:178–89.

70. Fricker, H., and Segal, S. Narcotic addiction, pregnancy, and the newborn. *American Journal of Diseases of Children* (1978) 132:360–66.

71. Lifschitz, M., Wilson, G., Smith, E., et al. Fetal and postnatal growth of children born to narcotic-dependent women. *Journal of Pediatrics* (1983) 102:686–91.

72. Robins, L. N., and Mills, J. L., Krulewitch, C., and Herman, A. A. Effects of in utero exposure to street drugs. *American Journal of Public Health* (December 1993) 83,12:S9.

73. Oleske, J. Experiences with 118 infants born to narcotic-using mothers. *Clinical Pediatrics* (1977) 16:418–23.

74. Dattel, B. J. Substance abuse in pregnancy. *Seminars in Perinatology* (1990) 14,2:179–87.

75. Bateman, D. A., Ng, S. K. C., Hansen, C. A., and Heagarty, M. C. The effects of intrauterine cocaine exposure in newborns. *American Journal of Public Health* (1993) 83,2:190–93.

76. Office for Substance Abuse Prevention. *Alcohol and other drugs can harm an unborn baby: Fact sheet and resource list.* Rockville, MD: National Clearinghouse for Alcohol and Drug Information, 1989, pp 1–19.

77. Fried, P. A., and Makin, J. E. Neonatal behavioral correlates of prenatal exposure to marijuana, cigarettes and alcohol in a low risk population. *Neurotoxicology and Teratology* (1986) 9:1–7.

78. Chasnoff, I. J., Landress, H. J., and Barrett, M. E. The prevalence of illicit-drug or alcohol use during pregnancy and discrepancies in mandatory reporting in Pinellas County, Florida. *New England Journal of Medicine* (1990) 322:1202–6.

79. Centers for Disease Control and Prevention. Statewide prevalence of illicit drug use by pregnant women—Rhode Island. *Morbidity and Mortality Weekly Report* (1990) 39,14:225–27.

80. Handler, A., Kistin, N., Davis, F., and Ferré, C. Cocaine use during pregnancy: Perinatal outcomes. *American Journal of Epidemiology* (1991) 133:818–25.

81. Zeitel, L., Bauer, T. A., and Brooks, P. *Infants at risk: Solutions within our reach.* New York: Greater New York March of Dimes/United Hospital Fund of New York, 1991.

82. U.S. General Accounting Office. *Drug abuse: The crack cocaine epidemic: Health consequences and treatment.* HRD-91–55FS. Washington, DC: GAO, 1991.

83. McCaul, M. E., Svikis, D. S., and Feng, T. Pregnancy and addition: Outcomes and interventions. *Maryland Medical Journal* (1991) 40:995–1001.

84. Newberger, E. H., Barkan, S. E., Leiberman, E. S., et al. Abuse of pregnant women and adverse birth outcome: Current knowledge and implications for practice. *Journal of the American Medical Association* (1992) 267,17:2370–72.

85. McAnarney, E. R., and Stevens-Simon, C. Maternal psychological stress/depression and low birth weight. *American Journal of Diseases of Children* (1990) 144:789–92.

86. Katch, F. I., and McArdle, W. E. *Introduction to nutrition, exercise and health.* 4th ed. Philadelphia: Lea and Febiger, 1993.

87. Dewey, K. G., and McCrory, M. A. Effects of dieting and physical activity on pregnancy and lactation. *American Journal of Clinical Nutrition* (1994) 59:446S–53S.

88. Jovanovic-Peterson, L., Durak, E. P., and Peterson, C. M. Randomized trial of diet versus diet plus cardiovascular conditioning on glucose levels in gestational diabetes. *American Journal of Obstetrics and Gynecology* (1989) 161:415–19.

89. Hall, D. C., and Kaufmann, D. A. Effects of aerobic and strength conditioning on pregnancy outcomes. *American Journal of Obstetrics and Gynecology* (1987) 157:1199–1203.

90. U.S. Bureau of the Census. *Work and family patterns of American women.* Current Population Reports, Series P-23, No. 165. Washington, DC: U.S. Government Printing Office, 1990.

91. Poerksen, A., and Petitti, D. B. Employment and low birth weight in black women. *Social Science and Medicine* (1991) 33:1281–96.

92. Simpson, J. L., Are physical activity and employment related to preterm birth and low birth weight? *American Journal of Obstetrics and Cynecology* (1993) 168:1231–38.

93. Helton, A. S., McFarlane, J., and Anderson, E. T. Battered and pregnant: A prevalence study. *American Journal of Public Health* (1987) 77,10:1337–39.

94. Mcfarlane, J., Parker, B., Soeken, K., and Bullock, L. Assessing for abuse during pregnancy: Severity and frequency of injuries and associated entry into prenatal care. *Journal of the American Medical Association* (1992) 267,23:3176–78.

95. Bullock, L. F., and Mcfarlane, J. The birthweight/battering connection. *American Journal of Nursing* (September 1989):1153–55.

96. Gibbs, R. S., Romero, R., Hillier, S. L., et al. A review of premature birth and subclinical infection. *American Journal of Obstetrics and Gynecology* (1992) 166:1515–28.

97. Carroll, J. C. Chalmaydia trachomatis during pregnancy: To screen or not to screen? *Canadian Family Physician* (1993) 39:97–102.

98. Kramer, M. S. The etiology and prevention of low birthweight: Current knowledge and priorities for future research. In *Advances in the prevention of low birthweight: An international symposium.* H. Berendes, S. Kessel, and S. Yaffe, eds. Washington, DC: National Center for Education in Maternal and Child Health, 1991, pp. 25–39.

99. Zygmunt, D. J. Toxoplasma gondii. *Infection Control and Hospital Epidemiology* (1990) 11,4:207–11.

100. Wegman, M. E. Annual summary of vital statistics—1992. *Pediatrics* (1993) 92,6:743–54.

Behaviors of a newborn can be traced to the fetus

The prenatal environment

Fetal research gives scientists unique insight into how behaviors and sensory systems develop.

By Beth Azar
Monitor staff

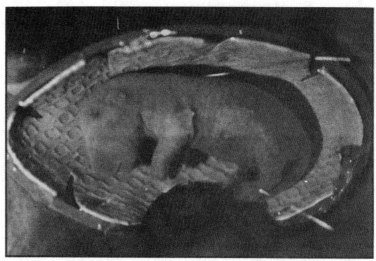

Studies of the rat fetus—kept alive outside its mother—find that touch is imperative to survival.

Some developmental researchers are so curious about how children's brains and behaviors develop that they're pushing the limits of technology to examine development prenatally. And over the past several years their efforts have borne fruit.

Researches are discovering how prenatal experiences affect child development. One of the most remarkable findings, say researchers, is that there isn't a dramatic shift in behavior and abilities from fetus to newborn.

"In some ways the newborn is a 'fetus exutero,'" says Cornell psychologist Steve Robertson, PhD. "Much of the behavior we see in the newborn can be traced directly back to behavior present in the fetus."

For example, Robertson has carefully examined and modeled fetal and then infant movements in humans and animals. He finds that there is a pattern to fetal movement that continues after birth. By age 2 or 3 months, babies' movements begin to appear more intentional. However, the spontaneous fetal movements continue to occur while they sleep.

These movements may play a role in priming animals for coordinated behavior, such as suckling, says Robertson. As part of a continuing collaboration between Robertson and Binghamton University psychologist William Smotherman, PhD, undergraduate students James Reilly and Ben MaClennan found that the waves of spontaneous motor activity seen in the rat fetus predict whether the fetus will respond to an artificial nipple put close to its mouth. "The fluctuations in movement seem to be playing a key role in how the fetus interacts with its environment," says Robertson.

Fetal experiences may also be crucial to survival outside the uterus, according to research by Indiana University psychologists April Ronca, PhD, and Jeffrey Alberts, PhD. In particular, the experience of birth appears to not only jump-start the fetus for the transition to the outside world but also to impart information important to survival, Ronca and Alberts find.

For example, up to 24 hours before a female rat goes into labor, she makes numerous movements, including frequently rearing onto her hind legs, vigorously licking her abdomen and scratching her belly. During this period the fetus is poked, stroked and shaken up, a process that turns out to be critical for development, Ronca and Alberts find.

If the researchers remove a pup from its mother's uterus and "deliver" it very gently, it never starts breathing and dies once the umbilical cord is cut. But when they provide the same tactile stimuli that the pup would receive inside the womb—squeezing it with a simulated uterine contraction, brushing it with an artificial tongue and tilting it to the same degree as when the mother rears—it breathes and develops normally.

Research in humans, including work by University of Miami psychologist Tiffany Field, PhD, finds that premature babies require touch to thrive. Alberts believes that tactile stimulation during and just after birth activates a chemical mechanism that prepares the body for the outside world. And work by researchers such as Saul Schanberg, PhD, MD, are beginning to elucidate those mechanisms.

The birth process may also impart important survival information, says Alberts. Years ago, psychologist Elliot Blass, PhD, now at the University of Massachusetts at Amherst, and his colleagues, found that the smell of the uterine environment is a crucial cue for suckling. When they injected a citrus smell into the amniotic fluid of a pregnant rat beginning 17 days into the pregnancy, her pups would suckle only nipples that were sprayed with citrus.

As an extension of that earlier research, Ronca and graduate student Regina Abel recently found that both smell and tactile stimulation just before birth are critical to suckling. They combined the citrus experiment with the tactile stimulation paradigm—externalizing fetuses and providing them with tactile stimulation in the presence of citrus or no tactile stimulation in the presence of citrus. They kept the pups that received no tactile stimulation alive by stimulating them postnatally.

The researchers found that around 80 percent of the pups that received both tactile stimulation and citrus successfully attached to their mothers' citrus-scented nipples. But few of the pups in the other group successfully suckled, even though they were exposed to citrus in utero, says Ronca.

"They're unprepared—they don't know what to do to feed themselves," adds Alberts. "This research shows us that experiences intrinsic to the birth process prime us for how we interact with the environment."

Rats in space

The prenatal experience also appears to determine how certain sensory systems develop, Alberts and Ronca find. In particular, they have studied the vestibular system—the sensors in the inner ear that keep track of gravity and body position, providing animals with a sense of balance. They examined how gravity affects the development of balance by studying rats that develop in a weightless environment.

Twice, they joined with a team of researchers funded by the National Institutes of Health and NASA to send a group of pregnant rats up in the space shuttle. The rats lived there in virtual weightlessness for about half of their pregnancy, returning to Earth and gravity soon before delivery. The researchers wanted to test how development might differ if it occurs without the constant gravitational cues experienced by organisms that develop and live on Earth.

The space rats' pups were born on time and were just as healthy as pups born to a group of control rats who stayed on Earth throughout their pregnancies, says Alberts. However, the researchers detected several differences in their sense of balance. For example, if rats are placed on their backs in a tank of warm water, they right themselves as they sink.

But when the researchers dropped the space pups in water, they responded poorly, even landing on their heads when failing to right themselves in time. This problem dissipated quickly, but it indicates that the pups' vestibular system was not initially prepared for the gravity-laden world.

"Examining behavior in the fetus is helping decipher how these sensory and behavioral systems develop and, perhaps, when development might go wrong," says Alberts.

Maternal emotions may influence fetal behaviors

One psychologist has shown that fetal behavior may predict infant temperament.

By Beth Azar
Monitor staff

Researchers are beginning to see behavioral effects of the uterine environment on fetal behavior. And they're finding that such behaviors in utero may predict behaviors in the newborn.

"While most people assume that the constitutional nature of infant temperament reflects genetic influences, I'm convinced that the intrauterine hormonal milieu, moderated by the mother's level of stress and other psychological characteristics, make an equally significant contribution," says Johns Hopkins University psychologist Janet DiPietro, PhD.

In a series of studies, she has found that fetal measures, such as movement and heart rate, may predict 20 percent to 60 percent of variation in temperament. In the first study to test this link, DiPietro and her colleagues examined 31 fetuses at six points during gestation and then mothers reported on their temperaments at 3 and 6 months after birth.

The babies who were more active prenatally were perceived by their mothers as being more irritable and more active at 3 and 6 months. And babies with higher heart rates in utero were less active and less predictable than babies with lower in-utero heart rates. Also, babies who never developed a regular sleep-wake pattern in the womb woke more at night at age 3 months than infants who began to regulate their sleep-wake pattern prenatally. DiPietro and her colleagues have begun a study to replicate these findings using a larger sample and laboratory-based observations of temperament.

Certain environmental factors, such as maternal stress and socioeconomic status, seem to affect the same fetal behaviors—heart rate and movement—that DiPietro finds help predict infant temperament.

For example, in a study of 103 infants and their mothers, now in press at *Developmental Psychobiology,* she finds that, prenatally, babies of women of low socioeconomic status were less active and had less heart-rate variability than babies of middle-class women. All of the fetuses fell within normal clinical values, but the differences between the two groups were consistent, says DiPietro.

Data collected on maternal perceptions of stress suggest that fetuses of women who report a lot of stress—regardless of socioeconomic status—have different patterns of movement and heart rate than fetuses of women under less stress. It's still unclear whether this difference affects postnatal development, says DiPietro.

But even small changes in mood seem to directly affect the fetus, according to preliminary data from a study by Columbia University psychologist William Fifer, PhD, and his colleagues. They showed pregnant women a videotape of a woman breast-feeding her baby. During the film, the women's heart rates and respiration increased, and as they did so did the heart rates of their fetuses. It's unclear how the change in heart rate is transmitted from mother to fetus, says Fifer. The fetus could be responding to movements, hormonal changes or simply the sound of its mother's increased heart rate.

An abundance of research shows that infant behavior is affected by the substances mothers consume during pregnancy. Now studies in the fetus find that the effects begin prenatally. For example, Emory University psychologist Eugene K. Emory, PhD, and his colleagues find that if a woman smokes, her fetus does not habituate to a vibrating stimulus but the fetuses of non-smokers do. This may indicate a difference in the stress response of fetuses of women who smoke, says Emory.

Drug-Exposed Infants

Lucy Salcido Carter
Carol S. Larson

Abstract

The problem of drug-exposed infants has been a societal concern for more than a decade. *The Future of Children* devoted its first journal issue in spring 1991[1] to this topic and has provided information updates in subsequent journal issues.[2] The 1991 issue reviewed the major trends in judicial, legislative, and treatment responses to this problem, reporting that, for the most part, appellate courts were rejecting attempts to prosecute pregnant substance-abusing women, and state and federal legislative efforts were creating more treatment programs for, rather than punishment of, these women. With only limited exceptions, these trends continue today. Evaluations of treatment programs funded through the federal initiatives of the late 1980s and early 1990s show some level of treatment effectiveness. However, they also highlight the continuing need for rigorous evaluations of treatment outcomes.

Lucy Salcido Carter, J.D., is a legal research analyst at the Center for the Future of Children.

Carol S. Larson, J.D., is director of foundation programs for the David and Lucile Packard Foundation, and special advisor to the Center for the Future of Children.

This update reviews recent judicial and legislative responses, and includes preliminary results from the major federal funding initiatives for treatment programs and evaluations. A local community treatment program funded under one of these initiatives is described briefly.

Judicial Activity

In 1997, it continues to be true that no state statute has created criminal laws specifically applicable to pregnant women who use illicit drugs. However, prosecutors continue to use other statutes protecting children to charge women for actions that potentially harm the fetus. Appellate courts reviewing guilty verdicts have typically ruled in favor of the mothers, finding that legislatures did not intend these statutes to apply to fetuses. A significant exception to this is the South Carolina Supreme Court case *Whitner v. State* decided on July 15, 1996.[3] In this case, the court affirmed conviction of the mother for criminal child neglect because her baby was born with cocaine in her system after the mother used cocaine in the third trimester of pregnancy. The court held that the broad language of South Carolina's criminal neglect statute and its underlying policy of prevention supported the legislature's intent to include viable fetuses within the definition of persons under the statute. The South Carolina Supreme Court did not address federal and state constitutional issues relating to due process and privacy, because these issues were not raised in the lower court. Attorneys for the mother have filed a motion for rehearing, claim-

---

In the late 1980s and early 1990s, heightened attention to perinatal substance abuse prompted significant federal efforts to increase the availability of drug abuse prevention and treatment programs for women.

---

ing that the South Carolina Supreme Court must reach a decision on the constitutional claims. At this time, the court has neither granted nor denied the motion for rehearing.[4]

Legislative Activity

State legislative activity continues to focus on increasing opportunities for treatment and creating task forces to further explore solutions to the problem of perinatal substance abuse.[5] For example, a law enacted in Arizona[6] in 1995 created an Advisory Council on Perinatal Substance Abuse to develop a statewide strategy for addressing substance abuse by pregnant women and mothers. A 1994 Michigan statute[7] requires that substance-abusing pregnant women and women with dependent children have priority in receiving treatment for substance abuse in state-funded facilities. And a 1995 Illinois statute[8] now permits counties in that state to retain revenues from drug-related fines to support community-based treatment for pregnant women addicted to alcohol and/or drugs. The American Academy of Pediatrics tracks such legislative developments.[5]

Federal Initiatives

In the late 1980s and early 1990s, heightened attention to this issue prompted significant federal efforts to increase the availability of drug abuse prevention and treatment programs for women.[9] The following describes briefly the four major federal initiatives and reports available to date for each.

Programs for Pregnant and Postpartum Women and Their Infants

Between 1989 and 1992, the federal Center for Substance Abuse Prevention initiated five-year grants for 147 Pregnant and Postpartum Women and Their Infants (PPWI) projects.[10] These projects provide comprehensive prevention, intervention, and treatment services to substance-abusing pregnant and postpartum women, as well as health and related services to their infants. An example of a PPWI program in Santa Clara County, California, is described in Box 1.

A 1997 evaluation of 90 PPWI demonstrations[11] claims that these programs have been highly successful in improving the coordination, availability, and accessibility of health care and alcohol and drug treatment for pregnant and postpartum women. The study also found that at least one-third of the women served by these programs reduced their drug use.[12]

The Perinatal 20 Projects

The National Institute on Drug Abuse (NIDA) funded a total of 20 projects in 1989 and 1990 to create new treatment opportunities for women with children and to conduct treatment research. These projects, which are no longer funded, were research driven; treatment approaches were designed to answer hypothetical research questions posed by the grantees.

Compilations of findings from project evaluations primarily address methodological issues related to research.[13] Individual program evaluators were encouraged to publish treatment outcomes in peer-review journals. An annotated bibliography on treatment outcomes for women lists many of these published studies.[14]

The Abandoned Infants Assistance Act

In 1988, Congress passed the Abandoned Infants Assistance Act (AIA)[15] to support comprehensive intervention programs to serve drug-exposed and HIV-affected infants and their families. Approximately 30 programs are funded annually. They provide a variety of services, including case

Box 1

One Community Treatment Response:
The Perinatal Substance Abuse Program (PSAP)

The Perinatal Substance Abuse Program (PSAP) is a county-administered, long-term outpatient treatment program with facilities in a hospital complex.[a] The program follows a one-stop shopping model of providing to substance-abusing pregnant women and mothers[b] a comprehensive array of services at one location. These services include individual case management and counseling, 12-step program meetings to help clients combat their addictions, parenting and prevocational skills (such as reading, math, and GED) classes, and on-site child care while mothers are in program activities. A program physician is available two days a week to all clients for consultation and to monitor the clients on methadone maintenance.

The treatment program is designed to take 18 months to complete; however, clients can remain in the program for a longer period of time if they are motivated and it is clear that they need extra time. In the program's first five years, 535 women were enrolled, and 177 births occurred.

Toxicological tests taken from July 1992 through June 1995 revealed that 84% of the women enrolled in the treatment program reduced their substance use. Eighty-two percent of infants born to 71 women (for whom data were available) had negative toxicological screens at birth. Seventy-five percent of births to women in treatment produced infants of normal birth weight. The designers of this program believe, based on their experience, that the number of drug-exposed infants and low birth weight infants would have been higher if the program had not been available to these pregnant women. However, it was beyond the scope of the evaluation to examine comparative birth weights and toxicology results for infants born to drug-abusing women who were not in treatment during pregnancy.

[a]For more information about this program, see the final report for CSAP grant #SPO1498–01, available through the Office of Women's Treatment Services, Perinatal Substance Abuse Program, Anthony J. Puentes Center, 2425 Enborg Lane, San Jose, CA 95128, telephone (408) 885–4060.

[b]Though self-referred women are welcome, most of PSAP's clients were either referred by child protective services or ordered by a court to attend a treatment program.

management, pediatric health care, housing assistance, and respite care for primary caregivers.[16]

Data on AIA programs compiled in annual reports are largely descriptive, rather than evaluative. Individual program evaluations have been conducted, and a monograph summarizing services outcomes for eight of the programs is forthcoming.[17] In October 1996, the collection of client-level outcome data was begun to better assess and refine AIA programs.[18]

Residential Treatment Grants

The federal Center for Substance Abuse Treatment (CSAT) initiated two demonstration residential programs in 1993: the Residential Treatment Grants for Pregnant and Postpartum Women and Their Infants (PPWI) and the Residential Treatment Grants for Women and Their Children (RWC). Both were designed to support comprehensive residential treatment services, including primary health care, mental health assessments and counseling, and other social services for substance-abusing women and their children. In 1996, some 74 residential programs were

funded and approximately 2,700 women and 2,900 children received services. In 1997, another 65 residential programs were funded.

A summary of evaluation data for both programs is available.[19] One of the key findings was that between October 1993 and June 1996 the number of women who reported the use of illicit drugs decreased by 73% to 80% from intake to postdischarge.[20]

Conclusion

Since the early 1990s, there has been considerably more experience in providing treatment to substance-abusing pregnant women and mothers. Although the results discussed above suggest some level of effectiveness, for the most part they rely on incomplete data. They demonstrate how difficult it is to study program effectiveness in a rigorous way.

There are many variations of community treatment programs; PSAP, described in Box 1, is just one example. The need for treatment services for substance-abusing pregnant women and mothers remains great. It is hoped that more experience in providing such services, as well as sound evaluations, will help to improve treatment approaches and the lives of these women and their children.

1. Behrman, R. E., ed. Drug Exposed Infants. *The Future of Children* (Spring 1991) 1,1:1–120.
2. Barth, R. P. Revisiting the issues: Adoption of drug-exposed children. *The Future of Children* (Spring 1993) 3,1:167–75; Revisiting the issues: Drug-exposed infants. *The Future of Children* (Summer/Fall 1993) 3,2:208–14; Shiono, P. H. Revisiting the issues: Prevalence of drug-exposed infants. *The Future of Children* (Summer/Fall 1996) 6,2:159–63.
3. *Whitner v. State*, WL 393164 (S.C. 1996). The mother was sentenced to eight years in prison.
4. Priscilla Smith, Center for Reproductive Law and Policy, New York City. Telephone conversation, March 11, 1997. CRLP staff represented the mother in the appellate case.
5. Seven such state bills were enacted from 1993 through 1995. See American Academy of Pediatrics. *Drug-exposed infants*. Elk Grove Village, IL: AAP, Division of State Government and Chapter Affairs, 1996.
6. Arizona Session Laws, 1995. Chapter 215, p. 1688.
7. Michigan Public Act Appropriation Bill for 1993–94, No. 201.
8. See 720 Illinois Compiled Statutes Annotated § 570/411.2 (Public Act 89-215, effective January 1, 1996).
9. Kumpfer, K. Treatment programs for drug-abusing women. In *The Future of Children*. R. E. Behrman, ed. (Spring 1991) 1,1:50–60. See especially the description of federal initiatives on pages 56 and 57.
10. Center for Substance Abuse Prevention, Division of Demonstrations for High Risk Populations. Executive summary: CSAP—PPWI demonstration program findings. Unpublished report. CSAP, October 1996.
11. See note no. 10, Center for Substance Abuse Prevention, pp. 1, 4. This evaluation included the 26 fully implemented PPWI programs that met data collection criteria. In on-site visits, evaluators collected both quantitative and qualitative data on more than 80 variables. Client outcome data on 3,641 women and 2,757 infants were collected by program grantees.
12. See note no. 10, Center for Substance Abuse Prevention, p. 9. Data on maternal drug use were limited to women who had positive toxicology test results at intake. These women were retested after having received program services.
13. Rahdert, E. R., ed. *Treatment for drug-exposed women and their children: Advances in research methodology*. NIDA Research Monograph 166. Rockville, MD: National Institute on Drug Abuse, 1996; Kilbey, M. M., and Asghar, K. *Methodological issues in epidemiological, prevention, and treatment research on drug-exposed women and their children*. NIDA Research Monograph 117. Rockville, MD: National Institute on Drug Abuse, 1992.
14. For more information about the results of the Perinatal Twenty project, contact Dr. E. R. Rahdert, NIDA, Division of Clinical and Service Research, 5600 Fishers Lane, Rockville, MD 20857, (310) 442–0107.
15. Abandoned Infants Assistance Act of 1988, Public Law 100–505, 42 U.S.C. § 670. This funding was reauthorized in 1991 under the Abandoned Infants Assistance Act Amendments of 1991, Public Law 102–236, 42 U.S.C. § 670 note.
16. Goldberg, S., Barth, R. P., and Hernandez, C. S. *Abandoned Infants Assistance programs: 1995 annual report*. Berkeley, CA: National Abandoned Infants Assistance Resource Center, Family Welfare Research Group, School of Social Welfare, University of California, December 1996.
17. For more information regarding this monograph, write to Reneé Robinson at the National Abandoned Infants Assistance Resource Center, Family Welfare Research Group, 1950 Addison, Suite 104, Berkeley, CA 94704, or call (510) 643–7020.
18. Sheryl Goldberg, National Abandoned Infants Assistance Resource Center. Personal communication, March 14, 1997.
19. Center for Substance Abuse Treatment, Department of Health and Human Services. Women and children's program accomplishments. Unpublished internal federal agency report. January 13, 1997. For more information, contact Maggie Wilmore at the Department of Health and Human Services' Center for Substance Abuse Treatment, Clinical Intervention Branch, in Rockville, MD, (301) 443–8216.
20. The analysis used *CSAT Quarterly Report Tracking System* data collected at intake, discharge, and postdischarge on 800 women from 45 programs. Only women with an intake record, discharge record, and at least one postdischarge record were included. On average, follow-up data were collected six months after discharge. All postdischarge records were aggregated. See note no. 19, Center for Substance Abuse Treatment, pp. 8–9.

SPERM UNDER SIEGE

MORE THAN WE EVER GUESSED, HAVING A HEALTHY BABY MAY DEPEND ON DAD

Anne Merewood

IT DIDN'T MAKE SENSE. Kate Malone's* first pregnancy had gone so smoothly. Yet when she and her husband Paul* tried to have a second child, their efforts were plagued by disaster. For two years, Kate couldn't become pregnant. Then she suffered an ectopic pregnancy, in which the embryo began to grow in one of her fallopian tubes and had to be surgically removed. Her next pregnancy heralded more heartache—it ended in miscarriage at four months and tests revealed that the fetus was genetically abnormal. Within months, she became pregnant and miscarried yet again. By this point, some four years after their troubles began, the couple had adopted a son; baffled and demoralized by the string of apparent bad luck, they gave up trying to have another child. "We had been to the top doctors in the country and no one could find a reason for the infertility or the miscarriages," says Kate.

Soon, however, thanks to a newspaper article she read, Kate uncovered what she now considers the likely cause of the couple's reproductive woes. When it all started, Paul had just been hired by a manufacturing company that used a chemical called paradichlorobenzene, which derives from benzene, a known carcinogen. The article discussed the potential effects of exposure to chemicals, including benzene, on a man's sperm. Kate remembered hearing that two other men in Paul's small office were also suffering from inexplicable infertility. Both of their wives had gone through three miscarriages as well. Kate had always considered their similar misfortunes to be a tragic coincidence. Now she became convinced that the chemical (which has not yet

been studied for its effects on reproduction) had blighted the three men's sperm.

Paul had found a new job in a chemical-free workplace, so the couple decided to try once more to have a baby. Kate conceived immediately—and last August gave birth to a healthy boy. The Malones are now arranging for the National Institute for Occupational Safety and Health (NIOSH), the federal agency that assesses work-related health hazards for the public, to inspect Paul's former job site. "Our aim isn't to sue the company, but to help people who are still there," says Kate.

The Malones' suspicions about sperm damage echo the concerns of an increasing number of researchers. These scientists are challenging the double standard that leads women to overhaul their lives before a pregnancy—avoiding stress, cigarettes and champagne—while men are left confident that their lifestyle has little bearing on their fertility or their future child's health. Growing evidence suggests that sperm is both more fragile and potentially more dangerous than previously thought. "There seems to have been both a scientific resistance, and a resistance based on cultural preconceptions, to accepting these new ideas," says Gladys Friedler, Ph.D., an associate professor of psychiatry and pharmacology at Boston University School of Medicine.

But as more and more research is completed, sperm may finally be stripped of its macho image. For example, in one startling review of data on nearly 15,000 newborns, scientists at the University of North Carolina in Chapel Hill concluded that a father's drinking and smoking habits, and even his age, can increase his child's risk of birth defects—ranging from cleft palates to *hydrocephalus*, an abnormal accumulation of spinal fluid in the brain. Other new and equally worrisome

---

*These names have been changed.

From *Health*, April 1991, pp. 53–57, 76–77. © 1991 by Anne Merewood. Reprinted by permission.

studies have linked higher-than-normal rates of stillbirth, premature delivery and low birthweight (which predisposes a baby to medical and developmental problems) to fathers who faced on-the-job exposure to certain chemicals. In fact, one study found that a baby was more likely to be harmed if the father rather than the mother worked in an unsafe environment in the months before conception.

The surprising news of sperm's delicate nature may shift the balance of responsibility for a newborn's well-being. The research may also have social and economic implications far beyond the concerns of couples planning a family. In recent years a growing number of companies have sought to ban women of childbearing age from jobs that entail exposure to hazardous substances. The idea is to protect the women's future children from defects—and the companies themselves from lawsuits. Already, the "fetal protection policy" of one Milwaukee-based company has prompted female employees to file a sex discrimination suit that is now before the U.S. Supreme Court. Conversely, if the new research on sperm is borne out, men whose future plans include fatherhood may go to court to *insist* on protection from hazards. Faced with potential lawsuits from so many individuals, companies may be forced to ensure that workplaces are safe for *all* employees.

SPERM UND DRANG

At the center of all this controversy are the microscopic products of the male reproductive system. Sperm (officially, spermatozoa) are manufactured by *spermatagonia*, special cells in the testes that are constantly stimulated by the male hormone testosterone. Once formed, a sperm continues to mature as it travels for some 80 days through the *epididymis* (a microscopic network of tubes behind the testicle) to the "waiting area" around the prostate gland, where it is expelled in the next ejaculation.

A normal sperm contains 23 chromosomes—the threadlike strands that house DNA, the molecular foundation of genetic material. While a woman is born with all the eggs she will ever produce, a man creates millions of sperm every day from puberty onwards. This awesome productivity is also what makes sperm so fragile. If a single sperm's DNA is damaged, the result may be a mutation that distorts the genetic information it carries. "Because of the constant turn-

over of sperm, mutations caused by the environment can arise more frequently in men than in women," says David A. Savitz, Ph.D., an associate professor of epidemiology and chief researcher of the North Carolina review.

If a damaged sperm fertilizes the egg, the consequences can be devastating. "Such sperm can lead to spontaneous abortions, malformations, and functional or behavioral abnormalities," says Marvin Legator, Ph.D., director of environmental toxicology at the department of preventative medicine at the University of Texas in Galveston. And in some cases, sperm may be too badly harmed even to penetrate an egg, leading to mysterious infertility.

Though the findings on sperm's vulnerability are certainly dramatic, researchers emphasize that they are also preliminary. "We have only a very vague notion of how exposure might affect fetal development, and the whole area of research is at a very early stage of investigation," says Savitz. Indeed, questions still far outnumber answers. For starters, there is no hard evidence that a chemical damages an infant by adversely affecting the father's sperm. A man who comes in contact with dangerous substances might harm the baby by exposing his partner indirectly—for example, through contaminated clothing. Another theory holds that the harmful pollutants may be carried in the seminal fluid that buoys sperm. But more researchers are becoming convinced that chemicals can inflict their silent damage directly on the sperm itself.

THE CHEMICAL CONNECTION

The most well-known—and most controversial—evidence that chemicals can harm sperm comes from research on U.S. veterans of the Vietnam war who were exposed to the herbicide Agent Orange (dioxin), used by the U.S. military to destroy foliage that hid enemy forces. A number of veterans believe the chemical is responsible for birth defects in their children. The latest study on the issue, published last year by the Harvard School of Public Health, found that Vietnam vets had almost twice the risk of other men of fathering infants with one or more major malformations. But a number of previous studies found conflicting results, and because so little is known about how paternal exposure could translate into birth defects, the veterans have been unsuccessful in their lawsuits against the government.

Scientific uncertainty also dogs investigations into other potentially hazardous chemicals and contaminants. "There seem to be windows of vulnerability for sperm: Certain chemicals may be harmful only at a certain period during sperm production," explains Donald Mattison, M.D., dean of the School of Public Health at the University of Pittsburgh. There isn't enough specific data to make definitive lists of "danger chemicals." Still, a quick scan of the research shows that particular substances often crop up as likely troublemakers. Chief among them: lead, benzene, paint solvents, vinyl chloride, carbon disulphide, the pesticide DBCP, anesthetic gases and radiation. Not surprisingly, occupations that involve contact with these substances also figure heavily in studies of sperm damage. For example, men employed in the paper, wood, chemical, drug and paint industries may have a greater chance of siring stillborn children. And increased leukemia rates have been detected among children whose fathers are medical workers, aircraft or auto mechanics, or who are exposed regularly to paint or radiation. In fact, a study of workers at Britain's Sellafield nuclear power plant in West Cambria found a sixfold leukemia risk among children whose fathers were exposed to the plant's highest radiation levels (about 9 percent of all employees).

Workers in "high-risk" industries should not panic, says Savitz. "The credibility of the studies is limited because we have no firm evidence that certain exposures cause certain birth defects." Yet it makes sense to be watchful for warning signs. For example, if pollution levels are high enough to cause skin irritations, thyroid trouble, or breathing problems, the reproductive system might also be at risk. Another danger signal is a clustered outbreak of male infertility or of a particular disease: It was local concern about high levels of childhood leukemia, for instance, that sparked the investigation at the Sellafield nuclear plant.

The rise in industrial "fetal protection policies" is adding even more controversy to the issue of occupational hazards to sperm. In 1984, employees brought a class-action suit against Milwaukee-based Johnson Controls, the nation's largest manufacturer of car batteries, after the company restricted women "capable of bearing children" from holding jobs in factory areas where lead exceeded a specific level. The suit—which the Supreme Court is scheduled to rule on this spring—focuses on the obstacles the policy creates for women's career advancement. Johnson Controls defends its regulation by pointing to "overwhelming" evidence that a mother's exposure to lead can harm the fetus.

In effect, the company's rule may be a case of reverse discrimination against men. Males continue to work in areas banned to women despite growing evidence that lead may not be safe for sperm either. In several studies over the past 10 years, paternal exposure to lead (and radiation) has been connected to Wilms' tumor, a type of kidney cancer in children. In another recent study, University of Maryland toxicologist Ellen Silbergeld, Ph.D., exposed male rats to lead amounts equivalent to levels below the current occupational safety standards for humans. The rats were then mated with females who had not been exposed at all. Results: The offspring showed clear defects in brain development.

Johnson Controls claims that evidence linking fetal problems to a father's contact with lead is insufficient. But further research into chemicals' effects on sperm may eventually force companies to reduce pollution levels, since *both* sexes can hardly be banned from the factory floor. Says Mattison: "The workplace should be safe for everyone who wants to work there, men and women alike!"

FATHER TIME

Whatever his occupation, man's age may play an unexpected role in his reproductive health. When researchers at the University of Calgary and the Alberta Children's Hospital in Canada examined sperm samples taken from 30 healthy men aged 20 to 52, they found that the older men had a higher percentage of sperm with structurally abnormal chromosomes. Specifically, only 2 to 3 percent of the sperm from men between ages 20 and 34 were genetically abnormal, while the figure jumped to 7 percent in men 35 to 44 and to almost 14 percent in those 45 and over. "The findings are logical," says Renée Martin, Ph.D., the professor of pediatrics who led the study. "The cells that create sperm are constantly dividing from puberty onwards, and every time they divide they are subject to error."

Such mistakes are more likely to result in miscarriages than in unhealthy babies. "When part of a chromosome is missing or broken, the embryo is more likely to abort as a miscarriage [than to carry to term]," Martin says.

Yet her findings may help explain why Savitz's North Carolina study noted a doubled rate of birth defects like cleft palate and hydrocephalus in children whose fathers were over 35 at the time of conception, no matter what the mothers' age.

Currently, there are no tests available to pre-identify sperm likely to cause genetic defects. "Unfortunately there's nothing offered, because [the research] is all so new," says Martin. But tests such as amniocentesis, alpha fetoprotein (AFP) and chorionic villi sampling (CVS) can ferret out some fetal genetic defects that are linked to Mom *or* Dad. Amniocentesis, for example, is routinely recommended for all pregnant women over 35 because with age a woman increases her risk of producing a Down's syndrome baby, characterized by mental retardation and physical abnormalities.

With respect to Down's syndrome, Martin's study provided some good news for older men: It confirmed previous findings that a man's risk of fathering a child afflicted with the syndrome actually drops with age. Some popular textbooks still warn that men over 55 have a high chance of fathering Down's syndrome babies. "That information is outdated," Martin insists. "We now know that for certain."

THE SINS OF THE FATHERS?

For all the hidden dangers facing a man's reproductive system, the most common hazards may be the ones most under his control.

Smoking. Tobacco addicts take note: Smoke gets in your sperm. Cigarettes can reduce fertility by lowering sperm count—the number of individual sperm released in a single ejaculation. "Most than half a pack a day can cause sperm density to drop by 20 percent," says Machelle Seibel, M.D., director of the Faulkner Centre for Reproductive Medicine in Boston. One Danish study found that for each pack of cigarettes a father tended to smoke daily (assuming the mother didn't smoke at all), his infant's birthweight fell 4.2 ounces below average. Savitz has found that male smokers double their chances of fathering infants with abnormalities like hydrocephalus, *Bell's palsy* (paralysis of the facial nerve), and mouth cysts. In Savitz's most recent study, children whose fathers smoked around the time of conception were 20 percent more likely to develop brain cancer, lymphoma and leukemia than were children whose fathers did not

smoke (the results still held regardless of whether the mother had a tobacco habit).

This is scary news—and not particularly helpful: Savitz's studies didn't record how frequently the fathers lit up, and no research at all suggests why the links appeared. Researchers can't even say for sure that defective sperm was to blame. The babies may instead have been victims of passive smoking—affected by Dad's tobacco while in the womb or shortly after birth.

Drinking. Mothers-to-be are routinely cautioned against sipping any alcohol while pregnant. Now studies suggest that the father's drinking habits just before conception may also pose a danger. So far, research hasn't discovered why alcohol has an adverse effect on sperm, but it does suggest that further investigation is needed. For starters, one study of laboratory rats linked heavy alcohol use with infertility because the liquor lowered testosterone levels. Another study, from the University of Washington in Seattle, discovered that newborn babies whose fathers drank at least two glasses of wine or two bottles of beer per day weighed an average of 3 ounces less than babies whose fathers were only occasional sippers—even when all other factors were considered.

Illicit Drugs. Many experts believe that a man's frequent use of substances such as marijuana and cocaine may also result in an unhealthy fetus, but studies that could document such findings have yet to be conducted. However, preliminary research has linked marijuana to infertility. And recent tests at the Yale Infertility Clinic found that long-term cocaine use led to both very low sperm counts and a greater number of sperm with motion problems.

WHAT A DAD CAN DO

The best news about sperm troubles is that many of the risk factors can be easily prevented. Because the body overhauls sperm supplies every 90 days, it only takes a season to get a fresh start on creating a healthy baby. Most experts advise that men wait for three months after quitting smoking, cutting out drug use or abstaining from alcohol before trying to sire a child.

Men who fear they are exposed to work chemicals that may compromise the health of future children can contact NIOSH. (Write the Division of Standards Development and Technology Transfer, Technical Information

Branch, 4676 Columbia Parkway, Mailstop C-19, Cincinnati, OH 45226. Or call [800] 356–4674.) NIOSH keeps files on hazardous chemicals and their effects, and can arrange for a local inspection of the workplace. Because it is primarily a research institution, NIOSH is most useful for investigating chemicals that haven't been studied previously for sperm effects (which is why the Malones approached NIOSH with their concerns about paradichlorobenzene). For better-known pollutants, it's best to ask the federal Occupational Safety and Health Administration (OSHA) to inspect the job site (OSHA has regional offices in most U.S. cities).

There is also advice for men who are concerned over exposure to radiation during medical treatment. Direct radiation to the area around the testes can spur infertility by halting sperm production for more than three years. According to a recent study, it can also triple the number of abnormal sperm the testes produce. Men who know they will be exposed to testicular radiation for medical reasons should consider "banking" sperm before the treatment, for later use in artificial in-semination. Most hospitals use lead shields during radiation therapy, but for routine X-rays, even dental X-rays, protection might not be offered automatically. If it's not offered, patients should be sure to request it. "The risks are really, really low, but to be absolutely safe, patients—male or female—should *always* ask for a lead apron to protect their reproductive organs," stresses Martin.

Though the study of sperm health is still in its infancy, it is already clear that a man's reproductive system needs to be treated with respect and caution. Women do not carry the full responsibility for bearing a healthy infant. "The focus should be on both parents—not on 'blaming' either the mother or the father, but on accepting that each play a role," says Friedler.

Mattison agrees: "Until recently, when a woman had a miscarriage, she would be told it was because she had a 'blighted ovum' [egg]. We never heard anything about a 'blighted sperm.' This new data suggests that both may be responsible. That is not unreasonable," he concludes, "given that it takes both an egg and a sperm to create a baby!"

Unit Selections

Key Points to Consider

❖ What are the intellectual potentials of babies?

❖ Is infant reactivity and temperamental style a factor in the development of personal and social behaviors?

❖ Can talking to infants shape their ability to compute the rules and structural principles of language? How do they discern meaning and decode patterns?

❖ How can environmental exposure and exercise help form the brain's circuitry for areas such as music and math?

❖ Why is empathy the trait that makes us human? Why is it critical to our survival?

❖ What are parents' views of early childhood development? Where do parents need more information and support?

 **Links**

www.dushkin.com/online/

These sites are annotated on pages 4 and 5.

Thousands of studies have linked environmental variables to development during infancy and early childhood over the past 120 years. With new technologies (e.g., tomography, magnetic resonance imaging, gene mapping, computational biology), hundreds of new studies are linking various biological variables to development during a child's early life. The articles selected for inclusion in this unit reflect both the influences of nurture (environment) and nature (biology).

Newborns are quite well developed in some areas and incredibly deficient in others. Babies' brains, for example, already have their full complement of neurons (worker cells). The neuroglia (supportive cells) are almost completely developed and will reach their final numbers by age one. In contrast, babies' legs and feet are tiny, weak, and barely functional. Looking at newborns from another perspective, however, makes their brains seem somewhat less superior. The neurons and neuroglia present at birth must last a lifetime. Neurons cannot replace themselves by mitosis after birth. By contrast, the cells of the baby's legs and feet (skin, fat, muscles, bones, blood vessels) are able to replace themselves by mitosis indefinitely.

The developing brain in infancy is a truly fascinating organ. At birth it is poorly organized. The lower (primitive) brain parts (brain stem, pons, medulla, cerebellum) are well enough developed to allow the infant to live. The lower brain directs vital organ systems (heart, lungs, kidneys, etc.). The higher (advanced) brain parts (cerebral hemispheres) have all their neurons, but the nerve cells and cell processes (axon, dendrites) are small, underdeveloped, and unorganized. During infancy, these higher (cerebral) nerve cells (that allow the baby to think, reason, and remember) grow at astronomical rates. Jean Piaget, the father of cognitive psychology, wrote that all brain activity in the newborn was reflexive, based on instincts for survival. Now researchers are discovering that fetuses can learn and that newborns can think as well as learn.

The first article in this unit addresses some of the new discoveries about brain development that have poured out of neuroscience labs recently. The role played by electrical activity of neurons in actively shaping the physical structure of the brain is particularly awe-inspiring. The neurons are produced prenatally. After birth, the flood of sensory inputs from the environment (sights, sounds, smells, tastes, touch, balance, and kinesthetic sensations) drives the neurons to form circuits and become wired to each other. Trillions of connections are established in a baby's brain. During childhood the connections that are seldom or never used are eliminated or pruned. J. Madeleine Nash suggests that the first 3 years are critical for establishing these connections. Environments that provide lots of sensory stimulation really do produce richer, more connected brains.

The second article in this unit invokes more attention to the development of social and emotional behaviors in infancy rather than to physical and cognitive development. Author Jerome Kagan is a Harvard professor with a worldwide reputation as an expert in socioemotional aspects of development. In this article, he contends that babies who are easily aroused and become distressed quickly are likely to grow into fearful and subdued preschoolers. Infants who remain motorically relaxed are apt to become bold and sociable in early childhood. However, he sees a danger in excusing conduct disorders and unrestrained emotions because they are due to inherited differences in reactivity. He stresses the need for socialization practices that focus on moral obligations to be civil and responsible.

The last selection on infancy deals with language development as it is affected by infant perceptions. Shannon Brownlee reviews research that suggests that infants as young as 18 months old can perceive differences in grammatically correct and incorrect speech. This supports the idea that the brain is biologically equipped to learn language before social learning (modeling, imitation) takes place. This article describes how infants decode patterns, discriminate rules, and cobble words together correctly. Deaf infants do this with sign language. The author reminds readers that in order to do this, infants need early and plentiful human language input. Recordings and television talk do not stimulate babies to compute the syntax of language.

The selections about toddlers and preschoolers in this anthology continue the trend of looking at development physically, cognitively, and socioemotionally. Each of the articles focuses on one topic and views the whole child across all three domains, considering hereditary and environmental factors.

"Your Child's Brain" continues the discussion of the rapid myelinization of neurons and their migration to permanent locations in the brain during early childhood. Sharon Begley contends that extra experience in the pursuit of an area of knowledge (e.g., math, language, music) can trigger more neurons to be sent to the area of the cerebral hemisphere involved in acquiring, storing, and retrieving that kind of information. This accommodation is a clear-cut example of nature–nurture interaction.

The next article, "Defining the Trait That Makes Us Human," focuses on empathy; the identification with and understanding of another person's situation and feelings. This is a cognitive achievement in early childhood. It requires that the preschooler has knowledge that he or she is separate from others, and that those separate others have their own feelings and positions. Researchers believe that a biological instinct for empathy exists, but it also requires environmental reinforcements to be learned well.

The concluding article in this unit addresses parental knowledge about raising young children in the 1990s. Parents may not recognize their power to affect their child's intellectual potential, or to affect his or her social development. Many parents feel that a child will catch up socially and that lack of social interaction from birth to age 3 is irrelevant. The author gives suggestions about helpful and welcome ways to support parents who are raising young children.

FERTILE MINDS

From birth, a baby's brain cells proliferate wildly,
making connections that may shape a lifetime of experience.
The first three years are critical

By J. MADELEINE NASH

RAT-A-TAT-TAT. RAT-A-TAT-TAT. RAT-A-tat-tat. If scientists could eavesdrop on the brain of a human embryo 10, maybe 12 weeks after conception, they would hear an astonishing racket. Inside the womb, long before light first strikes the retina of the eye or the earliest dreamy images flicker through the cortex, nerve cells in the developing brain crackle with purposeful activity. Like teenagers with telephones, cells in one neighborhood of the brain are calling friends in another, and these cells are calling their friends, and they keep calling one another over and over again, "almost," says neurobiologist Carla Shatz of the University of California, Berkeley, "as if they were autodialing."

But these neurons—as the long, wiry cells that carry electrical messages through the nervous system and the brain are called—are not transmitting signals in scattershot fashion. That would produce a featureless static, the sort of noise picked up by a radio tuned between stations. On the contrary, evidence is growing that the staccato bursts of electricity that form those distinctive rat-a-tat-tats arise from coordinated waves of neural activity, and that those pulsing waves, like currents shifting sand on the ocean floor, actually change the shape of the brain, carving mental circuits into patterns that over time will enable the newborn infant to perceive a father's voice, a mother's touch, a shiny mobile twirling over the crib.

Of all the discoveries that have poured out of neuroscience labs in recent years, the finding that the electrical activity of brain cells changes the physical structure of the brain is perhaps the most breathtaking. For the rhythmic firing of neurons is no longer assumed to be a by-product of building the brain but essential to the process, and it begins, scientists have established, well before birth. A brain is not a computer. Nature does not cobble it together, then turn it on. No, the brain begins working long before it is finished. And the same processes that wire the brain before birth, neuroscientists are finding, also drive the explosion of learning that occurs immediately afterward.

At birth a baby's brain contains 100 billion neurons, roughly as many nerve cells as there are stars in the Milky Way. Also in place are a trillion glial cells, named after the Greek word for glue, which form a kind of honeycomb that protects and nourishes the neurons. But while the brain contains virtually all the nerve cells it will ever have, the pattern of wiring between them has yet to stabilize. Up to this point, says Shatz, "what the brain has done is lay out circuits that are its best guess about what's required for vision, for language, for whatever." And now it is up to neural activity—no longer spontaneous, but driven by a flood of sensory experiences—to take this rough blueprint and progressively refine it.

During the first years of life, the brain undergoes a series of extraordinary changes. Starting shortly after birth, a baby's brain, in a display of biological exuberance, produces trillions more connections between neurons than it can possibly use. Then, through a process that resembles Darwinian competition, the brain eliminates connections, or synapses, that are seldom or never used. The excess synapses in a child's brain undergo a draconian pruning, starting around the age of 10 or earlier, leaving behind a mind whose patterns of emotion and thought are, for better or worse, unique.

Deprived of a stimulating environment, a child's brain suffers. Researchers at Baylor College of Medicine, for example, have found that children who don't play much or are rarely touched develop brains 20% to 30% smaller than normal for their age. Laboratory animals provide another provocative parallel. Not only do young rats reared in toy-strewn cages exhibit more complex behavior than rats confined to sterile, uninteresting boxes, researchers at the University of Illinois at Urbana-Champaign have found, but the brains of these rats contain as many as 25% more synapses per neuron. Rich experiences, in other words, really do produce rich brains.

The new insights into brain development are more than just interesting science. They have profound implications for parents and policymakers. In an age when mothers and fathers are increasingly pressed for time—and may already be feeling guilty about how many hours they spend away from their children—the results coming out of the labs are likely to increase concerns about leaving very young children in the care of others. For the data underscore the importance of hands-on parenting, of finding the time to cuddle a baby, talk with a toddler and provide infants with stimulating experiences.

The new insights have begun to infuse new passion into the political debate over early education and day care. There is an urgent need, say child-development experts, for preschool programs designed to boost the brain power of youngsters born into impoverished rural and inner-city households. Without such programs, they warn, the current drive to curtail welfare costs by pushing mothers with infants and toddlers into the work force may well backfire. "There is a time scale to brain development, and the most important year is the first," notes Frank Newman, president of the Education Commission of the States. By the age of three, a child who is neglected or abused bears marks that, if not indelible, are exceedingly difficult to erase.

But the new research offers hope as well. Scientists have found that the brain during the first years of life is so malleable that very young children who suffer strokes or injuries that wipe out an entire hemisphere can still mature into highly functional adults. Moreover, it is becoming increasingly clear that well-designed preschool programs can help many children overcome glaring deficits in their home environment. With appropriate therapy, say researchers, even serious disorders like dyslexia may be treatable. While inherited problems may place certain children at greater risk than others, says Dr. Harry Chugani, a pediatric neurologist at Wayne State University in Detroit, that is no excuse for ignoring the environment's power to remodel the brain. "We may not do much to change what happens before birth, but we can change what happens after a baby is born," he observes.

Strong evidence that activity changes the brain began accumulating in the 1970s. But only recently have researchers had tools powerful enough to reveal the precise mechanisms by which those changes are brought about. Neural activity triggers a biochemical cascade that reaches all the way to the nucleus of cells and the coils of DNA that encode specific genes. In fact, two of the genes affected by neural activity in embryonic fruit flies, neurobiologist Corey Goodman and his colleagues at Berkeley reported late last year, are identical to those that other studies have linked to learning and memory. How thrilling, exclaims Goodman, how intellectually satisfying that the snippets of DNA that embryos use to build their brains are the very same ones that will later allow adult organisms to process and store new information.

As researchers explore the once hidden links between brain activity and brain structure, they are beginning to construct a sturdy bridge over the chasm that previously separated genes from the environment. Experts now agree that a baby does not come into

Wiring Vision

WHAT'S GOING ON Babies can see at birth, but not in fine-grained detail. They have not yet acquired the knack of focusing both eyes on a single object or developed more sophisticated visual skills like dept perception. they also lack hand-eye coordination.
WHAT PARENTS CAN DO There is no need to buy high-contrast black-and-white toys to stimulate vision. But regular eye exams, starting as early as two weeks of age, can detect problems that, if left uncorrected, can cause a weak or unused eye to lose its functional connections to the brain.
WINDOW OF LEARNING Unless it is exercised early on, the visual system will not develop.

AGE (in years)	Birth	1	2	3	4	5	6	7	8	9	10
Visual acuity											
Binocular vision											

the world as a genetically preprogrammed automaton or a blank slate at the mercy of the environment, but arrives as something much more interesting. For this reason the debate that engaged countless generations of philosophers—whether nature or nurture calls the shots—no longer interests most scientists. They are much too busy chronicling the myriad ways in which genes and the environment interact. "It's not a competition," says Dr. Stanley Greenspan, a psychiatrist at George Washington University. "It's a dance."

THE IMPORTANCE OF GENES

THAT DANCE BEGINS AT AROUND THE THIRD week of gestation, when a thin layer of cells in the developing embryo performs an origami-like trick, folding inward to give rise to a fluid-filled cylinder known as the neural tube. As cells in the neural tube proliferate at the astonishing rate of 250,000 a minute, the brain and spinal cord assemble themselves in a series of tightly choreographed steps. Nature is the dominant partner during this phase of development, but nurture plays a vital supportive role. Changes in the environment of the womb—whether caused by maternal malnutrition, drug abuse or a viral infection—can wreck the clockwork precision of the neural assembly line. Some forms of epilepsy, mental retardation, autism and schizophrenia appear to be the results of developmental processes gone awry.

But what awes scientists who study the brain, what still stuns them, is not that things occasionally go wrong in the devel-

oping brain but that so much of the time they go right. This is all the more remarkable, says Berkeley's Shatz, as the central nervous system of an embryo is not a miniature of the adult system but more like a tadpole that gives rise to a frog. Among other things, the cells produced in the neural tube must migrate to distant locations and accurately lay down the connections that link one part of the brain to another. In addition, the embryonic brain must construct a variety of temporary structures, including the neural tube, that will, like a tadpole's tail, eventually disappear.

What biochemical magic underlies this incredible metamorphosis? The instructions programmed into the genes, of course. Scientists have recently discovered, for instance, that a gene nicknamed "sonic hedgehog" (after the popular video game Sonic the Hedgehog) determines the fate of neurons in the spinal cord and the brain. Like a strong scent carried by the wind, the protein encoded by the hedgehog gene (so called because in its absence, fruit-fly embryos sprout a coat of prickles) diffuses outward from the cells that produce it, becoming fainter and fainter. Columbia University neurobiologist Thomas Jessell has found that it takes middling concentrations of this potent morphing factor to produce a motor neuron and lower concentrations to make an interneuron (a cell that relays signals to other neurons, instead of to muscle fibers, as motor neurons do).

Scientists are also beginning to identify some of the genes that guide neurons in their long migrations. Consider the problem faced by neurons destined to become part of the cerebral cortex. Because they arise relatively late in the development of the mammalian brain, billions of these cells must push and shove their way through dense colonies established by earlier migrants. "It's as if the entire population of the East Coast decided to move en masse to the West Coast," marvels Yale University neuroscientist Dr. Pasko Rakic, and marched through Cleveland, Chicago and Denver to get there.

But of all the problems the growing nervous system must solve, the most daunting is posed by the wiring itself. After birth, when the number of connections explodes, each of the brain's billions of neurons will forge links to thousands of others. First they must spin out a web of wirelike fibers known as axons (which transmit signals) and dendrites (which receive them). The objective is to form a synapse, the gap-like structure over which the axon of one neuron beams a signal to the dendrites of another. Before this can happen, axons and dendrites must almost touch. And while the short, bushy dendrites don't have to travel very far, axons—the heavy-duty cables of the nervous system—must traverse distances that are the microscopic equivalent of miles.

What guides an axon on its incredible voyage is a "growth cone," a creepy, crawly sprout that looks something like an amoeba. Scientists have known about growth cones since the turn of the century. What they didn't know until recently was that growth cones come equipped with the molecular equivalent of sonar and radar. Just as instruments in a submarine or airplane scan the environment for signals, so molecules arrayed on the surface of growth cones search their surroundings for the presence of certain proteins. Some of these proteins, it turns out, are attractants that pull the growth cones toward them, while others are repellents that push them away.

THE FIRST STIRRINGS

UP TO THIS POINT, GENES HAVE CONTROLLED the unfolding of the brain. As soon as axons make their first connections, however, the nerves begin to fire, and what they do starts to matter more and more. In essence, say scientists, the developing nervous system has strung the equivalent of telephone trunk lines between the right neighborhoods in the right cities. Now it has to sort out which wires belong to which house, a problem that cannot be solved by genes alone for reasons that boil down to simple arithmetic. Eventually, Berkeley's Goodman estimates, a human brain must forge quadrillions of connections. But there are only 100,000 genes in human DNA. Even though half these genes—some 50,000—appear to be dedicated to constructing and maintaining the nervous system, he observes, that's not enough to specify more than a tiny fraction of the connections required by a fully functioning brain.

In adult mammals, for example, the axons that connect the brain's visual system arrange themselves in striking layers and columns that reflect the division between the left eye and the right. But these axons start out as scrambled as a bowl of spaghetti, according to Michael Stryker, chairman of the physiology department at the University of California at San Francisco. What sorts out the mess, scientists have established, is neural activity. In a series of experiments viewed as classics by scientists in the field, Berkeley's Shatz chemically blocked neural activity in embryonic cats. The result? The axons that connect neurons in the retina of the eye to the brain never formed the left eye–right eye geometry needed to support vision.

But no recent finding has intrigued researchers more than the results reported in October by Corey Goodman and his Berkeley colleagues. In studying a deceptively simple problem—how axons from motor neurons in the fly's central nerve cord establish connections with muscle cells in its limbs—the Berkeley researchers made an

Wiring Feelings

WHAT'S GOING ON Among the first circuits the brain constructs are those that govern the emotions. Beginning around two months of age, the distress and contentment experienced by newborns start to evolve into more complex feelings: joy and sadness, envy and empathy, pride and shame.
WHAT PARENTS CAN DO Loving care provides a baby's brain with the right kind of emotional stimulation. Neglecting a baby can produce brainwave patterns that dampen happy feelings. Abuse can produce heightened anxiety and abnormal stress responses.
WINDOW OF LEARNING Emotions develop in layers, each more complex than the last.

AGE (in years)	Birth 1 2 3 4 5 6 7 8 9 10
Stress Response	
Empathy, Envy	

unexpected discovery. They knew there was a gene that keeps bundles of axons together as they race toward their muscle-cell targets. What they discovered was that the electrical activity produced by neurons inhibited this gene, dramatically increasing the number of connections the axons made. Even more intriguing, the signals amplified the activity of a second gene—a gene called CREB.

The discovery of the CREB amplifier, more than any other, links the developmental processes that occur before birth to those that continue long after. For the twin processes of memory and learning in adult animals, Columbia University neurophysiologist Eric Kandel has shown, rely on the CREB molecule. When Kandel blocked the activity of CREB in giant snails, their brains changed in ways that suggested that they could still learn but could remember what they learned for only a short period of time. Without CREB, it seems, snails—and by extension, more developed animals like humans—can form no long-term memories. And without long-term memories, it is hard to imagine that infant brains could ever master more than rudimentary skills. "Nurture is important," says Kandel. "But nurture works through nature."

EXPERIENCE KICKS IN

WHEN A BABY IS BORN, IT CAN SEE AND HEAR and smell and respond to touch, but only dimly. The brain stem, a primitive region that controls vital functions like heartbeat and breathing, has completed its wiring. Elsewhere the connections between neurons are wispy and weak. But over the first few months of life, the brain's higher centers ex-

plode with new synapses. And as dendrites and axons swell with buds and branches like trees in spring, metabolism soars. By the age of two, a child's brain contains twice as many synapses and consumes twice as much energy as the brain of a normal adult.

University of Chicago pediatric neurologist Dr. Peter Huttenlocher has chronicled this extraordinary epoch in brain development by autopsying the brains of infants and young children who have died unexpectedly. The number of synapses in one layer of the visual cortex, Huttenlocher reports, rises from around 2,500 per neuron at birth to as many as 18,000 about six months later. Other regions of the cortex score similarly spectacular increases but on slightly different schedules. And while these microscopic connections between nerve fibers continue to form throughout life, they reach their highest average densities (15,000 synapses per neuron) at around the age of two and remain at that level until the age of 10 or 11.

This profusion of connections lends the growing brain exceptional flexibility and resilience. Consider the case of 13-year-old Brandi Binder, who developed such severe epilepsy that surgeons at UCLA had to remove the entire right side of her cortex when she was six. Binder lost virtually all the control she had established over muscles on the left side of her body, the side controlled by the right side of the brain. Yet today, after years of therapy ranging from leg lifts to math and music drills, Binder is an A student at the Holmes Middle School in Colorado Springs, Colorado. She loves music, math and art—skills usually associated with the right half of the brain. And while Binder's recuperation is not 100%—for example, she has never regained the use of her left arm—it comes close. Says UCLA pediatric neurologist Dr. Donald Shields: "If there's a way to compensate, the developing brain will find it."

What wires a child's brain, say neuroscientists—or rewires it after physical trauma—is repeated experience. Each time a baby tries to touch a tantalizing object or gazes intently at a face or listens to a lullaby, tiny bursts of electricity shoot through the brain, knitting neurons into circuits as well defined as those etched onto silicon chips. The results are those behavioral mileposts that never cease to delight and awe parents. Around the age of two months, for example, the motor-control centers of the brain develop to the point that infants can suddenly reach out and grab a nearby object. Around the age of four months, the cortex begins to refine the connections needed for depth perception and binocular vision. And around the age of 12 months, the speech centers of the brain are poised to produce what is perhaps the most magical moment of childhood: the first word that marks the flowering of language.

When the brain does not receive the right information—or shuts it out—the result can be devastating. Some children who display early signs of autism, for example, retreat from the world because they are hypersensitive to sensory stimulation, others because their senses are underactive and provide them with too little information. To be effective, then, says George Washington University's Greenspan, treatment must target the underlying condition, protecting some children from disorienting noises and lights, providing others with attention-grabbing stimulation. But when parents and therapists collaborate in an intensive effort to reach these abnormal brains, writes Greenspan in a new book, *The Growth of the Mind* (Addison-Wesley, 1997), three-year-olds who begin the descent into the autistic's limited universe can sometimes be snatched back.

Indeed, parents are the brain's first and most important teachers. Among other things, they appear to help babies learn by adopting the rhythmic, high-pitched speaking style known as Parentese. When speaking to babies, Stanford University psychologist Anne Fernald has found, mothers and fathers from many cultures change their speech patterns in the same peculiar ways. "They put their faces very close to the child," she reports. "They use shorter utterances, and they speak in an unusually melodious fashion." The heart rate of infants increases while listening to Parentese, even Parentese delivered in a foreign language. Moreover, Fernald says, Parentese appears to hasten the process of connecting words to the objects they denote. Twelve-month-olds, directed to "look at the ball" in Parentese, direct their eyes to the correct picture more frequently than when the instruction is delivered in normal English.

In some ways the exaggerated, vowel-rich sounds of Parentese appear to resemble the choice morsels fed to hatchlings by adult birds. The University of Washington's Patricia Kuhl and her colleagues have conditioned dozens of newborns to turn their heads when they detect the *ee* sound emitted by American parents, vs. the *eu* favored by doting Swedes. Very young babies, says Kuhl, invariably perceive slight variations in pronunciation as totally different sounds. But by the age of six months, American babies no longer react when they hear variants of *ee,* and Swedish babies have become impervious to differences in *eu.* "It's as though their brains have formed little magnets," says Kuhl, "and all the sounds in the vicinity are swept in."

TUNED TO DANGER

EVEN MORE FUNDAMENTAL, SAYS DR. BRUCE Perry of Baylor College of Medicine in Houston, is the role parents play in setting

Wiring Language

WHAT'S GOING ON Even before birth, an infant is tuning into the melody of its mother's voice. Over the next six years, its brain will set up the circuitry needed to decipher—and reproduce—the lyrics. A six-month-old can recognize the vowel sounds that are the basic building blocks of speech.

WHAT PARENTS CAN DO Talking to a baby a lot, researchers have found, significantly speeds up the process of learning new words. The high-pitched, singsong speech style known as Parentese helps babies connect objects with words.

WINDOW OF LEARNING Language skills are sharpest early on but grow throughout life.

AGE (in years)	Birth 1 2 3 4 5 6 7 8 9 10
Recognition of speech	
Vocabulary	

up the neural circuitry that helps children regulate their responses to stress. Children who are physically abused early in life, he observes, develop brains that are exquisitely tuned to danger. At the slightest threat, their hearts race, their stress hormones surge and their brains anxiously track the nonverbal cues that might signal the next attack. Because the brain develops in sequence, with more primitive structures stabilizing their connections first, early abuse is particularly damaging. Says Perry: "Experience is the chief architect of the brain." And because these early experiences of stress form a kind of template around which later brain development is organized, the changes they create are all the more pervasive.

Emotional deprivation early in life has a similar effect. For six years University of Washington psychologist Geraldine Dawson and her colleagues have monitored the brain-wave patterns of children born to mothers who were diagnosed as suffering from depression. As infants, these children showed markedly reduced activity in the left frontal lobe, an area of the brain that serves as a center for joy and other lighthearted emotions. Even more telling, the patterns of brain activity displayed by these children closely tracked the ups and downs of their mother's depression. At the age of three, children whose mothers were more severely depressed or whose depression lasted longer continued to show abnormally low readings.

Strikingly, not all the children born to depressed mothers develop these aberrant brain-wave patterns, Dawson has found. What accounts for the difference appears to be the emotional tone of the exchanges between mother and child. By scrutinizing hours of videotape that show depressed mothers interacting with their babies, Dawson has attempted to identify the links between maternal behavior and children's brains. She found that mothers who were disengaged, irritable or impatient had babies with sad brains. But depressed mothers who managed to rise above their melancholy, lavishing their babies with attention and indulging in playful games, had children with brain activity of a considerably more cheerful cast.

When is it too late to repair the damage wrought by physical and emotional abuse or neglect? For a time, at least, a child's brain is extremely forgiving. If a mother snaps out of her depression before her child is a year old, Dawson has found, brain activity in the left frontal lobe quickly picks up. However, the ability to rebound declines markedly as a child grows older. Many scientists believe that in the first few years of childhood there are a number of critical or sensitive periods, or "windows," when the brain demands certain types of input in order to create or stabilize certain long-lasting structures.

For example, children who are born with a cataract will become permanently blind in that eye if the clouded lens is not promptly removed. Why? The brain's visual centers require sensory stimulus—in this case the stimulus provided by light hitting the retina of the eye—to maintain their still tentative connections. More controversially, many linguists believe that language skills unfold according to a strict, biologically defined timetable. Children, in their view, resemble certain species of birds that cannot master their song unless they hear it sung at an early age. In zebra finches the window for acquiring the appropriate song opens 25 to 30 days after hatching and shuts some 50 days later.

WINDOWS OF OPPORTUNITY

WITH A FEW EXCEPTIONS, THE WINDOWS OF opportunity in the human brain do not close quite so abruptly. There appears to be a series of windows for developing language. The window for acquiring syntax may close as early as five or six years of age, while the window for adding new words may never close. The ability to learn a second language is highest between birth and the age of six, then undergoes a steady and inexorable decline. Many adults still manage to learn new languages, but usually only after great struggle.

The brain's greatest growth spurt, neuroscientists have now confirmed, draws to a close around the age of 10, when the balance between synapse creation and atrophy abruptly shifts. Over the next several years, the brain will ruthlessly destroy its weakest synapses, preserving only those that have been magically transformed by experience. This magic, once again, seems to be encoded in the genes. The ephemeral bursts of electricity that travel through the brain, creating everything from visual images and pleasurable sensations to dark dreams and wild thoughts, ensure the survival of synapses by stimulating genes that promote the release of powerful growth factors and suppressing genes that encode for synapse-destroying enzymes.

By the end of adolescence, around the age of 18, the brain has declined in plasticity but increased in power. Talents and latent tendencies that have been nurtured are ready to blossom. The experiences that drive neural activity, says Yale's Rakic, are like a sculptor's chisel or a dressmaker's shears, conjuring up form from a lump of stone or a length of cloth. The presence of extra material expands the range of possibilities, but cutting away the extraneous is what makes art. "It is the overproduction of synaptic connections followed by their loss that leads to patterns in the brain," says neuroscientist William Greenough of the University of Illinois at Urbana-Champaign. Potential for greatness may be encoded in the genes, but whether that potential is realized as a gift for mathematics, say, or a brilliant criminal mind depends on patterns etched by experience in those critical early years.

Wiring Movement

WHAT'S GOING ON At birth babies can move their limbs, but in a jerky, uncontrolled fashion. Over the next four years, the brain progressively refines the circuits for reaching, grabbing, sitting, crawling, walking and running.

WHAT PARENTS CAN DO Give babies as much freedom to explore as safety permits. Just reaching for an object helps the brain develop hand-eye coordination. As soon as children are ready for them, activities like drawing and playing a violin or piano encourage the development of fine motor skills.

WINDOW OF LEARNING Motor-skill development moves from gross to increasingly fine.

AGE (in years)	Birth	1	2	3	4	5	6	7	8	9	10
Basic motor skills	■	■	■								
Fine motor ability			■	■	■	■	■	■	■	■	
Musical fingering							■	■	■	■	■

Psychiatrists and educators have long recognized the value of early experience. But their observations have until now been largely anecdotal. What's so exciting, says Matthew Melmed, executive director of Zero to Three, a nonprofit organization devoted to highlighting the importance of the first three years of life, is that modern neuroscience is providing the hard, quantifiable evidence that was missing earlier. "Because you can see the results under a microscope or in a PET scan," he observes, "it's become that much more convincing."

What lessons can be drawn from the new findings? Among other things, it is clear that foreign languages should be taught in elementary school, if not before. That remedial education may be more effective at the age of three or four than at nine or 10. That good, affordable day care is not a luxury or a fringe benefit for welfare mothers and working parents but essential brain food for the next generation. For while new synapses continue to form throughout life, and even adults continually refurbish their minds through reading and learning, never again will the brain be able to master new skills so readily or rebound from setbacks so easily.

Rat-a-tat-tat. Rat-a-tat-tat. Rat-a-tat-tat. Just last week, in the U.S. alone, some 77,000 newborns began the miraculous process of wiring their brains for a lifetime of learning. If parents and policymakers don't pay attention to the conditions under which this delicate process takes place, we will all suffer the consequences—starting around the year 2010.

Temperament and the Reactions to Unfamiliarity

Jerome Kagan

The behavioral reactions to unfamiliar events are basic phenomena in all vertebrates. Four-month-old infants who show a low threshold to become distressed and motorically aroused to unfamiliar stimuli are more likely than others to become fearful and subdued during early childhood, whereas infants who show a high arousal threshold are more likely to become bold and sociable. After presenting some developmental correlates and trajectories of these 2 temperamental biases, I consider their implications for psychopathology and the relation between propositions containing psychological and biological concepts.

INTRODUCTION

A readiness to react to events that differ from those encountered in the recent or distant past is one of the distinguishing characteristics of all mammalian species. Thus, the events with the greatest power to produce both an initial orienting and sustained attention in infants older than 3 to 4 months are variations on what is familiar, often called discrepant events (Fagan, 1981; Kagan, Kearsley, & Zelazo, 1980). By 8 months of age, discrepant events can produce a vigilant posture of quiet staring and, occasionally, a wary face and a cry of distress if the event cannot be assimilated easily (Bronson, 1970). That is why Hebb (1946) made discrepancy a major basis for fear reactions in animals, why a fear reaction to strangers occurs in the middle of the first year in children growing up in a variety of cultural settings, and, perhaps, why variation in the initial behavioral reaction to novelty exists in almost every vertebrate species studied (Wilson, Coleman, Clark, & Biederman, 1993).

Recent discoveries by neuroscientists enrich these psychological facts. The hippocampus plays an important role in the detection of discrepant events (Squire & Knowlton, 1995). Projections from the hippocampus provoke activity in the amygdala and lead to changes in autonomic function and posture and, in older children, to reflection and anticipation (Shimamura, 1995). Because these neural structures and their projections are influenced by a large number of neurotransmitters and neuromodulators, it is reasonable to expect inherited differences in the neurochemistry of these structures and circuits and, therefore, in their excitability. Variation in the levels of, or receptors for, corticotropin releasing hormone, norepinephrine, cortisol, dopamine, glutamate, GABA, opioids, acetylcholine, and other molecules might be accompanied by differences in the intensity and form of responsivity to unfamiliarity (Cooper, Bloom, & Roth, 1991). This speculation is supported by research with infants and children (Kagan, 1994). This article summarizes what has been learned

From *Child Development*, February 1997, pp. 139-143. © 1997 by the Society for Research in Child Development. Reprinted by permission.

about two temperamental types of children who react in different ways to unfamiliarity, considers the implications of these two temperamental categories for psychopathology, and comments briefly on the relation between psychological and biological constructs.

INFANT REACTIVITY AND FEARFUL BEHAVIOR

About 20% of a large sample of 462 healthy, Caucasian, middle-class, 16-week-old infants became both motorically active and distressed to presentations of brightly colored toys moved back and forth in front of their faces, tape recordings of voices speaking brief sentences, and cotton swabs dipped in dilute butyl alcohol applied to the nose. These infants are called high reactive. By contrast, about 40% of infants with the same family and ethnic background remained motorically relaxed and did not fret or cry to the same set of unfamiliar events. These infants are called low reactive. The differences between high and low reactives can be interpreted as reflecting variation in the excitability of the amygdala and its projections to the ventral striatum, hypothalamus, cingulate, central gray, and medulla (Amaral, Price, Pitkanen, & Carmichael, 1992; Davis, 1992).

When these high and low reactive infants were observed in a variety of unfamiliar laboratory situations at 14 and 21 months, about one-third of the 73 high reactives were highly fearful (4 or more fears), and only 3% showed minimal fear (0 or 1 fear) at both ages. By contrast, one-third of the 147 low reactives were minimally fearful at both ages (0 or 1 fear), and only 4% displayed high levels of fear (Kagan, 1994).

The profiles of high and low fear to unfamiliar events, called inhibited and uninhibited, are heritable, to a modest degree, in 1- to 2-year-old middle-class children (DiLalla, Kagan, & Reznick, 1994; Robinson, Kagan, Reznick, & Corley, 1992). Further, high

reactives show greater sympathetic reactivity in the cardiovascular system than low reactives during the first 2 years (Kagan, 1994; Snidman, Kagan, Riordan, & Shannon, 1995).

As children approach the fourth and fifth years, they gain control of crying to and reflex retreat from unfamiliar events and will only show these responses to very dangerous events or to situations that are not easily or ethically created in the laboratory. Hence, it is important to ask how high and low reactive infants might respond to unfamiliar laboratory situations when they are 4–5 years old. Each species has a biologically preferred reaction to novelty. Rabbits freeze, monkeys display a distinct facial grimace, and cats arch their backs. In humans, restraint on speech seems to be an analogue of the immobility that animals display in novel situations (Panksepp, Sacks, Crepeau, & Abbott, 1991), for children often become quiet as an initial reaction to unfamiliar situations (Asendorpf, 1990; Kagan, Reznick, & Gibbons, 1989; Kagan, Reznick, & Snidman, 1988; Murray, 1971). It is also reasonable to expect that the activity in limbic sites provoked by an unfamiliar social situation might interfere with the brain states that mediate the relaxed emotional state that is indexed by smiling and laughter (Adamec, 1991; Amaral et al., 1992). When the children who had been classified as high and low reactive were interviewed at 4½ years of age by an unfamiliar female examiner who was blind to their prior behavior, the 62 high reactives talked and smiled significantly less often (means of 41 comments and 17 smiles) than did the 94 low reactives (means of 57 comments and 28 smiles) during a 1 hour test battery: $F(1, 152) = 4.51$, $p < .05$ for spontaneous comments; $F(1, 152) = 15.01$, $p < .01$ for spontaneous smiles. Although spontaneous comments and smiles were positively correlated ($r = 0.4$), the low reactives displayed significantly more smiles than would have been predicted from a regression of number of smiles on number of spontaneous comments. The high reactives

displayed significantly fewer smiles than expected. Every one of the nine children who smiled more than 50 times had been a low reactive infant.

However, only a modest proportion of children maintained an extreme form of their theoretically expected profile over the period from 4 months to 4½ years, presumably because of the influence of intervening family experiences (Arcus, 1991). Only 19% of the high reactives displayed a high level of fear at both 14 and 21 months (>4 fears), together with low values (below the mean) for both spontaneous comments and smiles at 4½ years. But not one low reactive infant actualized such a consistently fearful and emotionally subdued profile. By contrast, 18% of low reactive infants showed the opposite profile of low fear (0 or 1 fear) at both 14 and 21 months together with high values for both spontaneous smiles and spontaneous comments at 4½ years. Only one high reactive infant actualized that prototypic, uninhibited profile. Thus, it is uncommon for either temperamental type to develop and to maintain the seminal features of the other type, but quite common for each type to develop a profile that is characteristic of the less extreme child who is neither very timid nor very bold.

The 4½-year-old boys who had been high reactive infants had significantly higher resting heart rates than did low reactives, but the differences between high and low reactive girls at this older age took a different form. The high reactive girls did not show the expected high negative correlation (−0.6 to −0.8) between heart rate and heart rate variability. It is possible that the greater sympathetic reactivity of high reactive girls interfered with the usual, vagally induced inverse relation between heart rate and heart rate variability (Porges, Arnold, & Forbes, 1973; Richards, 1985).

Honest disagreement surrounds the conceptualization of infant reactivity as a continuum of arousal or as two distinct categories. The raw motor activity score at 4 months formed a continuum, but the distribution of distress cries did not. Some infants never fretted or cried; others cried a great deal. A more important defense of the decision to treat high and low reactivity as two distinct categories is the fact that within each of the two categories variation in motor activity and crying was unrelated to later fearfulness or sympathetic reactivity. If reactivity were a continuous trait, then a low reactive infant with extremely low motor and distress scores should be less fearful than one who showed slightly more arousal. But that prediction was not affirmed. Second, infants who showed high motor arousal but no crying or minimal motor arousal with frequent crying showed developmental profiles that were different from those who were categorized as low or high reactive. Finally, high and low reactives differed in physical and physiological features that imply qualitatively different genetic constitutions. For example, high reactives have narrower faces than low reactives in the second year of life (Arcus & Kagan, 1995). Unpublished data from our laboratory reveal that the prevalence of atopic allergies among both children and their parents is significantly greater among high than low reactive infants. Studies of monozygotic and dizygotic same-sex twin pairs reveal significant heritability for inhibited and uninhibited behavior in the second year of life (Robinson et al., 1992). These facts imply that the two temperamental groups represent qualitatively different types and do not lie on a continuum of arousal or reactivity to stimulation.

The decision to regard individuals with very different values on a construct as members of the discrete categories or as falling on a continuum will depend on the scientists' purpose. Scientists who are interested in the relation, across families and genera, between brain size and body mass treat the two measurements as continuous. However, biologists interested in the maternal

behavior of mice and chimpanzees regard these two mammals as members of qualitatively different groups. Similarly, if psychologists are interested in the physiological foundations of high and low reactives, it will be more useful to regard the two groups as categories. But those who are giving advice to mothers who complain about the ease of arousal and irritability of their infants may treat the arousal as a continuum.

IMPLICATIONS

The differences between high reactive-inhibited and low reactive-uninhibited children provoke speculation on many issues; I deal briefly with implications for psychopathology and the relation between psychological and biological propositions.

Anxiety Disorder

The high reactive infants who became very inhibited 4-year-olds—about 20% of all high reactives—have a low threshold for developing a state of fear to unfamiliar events, situations, and people. It is reasonable to expect that these children will be at a higher risk than most for developing one of the anxiety disorders when they become adolescents or adults. The childhood data do not provide a clue as to which particular anxiety profile will be most prevalent. However, an extensive clinical interview with early adolescents (13–14 years old), who had been classified 11 years earlier (at 21 or 31 months) as inhibited or uninhibited (Kagan et al., 1988), revealed that social phobia was more frequent among inhibited than among uninhibited adolescents, whereas specific phobias, separation anxiety, or compulsive symptoms did not differentiate the two groups (Schwartz, personal communication). This intriguing result, which requires replication, has interesting theoretical ramifications.

Research with animals, usually rats, suggests that acquisition of a

fear reaction (e.g., freezing or potentiated startle) to a conditioned stimulus (light or tone) that had been paired with electric shock is mediated by a circuitry that is different from the one that mediates the conditioned response to the context in which the conditioning had occurred (LeDoux, 1995).

Davis (personal communication) has found that a potentiated startle reaction in the rat to the context in which light had been paired with shock involves a circuit from the amygdala to the bed nucleus of the stria terminalis and the septum. The potentiated startle reaction to the conditioned stimulus does not require that circuit. A phobia of spiders or bridges resembles an animal's reaction of freezing to a conditioned stimulus, but a quiet, avoidant posture at a party resembles a fearful reaction to a context. That is, the person who is extremely shy at a party of strangers is not afraid of any particular person or of the setting. Rather, the source of the uncertainty is a situation in which the shy person had experienced anxiety with other strangers. Thus, social phobia may rest on a neurophysiology that is different from that of specific phobia.

Conduct Disorder

The correlation between social class and the prevalence of conduct disorder or delinquency is so high it is likely that the vast majority of children with these profiles acquired their risk status as a result of life conditions, without the mediation of a particular temperamental vulnerability. However, a small proportion—probably no more than 10%—who began their delinquent careers before age 10, and who often committed violent crimes as adolescents, might inherit a physiology that raises their threshold for the conscious experience of anticipatory anxiety and/or guilt over violating community standards for civil behavior (Tremblay, Pihl, Vitaro, & Dubkin, 1994). Damasio (1994) and Mountcastle (1995) have suggested that the surface of the ventromedial prefrontal cortex receives sensory information (from the amygdala) that originates in the peripheral targets, like heart, skin, gut, and muscles. Most children and adults who think about committing a crime experience a subtle feeling that accompanies anticipation of the consequences of an antisocial act. That feeling, which might be called anticipatory anxiety, shame, or guilt, provides an effective restraint on the action. However, if a small proportion of children possessed a less excitable amygdala, or a ventromedial surface that was less responsive, they would be deprived of the typical intensity of this feeling and, as a result, might be less restrained than the majority (Kochanska, Murray, Jacques, Koenig, & Vandegeest, 1996; Zahn-Waxler, Cole, Welsh, & Fox, 1995). If these children are reared in homes and play in neighborhoods in which antisocial behavior is socialized, they are unlikely to become delinquents; perhaps they will become group leaders. However, if these children live in families that do not socialize aggression consistently and play in neighborhoods that provide temptation for antisocial behavior, they might be candidates for a delinquent career.

Biology and Psychology

The renewed interest in temperament has brought some psychologists in closer intellectual contact with neuroscientists. Although this interaction will be beneficial to both disciplines, there is a tension between traditional social scientists who describe and explain behavioral and emotional events using only psychological terms and a smaller group who believe that an acknowledgment of biological events is theoretically helpful. The recent, dramatic advances in the neurosciences have led some scholars to go further and to imply that, in the future, robust generalizations about psychological processes might not be possible without study of the underlying biology (LeDoux, 1995).

Although some neuroscientists recognize that the psychological phenomena of thought, planning, and emotion are emergent—as a blizzard is emergent from the physics of air masses—the media suggest, on occasion, that the biological descriptions are sufficient to explain the psychological events. This publicity creates a misperception that the biological and psychological are competing explanations when, of course, they are not. Vernon Mountcastle notes that although "every mental process is a brain process, ... not every mentalistic sentence is identical to some neurophysiological sentence. Mind and brain are not identical, no more than lung and respiration are identical" (Mountcastle, 1995, p. 294).

Some neuroscientists, sensing correctly the community resistance to a strong form of biological determinism, are emphasizing the malleability of the neuron's genome to environmental events. A few neurobiologists have come close to declaring that the human genome, like Locke's image of the child's mind, is a tabula rasa that is subject to continual change. This position tempts citizens unfamiliar with neuroscience to conclude that there may be a linear cascade that links external events (e.g., loss of a loved one) directly to changes in genes, physiology, and, finally, behavior, with the psychological layer (e.g., a mood of sadness) between brain physiology and apathetic behavior being relatively unimportant. This error is as serious as the one made by the behaviorists 60 years ago when they assumed a direct connection between a stimulus and an overt response and ignored what was happening in the brain. Both corpora of evidence are necessary if we are to understand the emergence of psychological qualities and their inevitable variation. "The phenomena of human existence and experience are always simultaneously biological and social, and an adequate explanation must involve both" (Rose, 1995, p. 380).

ACKNOWLEDGMENTS

This paper represents portions of the G. Stanley Hall Lecture delivered at the annual meeting of the American Psychological Association, New York City, August 1995. Preparation of this paper was supported, in part, by grants from the John D. and Catherine T. MacArthur Foundation, William T. Grant Foundation, and NIMH grant 47077. The author thanks Nancy Snidman and Doreen Arcus for their collaboration in the research summarized.

ADDRESS AND AFFILIATION

Corresponding author: Jerome Kagan, Harvard University, Department of Psychology, Cambridge, MA 02138; e-mail: JK@WJH.HARVARD.EDU.

REFERENCES

Adamec, R. E. (1991). Anxious personality and the cat. In B. J. Carroll & J. E. Barrett (Eds.), *Psychopathology in the brain* (pp. 153–168). New York: Raven.

Amaral, D. J., Price, L., Pitkanen, A., & Carmichael, S. T. (1992). Anatomical organization of the primate amygdaloid complex. In J. P. Aggleton (Ed.), *The amygdala* (pp. 1–66). New York: Wiley.

Arcus, D. M. (1991). *Experiential modification of temperamental bias in inhibited and uninhibited children*. Unpublished doctoral dissertation, Harvard University.

Arcus, D. M., & Kagan, J. (1995). Temperament and craniofacial variation in the first two years. *Child Development, 66,* 1529–1540.

Asendorpf, J. B. (1990). Development of inhibition during childhood. *Developmental Psychology, 26,* 721–730.

Bronson, G. W. (1970). Fear of visual novelty. *Developmental Psychology, 2,* 33–40.

Cooper, J. R., Bloom, F. E., & Roth, R. H. (1991). *Biochemical basis of neuropharmacology*. New York: Oxford University Press.

Damasio, A. (1994). *Descartes' error*. New York: Putnam.

Davis, M. (1992). The role of the amygdala in conditioned fear. In J. P. Aggleton (Ed.), *The amygdala* (pp. 256–305). New York: Wiley.

DiLalla, L. F., Kagan, J., & Reznick, J. S. (1994). Genetic etiology of behavioral inhibition among two year olds. *Infant Behavior and Development, 17,* 401–408.

Fagan, J. F. (1981). Infant intelligence. *Intelligence, 5,* 239–243.

Hebb, D. O. (1946). The nature of fear. *Psychological Review, 53,* 259–276.

Kagan, J. (1994). *Galen's prophecy*. New York: Basic.

Kagan, J., Kearsley, R. B., & Zelazo, P. R. (1980). *Infancy*. Cambridge, MA: Harvard University Press.

Kagan, J., Reznick, J. S., & Gibbons, J. (1989). Inhibited and uninhibited types of children. *Child Development, 60*, 838–845.

Kagan, J., Reznick, J. S., & Snidman, N. (1988). Biological bases of childhood shyness. *Science, 240*, 167–171.

Kochanska, G., Murray, K., Jacques, T. Y., Koenig, A. L. & Vandegeest, K. A. (1996). Inhibitory control in young children and its role in emerging internalization. *Child Development, 67*, 490–507.

LeDoux, J. E. (1995). In search of an emotional system in the brain. In M. S. Gazzinaga (Ed.), *The cognitive neurosciences* (pp. 1049–1062). Cambridge, MA: MIT Press.

Mountcastle, V. (1995). The evolution of ideas concerning the function of the neocortex. *Cerebral Cortex, 5*, 289–295.

Murray, D. C. (1971). Talk, silence, and anxiety. *Psychological Bulletin, 75*, 244–260.

Panksepp, J., Sacks, D. S., Crepeau, L. J., & Abbott, B. B. (1991). The psycho and neurobiology of fear systems in the brain. In M. R. Denny (Ed.), *Fear, avoidance, and phobias* (pp. 17–59). Hillsdale, NJ: Erlbaum.

Porges, S. W., Arnold, W. R., & Forbes, E. J. (1973). Heart rate variability: An index of attention responsivity in human newborns. *Developmental Psychology, 8*, 85–92.

Richards, J. E. (1985). Respiratory sinus arrhythmia predicts heart rate and visual responses during visual attention in 14 to 20 week old infants. *Psychophysiology, 22*, 101–109.

Robinson, J. L., Kagan, J., Reznick, J. S., & Corley, R. (1992). The heritability of inhibited and uninhibited behavior: A twin study. *Developmental Psychology, 28*, 1030–1037.

Rose, R. J. 1995. Genes and human behavior. In J. T. Spence, J. M. Darley, & D. P. Foss (Eds.) *Annual review of psychology* (pp. 625–654). Palo Alto, CA: Annual Reviews.

Shimamura, A. P. (1995). Memory and frontal lobe function. In M. S. Gazzinaga (Ed.), *The cognitive neurosciences* (pp. 803–814). Cambridge, MA: MIT Press.

Snidman, N., Kagan, J., Riordan, L., & Shannon, D., 1995. Cardiac function and behavioral reactivity in infancy. *Psychophysiology, 31*, 199–207.

Squire, L. R., & Knowlton, B. J. (1995). Memory, hippocampus, and brain systems. In M. S. Gazzinaga (Ed.), *The cognitive neurosciences* (pp. 825–838). Cambridge, MA: MIT Press.

Tremblay, R. E., Pihl, R. O., Vitaro, F., & Dubkin, P. L. (1994). Predicting early onset of male antisocial behavior from preschool behavior. *Archives of General Psychiatry, 51*, 732–739.

Wilson, D. S., Coleman, K., Clark, A. B., & Biederman, L. (1993). Shy-bold continuum in pumpkinseed sunfish (*Lepomis gibbosus*): An ecological study of a psychological trait. *Journal of Comparative Psychology, 107*, 250–260.

Zahn-Waxler, C., Cole, P., Welsh, J. D., & Fox, N. A. (1995). Psychophysiological correlates of empathy and prosocial behavior in preschool children with behavioral problems. *Development and Psychopathology, 7*, 27–48.

Learning language, researchers are finding, is an astonishing act of brain computation—and it's performed by people too young to tie their shoes

By Shannon Brownlee

Inside a small, dark booth, 18-month-old Karly Horn sits on her mother Terry's lap. Karly's brown curls bounce each time she turns her head to listen to a woman's recorded voice coming from one side of the booth or the other. "At the bakery, workers will be baking bread," says the voice. Karly turns to her left and listens, her face intent. "On Tuesday morning, the people have going to work," says the voice. Karly turns her head away even before the statement is finished. The lights come on as graduate student Ruth Tincoff opens the door to the booth. She gives the child's curls a pat and says, "Nice work."

Karly and her mother are taking part in an experiment at Johns Hopkins University in Baltimore, run by psycholinguist Peter Jusczyk, who has spent 25 years probing the linguistic skills of children who have not yet begun to talk. Like most toddlers her age, Karly can utter a few dozen words at most and can string together the occasional two-word sentence, like "More juice" and "Up, Mommy." Yet as Jusczyk and his colleagues have found, she can already recognize that a sentence like "the people have going to work" is ungrammatical. By 18 months of age, most toddlers have somehow learned the rule requiring that any verb ending in *-ing* must be preceded by the verb *to be.* "If you had asked me 10 years ago if kids this young could do this," says Jusczyk, "I would have said that's crazy.

Linguists these days are reconsidering a lot of ideas they once considered crazy. Recent findings like Jusczyk's are reshaping the prevailing model of how children acquire language. The dominant theory, put forth by Noam Chomsky, has been that children cannot possibly learn the full rules and structure of languages strictly by imitating what they hear. Instead, nature gives children a head start, wiring them from birth with the ability to acquire their parents native tongue by fitting what they hear into a preexisting template for the basic structure shared by all languages. (Similarly, kittens are thought to be hard-wired to learn how to hunt.) Language, writes Massachusetts Institute of Technology linguist Steven Pinker, "is a distinct piece of the biological makeup of our brains." Chomsky, a prominent linguist at MIT, hypothesized in the 1950s that children are endowed from birth with "universal grammar," the fundamental rules that are common to all languages, and the ability to apply these rules to the raw material of the speech they hear—without awareness of their underlying logic.

The average preschooler can't tell time, but he has already accumulated a vocabulary of thousands of words—plus (as Pinker writes in his book, *The Language Instinct,*) "a tacit knowledge of grammar more sophisticated than the thickest style manual." Within a few months of birth, children have already begun memorizing words without knowing their meaning. The question that has absorbed—and sometimes divided—linguists is whether children need a special language faculty to do this or instead can infer the abstract rules of grammar from the sentences they hear, using the same mental skills that allow them to recognize faces or master arithmetic.

The debate over how much of language is already vested in a child at birth is far from settled, but new linguistic research already is transforming traditional views of how the human brain works and how language evolved. "This debate has completely changed the way we view the brain," says Elissa Newport, a psycholinguist at the University of Rochester in New York. Far from being an orderly, computer-like machine that methodically calculates step by step, the brain is now seen as working more like a beehive, its swarm of interconnected neurons sending signals back and forth at lightning speed. An infant's brain, it turns out, is capable of taking in enormous amounts of information and finding the regular patterns contained within it. Geneticists and linguists recently have begun to challenge the common-sense assumption that intelligence and language are inextricably linked, through research on a rare genetic disorder called Williams syndrome, which can seriously impair cognition while leaving language nearly intact (box, Rare Disorder Reveals Split between Language and Thought). Increasingly sophisticated technologies such as magnetic resonance imaging are allowing researchers to watch the brain in action, revealing that language literally sculpts and reorganizes the connections within it as a child grows.

Little polyglots. An infant's brain can perceive every possible sound in every language. By 10 months, babies have learned to screen out foreign sounds and to focus on the sounds of their native language.

The path leading to language begins even before birth, when a developing fetus is bathed in the muffled sound of its mother's voice in the womb. Newborn babies prefer their mothers' voices over those of their fathers or other women, and researchers recently have found that when very young babies hear a recording of their mothers' native language, they will suck more vigorously on a pacifier than when they hear a recording of another tongue.

At first, infants respond only to the prosody—the cadence, rhythm, and pitch—of their mothers' speech, not the words. But soon enough they home in on the actual sounds that are typical of their parents' language. Every language uses a different assortment of sounds, called phonemes, which combine to make syllables. (In English, for example, the consonant sound "b" and the vowel sound "a" are both phonemes, which combine for the syllable *ba*, as in *banana*.) To an adult, simply perceiving, much less pronouncing, the phonemes of a foreign language can seem impossible. In English, the p of *pat* is "aspirated," or produced with a puff of air; the p of *spot* or *tap* is unaspirated. In English, the two p's are considered the same; therefore it is hard for English speakers to recognize that in many other languages the two p's are two different phonemes. Japanese speakers have trouble distinguishing between the "l" and "r" sounds of English, since in Japanese they don't count as separate sounds.

Polyglot tots. Infants can perceive the entire range of phonemes, according to Janet Werker and Richard Tees, psychologists at the University of British Columbia in Canada. Werker and Tees found that the brains of 4-month-old babies respond to every phoneme uttered in languages as diverse as Hindi and Nthlakampx, a Northwest American Indian language containing numerous consonant combinations that can sound to a nonnative speaker like a drop of water hitting an empty bucket. By the time babies are 10 months to a year old, however, they have begun to focus on the distinctions among phonemes of their native language and to ignore the differences among foreign sounds. Children don't lose the ability to distinguish the sounds of a foreign language; they simply don't pay attention to them. This allows them to learn more quickly the syllables and words of their native tongue.

An infant's next step is learning to fish out individual words from the nonstop stream of sound that makes up ordinary speech. Finding the boundaries between words is a daunting task, because people don't pause ... between ... words ... when ... they speak. Yet children begin to note word boundaries by the time they are 8 months old, even though they have no concept of what most words mean. Last year, Jusczyk and his colleagues reported results of an experiment in which they let 8-month-old babies listen at home to recorded stories filled with unusual words, like *hornbill* and *python*. Two weeks later, the researchers tested the babies with two lists of words, one composed of words they had already heard in the stories, the other of new unusual words that weren't in the stories. The infants listened, on average, to the familiar list for a second longer than to the list of novel words.

The cadence of language is a baby's first clue to word boundaries. In most English words, the first syllable is accented. This is especially noticeable in words known in poetry as trochees—two-syllable words stressed on the first syllable—which parents repeat to young children (BA-by, DOG-gie, MOM-my). At 6 months, American babies pay equal amounts of attention to words with different stress patterns, like gi-RAFFE or TI-ger. By 9 months, however, they have heard enough of the typical first-syllable-stress pattern of English to prefer listening to trochees, a predilection that will show up later, when they start ut-

tering their first words and mispronouncing giraffe as *raff* and banana as *nana*. At 30 months, children can easily repeat the phrase "TOM-my KISS-ed the MON-key," because it preserves the typical English pattern, but

they will leave out the *the* when asked to repeat "Tommy patted the monkey." Researchers are now testing whether French babies prefer words with a second-syllable stress—words like *be-RET* or *ma-MAN*.

Decoding patterns. Most adults could not imagine making speedy progress toward memorizing words in a foreign language just by listening

to somebody talk on the telephone. That is basically what 8-month-old babies can do, according to a provocative study published in 1996 by the University of Rochester's Newport and her colleagues, Jenny Saffran

and Richard Aslin. They reported that babies can remember words by listening for patterns of syllables that occur together with statistical regularity.

The researchers created a miniature artificial language, which consisted of a handful of three-syllable nonsense words constructed from 11 different syllables. The babies heard a computer-generated voice repeating

Discriminating minds. Toddlers listen for bits of language like <u>the</u>, which signals that a noun will follow. Most 2-year-olds can understand "Find the dog," but they are stumped by "Find gub dog."

WILLIAMS SYNDROME

Rare disorder reveals split between language and thought

Kristen Aerts is only 9 years old, but she can work a room like a seasoned pol. She marches into the lab of cognitive neuroscientist Ursula Bellugi, at the Salk Institute for Biological Studies in La Jolla, Calif., and greets her with a cheery, "Good morning Dr. Bellugi. How are you today?" The youngster smiles at a visitor and says, "My name is Kristen. What's yours?" She looks people in the eye when

she speaks and asks questions—social skills that many adults never seem to master, much less a third grader. Yet for all her poise, Kristen has an IQ of about 79. She cannot write her address; she has trouble tying her shoes, drawing a simple picture of a bicycle, and subtracting 2 from 4; and she may never be able to live independently.

Kristen has Williams syndrome, a rare genetic disorder that affect both

body and brain, giving those who have it a strange and incongruous jumble of deficits and strengths. They have diminished cognitive capacities and heart problems, and age prematurely, yet they show outgoing personalities and a flair for language. "What makes Williams syndrome so fascinating," says Bellugis, "is it shows that the domains of cognition and language are quite separate."

Genetic gap. Williams syndrome, which was first described in 1961, results when a group of genes on one copy of chromosome 7 is deleted during embryonic development. Most people with Williams resemble each other more than they do their families, with wide-set hazel eyes, upturned noses, wide mouths. They also share a peculiar set of mental impairments. Most stumble over the simplest spa-

these words in random order in a monotone for two minutes. What they heard went something like "bidakupadotigolabubidaku." *Bidaku*, in this case, is a word. With no cadence or pauses, the only way the babies could learn individual words was by remembering how often certain syllables were uttered together. When the researchers tested the babies a few minutes later, they found that the infants recognized pairs of syllables that had occurred together consistently on the recording, such as *bida*. They did not recognize a pair like *kupa*, which was a rarer combination that crossed the boundaries of two words. In the past, psychologists never imagined that young infants had the mental capacity to make these sorts of inferences. "We were pretty surprised we could get this result with babies, and with only brief exposure," says Newport. "Real language, of course, is much more complicated, but the exposure is vast."

Learning words is one thing; learning the abstract rules of grammar is another. When Noam Chomsky first voiced his idea that language is hardwired in the brain, he didn't have the benefit of the current revolution in cognitive science, which has begun to pry open the human mind with so-phisticated psychological experiments and new computer models. Until recently, linguists could only parse languages and marvel at how quickly

children master their abstract rules, which give every human being who can speak (or sign) the power to express an infinite number of ideas from a finite number of words.

There also are a finite number of ways that languages construct sentences. As Chomsky once put it, from a Martian's-eye view, everybody on Earth speaks a single tongue that has thousands of mutually unintelligible dialects. For instance, all people make sentences from noun phrases, like "The quick brown fox," and verb phrases, like "jumped over the fence."

And virtually all of the world's 6,000 or so languages allow phrases to be moved around in a sentence to form questions, relative clauses, and passive constructions.

Statistical wizards. Chomsky posited that children were born knowing these and a handful of other basic laws of language and that they learn their parents' native tongue with the help of a "language acquisition de-

Masters of pattern. Researchers played strings of three-syllable nonsense words to 8-month-old babies for two minutes. The babies learned them by remembering how often syllables occurred together.

tial tasks, such as putting together a puzzle, and many cannot read or write beyond the level of a first grader.

In spite of these deficits, Bellugi has found that children with the disorder are not merely competent at language but extraordinary. Ask normal kids to name as many animals as possible in 60 seconds, and a string of barnyard and pet-store examples will tumble out. Ask children with Williams, and you'll get a menagerie or rare creatures, such as ibex, newt, yak, and weasel. People with Williams have the gift of gab, telling elaborate sto-

ries with unabashed verve and incorporating audience teasers such as "Gadzooks!" and "Lo and behold!"

This unlikely suite of skills and inadequacies initially led Bellugi to surmise that Williams might damage the right hemisphere of the brain, where spatial tasks are processed, while leaving language in the left hemisphere intact. That has not turned out to be true. People with Williams excel at recognizing faces, a job that enlists the visual and spatial-processing skills of the right hemisphere. Using functional brain

imaging, a technique that shows the brain in action, Bellugi has found that both hemispheres of the brains of people with Williams are shouldering the tasks of processing language.

Bellugi and other researchers are now trying to link the outward characteristics of people with Williams to the genes they are missing and to changes in brain tissue. They have begun concentrating on the neocerebellum, a part of the brain that is enlarged in people with Williams and that may hold clues to their engaging personalities and to the evolution

of language. The neocerebellum is among the brain's newest parts, appearing in human ancestors about the same time as the enlargement of the frontal cortex, the place where researchers believe rational thoughts are formulated. The neocerebellum is significantly smaller in people with autism, who are generally antisocial and poor at language, the reverse of people with Williams. This part of the brain helps make semantic connections between words, such as *sit* and *chair*, suggesting that it was needed for language to evolve.

vice," preprogrammed circuits in the brain. Findings like Newport's are suggesting to some researchers that perhaps children can use statistical regularities to extract not only individual words from what they hear but also the rules for cobbling words together into sentences.

This idea is shared by computational linguists, who have designed computer models called artificial neural networks that are very simplified versions of the brain and that can "learn" some aspects of language. Artificial neural networks mimic the way that nerve cells, or neurons, inside a brain are hooked up. The result is a device that shares some basic properties with the brain and that can accomplish some linguistic feats that real children perform. For example, a neural network can make general categories out of a jumble of words coming in, just as a child learns that certain kinds of words refer to objects while others refer to actions. Nobody has to teach kids that words like *dog* and *telephone* are nouns, while *go* and *jump* are verbs; the way they use such words in sentences demonstrates that they know the difference. Neural networks also can learn some aspects of the meaning of words, and they can infer some rules of syntax, or word order. Therefore, a computer that was fed English sentences would be able to produce a phrase like "Johnny ate fish," rather than "Johnny fish ate," which is correct in Japanese. These computer models even make some of the same mistakes that real children do, says Mark Seidenberg, a computational linguist at the University of Southern California. A neural network designed by a student of Seidenberg's to learn to conjugate verbs sometimes issued sentences like "He jumped me the ball," which any parent will recognize as the kind of error that could have come from the mouths of babes.

But neural networks have yet to come close to the computation power of a toddler. Ninety percent of the sentences uttered by the average 3-year-old are grammatically correct. The mistakes they do make are rarely random but rather the result of following the rules of grammar with excessive zeal. There is no logical reason for being able to say "I batted the ball" but not "I holded the rabbit," except that about 180 of the most commonly used English verbs are conjugated irregularly.

Strict grammarians. Most 3-year-olds rarely make grammatical errors. When they do, the mistakes they make usually are the result of following the rules of grammar with excessive zeal.

Yet for all of grammar's seeming illogic, toddlers' brains may be able to spot clues in the sentences they hear that help them learn grammatical rules, just as they use statistical regularities to find word boundaries. One such clue is the little bits of language called grammatical morphemes, which among other things tell a listener whether a word is being used as noun or as a verb. *The*, for instance, signals that a noun will soon follow, while the suffix *ion* also identifies a word as a noun, as in vibration. Psycholinguist LouAnn Gerken of the University of Arizona recently reported that toddlers know what grammatical morphemes signify before they actually use them. She tested this by asking 2-year-olds a series of questions in which the grammatical morphemes were replaced with other words. When asked to "Find the dog for me," for example, 85 percent of children in her study could point to the right animal in a picture. But when the question was "Find *was* dog for me," they pointed to the dog 55 percent of the time. "Find *gub* dog for me," and it dropped to 40 percent.

Fast mapping. Children may be noticing grammatical morphemes when they are as young as 10 months and have just begun making connections between words and their definitions. Gerken recently found that infants' brain waves change when they are listening to stories in which grammatical morphemes are replaced with other words, suggesting they begin picking up grammar even before they know what sentences mean.

Such linguistic leaps come as a baby's brain is humming with activity. Within the first few months of life, a baby's neurons will forge 1,000 trillion connections, an increase of 20-fold from birth. Neurobiologists once assumed that the wiring in a baby's brain was set at birth. After that, the brain, like legs and noses, just grew bigger. That view has been demolished, says Anne Fernald, a psycholinguist at Stanford University, "now that we can eavesdrop on the brain." Images made using the brain-scanning technique positron emission tomography have revealed, for instance, that when a baby is 8 or 9 months old, the part of the brain that stores and indexes many kinds of memory becomes fully functional. This is precisely when babies appear to be able to attach meaning to words.

Other leaps in a child's linguistic prowess also coincide with remarkable changes in the brain. For instance, an adult listener can recognize *eleph* as *elephant* within about 400 milliseconds, an ability called "fast mapping" that demands that the brain process speech sounds with phenomenal speed. "To understand strings of words, you have to identify individual words rapidly," says Fernald. She and her colleagues have found that around 15 months of age, a child needs more than a second to recognize even a familiar word, like *baby*. At 18 months, the child can get the picture slightly before the word is ending. At 24 months, she knows the word in a mere 600 milliseconds, as soon as the syllable *bay* has been uttered.

Fast mapping takes off at the same moment as a dramatic reorganization of the child's brain, in which language-related operations, particularly grammar, shift from both sides of the brain into the left hemisphere. Most adult brains are lopsided when it comes to language, processing grammar almost entirely in the left temporal lobe, just over the left ear. Infants and toddlers, however, treat language in both hemispheres, according to Debra Mills, at the University of California–San Diego, and Helen Neville, at the University of Oregon. Mills and Neville stuck electrodes to toddlers' heads to find that processing of words that serve special grammatical functions, such as prepositions, conjunctions, and articles, begins to shift into the left side around the end of the third year.

From then on, the two hemispheres assume different job descriptions. The right temporal lobe continues to perform spatial tasks, such as following the trajectory of a baseball and predicting where it will land. It also pays attention to the emotional information contained in the cadence and pitch of speech. Both hemispheres know the meanings of many words, but the left temporal lobe holds the key to grammar.

This division is maintained even when the language is signed, not spoken. Ursula Bellugi and Edward Klima, a wife and husband team at the Salk Institute for Biological Studies in La Jolla, Caiif., recently demonstrated this fact by studying deaf people who were lifelong signers of American Sign Language and who also had suffered a stroke in specific areas of the brain. The researchers found, predictably, that signers with damage to the right hemisphere had great difficulty with tasks involving spatial perception, such as copying a drawing of a geometric pattern. What was surprising was that right hemisphere damage did not hinder their fluency in ASL, which relies on movements of the hands and body in space. It was signers with damage to the left hemisphere who found they could no longer express themselves in ASL or understand it. Some had trouble producing the specific facial expressions that convey grammatical information in ASL. It is not just speech that's being processed in the left hemisphere, says MIT's Pinker, or movements of the mouth, but abstract language.

Nobody knows why the left hemisphere got the job of processing language, but linguists are beginning to surmise that languages are constructed the way they are in part because the human brain is not infinitely capable of all kinds of computation. "We are starting to see how the universals among languages could arise out of constraints on how the brain computes and how children learn," says Johns Hopkins linguist Paul Smolensky. For instance, the vast majority of the world's languages favor syllables that end in a vowel, though English is an exception. (Think of a native Italian speaking English and adding vowels where there are none.) That's because it is easier for the auditory centers of the brain to perceive differences between consonants when they come before a vowel than when they come after. Human brains can easily recognize *pad*, *bad*, and *dad* as three different words; it is much harder to distinguish *tab*, *tap*, and *tad*. As languages around the world were evolving, they were pulled along paths that minimize ambiguity among sounds.

Birth of a language. Linguists have never had the chance to study a spoken language as it is being constructed, but they have been given the opportunity to observe a new sign language in the making in Nicaragua. When the Sandinistas came to power in 1979, they established schools where deaf people came together for the first time. Many of the pupils had never met another deaf person, and their only means of communication at first was the expressive but largely unstructured pantomime each had invented at home with their hearing families. Soon the pupils began to pool their makeshift gestures into a system that is similar to spoken pidgin, the form of communication that springs up in places where people speaking mutually unintelligible tongues come together. The next generation of deaf Nicaraguan children, says Judy Kegl, a psycholinguist at Rutgers University, in Newark, N.J., has done it one better, transforming the pidgin sign into a full-blown language complete with regular grammar. The birth of Nicaraguan sign, many linguists believe, mirrors the evolution of all languages. Without conscious effort, deaf Nicaraguan children have created a sign that is now fluid and compact, and which contains standardized rules that allow them to express abstract ideas without circumlocutions. It can indicate past and future, denote whether an action was performed once or repeatedly, and show who did what to whom, allowing its users to joke, recite poetry, and tell their life stories.

Linguists have a long road ahead of them before they can say exactly how a child goes from babbling to banter, or what the very first languages might have been like, or how the brain transforms vague thoughts into concrete words that sometimes fly out of our mouths before we can stop them. But already, some practical conclusions are falling out of the new research. For example, two recent studies show that the size of toddlers' vocabularies depends in large measure on how much their mothers talk to them. At 20 months, according to a study by Janellen Huttenlocher of the University of Chicago, the children of talkative mothers had 131 more words in their vocabularies than children whose mothers were more taciturn. By age 2, the gap had widened to 295 words.

In other words, children need input and they need it early, says Newport. Parking a toddler in front of the television won't improve vocabulary, probably because kids need real human interaction to attach meaning to words. Hearing more than one language in infancy makes it easier for a child to hear the distinctions between phonemes of more than one language later on.

Newport and other linguists have discovered in recent years that the window of opportunity for acquiring language begins to close around age 6, and the gap narrows with each additional candle on the birthday cake. Children who do not learn a language by puberty will never be fluent in any tongue. That means that profoundly deaf children should be exposed to sign language as early as possible, says Newport. If their parents are hearing, they should learn to sign. And schools might rethink the practice of waiting to teach foreign languages until kids are nearly grown and the window on native command of a second language is almost shut.

Linguists don't yet know how much of grammar children are able to absorb simply by listening. And they have only begun to parse the genes or accidents of brain wiring that might give rise, as Pinker puts it, to the poet, the raconteur, or an Alexander Haig, a Mrs. Malaprop. What is certain is that language is one of the great wonders of the natural world, and linguists are still being astonished by its complexity and its power to shape the brain. Human beings, says Kegl, "show an incredible enthusiasm for discourse." Maybe what is most innate about language is the passion to communicate.

A baby's brain is a work in progress, trillions of neurons waiting to be wired into a mind. The experiences of childhood, pioneering research shows, help form the brain's circuits—for music and math, language and emotion.

Your Child's Brain

Sharon Begley

YOU HOLD YOUR NEWBORN SO his sky-blue eyes are just inches from the brightly patterned wallpaper. *ZZZt:* a neuron from his retina makes an electrical connection with one in his brain's visual cortex. You gently touch his palm with a clothespin; he grasps it, drops it, and you return it to him with soft words and a smile. *Crackle:* neurons from his hand strengthen their connection to those in his sensory-motor cortex. He cries in the night; you feed him, holding his gaze because nature has seen to it that the distance from a parent's crooked elbow to his eyes exactly matches the distance at which a baby focuses. *Zap:* neurons in the brain's amygdala send pulses of electricity through the circuits that control emotion. You hold him on your lap and talk . . . and neurons from his ears start hard-wiring connections to the auditory cortex.

And you thought you were just playing with your kid.

When a baby comes into the world her brain is a jumble of neurons, all waiting to be woven into the intricate tapestry of the mind. Some of the neurons have already been hard-wired, by the genes in the fertilized egg, into circuits that command breathing or control heartbeat, regulate body temperature or produce reflexes. But trillions upon trillions more are like the Pentium chips in a computer before the factory preloads the software. They are pure and of almost infinite potential, unprogrammed circuits that might one day compose rap songs and do calculus, erupt in fury and melt in ecstasy. If the neurons are used they become integrated into the circuitry of the brain by connecting to other neurons; if they are not used, they may die. It is the experiences of childhood, determining which neurons are used, that wire the circuits of the brain as surely as a programmer at a key-

board reconfigures the circuits in a computer. Which keys are typed—which experiences a child has—determines whether the child grows up to be intelligent or dull, fearful or self-assured, articulate or tongue-tied. Early experiences are so powerful, says pediatric neurobiologist Harry Chugani of Wayne State University, that "they can completely change the way a person turns out."

By adulthood the brain is crisscrossed with more than 100 billion neurons, each reaching out to thousands of others so that, all told, the brain has more than 100 trillion connections. It is those connections—more than the number of galaxies in the known universe—that give the brain its unrivaled powers. The traditional view was that the wiring diagram is predetermined, like one for a new house, by the genes in the fertilized egg. Unfortunately, even though half the genes—50,000—are involved in the central nervous system in some way, there are not enough of them to specify the brain's incomparably complex wiring. That leaves another possibility: genes might determine only the

brain's main circuits, with something else shaping the trillions of finer connections. That something else is the environment, the myriad messages that the brain receives from the outside world. According to the emerging paradigm, "there are two broad stages of brain wiring," says developmental neurobiologist Carla Shatz of the University of California, Berkeley: "an early period, when experience is not required, and a later one, when it is."

Yet, once wired, there are limits to the brain's ability to create itself. Time limits. Called "critical periods," they are windows of opportunity that nature flings open, starting before birth, and then slams shut, one by one, with every additional candle on the child's birthday cake. In the experiments that gave birth to this paradigm in the 1970s, Torsten Wiesel and David Hubel found that sewing shut one eye of a newborn kitten rewired its brain: so few neurons connected from the shut eye to the visual cortex that the animal was blind even after its eye was reopened. Such rewiring did not occur in adult cats

The Logical Brain

SKILL: Math and logic
LEARNING WINDOW: Birth to 4 years
WHAT WE KNOW: Circuits for math reside in the brain's cortex, near those for music. Toddlers taught simple concepts, like one and many, do better in math. Music lessons may help develop spatial skills.
WHAT WE CAN DO ABOUT IT: Play counting games with a toddler. Have him set the table to learn one-to-one relationships—one plate, one fork per person. And, to hedge your bets, turn on a Mozart CD.

The Language Brain

SKILL: Language

LEARNING WINDOW: Birth to 10 years

WHAT WE KNOW: Circuits in the auditory cortex, representing the sounds that form words, are wired by the age of 1. The more words a child hears by 2, the larger her vocabulary will grow. Hearing problems can impair the ability to match sounds to letters.

WHAT WE CAN DO ABOUT IT: Talk to your child—a lot. If you want her to master a second language, introduce it by the age of 10. Protect hearing by treating ear infections promptly.

---

whose eyes were shut. Conclusion: there is a short, early period when circuits connect the retina to the visual cortex. When brain regions mature dictates how long they stay malleable. Sensory areas mature in early childhood; the emotional limbic system is wired by puberty; the frontal lobes—seat of understanding—develop at least through the age of 16.

The implications of this new understanding are at once promising and disturbing. They suggest that, with the right input at the right time, almost anything is possible. But they imply, too, that if you miss the window you're playing with a handicap. They offer an explanation of why the gains a toddler makes in Head Start are so often evanescent: this intensive instruction begins too late to fundamentally rewire the brain. And they make clear the mistake of postponing instruction in a second language (see box, "Why Do Schools Flunk Biology?"). As Chugani asks, "What idiot decreed that foreign-language instruction not begin until high school?"

Neurobiologists are still at the dawn of understanding exactly which kinds of experiences, or sensory input, wire the brain in which ways. They know a great deal about the circuit for vision. It has a neuron-growth spurt at the age of 2 to 4 months, which corresponds to when babies start to really notice the world, and peaks at 8 months, when each neuron is connected to an astonishing 15,000 other neurons. A baby whose eyes are clouded by cataracts from birth will, despite cataract-removal surgery at the age of 2, be forever blind. For other systems, researchers know what happens, but not—at the level of neurons and molecules—how. They nevertheless remain confident that cognitive abilities work much like sensory ones, for the brain is parsimonious in how it conducts its affairs: a mechanism that works fine for wiring vision is not likely to be abandoned when it comes to circuits for music. "Connections are not forming willy-nilly," says Dale Purves of Duke University, "but are promoted by activity."

Language: Before there are words, in the world of a newborn, there are sounds. In English they are phonemes such as sharp ba's and da's, drawn-out ee's and ll's and sibilant sss's. In Japanese they are different—barked *hi's*, merged rr/ll's. When a child hears a phoneme over and over, neurons from his ear stimulate the formation of dedicated connections in his brain's auditory cortex. This "perceptual map," explains Patricia Kuhl of the University of Washington, reflects the apparent distance—and thus the similarity—between sounds. So in English-speakers, neurons in the auditory cortex that respond to "ra" lie far from those that respond to "la." But for Japanese, where the sounds are nearly identical, neurons that respond to "ra" are practically intertwined, like L.A. freeway spaghetti, with those for "la." As a result, a Japanese-speaker will have trouble distinguishing the two sounds.

Researchers find evidence of these tendencies across many languages. By 6 months of age, Kuhl reports, infants in English-speaking homes already have different auditory maps (as shown by electrical measurements that identify which neurons respond to different sounds) from those in Swedish-speaking homes. Children are functionally deaf to sounds absent from their native tongue. The map is completed by the first birthday. By 12 months," says Kuhl, "infants have lost the ability to discriminate sounds that are not significant in their language. And their babbling has acquired the sound of their language."

Kuhl's findings help explain why learning a second language after, rather than with, the first is so difficult. "The perceptual map of the first language constrains the learning of a second," she says. In other words, the circuits are already wired for Spanish, and the remaining undedicated neurons have lost their ability to form basic new connections for, say, Greek. A child taught a second language after the age of 10 or so is unlikely ever to speak it like a native. Kuhl's work also suggests why related languages such as Spanish and French are easier to learn than unrelated ones: more of the existing circuits can do double duty.

With this basic circuitry established, a baby is primed to turn sounds into words. The more words a child hears, the faster she learns language, according to psychiatrist Janellen Huttenlocher of the University of Chicago. Infants whose mothers spoke to them a lot knew 131 more words at 20 months than did babies of more taciturn, or less involved, mothers; at 24 months, the gap had widened to 295 words. (Presumably the findings would also apply to a father if he were the primary caregiver.) It didn't matter which words the mother used—monosyllables seemed to work. The sound of words, it seems, builds up neural circuitry that can then absorb more words, much as creating a computer file allows the user to fill it with prose. "There is a huge vocabulary to be acquired," says Huttenlocher, "and it can only be acquired through repeated exposure to words."

Music: Last October researchers at the University of Konstanz in Germany reported that exposure to music rewires neural circuits. In the brains of nine string players examined with magnetic resonance imaging, the amount of somatosensory cortex dedicated to the thumb and fifth finger of the left hand—the fingering digits—was significantly larger than in nonplayers. How long the players practiced each day did not affect the cortical map. But the age at which they had been introduced to their muse did: the younger the child when she took up an instrument, the more cortex she devoted to playing it.

Like other circuits formed early in life, the ones for music endure. Wayne State's

The Musical Brain

SKILL: Music

LEARNING WINDOW: 3 to 10 years

WHAT WE KNOW: String players have a larger area of their sensory cortex dedicated to the fingering digits on their left hand. Few concert-level performers begin playing later than the age of 10. It is much harder to learn an instrument as an adult.

WHAT WE CAN DO ABOUT IT: Sing songs with children. Play structured, melodic music. If a child shows any musical aptitude or interest, get an instrument into her hand early.

Chugani played the guitar as a child, then gave it up. A few years ago he started taking piano lessons with his young daughter. She learned easily, but he couldn't get his fingers to follow his wishes. Yet when Chugani recently picked up a guitar, he found to his delight that "the songs are still there," much like the muscle memory for riding a bicycle.

Math and logic: At UC Irvine, Gordon Shaw suspected that all higher-order thinking is characterized by similar patterns of neuron firing. "If you're working with little kids," says Shaw, "you're not going to teach them higher mathematics or chess. But they are interested in and can process music." So Shaw and Frances Rauscher gave 19 preschoolers piano or singing lessons. After eight months, the researchers found, the children "dramatically improved in spatial reasoning," compared with children given no music lessons, as shown in their ability to work mazes, draw geometric figures and copy patterns of two-color blocks. The mechanism behind the "Mozart effect" remains murky, but Shaw suspects that when children exercise cortical neurons by listening to classical music, they are also strengthening circuits used for mathematics. Music, says the UC team, "excites the inherent brain patterns and enhances their use in complex reasoning tasks."

Emotions: The trunk lines for the circuits controlling emotion are laid down before birth. Then parents take over. Perhaps the strongest influence is what psychiatrist Daniel Stern calls attunement—whether caregivers "play back a child's inner feelings." If a baby's squeal of delight at a puppy is met with a smile and hug, if her excitement at seeing a plane overhead is mirrored, circuits for these emotions are reinforced. Apparently, the brain uses the same pathways to generate an emotion as to respond to one. So if an emotion is reciprocated, the electrical and chemical signals that produced it are reinforced. But if emotions are repeatedly met with indifference or a clashing response—Baby is proud of building a skyscraper out of Mom's best pots, and Mom is terminally annoyed—those circuits become confused and fail to strengthen. The key here is "repeatedly": one dismissive harrumph will not scar a child for life. It's the pattern that counts, and it can be very powerful: in one of Stern's studies, a baby whose mother never matched her level of excitement became extremely passive, unable to feel excitement or joy.

Experience can also wire the brain's "calm down" circuit, as Daniel Goleman describes in his best-selling "Emotional Intelligence." One father gently soothes his crying infant, another drops him into his crib; one mother hugs the toddler who just skinned her knee, another screams "It's your own stupid fault!" The first responses are attuned to the child's distress; the others are wildly out of emotional sync. Between 10 and 18 months, a cluster of cells in the rational prefrontal cortex is busy hooking up to the emotion regions. The circuit seems to grow into a control switch, able to calm agitation by infusing reason into emotion. Perhaps parental soothing trains this circuit, strengthening the neural connections that form it, so that the child learns how to calm herself down. This all happens so early that the effects of nurture can be misperceived as innate nature.

Stress and constant threats also rewire emotion circuits. These circuits are centered on the amygdala, a little almond-shaped structure deep in the brain whose job is to scan incoming sights and sounds for emotional content. According to a wiring diagram worked out by Joseph LeDoux of New York University, impulses from eye and ear reach the amygdala before they get to the rational, thoughtful neocortex. If a sight, sound or experience has proved painful before—Dad's drunken arrival home was followed by a beating—then the amygdala floods the circuits with neurochemicals before the higher brain knows what's happening. The more often this pathway is used, the easier it is to trigger: the mere memory of Dad may induce fear. Since the circuits can stay excited for days, the brain remains on high alert. In this state, says neuroscientist Bruce Perry of Baylor College of Medicine, more circuits attend to nonverbal cues—facial expressions, angry noises—that warn of impending danger. As a result, the cortex falls behind in development and has trouble assimilating complex information such as language.

Movement: Fetal movements begin at 7 weeks and peak between the 15th and 17th weeks. That is when regions of the brain controlling movement start to wire up. The critical period lasts a while: it takes up to two years for cells in the cerebellum, which controls posture and movement, to form functional circuits. "A lot of organization takes place using information gleaned from when the child moves about in the world," says William Greenough of the University of Illinois. "If you restrict activity you inhibit the formation of synaptic connections in the cerebellum." The child's initially spastic movements send a signal to the brain's motor cortex; the more the arm, for instance, moves, the stronger the circuit, and the better the brain will become at moving the arm intentionally and fluidly. The window lasts only a few years: a child immobilized in a body cast until the age of 4 will learn to walk eventually, but never smoothly.

THERE ARE MANY MORE CIR-cuits to discover, and many more environmental influences to pin down. Still, neuro labs are filled with an unmistakable air of optimism these days. It stems from a growing understanding of how, at the level of nerve cells and molecules, the brain's circuits form. In the beginning, the brain-to-be consists of only a few advance scouts breaking trail: within a week of conception they march out of the embryo's "neural tube," a cylinder of cells extending from head to tail. Multiplying as they go (the brain adds an astonishing 250,000 neurons per minute during gestation), the neurons clump into the brain stem which commands heartbeat and breathing, build the little cerebellum at the back of the head which controls posture and movement, and form the grooved and rumpled cortex wherein thought and perception originate. The neural cells are so small, and the distance so great, that a neuron striking out for what will be the prefrontal cortex migrates a distance equivalent to a human's walking from New York to California, says developmental neurobiologist Mary Beth Hatten of Rockefeller University.

Only when they reach their destinations do these cells become true neurons. They grow a fiber called an axon that carries electrical signals. The axon might reach only to a neuron next door, or it might wend its way clear across to the other side of the brain. It is the axonal connections that form the brain's circuits. Genes determine the main highways along which axons travel to make their connection. But to reach particular target cells, axons follow chemical cues strewn along their path. Some of these chemicals attract: this way to the motor cortex! Some repel: no, *that* way to the olfactory cortex. By the fifth month of gestation most axons have reached their general destination. But like the prettiest girl in the bar, target cells attract way more suitors—axons—than they can accommodate.

How does the wiring get sorted out? The baby neurons fire electrical pulses once a minute, in a fit of what Berkeley's Shatz calls auto-dialing. If cells fire together, the target cells "ring" together. The target cells then release a flood of chemicals, called trophic factors, that strengthen the incipient connections. Active neurons respond better to trophic factors than inactive ones, Barbara Barres of Stanford University reported in October. So neurons that are quiet when others throb lose their grip on the target cell. "Cells that fire together wire together," says Shatz.

The same basic process continues after birth. Now, it is not an auto-dialer that sends signals, but stimuli from the senses. In experiments with rats, Illinois's Greenough found that animals raised with playmates and toys and other stimuli grow 25 percent more synapses than rats deprived of such stimuli.

Rats are not children, but all evidence suggests that the same rules of brain development hold. For decades Head Start has fallen short of the high hopes invested in it: the children's IQ gains fade after about three years. Craig Ramey of the University of Alabama suspected the culprit was timing: Head

Start enrolls 2-, 3-, and 4-year-olds. So in 1972 he launched the Abecedarian Project. Children from 20 poor families were assigned to one of four groups: intensive early education in a day-care center from about 4 months to age 8, from 4 months to 5 years, from 5 to 8 years, or none at all. What does it mean to "educate" a 4-month-old? Nothing fancy: blocks, beads, talking to him, playing games such as peek-a-boo. As outlined in the book "Learningames,"* each of the 200-odd activities was designed to enhance cognitive, language, social or motor development. In a recent paper, Ramey and Frances Campbell of the University of North Carolina report that children enrolled in Abecedarian as preschoolers still scored higher in math and reading at the age of 15 than untreated children. The children still retained an average IQ edge of 4.6 points. The earlier the children were enrolled, the more enduring the gain. And intervention after age 5 conferred no IQ or academic benefit.

All of which raises a troubling question. If the windows of the mind close, for the most part, before we're out of elementary school, is all hope lost for children whose parents did not have them count beads to stimulate their math circuits, or babble to them to build their language loops? At one level, no: the brain retains the ability to learn throughout life, as witness anyone who was befuddled by Greek in college only to master it during retirement. But on a deeper level the news is sobering. Children whose neural circuits are not stimulated before kindergarten are never going to be what they could have been. "You want to say that it is never too late," says Joseph Sparling, who designed the Abecedarian curriculum. "But there seems to be something very special about the early years."

And yet . . . there is new evidence that certain kinds of intervention can reach even the older brain and, like a microscopic screwdriver, rewire broken circuits. In January, scientists led by Paula Tallal of Rutgers University and Michael Merzenich of UC San Francisco described a study of children who have "language-based learning disabilities"—reading problems. LLD affects 7 million children in the United States. Tallal has long argued that LLD arises from a child's inability to distinguish short, staccato sounds—such as "d" and "b." Normally, it takes neurons in the auditory cortex something like .015 second to respond to a signal from the ear, calm down and get ready to respond to the next sound; in LLD children, it takes five to 10 times as long. (Merzenich speculates that the defect might be the result of chronic middle-ear infections in infancy: the brain never "hears" sounds clearly and so fails to draw a sharp auditory map.) Short sounds such as "b" and "d" go by too fast—.04 second—to process. Unable to associate sounds with letters, the children develop reading problems.

The scientists drilled the 5- to 10-year-olds three hours a day with computer-produced sound that draws out short consonants, like an LP played too slow. The result: LLD children who were one to three years behind in language ability improved by a full two years after only four weeks. The improvement has lasted. The training, Merzenich suspect, redrew the wiring diagram in the children's auditory cortex to process first sounds. Their reading problems vanished like the sounds of the letters that, before, they never heard.

Such neural rehab may be the ultimate payoff of the discovery that the experiences of life are etched in the bumps and squiggles of the brain. For now, it is enough to know that we are born with a world of potential—potential that will be realized only if it is tapped. And that is challenge enough.

With MARY HAGER

*Joseph Sparling and Isabelle Lewis *(226 pages. Walker. $8.95).*

Defining the trait that makes us human

The ability to empathize with others is critical to our survival as a species, behavioral researchers say.

By Beth Azar
Monitor staff

When a content newborn baby hears another baby crying, it also begins to wail. It's not just the loud noise, but also the sound of a fellow human in distress that triggers the baby's crying, researchers find.

New York University psychologist Martin Hoffman, PhD, believes this reflexive crying of newborns is a precursor to human empathy—the ability to observe the anguish or joy of another person and take it on as your own.

This ability has allowed humans to live as a communal species, say social scientists. The trait allows us to move beyond mere survival to helping our fellow humans.

"Empathy serves several major functions," says psychologist Janet Strayer, PhD, of Simon Fraser University. "It is a form of nonverbal communication, letting us know when others are distressed or in danger. It allows us to understand another's feelings, motivating a desire to help. And it gives people a sense of 'I am like

Nita Winter

Empathy develops along with a child's ability to understand the internal lives of others.

you and you are like me.' In short, we wouldn't be able to live without it."

Several developmental psychologists, including Carolyn Zahn-Waxler, PhD, of the National Institute of Mental Health, and Nancy Eisenberg, PhD, of the University of Arizona,

have begun to piece together the development of empathy, from basic biological instincts to the roles parents and society play in fostering empathy.

The precise definition of empathy varies depending on whom you talk to. But most psychologists agree that there are two aspects of empathy: an affective aspect—a person *feels* what another is feeling (either the exact emotion or a congruent emotion)—and a cognitive aspect—a person understands what another person is feeling and why.

Toward an outward focus

More than 20 years ago, Hoffman developed a five-stage model of empathy development based on anecdotal evidence from several children. Today, his theory is gaining support from empirical research.

"It turns out he was right on target," says Zahn-Waxler, who has been studying empathy for as long as Hoffman's been theorizing about it.

According to the model, empathy develops along with the ability to distinguish the self from others. Newborns

> # "There is . . . a lot of social scaffolding and experiences that can influence how empathy develops, which means we can do something about it."
>
> *Janet Strayer*
> *Simon Fraser University*

make no distinction between themselves and others. When they hear another infant cry, they start to cry far more from that than when they hear any other loud noise.

Sometime late in the first year, babies begin to understand that they are separate from others. When they hear or observe someone in distress, they understand that it's someone else who's upset. Even so, they often look upset and might run to their mothers.

As the self-other distinction becomes clearer—some time after the first year—babies begin trying to help people in distress, often using strategies they themselves find comforting. For example, they might offer their teddy bear or bring a crying child to their own mothers.

By the end of the second year, children are beginning to understand that everyone has their own internal feelings. They're able to use cognitively complex empathic mechanisms, including very early forms of role-taking (see sidebar). By age 4 or 5, children can understand the social situations that can cause people distress. This process continues to evolve throughout life.

"Self-recognition increases along with the development of a concern for others," says Zahn-Waxler, who, along with her colleagues, has followed more than 500 children over time to learn how they respond to distress in others.

These longitudinal studies provide strong support for the early stages described in Hoffman's model. Between the ages of 1 and 2, children develop empathic concern, cognitive understanding and a repertoire of helpful, comforting behaviors, says Zahn-Waxler.

Eisenberg, Richard Fabes, PhD, and their colleagues believe that whether people feel sympathy or personal distress—which stems from empathy, according to their model—when they observe someone else in distress depends, in part, on how well they can regulate their own emotions.

They've found that children who become overaroused when they witness others in distress show less sympathy than children who are able to regulate their emotional responses.

Children who feel personal distress are less likely to help a person in distress, while those who feel sympathy are more likely to help.

Nature *and* nurture

Most empathy researchers agree there's some biological disposition toward empathy. By 14 months, identical twins are more similar to each other on measures of empathy than fraternal twins, according to a study by Zahn-Waxler, JoAnn Robinson, PhD, of the University of Colorado Health Sciences Center, and their colleagues. Researchers also find significant individual differences in

---

Can your dog empathize with you?

Some researchers would say empathy is one of the emotions that sets humans apart from animals. It's an act of great sophistication requiring a complex cognitive analysis of another person's experience. But others argue that primordial empathy developed in all mammals as an instinctive reaction needed to rear young that require around-the-clock care.

New York University psychologist Martin Hoffman, PhD, believes both arguments might be right. At least five mechanisms are known to trigger empathy, he says. Some are more like reflexes, while others require complex cognition. They include:

• **Newborn cry:** Happy, content newborns will begin to cry when they hear another infant crying. This automatic reaction seems to be an inborn response to another human's distress.

• **Mimicry:** People automatically mimic the facial expressions and postures of others. When their facial and torso muscles move, nerves send the information to the brain, which triggers the emotions that correspond to the expression or posture. This mechanism is fairly automatic, dealing with relatively simple, universal emotions such as sadness and fear, and might be the basis of empathy in young children.

• **Simple classical conditioning:** When people observe others' experiences, they associate them with their own past experiences. That association automatically triggers an emotional reaction in the observer like that of the person having the experience.

• **Mediated association:** When people hear about another person's tragedy or good fortune the words remind them of a similar personal experience and trigger an emotional reaction. This is a more cognitive version of simple conditioning.

• **Role taking:** There are two types. With **self-focused role-taking** people put themselves in another person's place and imagine that what's happening to that person is happening to them. With **other-focused role-taking** people use what they know about the person—past, that individual's fears, financial situation—and imagine how he or she must feel in the situation.

Some researchers and philosophers argue that empathy is a purely human emotion. Others claim that many animals, from chimpanzees to dogs, show sure signs of empathic behavior. It depends on which empathetic mechanism you're talking about, says Hoffman.

There is evidence that some mammals—including chimpanzees and dolphins—mimic the postures and facial expressions of their peers. And many animals respond to conditioning. So, on that level, it's possible that some nonhuman animals have rudimentary versions of empathy, says Hoffman.

In contrast, few would argue that nonhuman animals have the cognitive abilities to experience role-taking or mediated association. Those forms of empathy may be restricted to humans, he says.

—Beth Azar

empathic reactions among children, beginning as early as age 2.

But, many studies also find that environment plays a significant role in shaping empathy, says Robinson. Parents can encourage empathy or discourage it.

For example, greater maternal warmth is associated with increases in empathy during the second year of life, Robinson and Strayer found in separate studies.

Also, mothers who provide forceful, clear messages about the consequences for others of hurtful behaviors tend to have more empathic children. And parents who discuss emotions tend to have children with high sympathy, find Eisenberg and Fabes.

In contrast, children whose mothers control them with anger tend to show decreases in empathy as they age, says Robinson.

Parents are more likely to explain to girls than boys the negative consequences for others of their harmful behaviors, even though young girls typically hurt others less often and show more empathy than boys, says Zahn-Waxler.

"Because empathic caregiving is important for survival, parents may begin early to prepare their girls for this role," she says.

With that said, it's not surprising that boys consistently score lower than girls on measures of empathy.

"Everyone is born with the capacity for empathy—it's part of our biological and cognitive wiring," says Strayer. "But there is also a lot of social scaffolding and experiences that can influence how empathy develops, which means we can do something about it."

The dark side of empathy

According to Hoffman's model, when parents point out the harmful consequences of hurtful behavior, children learn to pay attention to their empathic tendencies and feel empathy-based guilt—good guilt, says Hoffman. Some experimental evidence links guilt and empathy when children know they're the cause of another person's hurt, says Zahn-Waxler.

But too much empathy can be maladaptive, she adds. Children may begin to blur the distinction between empathy and guilt and begin to blame themselves for others' suffering, even if they are not the cause.

People tend to feel more empathy for people who are similar to themselves, says Hoffman, a potential down side to empathy. Men empathize more with men and women empathize more with women; members of an ethnic group empathize more with their group members; and people from one social stratum empathize more with others from their set.

And even if researchers give people a false sense of kinship, they are more empathic toward each other than if they view themselves as dissimilar, says Hoffman.

On the other side, Strayer and her colleague William Roberts, PhD, found that the more empathy a person feels for another person, the more similar that person seems.

In a study, they showed 73 children, ages 6 to 13, a video of people in distress. The children then had to place a picture of each person in the video on a grid, showing how similar they felt each person was to them. The more empathy a child had for a person, the more similar the children rated the person in the video, Strayer found.

"When we are empathic with somebody, it makes our dissimilarities similar," says Strayer.

Parents Speak:

Zero to Three's Findings from Research on Parents' Views of Early Childhood Development

Matthew Melmed

How much do parents of babies and toddlers know about their children's intellectual, social, and emotional development at the earliest ages? What are parents doing to encourage healthy development of their babies in these interrelated domains? Zero to Three commissioned a study that included focus groups and a national poll to determine what parents know and believe about early childhood development, where they go for information and support, and how receptive they are to new information.

Both the focus groups and the poll revealed that parents have much less knowledge and information about their children's emotional, intellectual, and social development than they do about their physical development. Parents thirst for more information on how to promote their young children's healthy development.

As new findings in brain research emerge (see *Young Children*, May 1997, pp. 4–9), they should provide a major impetus for parents to understand their own ability to im-

prove their children's lives and indeed to show all of us—parents, grandparents, other relatives, educators, child care providers, employers, policy-makers, and others—how we can positively impact children's development. Crafting such messages effectively requires knowledge of what parents know and value about early childhood development. Following are the major conclusions of our research, designed to address these questions.

1. Although parents recognize the importance of early childhood, they do not see its full significance.

There is much progress to be made to convince parents of babies that the period from birth to age three is *particularly* significant and provides a unique opportunity for growth and learning. In our study, parents said they felt that all of childhood is important, but they saw birth to three as important years of child development only in general terms and within limits. These parents lack much of the new information that can help them as their child's first teacher. The focus group parents understood that babies need more than love—including stimulation, consistency, and sense of security—but they were mostly unaware of the depth of their influences on their babies' long-term development.

2. Parents feel most able to impact babies' emotional development.

Our inquiry looked at attitudes and knowledge in three developmental domains: intellectual, emotional, and social. Of the three, *emotional development may be the area in which parents believe they can have the most impact.* The parents in our research groups stressed the importance of making babies feel secure and loved from the very beginning. They said babies' feelings can be hurt and that babies read and interpret their parents' and other people's emotional cues.

The national poll found that 39% of parents felt they had the greatest influence over their child's emotional development as compared to the child's intellectual (19%) or social (16%) development. However, one out of every four parents report having the least information on how a child develops emotionally.

3. Laying down a foundation for social growth in the early years is not seen as critical.

When it comes to social development, the attitudes expressed by the parents in this study were quite different. Parents were often unsure that what happens to a child from

Matthew Melmed is executive director of ZERO TO THREE: National Center for Infants, Toddlers and Families (formerly the National Center for Clinical Infant Programs), a national organization dedicated to advancing the healthy development of babies and young children that is based in Washington, D.C.

birth to age three has long-term impact on social development. They see *social development as an area where a child can "catch up,"* and they feel that this area is less crucial than the other domains.

4. *Parents may not recognize their power to shape their child's intellectual development.*

The parents in this study said their young children are always learning. Yet the parents felt *less able to impact intellectual development than any other area of childhood development.* The parents described intellectual development as a process of absorption rather than as a process of *creation* of more capacity or development of cognitive abilities, as suggested by emerging brain research. Some said that an unstimulating environment does not deny a child intellectual development, because much of the intellectual self is "nature" not "nurture."

The poll revealed that only 44% of the parents felt totally sure that they could tell if their infant or toddler's intellectual development was on track. Parents (53%) were more certain about signs to watch for to see if their child's physical develop-

ment was on track; 37% felt this way about milestones of social development and 38% about emotional development.

5. *Caregiver continuity and consistency is a hot-button issue for many parents.*

According to research, the individuals with whom an infant or toddler spends the most time play a critical role in that child's emotional, social, and intellectual development, and limiting the number of caregivers is important for creating strong relationships that form the basis of learning. Yet the focus groups found limiting the number of caregivers is a hot-button issue with parents. The suggestion that either the consistency or a limited number of caregivers really matters made some parents—particularly those with multiple child care arrangements—feel uncomfortable, guilty, or nervous. These feelings unfortunately may lead to some of these parents rejecting the notion that caregivers have important relationships with babies. Some parents believe that if a child has a stable home life, whatever happens during child care may not be as important.

The poll found that caregivers other than these mothers or fathers played a major role in the lives of their young children. Only one in five babies or toddlers were cared for since birth exclusively by a parent; 60% of babies and toddlers are currently cared for on a regular basis by someone other than their parents. Half of all parents surveyed thought that the more caregivers a child has before age three, the better that child will be at adapting and coping with change.

6. *Get parents the good news early on about the opportunity of children's first three years.*

The parents in the focus groups made it clear that they learned about child development *on the job* as parents. It is important to raise the consciousness of parents *before* they have children or when their babies are very young. Reaching parents early may avoid having to battle guilt feelings of parents who feel they have failed if they took few steps to enhance their child's development before the age of two or three.

Parental guilt and denial could thwart efforts to increase parents' involvement in their children's early development. Learning that the period from birth to age three is extremely important in child development and that parents can actively influence it is not good news for those parents who feel they have missed the boat. It is motivating, on the other hand, to new and expectant parents.

7. *Parents want specific information on what they can do with their child.*

These results suggest that many parents of young children may need guidance if they are to maximize experiences in the early years. What

---

Sources of Data and Further Information

Zero to Three used two different research methodologies—focus groups and in-depth telephone surveys—to collect information from parents of very young children.

Focus groups— The public opinion research firm Belden and Russonello conducted eight focus groups with parents of children younger than age three and expectant parents, exploring their knowledge and perceptions of child development. Held between October 1996 and February 1997, the groups convened parents of varying levels of education and income, segmented by gender and race.

In-depth telephone survey— Between March 21 and April 1, 1997, Peter D. Hart Research Associates conducted an in-depth telephone survey among a representative sample of 1,022 mothers and fathers and legal guardians of children aged 36 months and younger.

More detailed information about the results of both studies is available at the ZERO TO THREE Website: **http://www.zerotothree.org**; see the "newsroom."

Parents' Perspectives on Their Children's Development: Selected Comments of Focus Group Participants

"If they get the emotional—the proper attachments, the love, the support that they need—they will feel confident to go out in the social situations . . . explore things and learn intellectually."— *a mother, Richmond*

"No matter what you do . . . not everything is programmable. . . . Whether a child's going to be intelligent or not is more or less something they're born with, the level of intelligence they can achieve. That is kind of hardwired."—*a father, Boston*

"Really [it] is your innate abilities which affect how you do in school, more so than your experiences. But the more experience you have, that's going to give you more curiosity and interest. But your performance is really based on your native intelligence."—*a mother, New York*

"I hope [having a limited number of caregivers is] not that important, because my child's on her third [caregiver]. Just don't tell me that I'm wrong."—*a mother, Boston*

"I feel that I'm getting better—that when she was born I was just so new at everything—and I'm hoping I get better and better day by day, month by month, and year by year. It scares me to death thinking [that in] a year—that's it—my time is up."—*a mother, Richmond*

"[The statement about child development before age three] makes me paranoid. . . . Even though I'm trying, I do the best I can, like if I do one thing wrong . . . I'm an idiot. . . . So, I think you always question yourself, even though you do the best that you can for them."—*a mother, New York*

"It is like you communicate with someone who speaks a foreign language—basically that's what you're doing."—*a mother, Richmond*

"[Babies] don't have instructions."—*a mother, Boston*

---

they lack is not just information on the importance of the earliest years but also specific steps, ideas, activities, and concepts for making the most of this time. For example, the parents in the focus group research said they believe babies communicate and are interpretable almost from birth; however, parents have difficulty understanding what their babies are communicating and what their behaviors mean. Many said it is hard to read a baby's cues and would appreciate help in learning how to do so.

The poll indicated that 60% of the parents of babies and toddlers were extremely or very interested in information about early brain development and how children learn, and an additional 21% said that they were somewhat interested. According to the poll, parents relied most on their informal networks—their parents or friends and neighbors—for information or advice. Only 2% mentioned their child's caregiver as someone to whom they usually turned for help.

8. Many parents do not recognize that they can create capacity by stimulating a child's brain in ways that match the child's level and interest.

According to the focus group research, many parents see their role largely as keeping their children from harm. The participating parents often stressed the negative impact of a poor emotional or social environment, situations they seek to avoid. Making a creative difference in the lives of children, through *improving the quality of their experiences and their relationships with the important people in their lives*, is a different way of thinking for many parents than what they have traditionally held to be their obligations to their children.

Nearly all the parents (95% of those polled) recognized that children learn from the moment they are born. Most parents (87%) assumed that the more stimulation a baby receives, the better. But, in fact,

parents and caregivers need to carefully match the amount and kind of stimulation to a child's development, interests, temperament, and mood at the moment.

9. Many parents see time as a major barrier to better parenting.

In the poll, more than one-third of parents (37%) indicated that one of the chief reasons they may need to improve as parents is because they don't spend as much quality time with their child as they would like. Half of all parents said that they ended most days feeling that they had spent less time with their young child than they wanted to—either a lot less time (20%) or a little less (27%).

What these results mean to early childhood professionals

In this study, parents seemed well aware of the general importance of the love and time they give their infants and toddlers, but they wanted more information about exactly *how* to influence their children's emotional and intellectual development in positive ways. These moms and dads feel good about many aspects of being parents to young children. Yet they recognize their ability to improve, and they display a genuine interest in doing so.

Indeed, the data reveal these parents' desire to play the most positive role they can in their children's development. They want to understand how to prepare in advance for parenthood; where to turn for day-to-day information, especially when their children are young; how to provide the best care for their children, even when they cannot provide it exclusively themselves; how to recognize signals and cues that inform them about their children's development; how they can affect most positively a young and growing brain; and what specific strategies and techniques they can use to help practice better parenting and give their young children the best possible start in life.

Early childhood professionals, especially those working in programs that serve infants and toddlers, are in an excellent position to respond to parents' desire for more information and support. New and creative ways of providing this type of assistance may be needed, however, as most of the parents surveyed do not automatically turn to their child's caregiver as an information source.

Finally, early childhood professionals should recognize what parents think would help them become better parents: (1) information to help them understand their child's feelings or needs and ways to handle difficult situations, and (2) more quality time with their child. Actions and strategies that especially support parents in these ways are likely to be the most helpful and the most welcome.

Unit 3

Key Points to Consider

❖ How much do genes and environment matter for specific cognitive abilities and disabilities?

❖ Why should Piaget's cognitive constructivism be used to shape lesson plans for students?

❖ What is evolutional psychology and why is it a good metatheory for cognitive development?

❖ Why is *The Bell Curve* so controversial? Is it a scandalous idea?

❖ What is the postmodern conception of children? How can education best serve children today?

❖ How can television be used to empower students?

❖ Is school refusal due to a school phobia? What can be done to help school phobic children?

 **Links**   **www.dushkin.com/online/**

These sites are annotated on pages 4 and 5.

Cognition is the mental process of knowing. It includes aspects such as awareness, perception, reasoning, and judgment. Many kinds of achievement that require superb cognitive processes cannot be measured with intelligence tests or with achievement. Intelligence is the capacity to acquire and apply knowledge. It is usually assumed that intelligence can be measured. The ratio of tested mental age to chronological age is expressed as an intelligence quotient (IQ). For years, schoolchildren have been classified and tracked educationally by IQ scores. The links between IQ scores and school achievement are positive, but no significant correlations exist between IQ scores and life success. Consider, for example, the motor coordination and kinesthetic abilities of a baseball player such as Cal Ripken Jr. A Harvard psychologist, Howard Gardner, has suggested that there are at least seven different kinds of intelligences. These include the body-movement skills of athletes and dancers as well as musical, linguistic, logical/mathematical, spatial, self-understanding, and social understanding types. The 1990s have been host to a spate of research about the last two types of intelligences: self-understanding and social understanding.

Some psychologists have suggested that measuring one's emotional quotient (EQ) might make more sense than measuring one's intelligence quotient (IQ). The typical tests of intelligence only measure achievement and abilities in the logical/mathematical, spatial, and linguistic areas of intelligence. Jean Piaget, the Swiss founder of cognitive psychology, was involved in the creation of the world's first intelligence test, the Binet-Simon Scale. He became disillusioned with trying to quantify how much children knew at different chronological ages. He was much more intrigued with what they did not know, what they knew incorrectly, and how they came to know the world in the ways in which they knew it. Piaget discovered qualitative, rather than quantitative, differences in cognitive processes over the life span. Infants know the world through their senses and their motor responses. After language develops, toddlers and preschoolers know the world through their language/symbolic perspectives. Piaget likened early childhood cognitive processes to bad thought, or thought akin to daydreams. By school age, children know things in concrete terms, which allows them to number, seriate, classify, conserve, think backwards and forwards, and to think about themselves thinking (metacognition). They are able to use reason. However, Piaget believed that children do not acquire the cognitive processes necessary to think abstractly and to use clear, consistent, logical patterns of thought until early adolescence.

Contemporary cognitive researchers are refining Piaget's theories. They are discovering that children acquire many abilities in more sophisticated ways than Piaget postulated. In the first article in this unit, Robert Plomin and John DeFries review the role of genetic potentialities in determining how easily and in what ways (e.g., verbally, spatially) people process information. The authors do not refute the idea that learning affects cognitive processes. Rather they suggest that psychologists and educators take a balanced view and acknowledge that babies come into the world with different genetic attributes for learning. A teaching style that works for one child may be all wrong for another child. An appreciation of each child's cognitive heritabilities will make it easier to develop an appropriate learning environment and teaching modality. This could lessen or prevent many so-called learning disabilities, which might rather be viewed as learning differences.

The second article in this subsection on cognition explains Piaget's theory that learning originates from inside the child. Constance Kamii and Janice Ewing believe that school teaching should be based on Piaget's view of cognitive constructivism. Piaget makes a distinction between three kinds of knowledge: physical knowledge, social (conventional) knowledge, and logico-mathematical knowledge. The sources of each and their modes of being structured are very important building blocks for education. Teaching based on scientific theories of how children construct knowledge is more potent than teaching based on fads, pendulum swings, or superficial impressions of what works.

The third article on cognition introduces some of the basic principles of evolutionary psychology and suggests this as a new metatheory for cognitive development. David Bjorklund believes that a balanced view of nature–nurture resulting in species-typical behaviors in species-typical environments is the best starting point for new questions on cognitive development.

The first article in the schooling subsection of this unit addresses the issue of defining and testing intelligence for purposes of school placement and educational programming. Politicians play with the rhetoric about what our children should and should not learn in school. "Bell, Book, and Scandal" gives an historic overview of IQ testing and the use of IQ tests to differentiate children by achievement in the logical/mathematical type of intelligence. To what extent is this placement practice discriminating against other children who demonstrate high motivation and potential to achieve but have different types of intelligences?

The second article on schooling, by David Elkind, presents his belief that an educational system that believes every child is "regular" is a barrier to progress in a postmodern society. Behavioral genetics has enlightened us about the reality of irregular learning styles. Different subjects require different learning strategies. Educational innovators who view learning as creative and interactional are more effective as teachers.

The third schooling article suggests a creative, interactional means of teaching many subjects: use the power of television. The authors explain how you can do this. The last schooling article suggests a reason why many students fail to learn in school: school phobia. Bridget Murray explains what it is and what can be done about it in its many forms.

The Genetics of Cognitive Abilities and Disabilities

Investigations of specific cognitive skills can help clarify how genes shape the components of intellect

by Robert Plomin and John C. DeFries

People differ greatly in all aspects of what is casually known as intelligence. The differences are apparent not only in school, from kindergarten to college, but also in the most ordinary circumstances: in the words people use and comprehend, in their differing abilities to read a map or follow directions, or in their capacities for remembering telephone numbers or figuring change. The variations in these specific skills are so common that they are often taken for granted. Yet what makes people so different?

It would be reasonable to think that the environment is the source of differences in cognitive skills—that we are what we learn. It is clear, for example, that human beings are not born with a full vocabulary; they have to learn words. Hence, learning must be the mechanism by which differences in vocabulary arise among individuals. And differences in experience—say, in the extent to which parents model and encourage vocabulary skills or in the quality of language training provided by schools—must be responsible for individual differences in learning.

Earlier in this century psychology was in fact dominated by environmental explanations for variance in cognitive abilities. More recently, however, most psychologists have begun to embrace a more balanced view: one in which nature and nurture interact in cognitive development. During the past few decades, studies in genetics have pointed to a substantial role for heredity in molding the components of intellect, and researchers have even begun to track down the genes involved in cognitive function. These findings do not refute the notion that environmental factors shape the learning process. Instead they suggest that differences in people's genes affect how easily they learn.

Just how much do genes and environment matter for specific cognitive abilities such as vocabulary? That is the question we have set out to answer. Our tool of study is quantitative genetics, a statistical approach that explores the causes of variations in traits among individuals. Studies comparing the performance of twins and adopted children on certain tests of cognitive skills, for example, can assess the relative contributions of nature and nurture.

In reviewing several decades of such studies and conducting our own, we have begun to clarify the relations among specialized aspects of intellect, such as verbal and spatial reasoning, as well as the relations between normal cognitive function and disabilities, such as dyslexia. With the help of molecular genetics, we and other investigators have also begun to identify the genes that affect these specific abilities and disabilities. Eventually, we believe, knowledge of these genes will help reveal the biochemical mechanisms involved in human intelligence. And with the insight gained from genetics, researchers may someday develop environmental interventions that will lessen or prevent the effects of cognitive disorders.

Some people find the idea of a genetic role in intelligence alarming or, at the very least, confusing. It is important to understand from the outset, then, what exactly geneticists mean when they talk about genetic influence. The term typically used is "heritability": a statistical measure of the genetic contribution to differences among individuals.

Verbal and Spatial Abilities

Heritability tells us what proportion of individual differences in a population—known as variance—can be ascribed to genes. If we say, for example, that a trait is 50 percent heritable, we are in effect saying that half of the variance in that trait is linked to heredity. Heritability, then, is a way of explaining what makes people different, not what constitutes a given individual's intelligence. In general, however, if heritability for a trait is high, the influence of genes on the trait in individuals would be strong as well.

Attempts to estimate the heritability of specific cognitive abilities began with family studies. Analyses of similarities between parents and their children and between siblings have shown that cognitive abilities run in families. Results of the largest family study done on specific cognitive abilities, which was conducted in Hawaii in the 1970s, helped to quantify this resemblance.

The Hawaii Family Study of Cognition was a collaborative project between researchers at the University of Colorado at Boulder and the University of Hawaii and involved more than 1,000 families and sibling pairs. The study determined correlations (a statistical measure of resemblance) between relatives on tests of verbal and spatial ability. A correlation of 1.0 would mean that the scores of family members were identical; a correlation of zero would indicate that the scores were no more similar than those of two people picked at random. Because children on average share half their genes with each parent and with siblings, the highest correlation in test scores that could be expected on genetic grounds alone would be 0.5.

The Hawaii study showed that family members are in fact more alike than unrelated individuals on measures of specific cognitive skills. The actual correlations for both verbal and spatial tests were, on average, about 0.25. These correlations alone, however, do not disclose whether cognitive abilities run in families because of genetics or because of environmental effects. To explore this distinction, geneticists rely on two "experiments": twinning (an experiment of nature) and adoption (a social experiment).

Twin studies are the workhorse of behavioral genetics. They compare the resemblance of identical twins, who have the same genetic makeup, with the resemblance of fraternal twins, who share only about half their genes. If cognitive abilities are influenced by

---

TESTS OF VERBAL ABILITY

1. VOCABULARY: In each row, circle the word that means the same or nearly the same as the underlined word. There is only one correct choice in each line.

a.	arid	coarse	clever	modest	dry
b.	piquant	fruity	pungent	harmful	upright

2. VERBAL FLUENCY: For the next three minutes, write as many words as you can that start with F and end with M.

3. CATEGORIES: For the next three minutes, list all the things you can think of that are FLAT.

(Answers appear on last page of this article.)

JENNIFER C. CHRISTIANSEN

---

genes, identical twins ought to be more alike than fraternal twins on tests of cognitive skills. From correlations found in these kinds of studies, investigators can estimate the extent to which genes account for variances in the general population. Indeed, a rough estimate of heritability can be made by doubling the difference between identical-twin and fraternal-twin correlations.

Adoption provides the most direct way to disentangle nature and nurture in family resemblance, by creating pairs of genetically related individuals who do not share a common family environment. Correlations among these pairs enable investigators to estimate the contribution of genetics to family resemblance. Adoption also produces pairs of genetically un-

related individuals who share a family environment, and their correlations make it possible to estimate the contribution of shared environment to resemblance.

Twin studies of specific cognitive abilities over three decades and in four countries have yielded remarkably consistent results [see illustration, "Twin Studies"]. Correlations for identical twins greatly exceed those for fraternal twins on tests of both verbal and spatial abilities in children, adolescents and adults. Results of the first twin study in the elderly—reported last year by Gerald E. McClearn and his colleagues at Pennsylvania State University and by Stig Berg and his associates at the Institute for Gerontology in Jönköping, Sweden—show that the resemblances between identical and fraternal

---

How Do Cognitive Abilities Relate to General Intelligence?

by Karen Wright

Since the dawn of psychology, experts have disagreed about the fundamental nature of intelligence. Some have claimed that intelligence is an inherent faculty prescribed by heredity, whereas others have emphasized the effects of education and upbringing. Some have portrayed intelligence as a global quality that permeates all facets of cognition; others believe the intellect consists of discrete, specialized abilities—such as artistic talent or a flair for mathematics—that share no common principle.

In the past few decades, genetic studies have convinced most psychologists that heredity exerts considerable influence on intelligence. In fact, research suggests that as much as half of the variation in intelligence among individuals may be attributed to genetic factors.

And most psychologists have also come to accept a global conceptualization of intelligence. Termed general cognitive ability, or "g," this global quality is reflected in the apparent overlap among specific cognitive skills. As Robert Plomin and John C. DeFries point out, people who do well on tests of one type of cognitive skill also tend to do well on tests of other cognitive abilities. Indeed, this intercorrelation has provided the rationale for IQ (intelligence quotient) tests, which yield a single score from combined assessments of specific cognitive skills.

Because specific and general cognitive abilities are related in this manner, it is not surprising that many of the findings regarding specific abilities echo what is already known about general ability. The heritabilities found in studies of specific cognitive abilities, for example, are comparable with the heritability determined for g. The developmental trend described by the authors—in which genetic influence on specific cognitive abilities seems to increase throughout childhood, reaching adult levels by the mid-teens—is also familiar to researchers of general cognitive ability.

And because measures of g are derived from intercorrelations of verbal and spatial abilities, a gene that is linked with both those traits is almost guaranteed to have some role in general cognitive ability as well—and vice versa. This month in the journal *Psychological Science*, Plomin and various collaborators report the discovery of the first gene associated with general cognitive ability. Although the finding should further understanding of the nature of cognition, it is also likely to reignite debate. Indeed, intelligence research may be one realm where understanding does little to quell disagreement.

KAREN WRIGHT is a freelance writer living in New Hampshire.

twins persist even into old age. Although gerontologists have assumed that genetic differences become less important as experiences accumulate over a lifetime, research on cognitive abilities has so far demonstrated otherwise. Calculations based on the combined findings in these studies imply that in the general population, genetics accounts for about 60 percent of the variance in verbal ability and about 50 percent of the variance in spatial ability.

Investigations involving adoptees have yielded similar results. Two recent studies of twins reared apart—one by Thomas J. Bouchard, Jr., Matthew McGue and their colleagues at the University of Minnesota, the other an international collaboration headed by Nancy L. Pedersen at the Karolinska Institute in Stockholm—have implied heritabilities of about 50 percent for both verbal and spatial abilities.

In our own Colorado Adoption Project, which we launched in 1975, we have used the power of adoption studies to further characterize the roles of genes and environment, to assess developmental trends in cognitive abilities and to explore the extent to which specific cognitive skills are related to one another. The ongoing project compares the correlations between more than 200 adopted children and their birth and adoptive parents with the correlations for a control group of children raised by their biological parents [see illustration, "Colorado Adoption Project"].

These data provide some surprising insights. By middle childhood, for example, birth mothers and their children who were adopted by others are just as similar as control parents and their children on measures of both verbal and spatial ability. In contrast, the scores of adopted children do not resemble those of their adoptive parents at all. These results join a growing body of evidence suggesting that the common family environment generally does not contribute to similarities in family members. Rather family resemblance on such measures seems to be controlled almost entirely by genetics, and environmental factors often end up making family members different, not the same.

The Colorado data also reveal an interesting developmental trend. It appears that genetic influence increases during childhood, so that by the mid-teens, heritability reaches a level comparable with that seen in adults. In correlations of verbal ability, for example, resemblance between birth parents and their children who were adopted by others increases from about

TESTS OF SPATIAL ABILITY

1. IMAGINARY CUTTING: Draw a line or lines showing where the figure on the left should be cut to form the pieces on the right. There may be more than one way to draw the lines correctly.

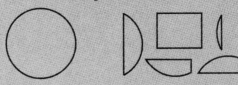

2. MENTAL ROTATIONS: Circle the two objects on the right that are the same as the object on the left.

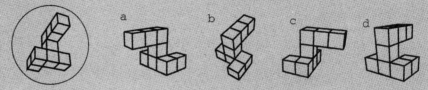

3. CARD ROTATIONS: Circle the figures on the right that can be rotated (without being lifted off the page) to exactly match the one on the left.

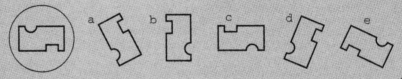

4. HIDDEN PATTERNS: Circle each pattern below in which the figure appears. The figure must always be in this position, not upside down or on its side.

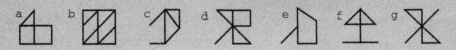

JENNIFER C. CHRISTIANSEN

0.1 at age three to about 0.3 at age 16. A similar pattern is evident in tests of spatial ability. Some genetically driven transformation in cognitive function seems to take place in the early school years, around age seven. The results indicate that by the time people reach age 16, genetic factors account for 50 percent of the variance for verbal ability and 40 percent for spatial ability—numbers not unlike those derived from twin studies of specific cognitive abilities.

The Colorado Adoption Project and other investigations have also helped clarify the differences and similarities among cognitive abilities. Current cognitive neuroscience assumes a modular model of intelligence, in which different cognitive processes are isolated anatomically in discrete modules in the brain. The modular model implies that specific cognitive abilities are also genetically distinct—that genetic effects on verbal ability, say, should not overlap substantially with genetic effects on spatial ability.

Psychologists, however, have long recognized that most specialized cognitive skills,

TESTS OF SPECIFIC ABILITIES administered to adolescents and adults include tasks resembling the ones listed here. The tests gauge each cognitive ability in several ways, and multiple tests are combined to provide a reliable measure of each skill. (Answers appear on last page of this article.)

including verbal and spatial abilities, intercorrelate moderately. That is, people who perform well on one type of test also tend to do well on other types. Correlations between verbal and spatial abilities, for example, are usually about 0.5. Such intercorrelation implies a potential genetic link.

From Abilities to Achievement

Genetic studies of specific cognitive abilities also fail to support the modular model. Instead it seems that genes are responsible for most of the overlap between cognitive skills. Analysis of the Colorado project data, for example, indicates that genetics governs 70 percent of the correlation between verbal and spatial ability. Similar results have been found in twin studies in childhood, young adulthood and middle age. Thus, there is a good chance that when genes associated with a particular cognitive ability are identified, the same genes will be associated with other cognitive abilities.

Research into school achievement has hinted that the genes associated with cognitive abilities may also be relevant to academic performance. Studies of more than 2,000 pairs of high school–age twins were done in the 1970s by John C. Loehlin of the University of Texas at Austin and Robert C. Nichols, then at the National Merit Scholarship Corporation in Evanston, Ill. In these studies the scores of identical twins were consistently and substantially more similar than those of fraternal twins on all four domains of the National Merit Scholarship Qualifying Test: English usage, mathematics, social studies and natural sciences. These results suggest that genetic factors account for about 40 percent of the variation on such achievement tests.

Genetic influence on school achievement has also been found in twin studies of elementary school–age children as well as in our work with the Colorado Adoption Project. It appears that genes may have almost as much effect on school achievement as they do on cognitive abilities. These results are surprising in and of themselves, as educators have long believed that achievement is more a product of effort than of ability. Even more interesting, then, is the finding from twin studies and our adoption project that genetic effects overlap between different

categories of achievement and that these overlapping genes are probably the very same genetic factors that can influence cognitive abilities.

This evidence supports a decidedly nonmodular view of intelligence as a pervasive or global quality of the mind and underscores the relevance of cognitive abilities in real-world performance. It also implies that genes for cognitive abilities are likely to be genes involved in school achievement, and vice versa.

Given the evidence for genetic influence on cognitive abilities and achievement, one might suppose that cognitive disabilities and poor academic achievement must also show genetic influence. But even if genes are involved in cognitive disorders, they may not be the same genes that influence normal cognitive function. The example of mental retardation illustrates this point. Mild mental retardation runs in families, but severe retardation does not. Instead severe mental retardation is caused by genetic and environmental factors—novel mutations, birth complications and head injuries, to name a few—that do not come into play in the normal range of intelligence.

Researchers need to assess, rather than assume, genetic links between the normal and the abnormal, between the traits that are

What Heritability Means

The implications of heritability data are commonly misunderstood. As the main text indicates, heritability is a statistical measure, expressed as a percentage, describing the extent to which genetic factors contribute to variations on a given trait among the members of a population.

The fact that genes influence a trait does not mean, however, that "biology is destiny." Indeed, genetics research has helped confirm the significance of environmental factors, which generally account for as much variance in human behavior as genes do. If intelligence is 50 percent heritable, then environmental factors must be just as important as genes in generating differences among people.

---

part of a continuum and true disorders of human cognition. Yet genetic studies of verbal and spatial disabilities have been few and far between.

Genetics and Disability

Most such research has focused on reading disability, which afflicts 80 percent of children diagnosed with a learning disorder. Children with reading disability, also known as dyslexia, read slowly, show poor comprehension and have trouble reading aloud [see "Dyslexia," by Sally E. Shaywitz, SCIENTIFIC AMERICAN, November 1996]. Studies by one of us (DeFries) have shown that reading disability runs in families and that genetic factors do indeed contribute to the resemblance among family members.

TWIN STUDIES have examined correlations in verbal *(top)* and in spatial (bottom) skills of identical twins and of fraternal twins. When the results of the separate studies are put side by side, they demonstrate a substantial genetic influence on specific cognitive abilities from childhood to old age; for all age groups, the scores of identical twins are more alike than those of fraternal twins. These data seem to counter the long-standing notion that the influence of genes wanes with time.

Jennifer C. Christiansen

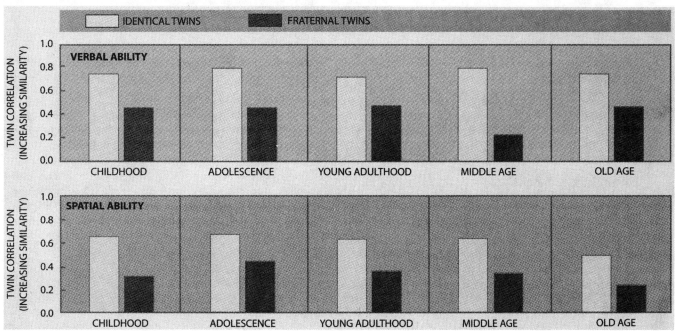

Moreover, even when genetic factors have an especially powerful effect, as in some kinds of mental retardation, environmental interventions can often fully or partly overcome the genetic "determinants." For example, the devastating effects of phenylketonuria, a genetic disease that can cause mental retardation, can often be nullified by dietary intervention.

Finally, the degree of heritability for a given trait is not set in stone. The relative influence of genes and environment can change. If, for instance, environmental factors were made almost identical for all the members of a hypothetical population, any differences in cognitive ability in that population would then have to be attributed to genetics, and heritability would be closer to 100 percent than to 50 percent. Heritability describes what is, rather than what can (or should) be.   —R.P. and J.C.D.

The identical twin of a person diagnosed with reading disability, for example, has a 68 percent risk of being similarly diagnosed, whereas a fraternal twin has only a 38 percent chance.

Is this genetic effect related in any way to the genes associated with normal variation in reading ability? That question presents some methodological challenges. The concept of a cognitive disorder is inherently problematic, because it treats disability qualitatively—you either have it or you don't—rather than describing the degree of disability in a quantitative fashion. This focus creates an analytical gap between disorders and traits that are dimensional (varying along a continuum), which are by definition quantitative.

During the past decade, a new genetic technique has been developed that bridges the gap between dimensions and disorders by collecting quantitative information about the relatives of subjects diagnosed qualitatively with a disability. The method is called DF extremes analysis, after its creators, DeFries and David W. Fulker, a colleague at the University of Colorado's Institute for Behavioral Genetics.

For reading disability, the analysis works by testing the identical and fraternal twins of reading-disabled subjects on quantitative measures of reading, rather than looking for a shared diagnosis of dyslexia [see illustration, "Reading Scores"]. If reading disability is influenced by genes that also affect variation within the normal range of reading performance, then the reading scores of the identical twins of dyslexic children should be closer to those of the reading-disabled group than the scores of fraternal twins are. (A single gene can exert different effects if it occurs in more than one form in a population, so that two people may inherit somewhat different versions. The genes controlling eye color and height are examples of such variable genes.)

It turns out that, as a group, identical twins of reading-disabled subjects do perform almost as poorly as dyslexic subjects on these quantitative tests, whereas fraternal twins do much better than the reading-dis-abled group (though still significantly worse than the rest of the population). Hence, the genes involved in reading disability may in fact be the same as those that contribute to the quantitative dimension of reading ability measured in this study. DF extremes analysis of these data further suggests that about half the difference in reading scores between dyslexics and the general population can be explained by genetics.

For reading disability, then, there could well be a genetic link between the normal and the abnormal, even though such links may not be found universally for other disabilities. It is possible that reading disability represents the extreme end of a continuum of reading ability, rather than a distinct disorder—that dyslexia might be quantitatively rather than qualitatively different from the normal range of reading ability. All this suggests that if a gene is found for reading disability, the same gene is likely to be associated with the normal range of variation in reading ability. The definitive test will come when a specific gene is identified that is associated with either reading ability or disability. In fact, we and other investigators are already very close to finding such a gene.

The Hunt for Genes

Until now, we have confined our discussion to quantitative genetics, a discipline that measures the heritability of traits without regard to the kind and number of genes involved. For information about the genes themselves, researchers must turn to molecular

---

COLORADO ADOPTION PROJECT, which followed subjects over time, finds that for both verbal (top) and spatial (bottom) abilities, adopted children come to resemble their birth parents (white bars) as much as children raised by their birth parents do (gray bars). In contrast, adopted children do not end up resembling their adoptive parents (black bars). The results imply that most of the family resemblance in cognitive skills is caused by genetic factors, not environment.

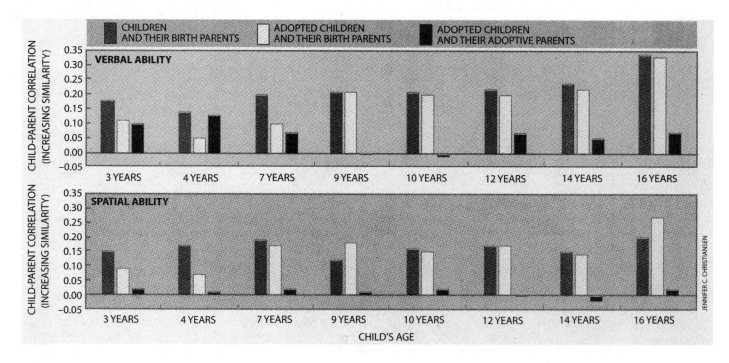

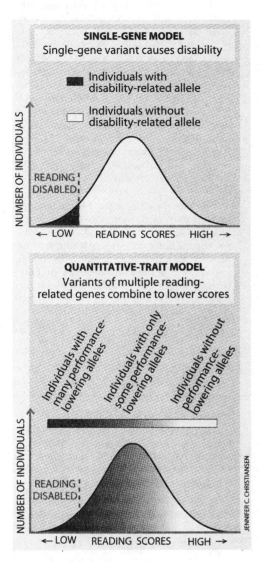

SINGLE-GENE MODEL
Single-gene variant causes disability

■ Individuals with disability-related allele

□ Individuals without disability-related allele

QUANTITATIVE-TRAIT MODEL
Variants of multiple reading-related genes combine to lower scores

Individuals with many performance-lowering alleles

Individuals with only some performance-lowering alleles

Individuals without performance-lowering alleles

TWO MODELS illustrate how genetics may affect reading disability. In the classic view (top), a single variant, or allele, of a gene is able to cause the disorder; everyone who has that allele becomes reading disabled (graph). But evidence points to a different model (bottom), in which a single allele cannot produce the disability on its own. Instead variants of multiple genes each act subtly but can combine to lower scores and increase the risk of disability.

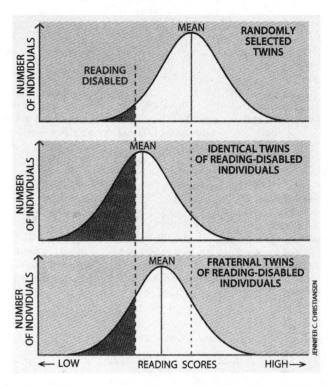

READING SCORES of twins suggest a possible genetic link between normal and abnormal reading skills. In a group of randomly selected members of twin pairs (top), a small fraction of children were reading disabled (gray). Identical (middle) and fraternal (bottom) twins of the reading-disabled children scored lower than the randomly selected group, with the identical twins performing worse than the fraternal ones. Genetic factors, then, are involved in reading disability. The same genes that influence reading disability may underlie differences in normal reading ability.

genetics—and increasingly, they do. If scientists can identify the genes involved in behavior and characterize the proteins that the genes code for, new interventions for disabilities become possible.

Research in mice and fruit flies has succeeded in identifying single genes related to learning and spatial perception, and investigations of naturally occurring variations in human populations have found mutations in single genes that result in general mental retardation. These include the genes for phenylketonuria and fragile X syndrome, both causes of mental retardation. Single-gene defects that are associated with Duchenne's mus-

cular dystrophy, Lesch-Nyhan syndrome, neurofibromatosis type 1 and Williams syndrome may also be linked to the specific cognitive disabilities seen in these disorders [see "Williams Syndrome and the Brain," by Howard M. Lenhoff, Paul P. Wang, Frank Greenberg and Ursula Bellugi; SCIENTIFIC AMERICAN, December 1997].

In fact, more than 100 single-gene mutations are known to impair cognitive development. Normal cognitive functioning, on the other hand, is almost certainly orchestrated by many subtly acting genes working together rather than by single genes operating in isolation. These collaborative genes are thought to affect cognition in a probabilistic rather than a deterministic manner and are called quantitative trait loci, or QTLs. The name, which applies to genes involved in a complex dimension such as cognition, emphasizes the quantitative nature of certain physical and behavioral traits. QTLs have already been identified for diseases such as diabetes, obesity and hypertension as well as for behavioral problems involving drug sensitivity and dependence.

But finding QTLs is much more difficult than identifying the single-gene mutations responsible for some cognitive disorders. Fulker addressed this problem by developing a method, similar to DF extremes analysis, in which certain known variations in DNA are correlated with sibling differences in quantitative traits. Because genetic effects are easier to detect at the extremes of a dimension, the method works best when at least one member of each sibling pair is known to be extreme for a trait. Investigators affiliated with the Colorado Learning Disabilities Research Center at the University of Colorado first used this technique, called QTL linkage, to try to locate a QTL for reading disability—and succeeded. The discovery was reported in 1994 by collaborators at Boulder, the University of Denver and Boys Town National Research Hospital in Omaha.

Like many techniques in molecular genetics, QTL linkage works by identifying differences in DNA markers: stretches of DNA that are known to occupy particular sites on chromosomes and that can vary somewhat from person to person. The different versions of a marker, like the different versions of a gene, are called alleles. Because people have two copies of all chromosomes (except for the gender-determining X and Y chromosomes in males), they have two alleles for any given DNA marker. Hence, siblings can share one, two or no alleles of a marker. In other words, for each marker, siblings can either be like identical twins (sharing both alleles), like fraternal twins (sharing half their alleles) or like adoptive siblings (sharing no alleles).

The investigators who found the QTL for reading disability identified a reading-disabled member of a twin pair and then obtained reading scores for the other twin—the "co-twin." If the reading scores of the co-twins were worse when they shared alleles of a particular marker with their reading-disabled twins, then that marker was likely to lie near a QTL for reading disability in the same chromosomal region. The researchers found such a marker on the short arm of chromosome 6 in two independent samples,

one of fraternal twins and one of non-twin siblings. The findings have since been replicated by others.

It is important to note that whereas these studies have helped point to the location of a gene (or genes) implicated in reading disability, the gene (or genes) has not yet been characterized. This distinction gives a sense of where the genetics of cognition stand today: poised on the brink of a new level of discovery. The identification of genes that influence specific cognitive abilities will revolutionize researchers' understanding of the mind. Indeed, molecular genetics will have far-ranging consequences for the study of all human behavior. Researchers will soon be able to investigate the genetic connections between different traits and between behaviors and biological mechanisms. They will be able to better track the developmental course of genetic effects and to define more precisely the interactions between genes and the environment.

The discovery of genes for disorders and disabilities will also help clinicians design more effective therapies and to identify people at risk long before the appearance of symptoms. In fact, this scenario is already being enacted with an allele called Apo-E4, which is associated with dementia and cognitive decline in the elderly. Of course, new knowledge of specific genes could turn up new problems as well: among them, prejudicial labeling and discrimination. And genetics research always raises fears that DNA markers will be used by parents prenatally to select "designer babies."

We cannot emphasize too much that genetic effects do not imply genetic determinism, nor do they constrain environmental interventions. Although some readers may find our views to be controversial, we believe the benefits of identifying genes for cognitive dimensions and disorders will far outweigh the potential abuses.

TEST ANSWERS VERBAL: 1a. dry; 1b. pungent SPATIAL: 1.   2. b, c; 3. a, c, d; 4. a, b, f

---

The Authors

ROBERT PLOMIN and JOHN C. DeFRIES have collaborated for more than 20 years. Plomin, who worked with DeFries at the University of Colorado at Boulder from 1974 to 1986, is now at the Institute of Psychiatry in London. There he is research professor of behavioral genetics and deputy director of the Social, Genetic and Developmental Psychiatry Research Center. DeFries directs the University of Colorado's Institute for Behavioral Genetics and the university's Colorado Learning Disabilities Research Center. The ongoing Colorado Adoption Project, launched by the authors in 1975, has so far produced three books and more than 100 research papers. Plomin and DeFries are also the lead authors of the textbook *Behavioral Genetics*, now in its third edition.

Further Reading

NATURE, NURTURE AND PSYCHOLOGY. Edited by Robert Plomin and Gerald E. McClearn. American Psychological Association, Washington, D.C., 1993.

GENETICS OF SPECIFIC READING DISABILITY. J. C. DeFries and Maricela Alarcón in *Mental Retardation and Developmental Disabilities Research Reviews,* Vol. 2, pages 39–47; 1996.

BEHAVIORAL GENETICS. Third edition. Robert Plomin, John C. DeFries, Gerald E. McClearn and Michael Rutter. W. H. Freeman, 1997.

SUSCEPTIBILITY LOCI FOR DISTINCT COMPONENTS OF DEVELOPMENTAL DYSLEXIA ON CHROMOSOMES 6 AND 15. E. L. Grigorenko, F. B. Wood, M. S. Meyer, L. A. Hart, W. C. Speed, A. Schuster and D. L. Pauls in *American Journal of Human Genetics,* Vol. 60, pages 27–39; 1997.

Basing Teaching on Piaget's Constructivism

Constance Kamii and Janice K. Ewing

Constance Kamii is Professor, Department of Curriculum and Instruction, University of Alabama at Birmingham. Janice K. Ewing is Assistant Professor, Department of Social Sciences and Education, Colby-Sawyer College, New London, New Hampshire.

Constructivism, the view that much of learning originates from *inside* the child, has become increasingly popular in recent years. Many educators, however, use the term "construct" loosely without knowing, for example, that children construct a system of writing very differently from how they construct mathematical understanding. And some people think that Piaget had nothing to do with constructivism, crediting him only with discovering the stages of children's development.

The purpose of this article is to explain three main reasons for basing teaching on Piaget's constructivism: 1) it is a scientific theory that explains the nature of human knowledge, 2) it is the only theory in existence that explains children's construction of knowledge from birth to adolescence and 3) it informs educators of how Piaget's distinction among the three kinds of knowledge changes the way we should teach many subjects.

From *Childhood Education*, Annual Theme Issue, 1996, pp. 260-264. © 1996 by the Association for Childhood Education International, 17904 Georgia Avenue, Suite 215, Olney, MD. Reprinted by permission.

A Scientific Explanation of Human Knowledge

Philosophers have debated for centuries about how human beings attain truth, or knowledge. The two main views—the empiricist and rationalist views—developed in answer to this question differ, especially in the way philosophers thought about the role of experience.

Empiricists (such as Locke, Berkeley and Hume) argued, in essence, that knowledge has its source outside the individual, and that it is acquired by internalization through the senses. Empiricists further argued that the individual at birth is like a clean slate on which experiences are "written" as he or she grows up. As Locke wrote in 1690, "The senses at first let in particular ideas, and furnish the yet empty cabinet, and the mind by degrees growing familiar with some of them, they are lodged in the memory..." (1690/1947, p. 22).

Although rationalists such as Descartes, Spinoza and Kant did not deny the necessity of experience, they argued that reason is more important than sensory experience because reason enables us to know with certainty many truths that observation can never ascertain. We know, for example, that every event has a cause, in spite of the fact that we cannot examine every event in the entire past and future of the universe. Rationalists also pointed out that since our senses often deceive us through perceptual illusions, the senses cannot be trusted to provide reliable knowledge. The rigor, precision and certainty of mathematics, a purely deductive system, was the rationalists' prime example supporting the power of reason. When asked to explain the origin of reason, many proclaimed it was innate in human beings.

As a biologist trained in scientific methods, Piaget decided that the way to resolve the debate between empiricism and rationalism was to study knowledge scientifically, rather than continuing to argue on the basis of speculation. Piaget also believed that to understand the nature of knowledge, we must study its formation rather than examining only the end product. This is why he wanted to study the evolution of science from its prehistoric beginning, to examine the roles of sensory information and reason. Prehistoric evidence did not exist anymore, however, and the closest data available to him were babies' and children's knowledge. For Piaget, the study of children was thus a means of explaining the nature of human knowledge (Bringuier, 1977/1980).

The outcome of more than 50 years of research was Piaget's sharp disagreement with empiricism. Although he did not agree completely with rationalism, he did align himself with rationalism when required to place himself in a broad sense in one tradition or the other. With regard to the empiricist belief that we know objects through our senses, he argued that we never know objects as they are "out there" in external reality. Objects can be known only by assimilation into the schemes that we bring to each situation.

The famous conservation-of-liquid task offers an example of Piaget's opposition to empiricism. Until children construct a certain level of logic from the inside, they are nonconservers because they can base their judgment only on what they can *see*. Their *reason* later enables them to *interpret* the empirical data and deduce that the amount

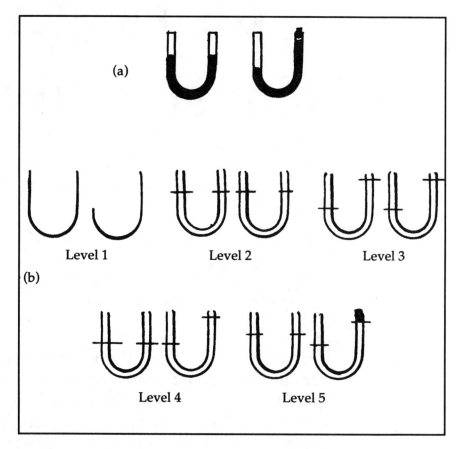

Figure 1

of liquid is the same even if one glass appears to have more than the other.

The Construction of Knowledge from Birth to Adolescence

To teach 3-year-olds, 7-year-olds or any other age group, educators must understand how children have acquired the knowledge they already have, and how this knowledge is related to that of adolescents and adults. The only theory in existence that shows this development from birth to adolescence is Piaget's. In his books about babies (Piaget, 1936/1952, 1937/1954, 1945,/1962), especially *The Construction of Reality in the Child*, we can read in meticulous detail about infants' construction of objects and of object permanence and the roots of logico-mathematical knowledge.

Although gaps are still being filled in Piaget's theory, we can clearly see children's subsequent construction of logic at ages 4–16 in *The Growth of Logical Thinking from Childhood to Adolescence* (Inhelder & Piaget, 1955/1958) and *The Early Growth of Logic in the Child* (Inhelder & Piaget, 1959/1964). An example related to the conservation-of-liquid task is given below to illustrate older children's construction of knowledge (Piaget & Inhelder, 1968/1973).

Children between 4 and 15 years of age were shown two U-shaped glass tubes (Figure 1a) mounted on a board and containing colored water. The subjects were asked to take a good look at the objects because they would later be asked to describe and draw them from memory.

Figure 1b shows examples of the children's drawings. At level 1, they drew only the containers (tubes) or the substance contained therein (liquid). At level 2, they made the water level the same everywhere. At level 3, while the water level became unequal, both tubes looked the same. The drawings became more accurate at level 4, but the children did not notice that the water level in the second tube went up on one side as much as it went down on the other side. At level 5, however, they inferred the initial equality of quantity in the two tubes, conserved this equality and noticed the significance of the stopper. As can be seen in Table 1, only the oldest children were frequently at levels 4 and 5.

Table 1

Relationship Between Ages and Levels in a Memory Task

	Levels					
Ages	1	2	3	4	5	Total number
4–5	12(54%)	6(27%)	2(9%)	2(9%)	0(0%)	22
6–7	4(22%)	4(22%)	1(5%)	8(44%)	1(5%)	18
8–15	0(0%)	1(5%)	1(5%)	9(45%)	9(45%)	20

This task is one of the countless examples that enable us to trace the roots of adolescents' knowledge all the way back to infancy. It again supports Piaget's view that we do not know objects as they are "out there" in external reality. Six-year-olds cannot even *see* the inequality of the water level in one of the tubes. When they can make more precise spatial relationships, they become able to notice what is obvious to older children.

Hundreds of other tasks can be found in Piaget's books that reveal the surprising process of children's construction of knowledge. In this process, children go from one level of being "wrong" to another, rather than simply accumulating more and more knowledge quantitatively. Nonconservation may be "wrong," but basing one's judgment on water level is an enormous achievement compared to what babies do, without even understanding the word "more."

The roles of sensory information and reason discussed earlier can be understood only in light of the distinction Piaget made among three kinds of knowledge. We, therefore, now turn to a discussion of the three kinds of knowledge and the difference this distinction can make to teaching.

Three Kinds of Knowledge

The three kinds of knowledge are physical, social (conventional) and logico-mathematical knowledge. Piaget's distinction among the three is based on their ultimate sources and modes of structuring.

Physical knowledge is knowledge of objects in external reality. The color and weight of a block are examples of physical properties that are in objects in external reality and can be known empirically by observation.

Examples of *social knowledge* are holidays, written and spoken languages, and the rule of saying "Good morning" under certain circumstances. The ultimate source of physical knowledge is partly in objects, and the ultimate source of social knowledge is partly in man-made conventions. The reason for saying "partly" is clarified shortly.

Logico-mathematical knowledge consists of relationships created by each individual and is the hardest kind to understand. When we are presented with a red block and a blue block and think that they are *similar,* for instance, the similarity is an example of logico-mathematical knowledge. Almost everybody thinks that the similarity between the blocks is observable, but this is not true. The blocks themselves are observable, but the similarity between them is not. The similarity exists neither *in* the red block nor *in* the blue one. If a person did not put the objects into this relationship, the similarity would not exist for him or her. The source of logico-mathematical knowledge, therefore, is *in* each child's mind. Other relationships the individual can create between the same blocks are *different, the same in weight* and *two.* Mathematical knowledge such as 2 + 2 = 4 and 3 × 4 = 12 is constructed by each child by making new relationships out of previously created relationships.

It was stated earlier that the source of physical knowledge is only *partly* in objects. Piaget's reason for saying "partly" was that a logico-mathematical framework, or a classificatory framework, is necessary even to recognize a block as a block or to recognize water as a liquid. Classification is also necessary to think about the color of an object and to recognize the color as blue. Without classification, it would be impossible to construct physical knowledge. Likewise, it would be impossible to construct social (conventional) knowledge without a logico-mathematical framework. To recognize a certain word as a "bad one," for example, the child has to categorize words into "good ones" and "bad ones."

The conservation of amount of liquid mentioned earlier is an example of the child's logico-mathematization of physical knowledge. The conservation of quantity of liquid involves spatio-temporal and other relationships, which belong to logico-mathematical knowledge. This is why we say that conservation is a logical deduction and not empirical knowledge.

Armed with Piaget's theory about the nature of logico-mathematical knowledge, Kamii set out to test the hypothesis that children can invent their own procedures for the four arithmetical operations . . .

The memory task described earlier also illustrates children's logico-mathematization of physical knowledge. We do not see facts only with our eyes. To the extent that we can make higher-level relationships and have more physical knowledge about contents such as air pressure, we obtain higher-level knowledge from the objects we see. In other

The Hindu Scratch Method for Solving 278 + 356 by Proceeding from Left to Right

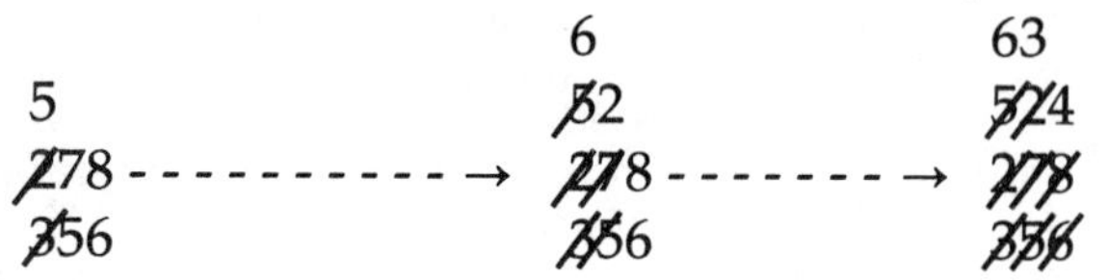

The rules followed:

1. Add 200 and 300, write the result (5 in the hundreds place), and cross out the 200 and 300.

2. Add 70 and 50, write the result (120), and cross out the 70 and 50. Because there was already a 5 in the hundreds place, this 5 was crossed out and changed to 6.

3. Add 8 and 6, write the result (14), and cross out the 8 and the 6. Because there was already a 2 in the tens place, this 2 was crossed out and changed to 3.

Figure 2

words, we observe the stopper in the task only if we bring a certain level of knowledge to it.

Physics and all the other branches of science involve the logico-mathematization of objects that are observable. Educators who understand the nature of science focus science education on children's reasoning about observable phenomena, rather than on transmission of scientific facts and terminology (social knowledge). An example of this emphasis on reasoning in physics can be found in Kamii and DeVries (1978/1993).

The teaching of mathematics also changes drastically when we understand the nature of logico-mathematical knowledge. Since 1980, Kamii (1985, 1989, 1994) has been developing an approach to primary mathematics based on Piaget's constructivism. This approach is described below as an example of how Piaget's theory can change the way we teach.

Elementary Mathematics Education

Traditional mathematics educators are usually not aware of Piaget's distinction among the three kinds of knowledge. Much of traditional elementary mathematics is therefore taught according to associationist-behavioristic principles, as if mathematics were social (conventional) knowledge. Teaching rules such as "carrying" and "borrowing" is an example of this social-knowledge approach.

Armed with Piaget's theory about the nature of logico-mathematical knowledge, Kamii set out to test the hypothesis that children can invent their own procedures for the four arithmetical operations, without any teaching of conventional rules. While this hypothesis was amply confirmed, an unexpected finding surfaced. The rules that are now taught in almost all the elementary schools throughout the United States are harmful to children's development of numerical reasoning.

Two reasons can be given to explain the harm. First, children have to give up their own thinking to use the rules of "carrying," "borrowing" and so forth. These rules make children proceed from right to left; that is, from the column of ones to those of tens, hundreds and so on. When children are free to do their own thinking, however, they invariably proceed in the opposite direction, from left to right. To add 38 + 16, for example, they typically do 30 + 10 = 40, 8 + 6 = 14, and 40 + 14 = 54. To subtract 18 from 32, they often say, "30 − 10 = 20. I can take only 2 from 2; so I have to take 6 more away from 20; so the answer is 14." In multiplication, likewise, children's typical way of doing 5 × 234, for example, is: 5 × 200 = 1,000, 5 × 30 = 150, 5 × 4 = 20, and 1,000 + 150 + 20 = 1170. Because a compromise is not possible between going from left to right and going from right to left, children have to give up their own thinking to obey their teachers.

The second reason for saying that algorithms are harmful is that these rules "unteach" place value and prevent children from developing number sense. While solving the preceding multiplication problem, for example, children who are taught algorithms say, "Five times four is twenty, put down the zero, and carry the two. Five times three is fifteen, plus two is seventeen, put down the seven, and carry the one. Five times two is ten," and so on. Treating every digit as ones is efficient for adults, who already know that the 2 in 234 is 200. For primary-age children, who have a tendency to think that the 2 in 234 means *two*, however, algorithms reinforce their "errors."

The history of computation is full of methods that are similar to the way today's children think. The Hindu Scratch Method shown in Figure 2 is an example of a method our ancestors used. It illustrates the constructive process through which the human species created knowledge (see Kamii, 1994, for other examples). Educators who impose algorithms on primary-age children think that mathematics is a cultural heritage that they must *transmit* to children. While their intentions are good, they impose on children in ready-made form the results of centuries of construction by adult mathematicians. An example of the outcome of this teaching is that the great majority of 4th-graders who had been taught algorithms gave outlandish answers such as 848, 783, 194 and 134 when asked to do 6 + 53 + 185 without paper and pencil (Kamii, 1994).

Conclusion

Education entered a scientific era when it embraced associationism and behaviorism. While both these theories are scientific, Piaget's constructivism has gone beyond them. Many educators cannot accept constructivism, however, because associationism and behaviorism seem too valid to reject.

It is not necessary to reject associationism and behaviorism completely to embrace constructivism. The reason is that Piaget's constructivism surpassed associationism and behaviorism in a way similar to the way Copernicus's theory went beyond the geocentric theory. Copernicus proved the geocentric theory wrong not by eliminating it, but by encompassing it. This is why even today we speak of sunrise and sunset, knowing perfectly well that the sun does not revolve around the earth. From the limited perspective of earth, it is still true that the sun rises and sets.

In a similar way, associationism and behaviorism still remain true from the limited perspective of surface behavior and specific bits of knowledge. In certain situations, therefore, associationism and behaviorism can still be used by educators. Science, too, advances by going through one level after another of being "wrong." Older, "wrong" knowledge is not eliminated completely. It is *modified* when we construct more adequate theories.

Although education has entered a scientific era, much of it remains at a stage of folk art based on opinions and trial-and-error. Because education is based mainly on opinions, it remains vulnerable to fads and the swinging of the pendulum. Progressive Education went out of fashion by the 1950s, for example, and came back in part in the 1960s as Open Education. But Open Education was quickly defeated by the forces of "back to basics."

Constructivist teaching has the potential of becoming another resurrection of Progressive Education. It is true that education cannot be based on scientific knowledge alone. But if education is to keep advancing and free itself from bandwagons and the swinging of the pendulum, we must study human knowledge with scientific rigor. Teaching will always remain an art, just as medicine is an art. But teaching must become an art based on scientific knowledge because science advances only in one direction and does not return to obsolete theories.

References

Bringuier, J.-C. (1980). *Conversations with Jean Piaget.* Chicago: University of Chicago Press. (Original work published 1977)

Inhelder, B., & Piaget, J. (1958). *The growth of logical thinking from childhood to adolescence.* New York: Basic Books. (Original work published 1955)

Inhelder, B., & Piaget, J. (1964). *The early growth of logic in the child.* New York: Harper & Row. (Original work published 1959)

Kamii, C. (1985). *Young children reinvent arithmetic.* New York: Teachers College Press.

Kamii, C. (1989). *Young children continue to reinvent arithmetic, 2nd grade.* New York: Teachers College Press.

Kamii, C. (1994). *Young children continue to reinvent arithmetic, 3rd grade.* New York: Teachers College Press.

Kamii, C., & DeVries, R. (1993). *Physical knowledge in preschool education.* New York: Teachers College Press. (Original work published 1978)

Locke, J. (1947). *Essay concerning human understanding.* Oxford, England: Oxford University Press. (Original work published 1690)

Piaget, J. (1952). *The origins of intelligence in children.* New York: Basic Books. (Original work published 1936)

Piaget, J. (1954). *The construction of reality in the child.* New York: Basic Books. (Original work published 1937)

Piaget, J. (1962). *Play, dreams, and imitation in childhood.* New York: Norton. (Original work published 1945)

Piaget, J., & Inhelder, B. (1973). *Memory and intelligence.* New York: Basic Books. (Original work published 1968)

In Search of a Metatheory for Cognitive Development (or, Piaget Is Dead and I Don't Feel So Good Myself)

David F. Bjorklund

With the waning of influence of Piaget's theory and the shortcomings of information-processing perspectives of cognitive growth, cognitive developmentalists lack a common set of broad, overarching principles and assumptions—a metatheory—to guide their research. Developmental biology is suggested as metatheory for cognitive development. Although it is important for developmentalists to understand proximal biological causes (e.g., brain development), most important for such a metatheory is an evolutionary perspective. Some basic principles of evolutionary psychology are introduced, and examples of contemporary research and theory consistent with these ideas are provided.

INTRODUCTION

The cognitive revolution changed the face of academic psychology, with developmental psychology being no exception. Success, however, had its cost. As Bruner (1990) pointed out, there was a focus to the cognitive revolution, and that was "meaning," a reaction to the mentalistically void behaviorism that had had a stranglehold on American psychology over most of the century. This focus has been lost in contemporary cognitive development. "Meaning" is now studied primarily by people interested in metacognition (e.g., Flavell, Green, & Flavell, 1995), the effects of cultural context on thinking (e.g., Rogoff, 1990), or by social developmentalists following variants of Bandura's (1986) social-cognitive theory, neo-Piagetian theory, or social information-processing approaches (e.g., Liben & Signorella, 1993; Stipek, Recchia, & McClintic, 1992). For psychologists such as these who study "meaning," to reduce cognitive devel-

opment much below this level of analysis results in an overabundance of details about children's performance on trivial tasks in unreal situations.

Other cognitive developmentalists have concluded that discerning meaning is not as simple as psychologists who study metacognition or social cognition believe, but involves a host of more elementary, or *basic processes*, most of which are unconscious (e.g., Dempster, 1993; Reyna & Brainerd, 1995). From this perspective, asking "bigger" questions may be inherently pleasing, but not scientifically fruitful. For example, inquiring about metacognition or the role of self-awareness is seen as providing only interesting descriptions of consciousness and leaves us with the feeling that the "ghost in the machine" is still in charge.

In addition to losing our common focus, we have also lost a common set of assumptions or principles about cognitive development; we have lost a *metatheory*. By

From *Child Development,* February 1997, pp. 144-148. © 1997 by the Society for Research in Child Development. Reprinted by permission.

metatheory, I do not mean a "theory about theories." Rather, I use the term much as Brainerd (1978) did in describing and evaluating Piagetian psychology to refer to some broad, overarching principles and assumptions—which may or may not be subject to experimental confirmation—that serve as a background for a host of more specific theories.

Piaget's metatheory was a great one. Researchers could heartily disagree about the specifics, but at the heart of development were still the functional invariants of organization and adaptation, the knowledge that development was a constructive process, and the principle of epigenesis. With the waning of Piaget's theory, a new metatheory took hold based on the assumptions of information-processing perspectives (e.g., limited capacity, serial processing of symbols, processing through a series of memory stores). Now, even this metatheory is crumbling in the face of evidence that calls into question some of the central tenets of the mind-as-a computer metaphor (e.g., the possibility of parallel processing, modularity of resources, rejection of strategic approaches to problem solving; see, for examples, Brainerd & Reyna, 1990; Stanovich, 1990). The result is a diversity of approaches to the study of thinking and its development, and this is a plus. Like all modern sciences, maturity means diversity and specialization. The cost of this specialization, however, has been the loss of the ability to communicate with others who call themselves cognitive developmentalists, and this is unfortunate.

What we need to bring us together again is a single focus, or metatheory. It is apparent, however, that the metatheories of the past will not work. A new metatheory is needed that makes sense in terms of what psychologists are doing today and what we will likely be doing during the next 20 years. Although I do not have a true metatheory to propose, I do have a focus that I think most contemporary theorists and researchers of cognitive development should consider, and that is developmental biology, particularly as it relates to the new field of evolutionary psychology.

DEVELOPMENTAL BIOLOGY AS A METATHEORY FOR COGNITIVE DEVELOPMENT

I use the term "developmental biology" broadly. As cognitive developmentalists, we should consider the development of the nervous system, the evolution of intelligence in the species, and the species-typical contexts in which cognition evolved and develops. This should be easy for developmentalists, for our entire discipline is implicitly based in biology. Development is a biological concept. Unlike other areas of experimental psychology that have their roots in physics, developmental psychology has its origins in turn-of-the-century embryology and evolutionary theory (Cairns, 1983).

Proximal Biological Causation

A knowledge of the developmental relation between brain and behavior has important implications, not only for theories of cognitive development, but also for societal practices. How pliable is human intelligence? When, in development, can children most benefit from certain educational experiences? Is earlier always better, or are there sensitive periods for particular experiences distributed throughout the course of development?

Evidence is accumulating showing greater plasticity of the mammalian brain than had been previously thought. This work, coupled with increasing knowledge of the course of human brain growth, has important implications for evaluating the role of experience on behavior and cognition (e.g., Greenough, Black, & Wallace, 1987). For example, Greenough and his associates (1987) pointed out how the nervous system of an animal is prepared for some experiences that all members of its species can expect, while other sets of neurons appear to await the idiosyncratic experiences that will vary from individual to individual. Such a distinction can be useful to the study of human development, particularly issues of plasticity and the types of experiences that are apt to be important in infancy and early childhood.

In a similar vein, having a knowledge of brain development should help us predict and understand what *type* of cognition should develop at what times. For example, knowing that the frontal lobe is associated with planfulness and the inhibition of prepotent responses (Diamond, 1991) clues us to when certain cognitive abilities will appear and mature. For stage theorists, knowledge of how the brain develops can be correlated with qualitative changes in cognitive abilities, giving the hypothesized discontinuities some basis in physical reality (e.g., Case, 1992).

Distal Biological Causation

As important as a knowledge of proximate biological causation is to understanding cognitive development, I doubt that this perspective alone could unite the diversity of people who today study cognitive development. A more likely candidate for this role is evolutionary theory. Evolution is the cornerstone of modern biology and could serve as the basis for a metatheory that unifies developmental psychologists of all ilk. Developmental psychology was begun by scholars interested in evolutionary concepts. Baldwin, Hall, and Piaget were among the more notable of our developmental forefathers who entered the field, in part, to get a better picture of human evolution. (Baldwin, in fact, has his name attached to an important evolutionary principle of preadaptation—the Baldwin effect.)

More recently, it has been suggested that cognitive psychology may be the "missing link" in the evolution of human behavior. Cosmides and Tooby (1987; Tooby & Cosmides, 1992) have proposed that it was information-processing mechanisms that evolved, and "these mechanisms in interaction with environmental input, generate manifest behavior. The causal link between evolution and behavior is made through psychological mechanisms" (Cosmides and Tooby, 1987, p. 277). According to Cosmides and Tooby, adaptive behavior is predicated on adaptive thought. Natural selection operates on the cognitive level—information-processing programs evolved to solve real-world problems. From this viewpoint, it becomes fruitful to ask what kind of cognitive operations an organism must have "if it is to extract and process information about its environment in a way that will lead to adaptive behavior" (Cosmides & Tooby, 1987, p. 285). Also, evolutionary theory suggests that most cognitive programs evolved to accomplish adaptive functions, what Cosmides and Tooby refer to as "Darwinian algorithms," and are domain-specific (i.e., modular) in nature.

Taking such an approach causes us to look at our data differently and to ask slightly different questions. For example, much research has focused on children's cognition on school-related tasks, often with the explicit aim of generalizing findings to education. Slightly different interpretations and prescriptions to educators may be made, however, by realizing that formal schooling is "unnatural" (e.g., Pellegrini & Bjorklund, in press). Children's cognitions evolved in environments where reading and math seat-work did not exist, and children's difficulty with such tasks should be viewed as the norm and not the exception. Similarly, evolutionary theory holds that some abilities may have evolved to deal with problems that the organism faced in specific environments at a particular time in development (ontogenetic adaptations; see Oppenheim, 1981). When we ask, "How are children's cognitions adapted for the cultural contexts in which they find themselves rather than the contexts experienced by adults?" we may find different answers to frequently asked questions. From this perspective, not all aspects of infancy and early childhood are preparations for later development (e.g., Bjorklund, 1995; Bjorklund & Green, 1992; Turkewitz & Kenny, 1982) but exist to serve the child at that specific point in time only.

Evolutionary theory also places an emphasis on *individual differences*. Variation among individuals within a population is the stuff upon which natural selection works. Developmentalists, concerned with universals, often treat variability only as error. Individual variation is not error, however, but is real; these differences are important to society and may have different causes than developmental universals (Plomin & Ho, 1991). Moreover, some substantial portion of individual differences have their origins in genetics and others in prenatal or postnatal hormone exposure. Much individual variability is also caused by general experiential factors, of course, but one must have a biological theory, such as found in contemporary behavioral genetics (Plomin, 1989) or the developmental-systems approach (e.g., Got-

tlieb, 1991) to know which is which, which characteristics are more pliable, and which are resistant to change.

CONTEMPORARY RESEARCH AND THEORY

The number of examples of theory and research that are taking the view I am proposing has increased sharply over the past decade. Several examples include:

Gardner's (1983) popular theory of multiple intelligences that considers intelligence and its development in terms of evolutionary theory, cross-cultural data, and neuropsychological evidence, particularly cases of brain damage;

Current research and theory relating development of the frontal lobes with cognitive accomplishments over infancy (e.g., Diamond, 1991) and childhood (e.g., Dempster, 1993; Harnishfeger & Bjorklund, 1993);

Siegler's (1995, 1996) recent adoption of the Darwinian metaphor of variation and selection to account for the development of children's strategies and as a general model of cognitive development; and

A proposal by Geary (1995) classifies cognitive abilities into two categories: *biologically primary*, which includes those abilities that have been selected for in evolution, and *biologically secondary*, which are abilities that have not been selected for in evolution but rather are culturally instilled practices. Geary provides examples of the two types of abilities from his own area of research, children's mathematics, but the classification can be applied to any set of cognitive abilities and has important implications not only for understanding the development of different skills but also for their educability.

I am not advocating that cognitive developmental psychologists retool to become developmental biologists. Developing a theory of the brain is important, of course, but that is not our job, and it is not enough. Having a theory of the brain does not obviate having a theory of the mind. Cognitive psychology is not just something to do until the biologists get better at their trade. What I am arguing is not a blind acceptance of all that biologists have to tell us, but merely that we be mindful of the proximal and distal biological causes of cognitive development and formulate our theories and design our experiments accordingly. Thus, for example, researchers concerned with the development of social perspective taking or of the origins of self-concept should be aware of the social context in which human intelligence develops and with theories that postulate social forces as providing a strong impetus for the evolution of human intelligence (e.g., Byrne & Whiten, 1988; Humphrey, 1976; see Tomasello, Kruger, & Ratner, 1993, for a recent theory that does this). Similarly, researchers concerned with the development of basic processes should consider the evolutionary pressures that may have produced these particular processes as well as the neurological systems that underlie them (e.g., Bjorklund & Harnishfeger, 1995; Geary, 1996).

CLOSING REMARKS

I realize that we could be criticized for getting into something that is none of our business. We are psychologists, and without further training we are apt to come up with naive theories based on oversimplified conceptions of the brain and evolution (see Morss, 1990). This is a criticism specialists in all fields make to interlopers; but I believe the errors we make will be worth the effort. By adopting a metatheory that views cognitive development as a natural consequence of species-typical behavior in a species-typical environment that has evolved to solve certain problems, we will make progress. We will ask better questions and collect better data.

I take this last point seriously. Having a "big picture" of cognitive development will mean that our questions will be posed not only to answer certain narrowly defined hypotheses, but to make sense in terms of our metatheory. Much data collected by contemporary cognitive developmentalists may be methodologically solid and yield "good" data, in that they nicely support or refute a hypothesis. But when the theory that generated the experiment dies, the data often are forgotten, and appropriately so. This is less apt to happen when there is a larger focus behind one's specific theory. Piaget's work is a case in point. Piaget's theory has been soundly criticized, to the point that much of it is regarded as flat-out wrong. Yet the data he collected remain important—they are significant independent of the theory—and this I believe is due, at least in part, to the broad, biologically based ideas that served as underpinnings of his theory. Much of what Piaget was concerned with involved children's developing understanding of the physical world—the permanence of objects, the conservation of physical quantities, the knowledge of numbers. Piaget studied cognitive problems that all members of our species face, and would have faced in our environment of evolutionary adaptiveness. Our own questions need not always share this universality, but they should address problems couched in a theory that is likely to be viewed as valid generations hence. Evolutionary theory, I believe, is such a theory.

Believing in biology will not make us into modern-day Piagets. Genius requires more than just a set of principles to follow. But it will, I believe, result in our collecting more important and long-lasting data, and perhaps getting us to communicate with one another again.

ACKNOWLEDGMENTS

An earlier version of this article was presented at the meetings of the Society for Research in Child Development, April 1991, Seattle, WA. I would like to thank Barbara R. Bjorklund, Katherine Kipp, and Rhonda Douglas for comments on drafts of the manuscript. This essay was completed while the author was supported by National Science Foundation research award SBR-9422177.

ADDRESS AND AFFILIATION

Corresponding author: David F. Bjorklund, Florida Atlantic University, Department of Psychology, Boca Raton, FL 33431; e-mail: BJORKLDF@FAU.EDU.

REFERENCES

Bandura, A. (1986). *Social foundations of thought and action: A social cognitive theory.* Englewood Cliffs, NJ: Prentice-Hall.

Bjorklund, D. F. (1995, September). *The adaptive nature of developmental immaturity.* Invited address at the German Psychological Conference (Developmental Psychology Group), Leipzig, Germany.

Bjorklund, D. F., & Green, B. L. (1992). The adaptive nature of cognitive immaturity. *American Psychologist, 47,* 46–54.

Bjorklund, D. F., & Harnishfeger, K. K. (1995). The role of inhibition mechanisms in the evolution of human cognition. In F. Dempster & C. Brainerd (Eds.), *New perspectives on interference and inhibition in cognition* (pp. 141–173). New York: Academic Press.

Brainerd, C. J. (1978). *Piaget's theory of intelligence.* Englewood Cliffs, NJ: Prentice-Hall.

Brainerd, C. J., & Reyna, V. F. (1990). Gist is the grist: Fuzzy-trace theory and the new intuitionism. *Developmental Review, 10,* 3–47.

Bruner, J. (1990). *Acts of meaning.* Cambridge, MA: Harvard University Press.

Byrne, R., & Whiten, A. (Eds.). (1988). *Machiavellian intelligence: Social expertise and the evolution of intellect in monkeys, apes, and humans.* Oxford: Clarendon.

Cairns, R. B. (1983). The emergence of developmental psychology. In W. Kessen (Ed.), P. H. Mussen (Series Ed.), *Handbook of child psychology: Vol. 1. History, theory, and methods* (pp. 41–102). New York: Wiley.

Case, R. (1992). The role of the frontal lobes in the regulation of cognitive development. *Brain and Cognition, 20,* 51–73.

Cosmides, L., & Tooby, J. (1987). From evolution to behavior: Evolutionary psychology as the missing link. In J. Dupre (Ed.), *The latest on the best essays on evolution and optimality* (pp. 277–306). Cambridge, MA: MIT Press.

Dempster, F. N. (1993). Resistance to interference: Developmental changes in a basic processing mechanism. In M. L. Howe & R. Pasnak (Eds.), *Emerging themes in cognitive development: Vol. 1. Foundations* (pp. 1–27). New York: Springer-Verlag.

Diamond, A. (1991). Frontal lobe involvement in cognitive changes during the first year of life. In K. R. Gibson & A. C. Petersen (Eds.), *Brain maturation and cognitive development: Comparative and cross-cultural perspectives* (pp. 127–180). New York: Aldine de Gruyter.

Flavell, J. H., Green, F. L., & Flavell, E. R. (1995). Young children's knowledge about thinking. *Monographs of the Society for Research in Child Development, 60* (1, Serial No. 243).

Gardner, H. (1983). *Frames of mind: The theory of multiple intelligences.* New York: Basic.

Geary, D. C. (1995). Reflections of evolution and culture in children's cognition: Implications for mathematical development and instruction. *American Psychologist, 50,* 24–37.

Geary, D. C. (1996). Sexual selection and sex differences in mathematical abilities. *Behavioral and Brain Sciences, 19,* 229–284.

Gottlieb, G. (1991). Experiential canalization of normal development: Theory. *Developmental Psychology, 27,* 4–13.

Greenough, W. T., Black, J. E., & Wallace, C. S. (1987). Experience and brain development. *Child Development, 58,* 539–559.

Harnishfeger, K. K., & Bjorklund, D. F. (1993). The ontogeny of inhibition mechanisms: A renewed approach to cognitive development. In M. L.

Howe & R. Pasnak (Eds.), *Emerging themes in cognitive development: Vol. 1. Foundations* (pp. 28–49). New York: Springer-Verlag.

Humphrey, N. K. (1976). The social function of intellect. In P. P. G. Bateson & R. A. Hinde (Eds.), *Growing points in ethology* (pp. 303–317). Cambridge: Cambridge University Press.

Liben, L. S., & Signorella, M. L. (1993). Gender-schematic processing in children: The role of initial interpretations of stimuli. *Developmental Psychology, 29,* 141–149.

Morss, J. R. (1990). *The biologising of childhood: Developmental psychology and the Darwinian myth.* Hillsdale, NJ: Erlbaum.

Oppenheim, R. W. (1981). Ontogenetic adaptations and retrogressive processes in the development of the nervous system and behavior. In K. J. Connolly & H. F. R. Prechtl (Eds), *Maturation and development: Biological and psychological perspectives* (pp. 73–108). Philadelphia: International Medical Publications.

Pellegrini, A. D., & Bjorklund, D. F. (in press). The place of recess in school: Issues in the role of recess in children's education and development: An introduction to the Special Issue. *Journal of Research in Childhood Education.*

Plomin, R. (1989). Environment and genes: Determinants of behavior. *American Psychologist, 44,* 105–111.

Plomin, R., & Ho, H-z. (1991). Brain, behavior, and developmental genetics. In K. R. Gibson & A. C. Petersen (Eds), *Brain maturation and cognitive development: Comparative and cross-cultural perspectives* (pp. 65–89). New York: Aldine de Gruyter.

Reyna, V. F., & Brainerd, C. J. (1995). Fuzzy-trace theory: An interim synthesis. *Learning and Individual Differences, 7,* 1–75.

Rogoff, B. (1990). *Apprenticeship in thinking: Cognitive development in social context.* New York: Oxford University Press.

Siegler, R. S. (1995). Children's thinking: How does change occur? In W. Schneider & F. E. Weinert (Eds.), *Research on memory development: State of the art and future directions* (pp. 405–430). Hillsdale, NJ: Erlbaum.

Siegler, R. S. (1996). *Emerging minds: The process of change in children's thinking.* New York: Oxford University Press.

Stanovich, K. E. (1990). Concepts in developmental theories of reading skill: Cognitive resources, automaticity, and modularity. *Developmental Review, 10,* 72–100.

Stipek, D. J., Recchia, S., & McClintic, S. (1992). Self-evaluation in young children. *Monographs of the Society for Research in Child Development, 57* (1, Serial No. 226).

Tomasello, M., Kruger, A. C., & Ratner, H. H. (1993). Cultural learning. *Behavioral and Brain Sciences, 16,* 495–511.

Tooby, J., & Cosmides, L. (1992). The psychological foundations of culture. In J. H. Barkow, L. Cosmides, & J. Tooby (Eds.), *The adapted mind: Evolutionary psychology and the generation of culture* (pp. 19–136). New York: Oxford University Press.

Turkewitz, G., & Kenny, P. (1982). Limitations on input as a basis for neural organization and perceptual development: A preliminary theoretical statement. *Developmental Psychobiology, 15,* 357–368.

Bell, book and scandal

For more than a century intelligence testing has been a field rich in disputed evidence and questionable conclusions. "The Bell Curve", by Charles Murray and Richard Herrnstein, has ensured it will remain so

THERE is plenty of room for debate about which was the most amusing book of 1994, or which the best written. But nobody can seriously quibble about which was the most controversial. "The Bell Curve: Intelligence and Class Structure in American Life", an 845-page tome by Charles Murray and Richard Herrnstein*, has reignited a debate that is likely to rage on for years yet, consuming reputations and research grants as it goes.

"The Bell Curve" is an ambitious attempt to resuscitate IQ ("intelligence quotient") testing, one of the most controversial ideas in recent intellectual

*The Free Press. New York, 1994

history; and to use that idea to explain some of the more unpalatable features of modern America. Mr Murray, a sociologist, and Herrnstein, a psychologist who died shortly before the book's publication, argue that individuals differ substantially in their "cognitive abilities"; that these differences are inherited as much as acquired; and that intelligence is distributed in the population along a normal distribution curve—the bell curve of the book's title—with a few geniuses at the top, a mass of ordinary Joes in the middle and a minority of dullards at the bottom (see chart).

Then, into this relatively innocuous cocktail, Messrs Murray and Herrnstein mix two explosive arguments.

The first is that different races do not perform equally in the IQ stakes—that, in America, Asians score, on average, slightly above the norm, and blacks, on average, substantially below it. The second is that America is calcifying into impermeable castes. The bright are inter-marrying, spawning bright offspring and bagging well-paid jobs; and the dull are doomed to teenage pregnancy, welfare dependency, drugs and crime.

For the past three months it has been almost impossible to pick up an American newspaper or tune into an American television station without learning more about Mr Murray's views. Dozens of academics are hard at work rebutting (they would say refuting) his arguments.

Thanks to the controversy, "The Bell Curve" has sold more than a quarter of a million copies.

Undoubtedly, Mr Murray has been lucky in his timing. Left-wingers point out that Americans have seldom been so disillusioned with welfare policy: the voters are turning not just to Republicans, but to Republicans who are arguing seriously about the merits of state orphanages and of compulsory adoption. Mr Murray's arguments answer to a feeling that social policies may have failed not because they were incompetently designed or inadequately funded, but because they are incompatible with certain "facts" of human nature.

Right-wingers retort that it is liberals' addiction to "affirmative action" that has supplied Mr Murray with much of his material. Affirmative action has institutionalised the idea that different ethnic groups have different cognitive abilities: "race norming", now *de rigueur* in academia, means that a black can perform significantly less well than, say, an Asian, and still beat him into a university. It has also resulted in America's having a compilation of statistics about race unequalled outside South Africa.

Differently weird

The regularity with which discussion of IQ testing turns into an argument that ethnic groups differ in their innate abilities, with blacks at the bottom of the cognitive pile, has done more than anything else to make theorists and practitioners of IQ testing into figures of academic notoriety reviled everywhere from Haight-Ashbury to Holland Park. The early 1970s saw a furious argument about "Jensenism", named after Arthur Jensen, a psychologist at the University of California, Berkeley, who published an article arguing, among other things, that the average black had a lower IQ than the average white. William Shockley, also known as a co-inventor of the transistor, drew the anti-Jensenists' fire by saying that blacks' and whites' brains were "differently wired".

But, even if it could be extricated from arguments about ethnic differences, IQ testing would remain controversial. One reason is that few people like the idea that inequality might be inevitable, the result of natural laws rather than particular circumstances (and the more so, perhaps, when economic inequalities seem likely to widen as labour markets put an ever-higher

premium on intelligence). The implication is that egalitarian policies are self-defeating: the more inherited prejudices are broken down, the more society resolves into intellectual castes.

A second reason for controversy is that IQ testers are all too prone to the fatal conceit of thinking that their discipline equips them to know what is best for their fellow men. To most parents the idea that a man with a book of tests and a clipboard can divine what is best for their children is an intolerable presumption (who can know a child as well as its parents?) and an insupportable invasion of lib-

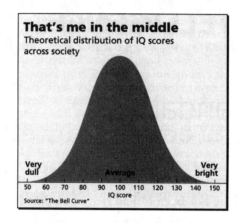

That's me in the middle
Theoretical distribution of IQ scores across society

Very dull   Average   Very bright

50 60 70 80 90 100 110 120 130 140 150
                    IQ score
Source: "The Bell Curve"

erty (surely people should be free to choose the best school for their children?). Nor has the IQ testers' image been helped by their having often been asked—as in England in the days of the 11-plus school entry examination—to help make already contentious decisions.

A third reason IQ testers excite concern is that they seem to make a fetish of intelligence. Many people feel instinctively that intelligence is only one of the qualities that make for success in life—that looks, luck and charm also play their part; they also like to feel that intelligence is less important than what they call "character", which can turn even a dull person into a useful citizen.

But the thing which, in the end, really frightens people about IQ testing is its message of genetic Calvinism: that IQ both determines one's destiny, and is dictated by one's genes. This flies in the face of the liberal notion that we are each responsible for fashioning our own fate. It also upsets two beliefs held particularly firmly in America: that anybody can win out, provided they have "the right stuff"; and that everybody

should be given as many educational chances as possible, rather than sorted out and classified at the earliest possible opportunity. (Thus "Forrest Gump", a film that appeared shortly before publication of "The Bell Curve", enjoyed great popularity and critical acclaim for its portrayal of a well-meaning simpleton who won all America's glittering prizes.)

Hunting down Sir Humphrey

How, then, did so widely distrusted a discipline originate? To answer that question means a trip to a rather unexpected place, the Whitehall of the mid-19th century. Traditionally, jobs in the British civil service had been handed out on the basis of family connections, in a sort of affirmative-action programme for upper-class twits. But as Britain developed a world-beating economy and a world-spanning empire, reformers argued that preferment should go to the most intelligent candidates, their identity to be discovered by competitive examinations.

This innovation proved so successful that policy-makers applied the same principle to the universities and schools. Their aim was to construct an educational system capable of discovering real ability wherever it occurred, and of matching that ability with the appropriate opportunities.

Ironically, it was children at the other end of the ability scale who inspired the first IQ tests as such. The introduction of compulsory schooling for the masses confronted teachers with the full variety of human abilities, and obliged them to distinguish between the lazy and the congenitally dull. Most investigators contented themselves with measuring children's heads. But in 1905 Alfred Binet, a French psychologist, came up with the idea of assigning an age level to a variety of simple intellectual operations, determined by the earliest age at which the average child could perform them, and ranking children both against their peers and against a normal development curve. Binet's idea was refined soon afterwards by introducing the arithmetical device of dividing mental age by chronological age and multiplying by 100.

Two English psychologists turned intelligence testing into a sort of scientific movement. The first was Francis Galton, a rich and well connected man (Charles Darwin was a cousin) who devoted his life to the nascent sciences of statistics and genetics. His motto was "wherever you can, count", and he measured everything from the distended buttocks of Hottentot women (with a theodolite) to the distribution of "pulchritude" in the British Isles. He compiled family trees of everybody from Cambridge wranglers to West Country wrestlers to prove his belief that "characteristics cling to families" and "ability goes by descent."

Combining his two passions, Galton speculated that abilities in the British population were distributed along a "bell curve", with the upper classes at the top and an underclass at the bottom. He was so worried that those at the bottom of the curve were outbreeding those at the top that he spent most of his fortune bankrolling another "science", eugenics.

Galton's mission was completed by a retired soldier, Charles Spearman. Deciding that the results of certain tests correlated with each other to a remarkable degree, Spearman concluded, in a seminal article published in 1904, that all mental abilities were manifestations of a single general ability, which he called "g": all individuals inherited a fixed quantity of mental energy, which infused every intellectual act they performed and determined what they were capable of in life. The right tests could capture how much "g" each individual possessed and express it as a single number.

Intelligence testing went on to enjoy decades of growing popularity. The American army used it on recruits in the first world war, employing more than 300 psychologists, and other armies followed. Schools used tests to help in streaming or selecting their pupils. Bureaucrats and businessmen used them to identify talented recruits. Tests were thought indispensable for discovering and diagnosing learning problems.

Only in the 1960s did opinion turn sharply against the IQ testers. Educationalists accused them of allowing an obsession with classification to blind them to the full range of human abilities. Sociologists (and sociologically minded psychologists) argued that intellectual differences owed more to social circumstances than to genes. In Britain, disillusionment with IQ tests hastened the introduction of comprehensive schools. In the United States, schools abandoned the use of IQ tests to classify children. In 1978 a district court in San Francisco even ruled unconstitutional the use of IQ tests to place children in classes for the backward if the use of such tests meant that

the classes contained a "grossly disproportionate" number of black children.

Dropping clangers

"The Bell Curve" thus represents an attempt to rehabilitate an idea that had fallen into two or three decades of disfavour. But have Messrs Murray and Herrnstein got their science right?

So far, the debate on "The Bell Curve" has been billed as if it were psychometrists (mind-measurers) versus the rest. In fact, IQ testers divide among themselves on all sorts of key issues, from the structure of the mind to the reliability of tests; moreover, Messrs Murray and Herrnstein occupy a rather eccentric position among psychometrists. They are unabashed supporters of Charles Spearman, believing that intelligence is a unitary quality expressible in a single number, such that people who are good at one thing will also be good at others. Yet this is one of the most hotly disputed topics within psychometry. A British pioneer, Godfrey Thomson, argued that the correlations which so excited Spearman might be explained by the laws of chance. He concluded that the mind had no fixed structure and that intelligence tests gave little more than a hint of a person's mental powers.

Among other psychologists, L.L. Thurstone argued for the existence of dozens of different types of mental abilities, such as mathematical, verbal and visio-spatial abilities. Liam Hudson has found IQ tests to reward a particular type of "convergent" thinker. Howard Gardner thinks there are many sorts of "intelligence".

Synaptitude

IQ testers have clashed and go on clashing over less arcane issues too. They endorse widely different estimates of the heritability of IQ, ranging from 40% to 80%. They squabble about the accuracy of IQ tests: some argue that such tests are nothing more than estimates that need to be repeated frequently and to be supplemented by personal interviews (and indeed, observably, children can learn, or be taught, to raise their IQ scores). Some of the most illustrious psychometrists are even starting to argue that IQ tests should be replaced by physical tests to measure the speed of reactions, the production of glucose in

the brain, the speed of neural transmission and even the size of the brain.

Psychometrists disagree, too, about the validity of generalising about groups in the way that Murray and Herrnstein do. It is widely accepted that differences within groups may reflect hereditary factors; but differences between groups are susceptible to other explanations (just as people in one place may be taller on average than people in another place, for example, but for reasons of nutrition, not genetics).

Oddly, Messrs Murray and Herrnstein have chosen to dispute (or ignore) one of the few arguments on which other psychometrists agree: that children do not necessarily have the same IQ as their parents. "The Bell Curve" argues that society is fixing itself into impermeable castes. But psychometry is a theory of social mobility, not social stasis. It tries to explain why bright people often have dull children and dull people often have bright children. Sex ensures that genes are resorted in each generation.

In fact, it is hereditarianism's sworn enemy, environmentalism, which is really a theory of social stasis: if the rich and educated can pass on their advantages to their children undisturbed by the dance of the chromosomes, then social mobility will always be something of a freak. Messrs Murray and Herrnstein are, perhaps, environmentalists in hereditarian clothing.

Politically, "The Bell Curve" has reinforced the impression that IQ testers are anti-welfare conservatives. Some are. But IQ tests have been invoked in defence of a wide variety of political positions, respectable and otherwise. American psychologists have popped up to support abominations such as compulsory sterilisation and ethnically sensitive immigration laws. Others have been socialists, keen on upward mobility, child-centred education and generous provision for the backward. In Britain between the wars Labour Party intellectuals such as R.H. Tawney argued for IQ testing as a way to ensure educational opportunities were allocated on the basis of innate ability rather than family connections; psychologists such as Cyril Burt have been passionate supporters of nursery-school education and better treatment of backward children. (The fusty T.S. Eliot, on the other hand, thought IQ tests were a plot to promote social mobility and debase education. A particularly crusty Cambridge don, Edward Welbourne, denounced them as "devices invented by Jews for the advancement of Jews.")

Too clever by half

What makes the IQ debate particularly frustrating is that both sides have long been addicted to exaggeration. The earliest IQ testers were guilty of hubris when they argued that they had invented an infallible technique for measuring mental abilities and distributing educational and occupational opportunities. As if that was not bad enough, they exacerbated their error by claiming that their method contributed to economic efficiency (by making the best use of human resources) and personal happiness (by ensuring that people were given jobs suited to their abilities).

The enemies of IQ testing were also guilty of terrible exaggeration when they accused testers of shoring up capitalism, perpetuating inequality, and justifying sexism, racism, even fascism. In fact, the IQ testers were never anywhere near as influential as they, or their opponents, imagined.

IQ theory played no part in persuading the American Congress to pass the Immigration Restriction Act of 1924; British grammar schools used IQ tests only to supplement other, more traditional selection procedures, such as scholastic examinations and interviews; Hitler and Mussolini had no time for IQ tests that were liable to contradict their own racial prejudices.

What the IQ debate needs now is a dash of cold water. Opponents of testing should forget their over-heated rhetoric about legitimising capitalism and racism. Supporters should fold up their more grandiose blueprints for building the meritocracy, and limit themselves to helping with practical problems. They should point out that IQ tests are useful ways of identifying and diagnosing mental deficiency, just so long as they are administered along with other diagnostic tools by a trained psychologist. They should add that IQ tests can also be useful in helping to allocate places in over-subscribed schools; that, indeed, they are less class-biased than scholastic tests (which favour the well-taught) or personal interviews (which favour the well-brought up). It is a pity that Charles Murray and Richard Herrnstein have chosen to douse the debate not with cold water but with petrol.

The Death of Child Nature

Education in the Postmodern World

By David Elkind

Mr. Elkind reviews the modern and postmodern conceptions of the child and the educational practices that follow from those conceptions. Becoming postmodern in education, he concludes, often means gaining a truer and deeper appreciation of the educational innovators of modernity.

EVERY CHILD, to paraphrase Clyde Kluckhohn and Henry Murray, is like all other children, like some other children, and like no other child.[1] Children are all alike in that they are members of the same species and share the same biological and physiological characteristics, walk upright, have the potential for speech, and so on. In this species sense, we can reasonably speak of the *biological* child who is like all other children. It is also true that only subgroups of children share the same language, culture, and physical environment. When considering children who are like some other children in this culture/environmental sense, we can speak of the *social* child. Finally, each child is different from every other in his or her unique genetic endowment and in the particular circumstances of his or her upbringing. When we speak of children in this unique, individual sense, we might speak of the *psychological* child.

Although it is unlikely that many would quarrel with this description of the three senses in which the term *child* may be used, the three are often confused, most notably in discussions of education. That is to say, individual psychological characteristics of chil-

DAVID ELKIND is a professor of child development at Tufts University, Medford, Mass.

Illustration by Mario Noche

From *Phi Delta Kappan*, November 1997, pp. 241-245.

dren are often treated as biological universals. In the past, the belief in a universal psychological child (which I will simply refer to as a belief in *child nature*) had some positive consequences. It contributed, for example, to the provision of free public education. Today, however, this very same belief in a universal child nature has become a barrier to achieving an individually appropriate pedagogy for children in all their personal, ethnic, racial, and cultural diversity. In this article I attempt to sub stantiate this thesis.

The critique of transcendent realities and overarching generalizations is a major thrust of the movement called *postmodernism*.[2] Although different writers define this movement in different ways, there is general agreement that many of the assumptions that fueled the modern view of the world were romantic ideals that now stand in need of correction. Postmodern critiques are already common in the arts, in architecture, in science, and in industry, but they are only now beginning to be heard in the social sciences and in education.[3]

Even without invoking postmodernism, a few contemporary education reform initiatives challenge the conception of normative education tailored to the needs of a uniform child nature.[4] Likewise, a number of contemporary educational practices reflect postmodern conceptions. Nonetheless, the modern assumption of an archetypal psychological child dies hard and underlies practices that are contributing to educational dysfunction among large numbers of children. In the succeeding pages, I will try to illustrate some of the educational practices that derive from the modern conception of a common (psychological) child nature and that impede, rather than further, children's academic achievement.

In preparation for that discussion, however, let me first briefly describe the major tenets of modernism and postmodernism and show how these differing paradigmatic assumptions about the world are reflected in the modern and postmodern conceptions of the child and in some of the educational practices that flow from them. That discussion will provide the context for a critique of those contemporary educational practices that remain wedded to a modern conception of a common child nature. Such practices miseducate children in the sense that they place them at risk with no purpose.

Modernity, Child Nature, And Modern Education

Modernity was built on three unquestioned assumptions about the world. The first idea was that of *progress*, the notion that societies inevitably moved forward in a positive direction from slavery and feudalism to individual freedom and democracy. From its inception in the 16th century, experimental science was the model for the modern conception of progress, with its gradual accumulation of knowledge serving to improve the quality of life for all members of society. Later, Darwin's theory of evolution offered a scientific explanation for this progress, suggesting that societies, like species, evolve by a process of variation and natural selection, with survival of the fittest as the end result.

The notion of progress shaped the modern conception of the child and of education. Although educational philosophers differed as to whether the child's mind was a blank tablet or a full book, none doubted that education was necessary to ensure the child's steady progress toward responsible and productive adulthood. John Locke, for one, saw the child as in need of adult tutelage if he or she was to become a socially responsible and culturally literate human being.[5] In contrast, Jean-Jacques Rousseau argued that experience itself was the best teacher and that adult instruction could well be delayed until children had acquired considerable knowledge on their own.[6] Both Locke and Rousseau, however, talked about children in a universal sense and with little attention to the differential progress that might be observed thanks to dissimilarities in ability, race, ethnicity, or culture.

The notion of progress was extended to pedagogy as well as to the child. It was the rationale for the metaphor of the "ladder" of education. Knowledge, values, and skills, it was assumed, are acquired in a uniform and stepwise fashion. Subject matters were also organized according to what was regarded as a natural progression—for example, arithmetic before algebra and algebra before trigonometry. The same held true for reading, and children were taught simple folk stories and fairy tales before they were introduced to true "literature." Not surprisingly, the rate at which a child ascended this educational ladder became the only measure of individual difference. The mentally "retarded" climbed at less than the average rate, whereas the mentally "gifted" skipped steps and rose more rapidly than the norm.

A second underlying conception of modernity was that of *universality*. The emergence of science, the scientific method, and the reliance on observation and experiment was encouraged by the modern belief that nature, rather than religious or imperial authority, was the only source of knowledge and truth. Nature was assumed to operate according to universal laws that could be discovered by diligent research. The scientific belief in universal natural laws was supported by such systematic descriptions of regularities as the Newtonian laws of gravitation, the periodic table of the elements, and the Darwinian principles of evolution.

The notion of universality was also incorporated into the modern conception of the child. Educators accepted the doctrine of "formal discipline," according to which the study of Greek, Latin, and mathematics was an effective method of training *all* children to think logically and rationally. Later, with the emergence of the social sciences, universality was given a scientific imprimatur. Educational psychology, like psychology as a whole, assumed that there were universal laws of learning that held across all species and that were the same for rats as they were for children and for adults. Rat psychology led to endless controversies over such issues as the benefits of *mass* versus *distributed learning and the extent of transfer of training.* Using human subjects, memory was studied by means of nonsense syllables so that content would not interfere with observation of the universal memory process. Problem solving was thought to involve only trial and error or insight, inasmuch as these were the processes employed by cats and chimpanzees in their attempts to remove barriers to desired goals.

The last undergirding assumption of the modern world was that of *regularity*. Nature was lawful, and the task of science was to uncover this lawfulness. As Einstein phrased this belief, "God does not play dice with the universe." Unlawful phenomena, from this perspective, were simply phenomena that had yet to be explained or could be explained at another "level." Irregular (unlawful) phenotypes, for example, could be explained by regular (lawful) genotypes. Taking the same "levels" approach to causality, Freud argued that slips of the tongue and pen (unlawful occurrences) could be explained by deeper-level unconscious (lawful) wishes and desires.

The idea of lawfulness was also assimilated into the modern conception of a child nature. Intelligence testing demonstrated that, although children varied considerably in their intellectual abilities, these abilities were nonetheless distributed according to the normal curve of probability. They were thus lawful phenomena. Many of children's behavior disorders were also explained according to the "levels" notion of causality. Seemingly idiosyncratic learning disabilities were frequently attributed to an underlying lawfulness, namely, "minimal brain damage." Thus children's observable irregular, unpredictable surface behavior could be explained by an underlying lawful relation between the human brain and human action.

Postmodernity, the Particular Child, and Postmodern Education

Postmodernism arose as a critique of modern ideas and as an effort to correct some of the overly idealistic and romantic views of the world that they created. In this century, after two world wars, the Holocaust, the atom bomb, the degradation of the environment, and the exploitation of the earth's natural resources, it is difficult to hold to the modern conception of progress as an unbroken march toward a better world and a more humane society. Even the progress toward individual freedom and self-fulfillment that did occur was often limited to certain groups (white, Anglo-Saxon males) and did not extend to women or to minorities. To be sure, progress still happens—say, in the conquest of disease—but it is particular and domain-specific rather than holding true for all of humanity.

What has come to the fore in postmodern times is the awareness of the importance of *difference*. In the modern era, difference was often seen from the standpoint of superiority. Non-Western societies, as an illustration, were regarded as inferior to Western "civilizations" because they had not progressed as far. This notion of superiority was implicit in the concept of the United States of America as a "melting pot" in which people (inferior) cultures would be melted down and then poured into a mold from which each would be dropped out as a purified, standard American. Today, however, we recognize that people do not melt and that other cultures, ethnic groups, and races are to be appreciated and valued rather than dissolved into some common amalgam. The postmodern conception of America as a cultural, ethnic, and racial "rainbow" celebrates the valuation of difference, in contrast to the feeling of superiority inherent in the modern conceptions of social progress and of the melting pot.

Unfortunately, the idea of progress is still omnipresent in education. Nonetheless, the appreciation of difference is beginning to make some headway. The new provisions for children with disabilities and for those who come to school with English as a second language are evidence that the needs of these "different" children are at last being recognized—if not fully or properly attended to. In other domains, such as the introduction of multicultural, gender-fair, and anti-bias curricula, the acceptance of difference has met more resistance in the schools and in the local communities. But the very fact that matters of race, gender, and ethnicity are not being openly talked about reflects a new, more accepting climate for a wide range of human differences.

Just as the conception of progress was challenged by the evidence of lack of progress, the assumption of universality has also undergone revision. This is particularly true in the social sciences. When Friedrich Nietzsche, an early postmodernist, proclaimed the death of God, he was railing against metaphysics and those who exploited the belief in universal supernatural beings.[7] In a similar tone, when Michel Foucault wrote about the end of man, he was arguing against the metaphysical idea of a universal human nature and for a fuller and deeper appreciation of human individuality.[8]

And the universals of social science are proving to be less than transcendent. The "grand" social/economic theories such as those of Marx and Engels have turned out to be less than prophetic and universal. Likewise, the "grand" histories of Spengler and Toynbee now appear as flawed individual theories of history rather than as discovered universal principles of societal progression. In a similar way, the recapitulation theory—which posited that the individual in his or her development recapitulates the development of the species—can no longer be maintained. While there are still universals, particularly in the physical and biological sciences, they are much less common in the social sciences, where particularity is more likely to be the rule.

The importance of particularity, as opposed to universals, is already being recognized in education. We now appreciate that different species learn in different ways and that, even within the same species, there are differences in learning *styles*.[9] We also recognize that different subject matters require their own specific learning strategies. The idea that there are "domain-specific" modes of learning has almost completely displaced the universal ideas of "formal discipline" and of "transfer of training." When we do encounter what appear to be universals in human behavior, they are often closely linked to maturational (biological child) characteristics, such as the Piagetian stages.[10]

Finally, the modern assumption of regularity and lawfulness has been modified by the postmodern acceptance of the normality of *irregularity*. We acknowledge today that some phenomena, such as the weather, are inherently irregular. So too are phenomena such as the dispersion of cream in a coffee cup. Each time we place cream in a coffee cup, the dispersion pattern is different from what it was before. Some phenomena are, by nature, chaotic and have no underlying regularity. The *DSM IV* definition of Attention Deficit Hyperactivity Disorder (ADHD) as involving any four or five out of 18 neurological, behavioral, or attentional symptoms is a recognition that this disorder has no underlying regularity. Likewise, the implementation of multi-age grouping in some schools is tacit acceptance of the fact that development is irregular and that we need flexible classroom arrangements to deal with the "normal irregularity" of growth.

The Modern Child in the Postmodern World

Although the postmodern conception of the child as different, particular, and irregular has been assimilated into some educational conceptions and practices, the modern conception of the child as progressive, universal, and lawful remains alive and well in many others. The following are but a few examples of the persistence of modern conceptions in contemporary educational practice.

Progress. The modern belief that children should progress uniformly through the grades is causing a major problem in kindergarten and first grade. At the heart of the problem is the fact that, in the postmodern world, the majority of children (about 85%) enter school after having been enrolled in one or another early childhood program. As a consequence, schools have tightened standards and now demand that all children know their letters and numbers before being accepted into the first-grade classroom. This demand is based on the modern assumption of a common child nature such that all children of the same age will profit equally from whatever type of early childhood program they have experienced.

Yet the truth lies elsewhere. The early childhood years, roughly from age 3 to age 8, are a period of rapid intellectual growth comparable to the period of rapid physical growth of early adolescence. At such times individual differences in growth rates are most evident. With adolescents, for example, some reach their full height at 13, some at 14, some at 15, and some at 16. They may all end up being the same height, but they get there at different rates. The same is true for young children's intellectual growth. Some may attain Piaget's concrete operations at 4, some at 5, some at 6, and some at 7. They will all attain concrete operations, but at different rates—even if they have the same intellectual ability. Because these operations are a necessary prerequisite to learning numbers and letters, children of the same intellectual ability will differ widely in their ability to acquire tool skills. Moreover, different early childhood programs vary widely in the extent to which they work on tool skills.

Because of these wide individual differences in growth rate and early childhood experience, children of school age vary tremendously in their readiness for formal instruction. As a consequence, in many communities some 10% to 20% of the children are being retained or placed in transition classes, and in some school districts the numbers are as high as 50%. This is a case in which a postmodern phenomenon—large numbers of children in early childhood programs—has elicited a modern notion of a common child nature that is having dysfunctional educational outcomes for large numbers of young children.

In a similar way, because of the belief that young people progress in a uniform fashion, there is little or no accommodation of the rather abrupt changes that come about in early adolescence. The middle school concept is supposed to speak more directly to the different needs of this age group,[11] but many middle schools are such in name only. Like the junior high school, misnamed middle schools fail to incorporate the team teaching, extended class times, and integrated curricula envisioned by the inventors of the middle school. The idea that children progress in uniform fashion throughout the grades dies hard, despite abundant knowledge of the differential growth spurts that characterize early adolescence as well as early childhood.

Unfortunately, the postmodern appreciation of difference is sometimes grafted onto modern ideas of progress and, as a result, is completely undermined. A case in point is the current emphasis on "inclusion" of children with special needs in the regular classroom. This practice frequently takes away from the child the special individuality that he or she has just been given. Too often, children are included without sufficient remedial support for

teachers and with too little regard to the appropriateness of inclusion of a given child in a particular classroom. Moreover, there is not accommodation to the fact that some children, such as those with spina bifida, may benefit from inclusion when they are young but not when they are teenagers. Nor is sufficient attention being paid to the number and variety of special-needs children in any given classroom. With too many special-needs children in a class, the teacher is overwhelmed and may not be able to meet the needs of other students. With too few special-needs children, the special child may stand out too much. Inclusion can be beneficial, but not for all children in all circumstances at all ages and in all ratios.

Universality. The universality component of the modern conception of the child is also difficult to dislodge. The current efforts to establish national standards presuppose that all children can attain the same standards. To be sure, those who are making up the assessment devices are making an effort to include not only quantitative tests but also qualitative measures such as portfolios, products, and performance.[12] Yet qualitative methods of assessment speak to the particularity of achievement rather than to its universality. Different children will attain and express their literacy in different ways. The real challenge of national standards, and one that has yet to be met, is how to reconcile assessments that presuppose individual differences—such as portfolios, projects, and performance—with assessments that presuppose uniformity, namely, standardized tests.

The idea of universality is also taken for granted by educational publishing, which provides standard textbooks with little acknowledgement of individual differences in learning styles, pace of learning, and so on. Publishers assume that it is the teachers' responsibility to individualize, but why should this be so? Those publishers who produce a "teacher-proof" curriculum of complete, day-to-day lesson plans and materials also presuppose a commonality or universality of learning. Yet the assumption of such universality is completely at variance with the diversity within even the most homogeneously grouped class. Educational publishers must begin to address the particularity of teachers and learners and the domain-specific nature of learning strategies. They also need to field-test their materials before they publish them.

Irregularity. While the new definition of ADHD and the introduction of multi-age grouping in some states and com-

munities are bows to the presence of irregularity, the belief in an underlying regularity is tenacious. Programs such as Benjamin Bloom's mastery learning, Madeline Hunter's model of effective teaching, Arthur Costa's program for teaching critical thinking, and Edward de Bono's CoRT all assume that learning is a regular process or, at least, that its products are.[13] As Richard Gibboney documents, all these innovations have been shown to be no more successful than the programs already in place.[14] One reason is that all these initiatives are founded on modern notions of learning as universal, progressive, and lawful.

From an individual (psychological child) perspective, however, learning is always a creative activity. The learner takes something from himself or herself, something from the external world, and puts them together into a product that cannot be reduced either to the learner or to the experience. Creativity, whether in classroom learning or in the arts or in the sciences, is necessarily chaotic and irregular. The artist cannot fully explain his or her art any more than the scientist can explain his or her insights. Portfolios, projects, and performance make sense only from the perspective of learning as an individual creative process.

To be sure, there are basic skills and common knowledge that all children must acquire. Sometimes the individual must subordinate his or her individual bent to acquire basic tools of the language, concepts and mores of the culture, and so on. But this is only part of learning, not the whole process. And even such learning always has an individual coloration. Put differently, the focus on mastery, skills, and outcomes acknowledges only the accommodative side of learning and totally ignores its assimilative, creative dimension. We need to encourage and to assess both types of learning.

Although we have yet to fully appreciate the fact, the classroom is a chaotic phenomenon as well. Each time a group meets, each member of the group is in some ways different from the time the group met before. Each has had experiences that no other member of the group has encountered. In many ways, every class meeting is like every dispersion of cream in a coffee cup. This does not mean that we cannot or should not study classrooms—only that we should explore them as irregular, chaotic, and social (not as recurring physical) events. Educational research, as long as it operates according to the modern idea of regularity, will fail to capture the true dynamics of classroom interactions.

Summary and Conclusion

I have briefly reviewed here the modern and postmodern conceptions of the child and the educational practices that follow from those conceptions. The modern conception confused and merged the universal biological child with the individual psychological child. While this identification of the two different conceptions of child nature was probably necessary to the establishment of free public education, it is often a hindrance to effective contemporary educational practice. Despite a growing recognition of children as different, as particular, and as irregular, the modern conception of child nature as progressive, universal, and regular still dominates educational theory and practice. In this article, I have given only a few of the many possible examples to illustrate how modern ideas continue to undermine effective pedagogy and authentic education reform.

For purposes of space, I have limited my discussion to those aspects of education that revolve around the conception of a common child nature. Postmodern ideas, however, have implications for many other educational issues. I have already addressed the issue of school and family from this perspective,[15] but it also has implications for teacher training, curricula, school organization, and so on that cannot be dealt with here. But rethinking the conception of child nature seems a useful starting point for a broader and more wide-ranging critique of modern education.

In closing, it is important to emphasize that I am not arguing that everything postmodern is good and that everything modern is bad. There is much to be valued in modern education. Many of our foremost educational innovators were already quite postmodern. This is certainly true of John Dewey, whose project method foreshadowed the integrated curriculum.[16] It is equality true of Maria Montessori, whose recognition of young children's learning ability is now accepted in our postmodern perception of childhood competence.[17] Likewise, Jean Piaget's contention that children create their reality out of their experiences with the environment[18] is echoed in the postmodern view that all concepts are human constructions, not copies of a preexisting reality. Becoming postmodern in education, therefore, often means gaining a truer and deeper appreciation of the educational innovators of modernity.

1. Clyde Kluckhohn and Henry A. Murray, "Personality Formation: The Determinants," in idem, eds., *Personality in Nature, Society, and Culture* (New York: Knopf, 1950), pp. 35–48.
2. See, for example, Steven Connor, *Postmodern Culture* (Oxford: Basil Blackwell, 1989); and Steven Best and Douglas Kellner, *Postmodern Theory* (New York: Guilford, 1991).
3. Henry Giroux, "Postmodernism and the Discourse of Educational Criticism," *Journal of Education*, vol. 170, no. 3, 1988, pp. 6–29; and Stanley Aronowitz and Henry Giroux, *Postmodern Education* (Minneapolis: University of Minnesota Press, 1991).
4. See, for example, James Comer, "Educating Poor Minority Children," *Scientific American*, vol. 295, no. 5, 1988, pp. 42–48; and Theodore Sizer, *Horace's School: Redesigning the American High School* (Boston: Houghton Mifflin, 1992).
5. John Locke, *Some Thoughts Concerning Education*, in Charles Eliot, ed., *The Harvard Classics* (New York: Collier, 1930), pp. 9–200.
6. Jean-Jacques Rousseau, *Emile*, trans. W. Payne (New York: Appleton, 1911).
7. Friedrich Nietzsche, *Thus Spoke Zarathustra* (New York: Viking, 1966).
8. Michel Foucault, *The Order of Things* (New York: Vintage, 1973).
9. Thomas Debello, "Comparison of Eleven Major Learning Style Models: Variables, Appropriate Populations, Validity of Instrumentation, and the Research Behind Them," *Journal of Reading, Writing, and Learning Disabilities International*, vol. 6, 1990, pp. 203–22.
10. Jean Piaget, *The Psychology of Intelligence* (London: Routledge & Kegan Paul, 1950).
11. See, for example, Task Force on Education of Young Adolescents, *Turning Points: Preparing American Youth for the 21st Century* (Washington, D.C.: Carnegie Council on Adolescent Development, 1989); and Jeffrey Wiles and James Bondi, *The Essential Middle School*, 2nd ed. (New York: Macmillan, 1993).
12. Gary Sykes and Phillip Plastrik, *Standard Setting and Educational Reform* (Washington, D.C.: ERIC Clearinghouse on Teacher Education, 1993).
13. Benjamin Bloom, *Human Characteristics and School Learning* (New York: McGraw-Hill, 1976); Madeline Hunter, "Knowing, Teaching, and Supervision," in Peter L. Hosford, 3d., *Using What We Know About Teaching* (Alexandria, Va.: Association for Supervision and Curriculum Development, 1984), pp. 165–76; Arthur L. Costa, *Developing Minds* (Alexandria, Va.: Association for Supervision and Curriculum Development, 1985); and Edward de Bono, *CoRT Program* (San Diego: Pergamon Press, 1988).
14. Richard A. Gibboney, *The Stone Trumpet* (Albany: State University of New York Press, 1994).
15. David Elkind, "School and Family in the Postmodern World," *Phi Delta Kappan*, September 1995, pp. 8–14.
16. John Dewey, *The Child and the Curriculum/The School and Society* (1915; reprint, Chicago: University of Chicago Press, 1956).
17. Maria Montessori, *The Absorbent Mind* (New York: Delta, 1967).
18. Jean Piaget, *Science of Education and the Psychology of the Child* (New York: Viking, 1969).

Teaching Television to Empower Students

David B. Owen, Charles L. P. Silet, and Sarah E. Brown

One of the most effective ways to cultivate cooperative learning is to teach television. When you teach television, you can transform the dynamics of the traditional classroom where the teacher knows the subject, the students do not, and motivation is always an issue. Effective teachers have always been able to create a motivating connection between their subject matter and the students' world. With television, however, that connection is already present, and the teacher's role is to use and shape an existing interest, not create it in the first place.

As we all know, students enter the classroom with thousands of hours of viewing experience, the raw data of television, and teachers come with knowledge of the analytic and critical skills that can transform students' preconceived attitudes toward television into real understanding of the medium.

WHAT DO STUDENTS KNOW?

We find that the best way to begin media analysis is to have our students complete an inventory of their viewing and reading habits. In the first class meeting we pass out a two-page questionnaire in which we ask them to provide us information about what they read and view aside from school assignments. The purpose of this is both for us to learn which media sources our students consume and, equally important, for our students to become aware of how they gain access to information and entertainment.

For instance, we ask about the books, newspapers, and magazines they read. We are interested in both the frequency (often, occasionally, rarely, never) as well as the specific titles. We also ask them about movies (in theaters and on videos), concerts (popular and classical), theater, CDs purchased and listened to, radio, any source from which they derive information or entertainment. Finally, we ask them about their television-viewing habits: what shows they watch, how often, and who their favorite television personalities are. We even inquire whether they take the trouble to record shows they cannot see when broadcast, such as soap operas.

This gives us a reasonably detailed knowledge of our students' media exposure, which provides us with a context within which to communicate with our students about the media world they inhabit.

Periodically we ask the students to participate in more directed television viewing. We ask them to keep a video log for a week in which they not only list the shows they watch but also comment on the characters and themes and on their reactions to them. While the media surveys listed above are general in nature, these logs are much more formally directed and detailed and can be used for class discussion and reflection.

Our students are experienced consumers of television. How can we harness their expertise?

rected and detailed and can be used for class discussion and reflection.

Finally, we conduct another kind of survey when we are through teaching television and ask our students some evaluative questions concerning how their viewing habits have changed. For instance, we ask them, "When you watch television now, how is the experience different than before?" We also ask students if they notice a difference in their television viewing habits: do they watch different shows, are there shows they no longer watch, do they watch more or less television now, and so on. In general, this last survey allows us to judge how successful our teaching has been and also indicates to the students how their critical viewing skills have empowered them.

THREE PRINCIPLES

We have discovered that teaching television is a circular process which revolves around three principles. First, most students have preconceived viewing habits which lead them to believe that television is essentially "just entertainment." Second, students must change their initial viewing habits in order to become critical viewers. And third, if students develop active, critical viewing habits, they will come of their own accord to begin to understand the breadth and subtlety of televi-

sion's power and the serious personal and cultural consequences it has for all of us.

Television as Entertainment

Most students come to school having watched an extraordinary amount and variety of television. They have a stupefying amount of what we call "telinfo" (television information). For instance, they bring the ability to sing or whistle theme songs from shows like "Friends" or "The Simpsons" or "The Brady Bunch" as well as advertising jingles like "You deserve a break today" (McDonalds). They can instantly recognize products' slogans ("Just do it!" [Coke] "Pizza! Pizza! [Little Caesar's Pizza]), logos (the Swoosh [Nike]), color associations ("If it's yellow, it's Cheerios!" "If it's orange, it's Wheaties!"). They know in extraordinary detail the history of their favorite television characters and their relations with other characters (what they wear, what they eat, who their friends are and have been, what they do, favorite expressions). Because stu-

SELECTED READINGS

Abercrombie, N. 1996. *Television and Society.* Cambridge, MA: Polity Press. A textbook designed to introduce students to the role of television in a contemporary society. Explores the structure of the television text, the way in which that text is produced, and the way it is consumed.

Barbour, W., ed. 1994. *Mass Media: Opposing Viewpoints.* San Diego, CA: Greenhaven Press. Part of the "Opposing Viewpoints" series, it takes an issue dealing with mass media and presents both sides using two essays, one representing each viewpoint, often from the popular press.

Dunn, J. L. 1994. "Teaching Television Watchers." *Instructor* 103: 50–54. Geared for children, this piece includes activities to help address the needs and behaviors of a generation brought up on television and resources to help you do this.

Fehlman, R. H. 1992. "Making Meanings Visible: Critically Reading TV." *English Journal* 81.7 (Nov.): 19–24. An in-depth discussion of how one teacher has taught students to analyze television critically. He hopes that these modes of inquiry will be options, that they will be companions to literary criticism, and that they will value student voice, error and experience.

Flint-Ferguson, J. 1995. "And Now, a Word from Our Sponsors." *English Journal* 84.2 (Feb.): 107–110. A "Teaching Ideas" section of *EJ*, it lists many activities for teaching about advertising in both print and non-print media.

Minow, N. N. and C. L. Lamay. 1995. *Abandoned in the Wasteland: Children, Television, and the First Amendment.* New York: Hill and Wang. The product of a study conducted for the American Academy of Arts and Sciences. Explores the "vast wasteland" (Mi-

now introduced the term) our children have been left in because of the commercial interests which dominate television.

Morris, B. S. 1993. "Two Dimensions of Teaching Television Literacy: Analyzing Television Content and Analyzing Television Viewing." *Canadian Journal of Educational Communication* 22: 37–45. An approach to teaching television literacy in the classroom based on forming a research question about television text, hypothesizing, logging, and categorizing data and finally presenting the findings using evidence. Viewer analysis is also conducted.

Newcomb, H. 1994. *Television: The Critical View,* Fifth edition. New York: Oxford University Press. A sophisticated collection of academic, critical essays on television and its place in popular culture.

Palmer, E. L. 1988. *Television & America's Children: A Crisis of Neglect.* New York: Oxford University Press. A simply written, mildly critical overview of the influence television has on children.

Sorenson, M. 1989. "Television: Developing the Critical Viewer and Writer." *English Journal* 78.8: 42–46. Describes a unit on developing a critical viewer. The author offers extensive information about teaching advertising, especially in identifying the audience and emotional appeals, and on teaching the news.

Weedman, R. Z. 1988. "Mass Appeal: Pop Culture in the Composition Classroom." *English Journal* 77.7: 96–97. A rationale for using pop culture, such as television, in the classroom. Reasons cited include student expertise and classroom cohesiveness.

Witkin, M. 1994. "A Defense of Using Pop Media in the Middle-School Classroom." *English Journal* 83.1: 30–33. Rationalizes using pop culture in the classroom. Describes in detail many of the ways pop culture is incorporated in her classroom, some of which specifically deal with television.

dents know so much detail, they think they already understand television.

Change of Viewing Habits

Our first task, consequently, is to jolt our students out of their customary viewing habits and help them develop a reflective attitude. We do that by starting quite simply. We begin teaching television by having the students analyze color magazine advertisements, for instance, ones for Stetson perfume, a Mont Blanc fountain pen, and a Dodge automobile. We project a color image of the ad and ask the students to do two things. First, we have them describe without any analysis, commentary, or evaluation what they see and write those things down individually. Then, in a class discussion, we ask them to use their lists to say what they see and write their observations on the board. We keep asking them, whatever they respond, "What else?," until they have fairly exhausted describing the ad. As we have already said, at this stage we do not allow students to use any evaluative language in their descriptions.

The next step, after establishing this exhaustive description, is to have students begin to analyze and evaluate what they see. Once again we have them make a list, this time of what the various details *mean* to the viewer, and then share their insights in a class discussion. For example, in the fountain pen ad, where in their first list they would mention merely that the decoration on the pen was of a gold color, in the second list they might comment that the gold suggests something about wealth, status, power, and so on. In addition, they might observe that the gold color also appears elsewhere in the ad, as on the pen's tip and the reflection along the barrel, which thereby not only shapes the ad's meaning but also its composition as a whole. We tend to spend 30 to 45 minutes on this single exercise.

When we are through, students often comment that they had no idea one could look at a single picture meaningfully in such detail and depth. This simple ad exercise, then, provides a paradigm for how to look at all visual images, including television. It also exemplifies the three guidelines which we have formulated from our experience and which help us shape our pedagogy:

1. start with the students' own experience and perceptions;

2. move from the simple to the complex;
3. shift the students' viewing from passive to active.

This initial exercise begins the process of transforming viewing habits from a casual, uncritical acceptance of visual material to a more attentive, analytical questioning of what is being presented to them. This is essential for creating visual literacy.

Recognition of Television's Power

For our students to reach the point where they can recognize television's sophisticated messages, they must become active, critical, reflective viewers. The catch phrase we use to describe our two-step learning process is "What do you see, and what does it mean?"

The second step is to develop habits of critical viewing. Once students are seeing more detail, then we repeatedly encourage them to interpret what this detail means. For example, again in the same activity, the insights growing out of cooperative interaction reveals a much greater complexity of meaning than what they as individuals had first noted. As students become better observers and learn to analyze what they have observed, they will spontaneously come to recognize that television is a powerful cultural force. Once sensitized to viewing critically, they are never again able, as they frequently tell us, "to watch television in the same way." When we start hearing students volunteer this observation, we know that by working together we have all succeeded.

A SAMPLE UNIT

After having surveyed our students' viewing experience and having completed the exercise on viewing print advertisements, students are ready to move on to use the same process but apply it now to advertisements that appear on television, advertisements which incorporate all of the visual materials from the print medium but add to them the qualities of movement and sound. Since ads "tell a story," we begin focusing on questions of narrative that the visual produces, and the examination of narrative becomes one of the foundations of our approach to television. As the students soon learn, this is a vastly more complicated visual experience to understand.

From the ads we move on to an examination of news broadcasts—local, national, PBS, CNN, "60 Minutes," "Nightline," "20/20," etc. From there we turn to dramas. We begin with soap operas because their deliberate narrative and visual pacing makes them the most accessible drama to analyze. Next we examine the increasingly complex world of drama from shows like "Dr. Quinn, Medicine Woman" to the more visually and thematically sophisticated shows like "ER," "NYPD Blue," "Homicide," or "The X-Files." We complete the unit by looking at situation comedies, which we have found to be the most difficult for our students to take seriously enough to analyze. We examine sitcoms all the way from the animated "Simpsons," with their cartoon characters, through "Seinfeld" and "Friends" to the much more complex and socially critical comedies like the recently concluded "Roseanne."

We have discovered that this progression of genres from ads to news to dramas to sitcoms is important in developing our students' willingness to take television seriously enough to give it the critical attention it deserves. Students *know* ads are manipulating them, but they discover right at the beginning how much more extensively and subtly they are doing so than they first suspected. News programs, from the students' perspective, are by definition serious television since they give us the "facts" about our world. Here, again, their analysis reveals to them how complex the relation is between the viewer and what is on the screen, how the "facts" of the news program are shaped by the ways in which they are selected and presented.

Students are now ready to deal with the even more complex and problematic programming of "fictional" television. Because dramas obviously take on serious issues such as crime, poverty, sexuality, family relationships, and other social issues, students are open to the idea that these programs have meaning beyond their entertainment value.

Finally, we save comedy for last because students have the most difficulty in seeing the social content and "seriousness" there. Our experience is that by following this sequence, students are ready on their own initiative at the end to watch comedy shows more closely, think about what they see, and recognize that they are more than just a way to pass time. Past episodes of "Roseanne," for instance, are not only funny but also are richly nuanced presentations of genuine problems that the students are actually encountering in their everyday worlds.

Student Activities

Students actively engage in selecting and evaluating television examples. We as teachers may choose the genres to be studied and the general approach, but students select specific shows to work with within those broad categories. Students seem much more motivated when they can pick shows they feel they know something about and then, by analyzing them in detail, learn that the shows are much more complex than they had originally believed. We also have students work in groups both when analyzing and when presenting their findings. Our experience has been that this active approach is essential for students to develop true media literacy.

Student Contracts

Each student submits a contract which indicates his/her commitment to the unit based on one of the following conditions:

1. I will choose four shows which all appear in the same time slot but on different channels, e.g., Thursday at 7:00 p.m. on ABC, CBS, NBC, FOX, or PBS.
2. I will choose four shows which all fall under the same category. At least two will appear at different time slots. I will choose one of the following categories: news, drama (crime shows, medical shows, lawyer shows), soap opera (daytime), melodrama (evening), science fiction, situation comedy, sports, MTV, talk show, or verisimilitude (tabloid journalism).
3. I will choose four different shows which all appear during a specific block of time, say, two hours (for example, weekdays from 7:00–9:00 a.m. or 3:00–5:00 p.m.), and I will make inferences about what characterizes this time frame.
4. Whichever choice I make, I will prepare a written report which summarizes my understanding of the shows, their relationships, and the consequences for television viewers.

Analysis of Show

Following the submission of this commitment, students prepare to bring to each cooperative learning/discussion group meeting an analysis of one of their shows which is based on questions such as these:

1. What is the plot of the show? Write a concise plot summary.

2. What is the audience focus of this show? Age? Sex? Education? Economic status? Primary interests? Occupation? Size of audience? Social group?
3. Is this the appropriate viewing audience? Why or why not? What is the appropriate viewing audience?
4. What emotional appeals do the producers of the show use to get its viewers "hooked," e.g., power, family life, humor, drama, vicarious living, emotions?
5. How is violence portrayed in this show? Is it appropriate? Is it realistic?
6. How is sex portrayed in this show? Is it appropriate? Is it realistic?
7. How does the show address issues of diversity, racism, and sexism?
8. Are these accurate depictions of society and real life?
9. How can you tell the difference between fantasy and fiction in this show?
10. What have you learned by analyzing this show? Write a brief summary, including what surprised you, what angered you, and whether your opinion of this show has changed. Use specific evidence to support your answers.

In addition to such higher-order thinking, students use specific techniques first practiced in class such as these: taking notes on scratch

There appears to be a direct, inverse relation between the decline in professional attention to television and its ascent in cultural influence.

paper while watching; viewing the show more than once; paying close attention to commercials for audience focus; rewinding and replaying specific areas of the show; keeping tallies of violent acts, sexually explicit content, or inaccurate depiction of diversity issues regarding gender, race, and class; and asking someone else's opinion, such as talking about findings with others or watching the show with a friend or family member.

Discussion Topics

Given this individual preparation, the learning/discussion groups meet four times.

Each meeting serves as a cooperative effort to answer questions pertaining to a different focus topic for that meeting. This is important so that students are continually building upon their knowledge and covering in depth these four "core" areas. The four topics follow.

Meeting One: Advertising. How did advertising affect your viewing? Who was the target audience? How did it fit into the program that you were watching? Was it effective? Was it misleading? Come to a group consensus about the role of advertising in television based on each individual's work and the group's discussion. Use specific examples from both to support answers.

Meeting Two: Diversity. How were the issues of diversity handled in the shows watched? What kind of ethnic groups were represented? Were they treated fairly? Were their roles realistic? Was one particular race or ethnic group always playing the same role? How does that make you feel? What does this say about our society? Come to a group consensus about the way the television industry treats different races and ethnic groups based on each individual's work and the group's discussion. Use specific examples from both to support answers.

Meeting Three: Gender Roles. How were the issues of gender roles handled in the shows watched? What roles did men play? Women? Are they realistic? Are they fair? Do they accurately reflect society? Does the portrayal of gender roles on television influence the way people perceive roles in real life? Come to a group consensus about the way television treats the sexes based on each individual's work and the group's discussion. Use specific examples from both to support answers.

Meeting Four: Violence and Sex. How are violence and sex portrayed in the shows watched? Were they portrayed together? What do we learn about sex and violence from the television? How are we supposed to know what is real and what is not real? What is acceptable and what is not acceptable? Does television accurately reflect society's view of violence and sex? Come to a group consensus about the way violence and sex are portrayed on television based on each individual's work and the group's discussion. Use specific examples from both to support answers.

When the groups meet, each member of the group has a specific job. A *recorder* is responsible for filling out the group's answers on the worksheet to be turned in. An *instigator* is responsible for keeping the discussion moving along and monitoring the time. A *questioner* is the "devil's advocate" in the discussion, questioning and probing those who are talking. Finally, a *reporter* is responsible for sharing with the class as a whole some of the most interesting things the group discussed. In addition, each group is to prepare a written report of its findings on each of the topics.

STUDENT PROJECTS

In addition to the genre and topical activities listed above, innumerable other kinds of projects are possible.

Epitaphs: Students construct two epitaphs, putting to rest a television show they have analyzed. The epitaphs are to contain style techniques from a poet they had recently studied. Of the two epitaph creations, one is to be transformed into a symbolic and representative gravestone.

Pilot show based on short-story techniques: Students create a pilot for a sitcom or drama using aspects of short story construction such as plot, character, setting, fantasy and escape, and imagination. After writing their pilot, they find actors, produce and edit it. They must take into consideration all aspects of the television process: advertising, camera angles, lighting, sound, and so on.

Transcript exercise: In order to help make students aware of the powerful images they see on television, students transcribe a talk show or sitcom. Have students first read portions of the transcript, then watch the actual footage. Compare and contrast the differences between the written text and the text as performed.

Role-play and conflict management: Take a scene from a sitcom or drama. Set it up in class and have students role-play a realistic outcome. Other student "observers" pay close attention to how the conflict is resolved and whether it is resolved realistically. Then watch the clip from the actual television show. Does the role-play mirror the way the situation was resolved on television? Is either realistic? Does television even influence how students solve problems in their real lives?

Plan a day's programming. Students must plan one entire programming day for a television station. It should be programmed in terms of an "ideal" broadcast day. They must take into consideration FCC regulations of quality children's programming and what kind of advertising they will allow and when.

They may want to cancel shows they feel are harmful to children or change time slots of adult programming to later hours. Finally, they may create their own plot lines for shows which they feel need a voice on their station.

GETTING STARTED TO TEACH TELEVISION

We make three suggestions.

First, you have to know what is on television. Even if you do not watch much television, the vast majority of your students do. So, you must have some general notion of what shows are on, when they appear, who is in them, and what they are about. You need to have some familiarity with sitcoms, evening dramas, soap operas, talk shows, game shows, sports, news, advertising, the lot. This way you can demonstrate your knowledge of your subject in class and be able to respond intelligently to students' observations about the shows they watch. You should not feel compelled to know *more* than your students do about various shows because, quite frankly, you probably will not be able to do so. Nevertheless, you need to demonstrate a "good faith" effort to understand the media world that they live in.

Second, you need to read about television. This you can do on three levels. On the easiest level, read the articles on television that appear in the daily newspaper. Some of them will simply be celebrity profiles, others might describe a new show, while still others might provide items of information, such as discussions of violence on television or the new ratings system. On a more sophisticated level you can also find in the popular press extended critiques and analyses of individual shows, of series, of trends, of the industry as a whole, and so on. Lastly, a body of criticism published in professional journals examines television from a variety of intellectual disciplines: aesthetics, psychology, cultural studies, sociology, etc. These journal articles can provide background and a diversity of approaches that will help you develop your own critical viewing skills.

Third, you need to be sensitive that critically examining television may involve controversy. Prepare yourself, your administrators, and the parents of your students for whatever examination of television you intend to pursue. Discuss with the appropriate administrators what you plan to do so that both you and they can be aware of potential problems. It is important to realize that some parents greatly restrict the television their children watch, censor it, or even forbid watching it. These restrictions can arise for religious, moral, or practical reasons; and, of course, they need to be addressed. In your planning, you may need to provide alternative activities at various points to accommodate any students who might, for whatever reason, have restrictions on viewing. As always in the public schools, teachers walk a very fine line between challenging students and alienating their parents. You need to remember that television is a "hot-button" topic.

CONCLUSION

Almost every large-scale analysis of education from the 1960s on to the current administration's Department of Education report, *Strong Families, Strong Schools: Building Community Partnerships for Learning* (1994, Washington, DC: U.S. Department of Education), mentions the central importance of children's television viewing as one of the most powerful—possibly *the* most powerful—factors in developing their definitions of self and connection with the world. If television is largely responsible for forming the students who populate our nation's classrooms, should not we, as educators, be training ourselves and

our students to understand and cope with the power of the medium?

Since its beginnings after World War II, television has attracted the attention of educators, social critics, and the public. In the 1970s, however, the number of critical commentaries began to decline, and with the widespread use of the personal computer in the 1980s, focus has largely shifted away from television's cultural role. Yet, there appears to be a direct, inverse relation between the decline in professional attention to television and its ascent in cultural influence. We all are convinced that television today is the most powerful educator in America. Therefore, we think it needs to be viewed with the greatest attention and concern, and to develop such reflective viewing we need to make television studies a routine, perhaps central, part of public education. Either we empower ourselves and our students by understanding television or television will retain its power over us.

Note

We want to acknowledge the help of Julie Freed and Robert Yuetz, who read an earlier version of our essay and provided a number of helpful suggestions.

David P. Owen, Charles L. P. Silet, and Sarah E. Brown teach at Iowa State University in Ames, Iowa.

School phobias hold many children back

It takes a team effort to help children overcome fear of school.

By Bridget Murray
Monitor staff

As millions of school children head back to school this month, many eagerly await reuniting with friends and starting new academic challenges. But others bemoan leaving the comfort of home for the trials of school—a place where they might wear the wrong clothes or give the wrong answer in class. Some even refuse to go, throwing tantrums or complaining of stomachaches, headaches or nausea.

These children suffer from what's commonly known as school phobia, although many psychologists prefer calling it school refusal. Affecting between 5 percent and 10 percent of U.S. school children in its mildest form—and 1 percent of them in its severest form—the phobia can lead to serious problems with school absenteeism, psychologists say.

Chronic absence puts students at risk for psychological problems later

PUBLIC SCHOOL № 13

JOHN MICHAEL YANSON

in life, such as alcohol abuse and criminal behavior, as well as underemployment and even marital difficulties, says psychologist Christopher Kearney, PhD, a school refusal researcher at the University of Nevada, Las Vegas.

Broadly defined, school phobia is anxiety and fear related to being in school. In addition to throwing tantrums and feigning sickness, other typical school-refusal behaviors include panic attacks, crying, shyness, unhappiness, demands for parental attention, petulance and clinginess, psychologists report.

Most often the problems emerge after children have had long breaks from school, says Kearney. As their vacation dwindles to an end, some children dread the return to peers, teachers and homework. They may feel safer in the sanctity of home, where they feel loved by their parents instead of judged by their peers and teachers, psychologists say.

A closer look at the problem reveals that some children experience "generalized" anxiety about their abilities. They fear softball games, quizzes, science projects—anything that tests their mettle. Other children have distinct types of anxiety-related school refusal, says Kearney. One type stems from childhood anxiety about separating from mother and family. Another type—social phobia—involves worry over peer relations or public speaking. And simple phobias are fears about specific aspects of school, such as the wail of the fire-alarm or the walk down the hallway between classes. Several warning signs can alert teachers that a child is school phobic, says psychologist Robert Deluty, PhD, director of clinical training at the University of Maryland–Baltimore County. These include crying fits in class, withdrawn behavior and excessive time spent in the nurse's office. Teachers play a crucial role in flagging the problem and consulting parents and psychologists about treatment, notes Deluty. Overcoming the problem requires a team effort involving teachers, parents and psychologists, he says.

Separation anxiety

Separation anxiety typically affects young children. Those afflicted worry excessively when separated from their home and parents, often fearing for their life or their parents' lives, says Deluty. They worry that their parents will be kidnapped, attacked by monsters or killed in a car accident. To allay their worries, they cling to adults and demand constant attention.

Children with the problem experience such high levels of anxiety that their muscles tense up and their stomachs ache—they feel too ill to attend school but doctors find no evidence of physical illness, says Deluty.

Causes of separation anxiety are hard to pinpoint, but anxiety-prone children and depressive children with low self-confidence are particularly susceptible, researchers say. The same is true of phobic children, they note. In many cases, parents unwittingly reinforce the problem by catering to their children's every whim, coddling and pampering them instead of encouraging them to think independently and solve their own problems, says Achenbach. Often the parent—in many cases the mother—becomes dependent on the child's company as well, Achenbach says.

In fact, mothers of anxious children often themselves have histories of school refusal, found psychologist Cynthia Last, PhD, director of the School Phobia program at Nova Southeastern University in Fort Lauderdale, Fla., in a study of 145 anxious children and adolescents. The study was published in 1990 in the *Journal of the American Academy of Child and Adolescent Psychiatry* (Vol. 29, No. 1, pp. 31–35). Unhealthy cycles of dependency tend to run in families, she says.

Illustrating this phenomenon is the case of a 6-year-old school-phobic boy, treated by psychologist Larazo Garcia, PhD, of the Miami Psychological and Behavioral Center. The boy and his mother spent their days together "like one unit," says Garcia. The boy balked at attending school,

and his mother, who was single and on welfare, didn't make him go.

Garcia used desensitization, a common anxiety treatment, to conquer the boy's fear of mother separation. He first introduced the boy to play with neighborhood children, then brought the boy to school and sat in class with him for 10 minutes.

On subsequent days he increased the time they spent together in school to gradually ease that child into a daily routine. Noting that regular, extended separations from him mother hurt neither him nor her, the boy learned to spend his days at school. Anxious children typically spend too little time at school to realize that their parents are safe without them, Garcia notes. Garcia also involved the school's staff, a crucial aspect of treatment, says Kearney. Teachers and school nurses can encourage children to stay in class and urge them to check their anxiety by talking through it or using breathing exercises to calm their rapid breathing. Calling their parents should be the last resort, he says.

For their part, parents can more firmly set and enact rules about school attendance. Creating a regular morning routine prevents children from dwelling on anxiety and developing school-related aches and pains, says Kearney. Psychotherapy can also be used to help children face their fears, including the use of dolls to help them act out unrealistic fears about their parents getting injured or sick.

Social and simple phobias

Garcia's young patient also had an acute fear of interacting with peers and unknown adults, a form of social phobia. The child was extremely obese, which made him feel like a misfit.

"Some children are extremely fearful of being humiliated or embarrassed," says Last. "Peers' opinions are everything to them and children obsess over how others judge them."

In fact, most social phobias begin at around ages 11 or 12, a time when children tend to most viciously insult and pick on each other.

> ## Adding to the problem of peer-related phobias is an increasingly hostile school environment. "It used to be that nastiness was mostly in middle schools, but the teasing and taunting starts in kindergarten these days."
>
> *Cynthia Pilkington, PhD*
> *Central Plains Clinic*
> *Sioux Falls, S.D.*

This cruelty, Last says, can seriously harm sensitive children. Particularly at-risk for developing peer-related phobias are children harassed for physical traits, such as obesity, skinniness or physical disabilities. Intellectual ability is also a source of heckling from peers: Some children suffer for their braininess while others get teased for their academic slowness, Last notes.

Adding to the problem of peer-related phobias is an increasingly hostile school environment, adds Cynthia Pilkington, PhD, a child and school psychologist at the Central Plains Clinic in Sioux Falls, S.D. Her patients experience aggression and name-calling at increasingly younger ages. "It used to be that nastiness was mostly in middle schools, but the teasing and taunting starts in kindergarten these days," says Pilkington.

Children with performance-related phobias may fear public speaking, tests or being questioned by teacher in class. Some develop unreasonable fears about their grades and academic performance, becoming so paralyzed with fear that they can't perform at all. Most of these children are perfectionists who fear earning a "B," Last says.

A number of treatments are available for the various phobias. As with separation anxiety, desensitization helps children grow accustomed to peers and eases them into the academic cycle of testing and grading. Some treatments focused on increasing competence are relatively straightforward, Deluty adds. For example, the child who fears public speaking will likely benefit from help giving speeches and the child who fears failing math class may simply need extra math tutoring, he says.

Also beneficial is coping-skills training that helps children avert or counter bullying remarks. The training teaches children to respond to insults with a firm voice and direct eye contact, instead of with violence or passive weeping, says Deluty. Teachers can also help by giving phobic students "a way to shine," says Pilkington. Such tasks as decorating a class bulletin board give anxious children a positive sense of identity, she says.

Drug treatments are also available to treat school phobia. Some psychiatrists have been using imipramine, which has antipanic and antidepressive effects. Thus far, though, studies of the drug's effects are inconclusive.

It's hard to tell what treatment works best because school phobia is an under-researched area, says Last. Behavioral therapy shows promise, but even those results are based largely on case studies, she says. However, notes Last, one thing is certain. With dogged cooperation from parents and school staff, most school phobias can be conquered.

Unit 4

Unit Selections

Key Points to Consider

❖ How important are fathers in the lives of their children?

❖ What can parents do to turn a foundering child into a thriving survivor?

❖ Do parents really matter? Can they work with children's inherited personalities? Explain your answer.

❖ What are the effects of poverty on children?

❖ What are the myths and what is the reality about viewing televised violence?

❖ What is "The Biology of Soul Murder"? Does stress have a devastating effect on biological processes in childhood?

❖ Can parents today afford children? Why or why not?

 **Links**   **www.dushkin.com/online/**

These sites are annotated on pages 4 and 5.

Most people accept the proposition that families and cultures have substantial effects on children's outcomes. Do they? New interpretations of behavioral genetic research suggest that genetically predetermined children's behaviors may be having substantial effects on how families parent and on how cultures are evolved.

If parents and societies have a significant impact on children's outcomes, is there a set of family values that is superior to another set of family values? Is there a culture that has more correct answers than another culture? It is often assumed by the layperson that children's behaviors and personalities have a direct correlation with the behaviors and personalities of the person or persons who provided their socialization during infancy and childhood. Are you a mirror image of the person or persons who raised you? Why or why not? How many of their behaviors do you reflect?

During childhood, a person's family values get compared to, and tested against, the values of school, community, and culture. Peers, schoolmates, teachers, neighbors, extracurricular activity leaders, religious leaders, even shopkeepers, play increasingly important roles. Culture influences and is influenced by children through holidays, styles of dress, music, television, movies, slang, games played, parents' jobs, transportation, and exposure to sex, drugs, and violence. The ecological theorist, Urie Bronfenbrenner, calls these cultural variables exosystem and macrosystem influences. The developing personality of a child has multiple interwoven influences: from genetic potentialities through family values and socialization practices to community and cultural pressures for behaviors.

The first article in this unit appeals to partnerships in parenting: fathers plus mothers. Fathers have been relegated to "second banana" position, often viewed as breadwinners and disciplinarians. School-age children need parents both of whom are responsive and demanding. Discipline is crucial to a healthy personality. However, mothers as well as fathers need to be disciplinarians, and fathers as well as mothers need to provide tender, loving, and responsive caregiving. The authors are both fathers who have important things to say about their roles in their children's lives.

The second article reviews several important parenting factors that can help children develop resiliency and healthy self-esteem. Bad environments (e.g., poverty, poor nutrition, use of drugs, violence) do not always signal calamity for children. Good parenting can help children overcome, and even grow stronger, in times of adversity. Joseph Shapiro and his coauthors review research on resiliency-building factors, which are assets for children. They give vignettes of strengths in the lives of several people.

The third article in the family subsection of this unit asks, "Do Parents Really Matter?" It reviews some of the controversy engendered by some of the recent research findings of behavioral geneticists. Another way to look at the nature–nurture question is to ask "What can parents do?" to offset evocative genes (genes which evoke particular behaviors/personality traits). Can changing the environment change the expression of the genes? If so, how do parents learn to work with the innate tendencies of each unique, irregular, highly individualistic child to assure that he or she will have a happy, healthy and productive life?

The first article in the culture section of this unit is a review of recent, detailed, longitudinal data sets that deal with the effects of poverty on children. It includes information on the differential effects of poverty related to timing, depth, and duration of poverty and to parental factors such as age and education.

The second article deals with the question of television as a pervasive influence on the psyche of the school-age child. The reality is that the average child spends more time in front of a television set than in a school classroom. Current research explicitly demonstrates that children learn violent behaviors from television and practice them in their real worlds.

The third article, "The Biology of Soul Murder," looks at the stresses engendered by the contemporary culture of childhood. School-aged children base decisions about right and wrong on criteria such as the approval of others, relationship and social order maintenance, and respect for authority. When adult role models condone an environment that includes violence, drugs, and sexual promiscuity, children come to think of these behaviors as socially and morally acceptable. Some children experience a great deal of stress in trying to figure out why what they hear and see all around them is labeled wrong by some parents, teachers, peers, and religious leaders. Is a loved adult's opinion more important than the majority opinion? What is the opinion of the greater society in a rapidly changing culture? What beliefs continue to exert pressure? What social climate should be maintained? The presence of a loving adult can be a powerful antidote for some stress-ridden children. Nevertheless, too much culture shock and stressful living can cause brain changes that may or may not be reversible.

The last article in this unit is a hard-headed, but not hard-hearted, inquiry into "The Cost of Children." Phillip Longman makes it clear that children bring intangible, priceless pleasures to our families, communities, and culture. However, they cost money. He lists food, clothing, shelter, child care, health care, transportation, education, and even toys as some of the variables to be considered when contemplating parenthood. Children in our culture expect comparable, if not equivalent, treatment as their peers receive. Even low-income families pay steep prices to raise children.

Fathers' Time

Their style is vastly different, but dads can no longer be looked on as second bananas in the parenting biz. New studies show fathers are crucial for the emotional and intellectual growth of their kids, influencing how they ultimately turn out. Writer/father PAUL ROBERTS reports on the importance of being a papa. Actor/father BILL MOSELEY's dispatches reveal what it's like on the front lines.

Paul Roberts

PAUL ROBERTS is a Seattle-based freelance writer. Actor BILL MOSELEY interviewed Timothy Leary for *PT* in 1995.

This was supposed to be the Golden Era of Paternity. After decades of domestic aloofness, men came charging into parenthood with an almost religious enthusiasm. We attended Lamaze classes and crowded into birthing rooms. We mastered diapering, spent more time at home with the kids, and wallowed in the flood of "papa" literature unleashed by Bill Cosby's 1986 best-seller Fatherhood.

Yet for all our fervor, the paternal revolution has had a slightly hollow ring. It's not simply the relentless accounts of fatherhood's dark side—the abuse, the neglect, the abandonment—that make us so self-conscious. Rather, it's the fact that for all our earnest sensitivity, we can't escape questions of our psychological necessity: What is it, precisely, that fathers do? What critical difference do we make in the lives of our children?

Think about it. The modern mother, no matter how many nontraditional duties she assumes, is still seen as the family's primary nurturer and emotional guardian. It's in her genes. It's in her soul. But mainstream Western society accords no corresponding position to the modern father. Aside from chromosomes and feeling somewhat responsible for household income, there's no similarly celebrated deep link between father and child, no

widely recognized "paternal instinct." Margaret Mead's quip that fathers are "a biological necessity but a social accident" may be a little harsh. But is does capture the second-banana status that many fathers have when it comes to taking their measure as parents.

Happily, a new wave of research is likely to substantially boost that standing. Over the

Diary of a Dad

I love this time. Jane Moseley puts her hunter mare through its paces. Time slows to a trot, works up to a canter, drops to a lazy walk.

She announces she won't wear her riding hat. I insist she must. She refuses, would rather not ride. I can't believe she'd give up The Most Important Thing in her life over this. Fine, don't ride. This triggers an outpouring of vitriol. I pay attention, but don't take it personally. Thirty minutes later she's holding my hand as we walk down Melrose.

last decade, researchers like Jay Belsky, Ph.D., at Pennsylvania State University, and Ross Parke, Ph.D., of the University of California/Riverside Center for Family Studies, have been mapping out the psychology of the father-child bond, detailing how it functions and how it differs—sometimes substantially—from the bond between mother and child. What emerges from their work is the beginning of a truly modern concept of paternity, one in which old assumptions are overturned or, at the very least, cast in a radically different light. Far from Mead's "social accident," fatherhood turns out to be a complex and unique phenomenon with huge consequences for the emotional and intellectual growth of children.

Key to this new idea of fatherhood is a premise so mundane that most of us take it for granted: Fathers parent differently than mothers do. They play with their children more. Their interactions tend to be more physical and less intimate, with more of a reliance on humor and excitement. While such distinctions may hardly seem revelatory, they can mean a world of difference to kids. A father's more playful interactive style, for example, turns out to be critical in teaching a child emotional self-control. Likewise, father-child interactions appear to be central to the development of a child's ability to maintain strong, fulfilling social relationships later in life.

But it's not simply a matter of paternal behavior differing from maternal methods. The fabric of the father-child bond is also different. Studies show that fathers with low self-esteem have a greater negative impact on their children than do mothers who don't like themselves. In addition, the father-child bond seems to be more fragile—and therefore more easily severed—during periods of strife between parents.

Amid this welter of findings two things are clear. First, given our rapidly evolving conceptions of "father" and "family," fatherhood in the 1990s is probably tougher, psychologically, than at any other time in recent history. Plainly put, there are precious few positive role models to guide today's papas. Yet at the same time, the absence of any guidance holds hidden promise. Given the new information on fatherhood, the potential for a rich and deeply rewarding paternal experience is significantly greater today than even a generation ago. "The possibilities for fathering have never been better," Belsky says. "Culturally

After Jane and I had a walk, she wanted to box. So we waltzed around for 20 minutes, floating like a butterfly (me), stinging like a bee (Jane). I've taught her the rudiments of pugilism: how to make a fist (don't wrap your fingers around your thumb); how she should always stand sideways to her opponent, watching the hands not the eyes, etc. After a few fun-filled injury-free rounds, I came to my senses and ended our play.

Jane is an only child, so I figure it's my job to play with her as a brother or provide her with a sibling—playing with her is easier!

speaking, there is so much more that fathers are 'allowed' to do."

Our Forefathers

The surge of interest in fatherhood has a distinctly modern feel, as if after thousands of years of unquestioned maternal preeminence, men are just now discovering and asserting their parental prerogatives. But in fact, this unquestioned maternal dominance is itself a relatively recent development. Up until the mid-1700s, when most fathers worked in or near the home and took a much greater hand in child rearing, Western culture regarded them and not mothers as the more competent parent—and ultimately held them more responsible for how their children turned out. Not only were books and manuals on parenting written chiefly for men, according to R. L. Griswold, author of *Fatherhood in America*, men were routinely awarded custody of their kids in cases of divorce.

With the Industrial Revolution, however, more fathers began working outside their homes and thus were effectively removed from domestic life. As Vicky Phares, Ph.D., assistant professor of psychology at the University of South Florida, wrote in *Fathers and Developmental Psychopathology*, industrialization ushered in the "feminization of the domestic sphere and the marginalization of fathers' involvement with their children." By the mid-1800s, Phares notes, "child-rearing manuals were geared toward mothers, and this trend continued for the most part until the mid 1970s."

The implication here—that parental roles have largely been defined by economics—is still a subject of cultural debate. Less arguable, however, is the fact that by the turn of the twentieth century, both science and society saw the psychology of parenting largely as the psychology of motherhood. Not only were mothers somehow more "naturally" inclined to parent, they were also genetically better prepared for the task. Indeed, in 1916, Phares notes, one prominent investigator went so far as to "prove" the existence of the maternal instinct—and the lack of paternal equivalent—largely based on the notion that "few fathers were naturally skilled at taking care of infants."

Granted, bogus scientific claims were plentiful in those times. But even Freud, who believed fathers figured heavily in children's development of conscience and sexual identity, dismissed the idea that they had any impact until well past a child's third year. And even then, many psychologists argued, these paternal contributions consisted primarily of providing income, discipline, and a masculine role model, along with periodic injections of what might be called "real world" experience—that is, things that took place outside the home. "The classical psychological view held that a father's 'job' was to expand his children's horizon beyond the bosom of the family and the mother-child relationship," Belsky observes. "Mothers preserved and protected children from discomfort. But fathers imposed a realistic, the world-is-tough perspective."

By the 1920s, the classic "mother-centric" view was showing its cracks. Not only did subsequent empirical studies find little hard evidence of any unique maternal instinct but, as Phares points out, the phenomenon of "mother-blaming"—that is, blaming mothers for all the emotional and behavioral problems of their children—prodded some researchers (and, no doubt, a good many mothers) to ask whether fathers might share some of the responsibility.

I crave adult company, but I don't have a baby-sitter for tonight. So I'm trying to lug Jane all the way to Santa Monica to see Wing Chung, a kung-fu movie she says she doesn't want to see. Oh, no you don't, kid, it's my time now; and we're going to Santa Monica. Of course, Jane winds up loving the movie. Later that night we watch a video of Captains Courageous. I am reminded of all the songs that the two of us have made up over the past several years: "Feed Lot," "Ain't No Bridge," "Don't Drink the Water," "When the Vulture Swoops," etc. (Lyrics upon request).

By the 1950s, science began to recognize that there was some paternal impact on early childhood—even if it was only in the negative context of divorce or the extended absence of a father. Psychologist Michael Lamb, Ph.D., research director at the National Institute for Child Health and Human Development in Bethesda, Maryland, explains: "The assumption was that by comparing the behavior and personalities of children raised with and without fathers, one could—essentially by a process of subtraction—estimate what sort of influence fathers typically had."

What Dads Do

It wasn't until the feminist movement of the 1970s that researchers thought to ask whether dads could be as nurturing as moms. To everyone's astonishment, the answer was yes.

Actually, that was half the answer. Subsequent inquiries showed that while fathers could be as nurturing as mothers, they tended to leave such duties to moms. Hardly news to millions of overworked women, this finding was crucial. For the first time, researchers began systematically studying how and why male and female parenting strategies diverged, and more to the point, what those differences meant for children.

Although the total fatherhood experience runs from conception on, research has focused most keenly on the first few years of the parent-child relationship. It's here that children are most open to parental influence; they function primarily as receivers, consuming not only huge quantities of nourishment and comfort but stimuli as well. For decades, investigators have understood that infants not only enjoy taking in such rudimentary knowledge but absolutely require it for intellectual, physical, and especially emotional growth.

Without such constant interaction, argues W. Andrew Collins, Ph.D., of the University of Minnesota's Institute for Child Development, infants might never fully develop a sense of comfort and security. As important, they might not develop a sense of being connected to—and thus having some degree of control over—the world around them. "The key ingredient is a 'contingent responsiveness,'" says Collins, "where infants learn their actions will elicit certain reliable responses from others."

It's also during this crucial period that one of the most fundamental differences between male and female parenting styles takes place. Work by several psychiatrists, including San Diego's Martin Greenberg, M.D., and Kyle Pruett, M.D., a professor of psychiatry at the Yale Child Study Center, suggests that while new mothers are inclined to relate to their infants in a more soothing, loving, and serious way, new fathers "hold their children differ-

Made Jane cry—down on her for not helping me put away the groceries, make dinner. She wanted to play Super Mario Bros. (So did I.) She called me an idiot. I yelled at her about not pulling her oar—sounded just like my dad—and sent her to her room. I kept her in there for a few minutes, felt bad, knocked on the door, and sat on her bed and apologized for losing my temper. "You hurt my feelings," she sniffed.

CREATING A NEW PATRIARCHY

Even the most dedicated dads quickly discover that the road to modern fatherhood is strewn with obstacles. Positive role models are in short supply and personal experiences are usually no help. Jerrold Lee Shapiro, Ph.D., professor of psychology at Santa Clara University, says understanding your relationship with your own father is the first step. If not, you're bound to automatically and unconciously replicate things from your childhood.

Here are several strategies both parents can use to strengthen the father-child bond.

◆ Start early. While involvement doesn't always equal intimacy, fathers who immerse themselves in all aspects of parenting from birth on are more likely to be closer to their children. Take part in as many prenatal activities as possible and schedule at least a week away from work after the baby is born to practice parenting skills and overcome anxieties about handling the baby.

◆ Create "fathering space": Schedule times and activities in which you take care of your newborn entirely on your own. The traditional practice of deferring to mothers as "experts" gives new fathers few chances to hone their parenting skills, bolster their confidence, and build solid bonds with baby.

Sue Dickinson, M.S.W., a marriage and family therapist in Cle Elum, Washington, suggests persuading mom to go out of the house so you can have the experience of being the parent. Martin Greenberg, M.D., recommends bundling your baby in a chest pack and going for walks. The feeling of a baby's body—together with his or her warmth and smell—is captivating.

◆ Articulate feelings. Although fatherhood is routinely described as "the most wonderful experience" a man can have, new fathers may feel anxious, fearful, and frustrated. They may also be jealous of the time their wives spend with the baby and of their wives' "natural" parenting skills. These feelings may only make it harder for you to wholeheartedly participate in parenting and create distance between you and your child. New fathers need to identify such feelings and discuss them with their wives.

◆ Mind the details. Tune in to your children and avoid relying on mom to "read" what your baby wants.

◆ Respect diversity. Accept your partner's parenting style without criticizing. Mothers often regard fathers' more boisterous, style as too harsh or insensitive. But such criticism can derail a dad's desire for involvement. "Just because he's doing something you wouldn't do doesn't make it wrong," says Jay Belsky, Ph.D. Mothers have to temper their need to protect and remember dads offer things moms don't.

◆ Be realistic. Fathers who want to adopt a more hands-on approach than they themselves experienced are often frustrated when kids don't immediately respond. But children accustomed to having mom as the primary caregiver simply cannot adapt to "sudden" paternal involvement overnight. Above all, parenting requires patience.

ently and have a different kind of patience and frustration cycle than mothers," Pruett observes.

Why it is fathers behave this way isn't entirely clear. (And when fathers are primary caregivers, they are likely to display many of the so-called maternal traits.) Some studies suggest these gender differences are part of a larger male preference for stimulating, novel activities that arises from neurobiological differences in the way stimuli and pleasure are linked in male and female brains, and likely a result of genetics. Individuals high in the sensation-seeking trait are far more likely to engage in new and exciting pastimes. Though not all guys qualify as sensation seekers, the trait is far more common in men—particularly young ones—than it is in women, and might help explain why [m]any young fathers start off having a parenting style that's stimulating for them as well as their child.

THE DADDY DYNAMIC

Whatever its origins, this more playful, jocular approach carries major consequences for developing children. Where the "average" mother cushions her baby against irritating stimulation, the "average" father heaps it on, consistently producing a broader range of arousal. The resulting ups and downs force children to "stretch," emotionally and physically.

This emotion-stretching dynamic becomes more pronounced as father-child relationships enter into their second and third years. When playing, fathers tend to be more physical with their toddlers—wrestling, playing tag, and so on—while mothers emphasize verbal exchanges and interacting with objects, like toys. In nearly all instances, says Lamb, fathers are much more likely "to get children worked up, negatively or positively, with fear as well as delight, forcing them to learn to regulate their feelings."

In a sense, then, fathers push children to cope with the world outside the mother-child bond, as classical theory argued. But more than this, fathering behavior also seems to make children develop a more complex set of interactive skills, what Parke calls "emotional communication" skills.

First, children learn how to "read" their father's emotions via his facial expressions, tone of voice, and other nonverbal cues, and respond accordingly. Is Daddy really going to chase me down and gobble me up, or is he joking? Did I really hurt Daddy by poking him in the eye? Is Daddy in the mood to play, or is he tired?

Second, children learn how to clearly communicate their own emotions to others. One common example is the child who by crying lets her daddy know that he's playing too roughly or is scaring her. Kids also learn to indicate when interactions aren't stimulating enough; they'll show they've lost interest by not responding or wandering off.

Finally, children learn how to "listen" to their own emotional state. For instance, a child soon learns that if he becomes too "worked up" and begins to cry, he may in effect drive his play partner away.

The consequences of such emotional mastery are far-reaching. By successfully coping with stimulating, emotionally stretching interactions, children learn that they can indeed effect change both on internal matters (their feelings) and in the outside world (their father's actions). In that regard, links have been found between the quality of father-child interactions and a child's later development of certain life skills, including an ability to manage frustration, a willingness to explore new things and activities, and persistence in problem solving.

Anna's sleeping over. Earlier in the evening, Jane was on the floor of her bedroom looking up my shorts, laughing, saying she saw my penis. Later, I spy Jane and Anna holding up our cat Jackson. Must be a penis hunt, little-girl style. It's already in full swing and they're seven and eight!

In addition to being cook, chauffeur, maid, and spiritual protector, I am also Sex Authority! Two years ago, I explained, in a general way, the birds and the bees to Jane, correcting the misinformation she'd been given by her good friend Olivia.

As important as learning to regulate the emotional intensity of their interactions is children's ability to master the larger interactive process, the give and take that makes up social communication. "Kids who learn how to decode and encode emotions early on will be better off later when it comes to any social encounter," Parke says.

Such benefits have been intensely studied in the area of sibling relationships. Work by Belsky and Brenda Volling, Ph.D., an assistant professor of psychology at the University of Michigan, suggests that the emotion-management "lessons" learned by children from their fathers during play are applied later in interactions with siblings—and ultimately with people outside the family—and lead to more cooperation and less fighting. The press release announcing Belsky and Volling's research quipped, "If Adam had been a better father, things might have turned out differently for Cain and Abel."

Such findings come with plenty of caveats. A mother's more comforting manner is just as crucial to her children, helping them foster, among other things, a critical sense of security and self-confidence. Indeed, a mere preference for stimulating activities does not a good father make; obviously, the quality of father-child interactions is important. Successful fathers both monitor and modulate their play, maintaining a level of stimulation that keeps children engaged without making them feel like they've been pushed too far. This requires complete engagement—something many of today's busy fathers find difficult to manage. "What often happens is fathers don't pay attention to the cues their kids are sending," Belsky says. "A kid is crying 'uncle' and his father doesn't hear it."

Of course, fathers aren't the only parent who can teach these coping skills. Mothers physically play with their kids and, depending on the dynamics and history of the family, may also be the ones providing more of a "paternal" influence—teaching coping skills through play. Yet this "stretching" role typically falls to fathers because men gravitate toward less intimate, more physical interactions. And, as Reed Larson, Ph.D., a psychologist at the University of Illinois-Champagne, observes, "when dads stop having fun interacting with their kids, they're more likely than mothers to exit."

Whether these differences are genetic, cultural, or, more likely, a combination of the two, is still hotly debated. But the fact remains

Jane's legs hurt tonight; she calls them growing pains. I got mad, then simmered down (when my fear subsided), gave her Tylenol after she brushed her teeth. Read her a chapter from Great Expectations.

When Jane's sick, her mother takes such good care of her with medicines, doctors. I was raised Christian Scientist, taught that sickness and injury are illusions that should be healed with prayer and proper thinking. I'm just getting over my anger, my fear of disease, doctors, medicine.

that in terms of time spent with children, fathers typically spend more of it playing with their kids than mothers do—a difference that from very early on, children pick up on. Studies show that during stressful situations, one-year-old and 18-month-old babies more often turn to their primary caretaker—in most families, mom—for help. By contrast, when researchers measured so-called affiliative behaviors like smelling and vocalizing, during their first two years, babies showed a preference for their fathers. Just as dramatic, almost as soon as a child can crawl or walk, he or she will typically seek out dad for play and mom for comfort and other needs.

Downside of The Daddy Track

On the face of it, fathers would seem to enjoy considerable advantages over mothers during their children's first years. Not only do they do less of the dirty work, but it's almost as if they've been anointed to handle the fun art of parenting. Yet as time goes on this situation changes dramatically. While a mother's more intimate, need-related approach to parenting generally continues to cement her bond with her children, a father's more playful and stimulating style steadily loses its appeal. By the age of eight or nine, a child may already be angry at his father's teasing, or bored or annoyed by his I'm-gonna-gitcha style.

This discrepancy often becomes quite pronounced as children reach adolescence. Research suggests that preteens and teens of both sexes continue to rely on their mothers for intimacy and needs, and increasingly view her as the favored parent for topics requiring sensitivity and trust. By contrast, Parke says, the joking, playful style that serves fathers so well during children's first years may begin to alienate teens, giving them the impression that their father doesn't take their thoughts and needs seriously.

Adding to this tension is the father's traditional role as the dispenser of discipline and firmness. It's hypothesized that fathers' less intimate interactive style may make it easier—although not more pleasant—for them to play the "heavy." In any case, adolescents come to see their fathers as the harsher, more distant parent. This feeling may increase teenagers' tendency to interact more often and intimately with their mothers, which in turn only heightens the sense of estrangement and tension between fathers and their kids.

As to whether fathers' possibly not being at home as much as mothers makes it easier or more difficult for them to be the disciplinarian, Parke says there are too many other factors involved to make such a determination. He does note, however, that many mothers faced with unruly kids still employ the threat, "Wait 'til your father gets home."

Clearly, the distance between fathers and adolescent children is not solely a result of fathers' playfulness earlier on. A central function of adolescence is a child's gradual movement toward emotional and physical autonomy from both parents. But studies suggest this movement is more directly and forcefully spurred by fathers' less intimate ways.

Does a father's parenting style during adolescence produce more closeness between father and child? The answer is probably no, says Parke. But if the question is, does a father's style serve a launching, independence-gaining function, the answer is probably yes. "Mothers' continued nurturance maintains a child's connectedness to the family, while fathers encourage differentiation," Parke says. In fact, according to a recent survey of adolescents by Israeli researchers Shmuel Shulman, Ph.D., and Moshe Klein, Ph.D., most perceived their fathers as being the primary source of support for their teenage autonomy.

Such notions will undoubtedly strike some as disturbingly regressive, as if researchers have simply found new, complex ways to justify outdated stereotypes of paternal behavior. For as any sensitive observer knows, the totality of fatherhood goes well beyond a tendency toward stimulating interactions and away from intimacy. Nonetheless, this does appear to be a central component of fathering behavior and may help explain why some seemingly antiquated modes of fathering persist. Despite evolution in gender roles, Belsky says, fathers are still more likely to provide less sensitivity, require kids to adjust to 'tough' realities, and perhaps be less understanding and empathetic.

Yet if the father-child bond truly serves as a mechanism for preparing children for the external world, the bond itself seems remarkably sensitive, even vulnerable, to that world. External variables, such as a father's relationships beyond his family—and in particular his experience in the workplace—appear to be linked to both the kind of fathering behavior he exhibits and the success he achieves with it. Some of these links are obvious. Few would be surprised to learn that fathers with high-stress jobs are apt to be more distant from their kids or use harsher, physical discipline when dealing with youthful infractions.

Other links between a man's external world and the way he fathers are more subtle. According to Parke, there are significant and intriguing fathering differences between men whose jobs involve a great degree of independence and those who are heavily managed. Fathers with workplace autonomy tend to expect and encourage more independence in their children. Moreover, they generally place grater emphasis on a child's intent when assessing misbehavior, and aren't inclined toward physical discipline. By contrast, men in highly supervised jobs with little autonomy are more likely to value and expect conformity from their kids. They're also more likely to consider the consequences of their children's misbehavior when meting out punishment, and discipline them physically.

This so-called spillover effect is hardly mysterious. We would expect parents whose jobs reward them for creativity, independence, and intent to value those qualities, and to emphasize them in their interactions with their children. Not that men have a monopoly on job spillover. A mother whose job is stressful probably isn't able to parent at one hundred percent either.

Lately, I've felt a little more thin-skinned with Jane. I think it dates back to around the time of her Christmas break. Jane's not as cuddly, pliable, obedient as she was before. Rather, she's more headstrong, defiant, sometimes openly mocking of me, my authority.

I guess she's becoming independent, setting her own boundaries. Yipes! Thankfully, Lucinda explained this. I figured Jane was going through a bad patch, or maybe her friends or mother were encouraging her to resist my fine parenting! Instead, it's my parenting that's helped foster her confidence.

Bill Moseley

Dads Who Disconnect

Other factors may also have a greater impact on the father-child bond than on the bond between mother and child. "If things aren't going well in a marriage," says Lamb, "it's more likely to have a negative impact on a father's relationship with his child." This is surely due in part to a child's history of intimacy with his or her mother. But Lamb also speculates that fathers simply find it easier to "disconnect" from their kids during times of conflict.

Speculations like these raise the specter of some genetic explanation. If fathers are inclined to relate to their children in a less intimate way, they may naturally be less capable of building and maintaining strong parent-child bonds. Yet while Lamb and Parke acknowledge some degree of innate, gender-related parenting differences, they place far more emphasis on cultural or learned factors.

Of these, the most important may be the parenting models today's men and women have from their own childhoods—models that very likely ran along traditional lines, and most significantly indicated mothering was mandatory and fathering far more discretionary. A mother may be angry and depressed, Lamb says, "but parenting has to be done and the buck stops with her, whereas dads have traditionally been given leeway."

It's changing, of course. New legal sanctions, such as those against deadbeat dads, coupled with a rising sense—not just among conservatives—of fathers' familial obligations, are making it tougher for men to simply walk away physically or emotionally. Today men getting divorced are likely to fight for primary or joint custody of their kids. We may even reach a point where one parent isn't deemed mandatory and the other "allowed" to drop back.

Bringing the Revolution Home

Researchers say the more compelling changes in fathering are, or ought to be, taking place not just on a social level but on a personal one. One of the simplest steps is refiguring the division of parental duties: mom takes on some of the play master role, while dad does more of the need-based parenting—everything from changing diapers to ferrying the kids to dance lessons. By doing more of the "mandatory" parenting, Parke says, fathers will encourage their kids to see them not simply as a playmate, but as a comfort provider too.

No one's advocating a complete role reversal, or suggesting a complete shift is possible. Parke says men have difficulty "giving up their robust interactive styles, even when they are the parent staying at home." Instead, families should take advantage of the difference between men's and women's parenting approaches. Since fathers' boisterous antics seem to help prepare children for life outside the family, mothers shouldn't cancel this out by intervening or being overly protective.

At the same time, a more androgynous approach has its advantages. Children will be less inclined to mark one parent for fun and the other for comfort. For fathers this might mean more opportunities to deal with emotional ups and downs and develop the empathy and emotional depth.

Of course, fathers will experience difficulties making this shift. Yet the potential rewards are huge. Not only will we give our children more progressive examples of parenting—examples that will be crucial when they raise their own children—but we'll greatly enhance our own parenting experiences.

Fatherhood may be more confusing and open-ended than ever before, but the possibilities—for those willing to take the risks—are endless. "In the theater of modern family life," says Belsky, "there are just many more parts that fathers can play."

CULTURE & IDEAS

INVINCIBLE KIDS

*Why do some children survive
traumatic childhoods unscathed?
The answers can help every child*

Child psychologist Emmy Werner went looking for trouble in paradise. In Hawaii nearly 40 years ago, the researchers began studying the offspring of chronically poor, alcoholic, abusive and even psychotic parents to understand how failure was passed from one generation to the next. But to her surprise, one third of the kids she studied looked nothing like children headed for disaster. Werner switched her focus to these "resilient kids," who somehow beat the odds, growing into emotionally healthy, competent adults. They even appeared to defy the laws of nature: When Hurricane Iniki flattened Kauai in 1992, leaving nearly 1 in 6 residents homeless, the storm's 160-mpg gusts seemed to spare the houses of Werner's success stories.

Werner's "resilient kids," in their late 30s when Iniki hit, helped create their own luck. They heeded storm warnings and boarded up their properties. And even if the squall blew away their roofs or tore down their walls, they were more likely to have the financial savings and insurance to avoid foreclosure—the fate of many of Iniki's victims. "There's not a thing you can do personally about being in the middle of a hurricane," says the University of California–Davis's Werner, "but [resilient kids] are planners and problem solvers and picker-uppers."

For many of America's children, these are difficult times. One in five lives in poverty. More than half will spend some of their childhood living apart from one parent—the result of divorce, death or out-of-wedlock birth.

Child abuse, teen drug use and teen crime are surging. Living in an affluent suburb is no protection: Suburban kids are almost as likely as those in violent neighborhoods to report what sociologists call "parental absence"—the lack of a mother and father who are approachable and attentive, and who set rules and enforce consequences.

In the face of these trends, many social scientists now are suggesting a new way of looking at kids and their problems: Focus on survivors, not casualties. Don't abandon kids who fail, but learn from those who succeed.

Such children, researchers find, are not simply born that way. Though genes play a role, the presence of a variety of positive influences in a child's environment is even more crucial; indeed, it can make the difference between a child who founders and one who thrives.

The implications of such research are profound. The findings mean that parents, schools, volunteers, government and others can create a pathway to resiliency, rather than leaving success to fate or to hard-wired character traits. Perhaps most important, the research indicates that the lessons learned from these nearly invincible kids can teach us how to help *all* kids—regardless of their circumstances—handle the inevitable risks and turning points of life. The Search Institute, a Minneapolis-based children's research group, identified 30 resiliency-building factors. The more of these "assets" present in a child's environment, the more likely the child was to avoid school problems, alco-

hol use, early sexual experimentation, depression and violent behavior.

Like the factors that contribute to lifelong physical health, those that create resilience may seem common-sensical, but they have tremendous impact. Locate a resilient kid and you will also find a caring adult—or several—who has guided him. Watchful parents, welcoming schools, good peers and extracurricular activities matter, too, as does teaching kids to care for others and to help out in their communities.

From thug to Scout. The psychologists who pioneered resiliency theory focused on inborn character traits that fostered success. An average or higher IQ was a good predictor. So was innate temperament—a sunny disposition may attract advocates who can lift a child from risk. But the idea that resiliency can be molded is relatively re-

ROBERT DOLE. He came of age during the tough years of the Great Depression. Later, he overcame a nearly fatal war injury.

"Why me, I demanded? ... Maybe it was all part of a plan, a test of endurance and strength and, above all, of faith."

 From *U.S. News & World Report,* November 11, 1996, pp. 60-71. © 1996 by U.S. News & World Report. Reprinted by permission.

cent. It means that an attentive adult can turn a mean and sullen teenage thug—a kid who would smash in someone's face on a whim—into an upstanding Boy Scout.

That's the story of Eagle Scout Rudy Gonzalez. Growing up in Houston's East End barrio, Gonzalez seemed on a fast track to prison. By the time he was 13, he'd already had encounters with the city's juvenile justice system—once for banging a classmate's head on the pavement until blood flowed, once for slugging a teacher. He slept through classes and fought more often than he studied. With his drug-using crew, he broke into warehouses and looted a grocery store. His brushes with the law only hardened his bad-boy swagger. "I thought I was macho," says Gonzalez. "With people I didn't like, [it was], 'Don't look at me or I'll beat you up.' "

Many of Gonzalez's friends later joined real gangs. Several met grisly deaths; others landed in prison for drug dealing and murder. More than a few became fathers and dropped out of school. Gonzalez joined urban scouting, a new, small program established by Boy Scouts of America to provide role models for "at risk" youth. At first glance, Gonzalez's path could hardly seem more different than that of his peers. But both gangs and Boy Scouts offer similar attractions: community and a sense of purpose, a hierarchical system of discipline and a chance to prove loyalty to a group. Gonzalez chose merit badges and service over gang colors and drive-by shootings.

Now 20, Gonzalez wears crisply pressed khakis and button-down shirts and, in his sophomore year at Texas A&M, seems well on his way to his goal of working for a major accounting firm. Why did he succeed when his friends stuck to crime? Gonzalez's own answer is that his new life is "a miracle." "Probably, God chose me to do this," he says.

There were identifiable turning points. Scoutmaster John Trevino, a city policeman, filled Gonzalez's need for a caring adult who believed in him and could show him a different way to be a man. Gonzalez's own father was shot and killed in a barroom fight when Rudy was just 6. Fate played a role, too. At 14, using survival skills he'd learned in scouting, Gonzalez saved the life of a younger boy stuck up to his chin in mud in a nearby bayou. The neighborhood hero was lauded in the newspaper and got to meet President Bush at the White House. Slowly, he began to feel the importance of serving his community—another building block of resiliency. For a Scout project he cleaned up a barrio cemetery.

Something special. Once his life started to turn around, Gonzalez felt comfortable enough to reveal his winning personality and transcendent smile—qualities that contributed further to his success. "When I met him, I wanted to adopt him," says his high school counselor, Betty Porter. "There's something about him." She remembers Gonzalez as a likable and prodigious networker who made daily visits to her office to tell her about college scholarships—some she didn't even know about.

> BILL CLINTON. He lost his father in an auto wreck before he was born. Later, he coped with an alcoholic, occasionally violent stepfather.
>
> "My mother taught me about sacrifice. She held steady through tragedy after tragedy and, always, she taught me to fight."

A little bit of help—whether an urban scouting program or some other chance to excel—can go a long way in creating resiliency. And it goes furthest in the most stressed neighborhoods, says the University of Colorado's Richard Jessor, who directs a multimillion-dollar resiliency project for the John D. and Catherine T. MacArthur Foundation. Looking back, Gonzalez agrees. "We were just guys in the barrio without anything better to do," he says. "We didn't have the YMCA or Little League, so we hung out, played sports, broke into warehouses and the school." Adds Harvard University's Katherine Newman: "The good news is that kids are motivated. They want to make it. The bad news is that there are too few opportunities."

Resiliency theory brightens the outlook for kids. Mental health experts traditionally have put the spotlight on children who emerge from bad childhoods damaged and scarred. But statistics show that many—if not most—children born into unpromising circumstances thrive, or at least hold their own. Most children of teen mothers, for example, avoid becoming teen parents themselves. And though the majority of child abusers were themselves abused as children, most abused children do not become abusers. Similarly, children of schizophrenics and children who grew up in refugee camps also tend to defy the odds. And many Iowa youths whose families lost their farms during the 1980s farm crisis became high achievers in school.

Living well. A person who has faced childhood adversity and bounced back may even fare *better* later in life than someone whose childhood was relatively easy—or so Werner's recently completed follow-up of the Kauai kids at age 40 suggests. Resilient children in her study reported stronger marriages and better health than those who enjoyed less stressful origins. Further, none had been on welfare, and none had been in trouble with the law. Many children of traumatic, abusive or neglectful childhoods suffer severe consequences, including shifts in behavior, thinking and physiology that dog them into adulthood. But though Werner's resilient kids turned adults tended to marry later, there was little sign of emotional turmoil. At midlife, these resilient subjects were more likely to say they were happy and only one third as likely to report mental health problems.

Can any child become resilient? That remains a matter of debate. Some kids, researchers say, simply may face too many risks. And the research can be twisted to suggest that there are easy answers. "Resiliency theory assumes that it's all or nothing, that you have it or you don't," complains Geoffrey Canada, who runs neighborhood centers for New York's poorest youth. "But for some people it takes 10,000 gallons of water, and for some kids it's just a couple of little drops."

In fact, as Canada notes, most resilient kids do not follow a straight line to success. An example is Raymond Marte, whom Canada mentored, teaching the youth karate at one of his Rheedlen Centers for Children and Families. Today, Marte, 21, is a freshman at New York's Bard College. But only a few years ago, he was just another high school dropout and teenage father, hanging out with gang friends and roaming the streets with a handgun in his pocket. "This is choice time," Canada told

DR. RUTH WESTHEIMER. The sex therapist fled the Nazis at 10; her parents died in the Holocaust, and she grew up in a Swiss orphanage.

"The values my family [instilled] left me with the sense I must make something out of my life to justify my survival."

Marte after five of the boy's friends were killed in three months. Marte re-enrolled in school, became an Ameri-Corps volunteer and won a college scholarship. Today, when he walks the streets of his family's gritty Manhattan neighborhood, he is greeted as a hero, accepting high-fives from friends congratulating the guy who made it out.

Good parenting can trump bad neighborhoods. That parents are the first line in creating resilient children is no surprise. But University of Pennsylvania sociologist Frank Furstenberg *was* surprised to find that adolescents in the city's most violence prone, drug-ridden housing projects showed the same resilience as middle-class adolescents. The expectation was that the worst neighborhoods would overwhelm families. Inner-city housing projects do present more risk and fewer opportunities. But good parenting existed in roughly equal proportions in every neighborhood.

Sherenia Gibbs is the type of dynamo parent who almost single-handedly can instill resiliency in her children. The single mother moved her three children from a small town in Illinois to Minneapolis in search of better education and recreation. Still, the new neighborhood was dangerous, so Gibbs volunteered at the park where her youngest son, T. J. Williams, played. Today, six years later, Gibbs runs a city park, where she has started several innovative mentoring programs. At home, Gibbs sets aside time to spend with T. J., now 14, requires him to call her at work when he gets home from school or goes out with friends and follows his schoolwork closely. Indeed, how often teens have dinner with their family and whether they have a curfew are two of the best predictors of teen drug use, according to

the National Center on Addiction and Substance Abuse at Columbia University. How often a family attends church—where kids are exposed to both values and adult mentors—also makes a difference. Says Gibbs: "The streets will grab your kids and eat them up."

Some resiliency programs study the success of moms like Gibbs and try to teach such "authoritative parenting" skills to others. When a kid has an early brush with the law, the Oregon Social Learning Center brings the youth's whole family together to teach parenting skills. Not only is the training effective with the offending youth, but younger brothers and sisters are less likely to get in trouble as well.

Despite the crucial role of parents, few—rich or poor—are as involved in their children's lives as Gibbs. And a shocking number of parents—25 percent—ignore or pay little attention to how their children fare in school, according to Temple University psychology professor Laurence Steinberg. Nearly one third of students across economic classes say their parents have no idea how they are doing in school. Further, half the parents Steinberg surveyed did not know their children's friends, what their kids did after school or where they went at night. Some schools are testing strategies for what educator Margaret Wang, also at Temple, calls "educational resilience."

One solution: teaching teams, which follow a student for a few years so the child always has a teacher who knows him well. In Philadelphia, some inner-city schools have set up "parents' lounges," with free coffee, to encourage moms and dads to be regular school visitors.

Given the importance of good parenting, kids are at heightened risk when parents themselves are troubled. But it is a trait of resilient kids that in such circumstances, they seek out substitute adults. And sometimes they become substitute adults themselves, playing a parental role for younger siblings. That was true of Tyrone Weeks. He spent about half his life without his mother as she went in and out of drug rehabilitation. Sober now for three years, Delores Weeks maintains a close relationship with her son. But Tyrone was often on his own, living with his grandmother and, when she died, with his basketball coach, Tennis Young. Young and Dave Hagan, a neighborhood priest in north

Philadelphia, kept Weeks fed and clothed. But Weeks also became a substitute parent for his younger brother, Robert, while encouraging his mother in her struggle with cocaine. Says Weeks, "There were times when I was lost and didn't want to live anymore."

Like many resilient kids, Weeks possessed another protective factor: a talent. Basketball, he says, gave him a self-confidence that carried him through the lost days. Today, Weeks rebounds and blocks shots for the University of Massachusetts. Obviously, not all kids have Weeks's exceptional ability. But what seems key is not the level of talent but finding an activity from which they derive pride and sense of purpose.

Mon Ye credits an outdoor leadership program with "keeping me out of gang life." Born in a Cambodian refugee camp, Ye has lived with an older brother in a crime-ridden Tacoma, Wash., housing project since his mother's death a few years ago. Outdoor adventure never interested him. But then parks worker LeAnna Waite invited him to join a program at a nearby recreation center (whose heavy doors are dented with bullet marks from gang fights). Last year, Ye led a youth climb up Mount Rainier and now plans to go to college to become a recreation and park supervisor.

It helps to help. Giving kids significant personal responsibility is another way to build resiliency, whether it's Weeks pulling his family together or Ye supervising preteens. Some of the best youth programs value both service to others and the ability to plan and make choices, according to Stanford University's Shirley Brice Heath. The Food Project—in which kids raise 40,000 pounds of vegetables for Boston food kitchens—is directed by the young par-

KWEISI MFUME. The NAACP chief's stepdad was abusive. After his mom died, he ran with gangs and had five sons out of wedlock.

"We're all inbred with a certain amount of resiliency. It's not until it's tested . . . that we recognize inner strength."

ticipants, giving them the chance to both learn and then pass on their knowledge. Older teens often find such responsibility through military service.

Any program that multiplies contacts between kids and adults who can offer advice and support is valuable. A recent study of Big Brothers and Big Sisters found that the nationwide youth-mentoring program cuts drug use and school absenteeism by half. Most youth interventions are set up to target a specific problem like violence or teen sex—and often have little impact. Big Brothers and Big Sisters instead succeeds with classic resiliency promotion: It first creates supportive adult attention for kids, then expects risky behavior to drop as a consequence.

The 42,490 residents of St. Louis Park, Minn., know all about such holistic approaches to creating resiliency. They've made it a citywide cause in the ethnically diverse suburb of Minneapolis. Children First is the city's call for residents to think about the ways, big and small, they can help all kids succeed, from those living in the city's Meadowbrook housing project to residents of parkside ranch houses. The suburb's largest employer, HealthSystem Minnesota, runs a free kids' health clinic. (Doctors and staff donate their time.) And one of the smallest businesses, Steve McCulloch's flower shop,

DIANNE FEINSTEIN. The California senator was raised in privilege, but her mother was mentally ill and at times violent.

"I've never believed adversity is a harbinger of failure. On the contrary, [it] can provide a wellspring of strength."

gives away carnations to kids in the nearby housing project on Mother's Day. Kids even help each other. Two high school girls started a Tuesday night baby-sitting service at the Reformation Lutheran Church. Parents can drop off their kids for three hours. The cost: $1.

The goal is to make sure kids know that they are valued and that several adults outside their own family know and care about them. Those adults might include a police officer-volunteering to serve lunch in the school cafeteria line. Or Jill Terry, one of scores of volunteers who stand at school bus stops on frigid mornings. Terry breaks up fights, provides forgotten lunch money or reassures a sad-faced boy about his parents' fighting. The adopt-a-bus-stop program

was started by members of a senior citizens' group concerned about an attempted abduction of a child on her way to school.

Another volunteer, Kyla Dreier, works in a downtown law firm and mentors Angie Larson. The 14-year-old has long, open talks with her mother but sometimes feels more comfortable discussing things with another adult, like Dreier.

Spreading out. St. Louis Park is the biggest success story of over 100 communities nationwide where the Search Institute is trying to develop support for childhood resiliency. In a small surburb, it was relatively easy to rally community leaders. Now Search is trying to take such asset building to larger cities like Minneapolis and Albuquerque, N.M.

In St. Louis Park, resiliency is built on a shoestring budget. About $60,000 a year—all raised from donations—covers the part-time staff director and office expenses. But that's the point, says Children First Coordinator Karen Atkinson. Fostering resiliency is neither complicated nor costly. It's basic common sense—even if practiced too rarely in America. And it pays dividends for all kids.

By Joseph P. Shapiro with Dorian Friedman in New York, Michele Meyer in Houston and Margaret Loftus

Do Parents Really Matter?

Once, parents were given all the credit—and all the blame—for how their children turned out. Then researchers told us that heredity determines who we are. The latest take: parents can work with their children's innate tendencies to rear happy, healthy kids. It's a message many parents will find reassuring—but it may make others very nervous.

By Annie Murphy Paul

David Reiss, M.D., didn't want to believe it. The George Washington University psychiatrist had worked for more than 12 years on a study of adolescent development—just completed—and its conclusions were a surprise, to say the least. "I'm talking to you seven or eight years after the initial results came out, so I can sound very calm and collected now," says Reiss. "But I was shocked." This, even though other scientists had previously reached similar conclusions in many smaller-scale studies. "We knew about those results, but we didn't believe it," says Reiss, speaking of himself and one of his collaborators, E. Mavis Heatherington, Ph.D. "Now we've done the research ourselves, so . . ." He sighs. "We're not ever going to believe it, but we're going to have to act as if we do."

What Reiss and his colleagues discovered, in one of the longest and most thorough studies of child development ever attempted, was that parents appear to have relatively little effect on how children turn out, once genetic influences are accounted for. "The original objective was to look for environmental differences," says Reiss. "We didn't find many." Instead, it seems that genetic influences are largely responsible for how "adjusted" kids are: how well they do in school, how they get along with their peers, whether they engage in dangerous or delinquent behavior. "If you follow the study's implications through to the end, it's a radical revision of contemporary theories of child development," says Reiss. "I can't

---

The way heredity shapes who we are is less like one-way dictation and more like spirited rounds of call and response.

---

even describe what a paradigm shift it is."

The only member of the research team who wasn't surprised by the results, Reiss recalls, was Robert Plomin, Ph.D., a researcher at the Institute of Psychiatry in London. Plomin is a behavioral geneticist, and he and others in his field have been saying for years what Reiss has just begun to accept: genes have a much greater influence on our personalities than previously thought, and parenting much less. The work of behavioral geneticists has been the focus of considerable controversy among psychologists, but it has been mostly ignored by parents, despite ample attention from the media. That may be because such coverage has rarely described just how genes are thought to wield their purported influence. Behavioral geneticists don't claim that genes are blueprints that depict every detail of our personality and behavior; rather, they propose that heredity reveals itself through complex interactions with the environment. Their theories are far more subtle, and more persuasive, than the simple idea of heredity as destiny. It is by participating in these very interactions, some scientists now say, that parents exert their own considerable influence—and they can learn to exert even more.

NATURE MEETS NURTURE

As behavioral geneticists understand it, the way heredity shapes who we are is less like one-way dictation and more like spirited rounds of call and response, with each

phrase spoken by heredity summoning an answer from the environment. Scientists' unwieldy name for this exchange is "evocative gene-environment correlations," so called because people's genetic makeup is thought to bring forth particular reactions from others, which in turn influence their personalities. A baby with a sunny disposition will receive more affection than one who is difficult; an attractive child will be smiled at more often than a homely one. And the qualities that prompt such responses from parents are likely to elicit more of the same from others, so that over time a self-image is created and confirmed in others' eyes.

Even as genes are calling forth particular reactions, they're also reaching out for particular kinds of experience. That's because each person's DNA codes for a certain type of nervous system: one that feels alarm at new situations, one that craves strong sensations, or one that is sluggish and slow to react. Given an array of opportunities, some researchers say, children will pick the ones that are most suited to their "genotype," or genetic endowment. As they grow older, they have more chances to choose—friends, interests, jobs, spouses—decisions that both reflect and define personality.

In order for genes and environment to interact in this way, they need to be in constant conversation, back and forth. Since parents usually raise the children to whom they have passed on their genes, that's rarely a problem: they are likely to share and perhaps appreciate the qualities of their offspring. And the environment they provide their children with may further support their natural abilities: highly literate parents might give birth to an equally verbal child, then raise her in a house full of books. Developmental psychologists call this fortunate match "goodness of fit." But problems may arise if nurture and nature aren't on speaking terms—if a child's environment doesn't permit or encourage expression of his natural tendencies. That may happen when children's abilities don't match their parents' expectations; when their genetically-influenced temperament clashes with that of their parents; or when their environment offers them few opportunities to express themselves constructively, as is often the case with children who grow up in severe poverty. Research has shown that a poor person-to-environment match can lead to decreased motivation, diminished mental health, and rebellious or antisocial behavior.

The dialogue between genes and environment becomes more complicated when a sibling adds another voice. Although siblings share an average of 50 percent of their genes, the half that is different—and the kaleidoscopic ways that genes can combine—leads their genotypes to ask different

questions and get different answers from what would seem to be the same environment. In fact, siblings create individual environments of their own by seeking out different experiences and by evoking different responses from parents, friends, and others. Like the proverbial blind men touching the leg, the trunk, or the tail of an elephant, they "see" different parts of the same animal. "Our studies show that parents do indeed treat their children differently, but that they are in large measure responding to differences that are already there," says Robert Plomin. "Family environment does have an effect on personality development, but not in the way we've always thought. It's the experiences that siblings *don't* share that matter, not the ones they do."

KIDS IN CHARGE?

One intriguing implication of behavioral genetic research is that children are in many ways driving their own development, through the choices they make, the reactions they elicit, even the friends they pick (see "The Power of Peers"). But parents are crucial collaborators in that process, and that means that their role in shaping their children may actually be larger than it first appears. *How* a parent responds to a child's genetically-influenced characteristics may make all the difference in how those traits are expressed, says David Reiss. In his formulation, the parent-child relationship acts as a sort of translator of genetic influence: the genotype provides the basic plot, but parenting gives it tone and inflection, accent and emphasis. He calls this conception of gene-environment correlation "the relationship code," and says that it returns to parents some of the influence his study would seem to give to genes. "Our data actually give the role of parents a real boost—but it's saying that the story doesn't necessarily start with the parent," says Reiss. "It starts with the kid, and then the parent picks up on it."

To Reiss, parents' role as interpreters of the language of heredity holds out an exciting possibility. "If you could intervene with parents and get them to respond differently to troublesome behavior, you might be able to offset much of the genetic influence" on those traits, he says. In other words, if genes become behavior by way of the environment, then changing the environment might change the expression of the genes. Although such intervention studies are years away from fruition, small-scale research and clinical experience are pointing the way toward working with children's hereditary strengths and weaknesses. Stanley Greenspan, M.D., a pediatric psychiatrist at George Washington Medical School and author of *The Growth of the Mind,* is actively applying the discoveries of genetics to parenting. "Genes do create certain general tendencies, but parents can work with these by tailoring their actions to the nervous system of the child," says Greenspan. He believes that the responses children "naturally" elicit may not be in their best interests—but that parents can consciously and deliberately give them the ones that are. "You have to pay attention to what you're doing intuitively, and make sure that is what the kids really need," he says.

The exact same temperament that might predispose a kid to become a criminal can also make for a hot test pilot.

A baby with a sluggish temperament, for example, won't respond as readily to his parents' advances as a child with a more active nervous system. Disappointed at their offsprings' lack of engagement, parents may respond with dwindling interest and attention. Left to his own devices, the baby may become even more withdrawn, failing to make crucial connections and to master developmental challenges. But if the parents resist their inclinations, and engage the baby with special enthusiasm, Greenspan has found that the child will change his own behavior in response. The same principle of working against the grain of a child's genotype applies to those who are especially active or oversensitive, suggests Greenspan, comparing the process to a right-handed baseball player who practices throwing with his left hand. "It feels funny at first, but gradually you build up strength in an area in which you would naturally be weak," he says.

Of course, honing a right-handed pitch is important, too. Parents can improve on their children's hereditary strengths by encouraging their tendency to seek out experiences in tune with their genes. "Parents should think of themselves as resource providers," says Plomin. "Expose the child to a lot of things, see what they like, what they're good at, and go with that." By offering opportunities congenial to children's genetic constitutions, parents are in a sense improving their "goodness of fit" with the environment.

WILL YOUR KID GO TO YALE—OR TO JAIL?

For those traits that could easily become either assets or liabilities, parenting may be especially critical to the outcome. "The same temperament that can make for a criminal can also make for a hot test pilot or astronaut," says David Lykken, Ph.D., a behavioral geneticist at the University of Minnesota. "That kind of little boy—ag- gressive, fearless, impulsive—is hard to handle. It's easy for parents to give up and let him run wild, or turn up the heat and the punishment and thereby alienate him and lose all control. But properly handled, this can be the kid who grows up to break the sound barrier." Lykken believes that especially firm, conscientious, and responsive parents can make the difference—but not all behavioral geneticists agree. David Rowe, Ph.D., a University of Arizona psychologist and author of *The Limits of Family Influence,* claims that "much of the effort of 'superparents' may be wasted, if not counter-productive." And as for exposing children to a variety of experiences, Rowe thinks that this can give genetically talented children the chance they need, "but not many children have that much potential. This may not be so in Lake Wobegon [where every child is "above average"], but it is true in the rest of the world."

But with an optimism worthy of Garrison Keillor, advocates of parental influence insist that genes aren't the end of the story "The old idea is that you tried to live up to a potential that was set by genes," says Greenspan. "The new idea is that environment helps create potential." His view is supported by recent research that suggests a baby is born with only basic neural "wiring" in place, wiring whose connections are then elaborated by experience. Both sides will have to await the next chapter of genetic research, which may reveal even more complicated interactions between the worlds within and without. In the long-running debate between genes and the environment, neither one has yet had the last word.

The Effects of Poverty on Children

Jeanne Brooks-Gunn
Greg J. Duncan

Jeanne Brooks-Gunn, Ph.D., is Virginia and Leonard Marx professor of child development and education, and is director of the Center for Young Children and Families at Teachers College, Columbia University.

Greg J. Duncan, Ph.D., is a professor of education and social policy, and is a faculty associate at the Institute for Policy Research, Northwestern University.

Abstract

Although hundreds of studies have documented the association between family poverty and children's health, achievement, and behavior, few measure the effects of the timing, depth, and duration of poverty on children, and many fail to adjust for other family characteristics (for example, female headship, mother's age, and schooling) that may account for much of the observed correlation between poverty and child outcomes. This article focuses on a recent set of studies that explore the relationship between poverty and child outcomes in depth. By and large, this research supports the conclusion that family income has selective but, in some instances, quite substantial effects on child and adolescent well-being. Family income appears to be more strongly related to children's ability and achievement than to their emotional outcomes. Children who live in extreme poverty and who live below the poverty line for multiple years appear, all other things being equal, to suffer the worst outcomes. The timing of poverty also seems to be important for certain child outcomes. Children who experience poverty during their preschool and early school years have lower rates of school completion than children and adolescents who experience poverty only in later years. Although more research is needed on the significance of the timing of poverty on child outcomes, findings to date suggest that interventions during early childhood may be most important in reducing poverty's impact on children.

In recent years, about one in five American children—some 12 to 14 million—have lived in families in which cash income failed to exceed official poverty thresholds. Another one-fifth lived in families whose incomes were no more than twice the poverty threshold.[1,2] For a small minority of children—4.8% of all children and 15% of children who ever became poor—childhood poverty lasted 10 years or more.[3]

From *The Future of Children*, Summer/Fall 1997, pp. 55-71. © 1997 by the Center for the Future of Children of the David and Lucile Packard Foundation. Reprinted by permission. *The Future of Children* journals and executive summaries are available free of charge by faxing mailing information to: Circulation Department (650) 948-6498.

Income poverty is the condition of not having enough income to meet basic needs for food, clothing, and shelter. Because children are dependent on others, they enter or avoid poverty by virtue of their family's economic circumstances. Children cannot alter family conditions by themselves, at least until they approach adulthood. Government programs, such as those described by Devaney, Ellwood, and Love in this journal issue, have been developed to increase the likelihood that poor children are provided basic necessities. But even with these programs, poor children do not fare as well as those whose families are not poor.[4]

What does poverty mean for children? How does the relative lack of income influence children's day-to-day lives? Is it through inadequate nutrition; fewer learning experiences; instability of residence; lower quality of schools; exposure to environmental toxins, family violence, and homelessness; dangerous streets; or less access to friends, services, and, for adolescents, jobs? This article reviews recent research that used longitudinal data to examine the relationship between income low-poverty and child outcomes in several domains.

Hundreds of studies, books, and reports have examined the detrimental effects of poverty on the well-being of children. Many have been summarized in recent reports such as *Wasting America's Future* from the Children's Defense Fund and *Alive and Well?* from the National Cenier for Children in Poverty.[5] However, while the literature on the effects of poverty on children is large, many studies lack the precision necessary to allow researchers to disentangle the effects on children of the array of factors associated with poverty. Understanding of these relationships is key to designing effective policies to ameliorate these problems for children.

This article examines these relationships and the consequences for children of growing up poor. It begins with a long, but by no means exhaustive, list of child outcomes (see Table 1) that have been found to be associated with poverty in several large, nationally representative, cross-sectional surveys. This list makes clear the broad range of effects poverty can have on children. It does little, however, to inform the discussion of the causal effects of income poverty on children because the studies from which this list is derived did not control for other variables associated with poverty. For example, poor families are more likely to be headed by a parent who is single, has low educational attainment, is unemployed, has low earning potential and is young. These parental attributes, separately or in combination, might

account for some of the observed negative consequences of poverty on children. Nor do the relationships identified in the table capture the critical factors of the timing, depth, and duration of childhood poverty on children.[6,7]

This article focuses on studies that used national longitudinal data sets to estimate the effects of family income on children's lives, independent of other family conditions that might be related to growing up in a low-income household. These studies attempt to isolate the effect of family income by taking into account, statistically, the effects of maternal age at the child's birth, maternal education, marital status, ethnicity, and other factors on child outcomes.[2,8] Many used data on family income over several years and at different stages of development to estimate the differential effects of the timing and duration of poverty on child outcomes. The data sets analyzed include the Panel Study of Income Dynamics (PSID), the National Longitudinal Survey of Youth (NLSY), Children of the NLSY (the follow-up of the children born to the women in the original NLSY cohort), the National Survey of Families and Households (NSFH), the National Health and Nutrition Examination Survey (NHANES), and the Infant Health and Development Program (IHDP). These rich data sets include multiple measures of child outcomes and family and child characteristics.

This article is divided into four sections. The first focuses on the consequences of poverty across five child outcomes. If income does, in fact, affect child outcomes, then it is important not only to identity these outcomes but also to describe the pathways through which income operates. Accordingly, in the second section, five pathways through which poverty might operate are described. The third section focuses on whether the links between poverty and outcomes can reasonably be attributed to income rather than other family characteristics. The concluding section considers policy implications of the research reviewed.

Effects of Income on Child Outcomes

Measures of Child Well-Being

As illustrated in Table 1, poor children suffer higher incidences of adverse health, developmental, and other outcomes than non-poor children. The specific dimensions of the well-being of children and youths considered in some detail in this article include (1) physical health (low birth weight, growth stunting, and lead poisoning), (2) cognitive ability (intelligence, verbal ability, and achievement test scores), (3) school achievement (years of schooling, high school completion), (4) emotional and behavioral outcomes, and (5) teen-age out-of-wedlock childbearing. Other outcomes are not addressed owing to a scarcity of available research, a lack of space, and because they overlap with included outcomes.

While this review is organized around specific outcomes, it could also have been organized around the various ages of childhood.[9-11] Five age groups are often distinguished—prenatal to 2 years, early childhood (ages 3 to 6), late childhood (ages 7 to 10), early adolescence (ages 11 to 15), and late adolescence (ages 16 to 19). Each age group covers one or two major transitions in a child's life, such as school entrances or exits, biological maturation, possible cognitive changes, role changes, or some combination of these. These periods are characterized by relatively universal developmental challenges that require new modes of adaptation to biological, psychological, or social changes.[10]

Somewhat different indicators of child and youth well-being are associated with each period. For example, grade retention is more salient in the late childhood years than in adolescence (since most schools do not hold students back once they reach eighth grade[12]). Furthermore, low income might influence each indicator differently. As an illustration, income has stronger effects on cognitive and verbal ability test scores than it has on indices of emotional health in the childhood years.

Physical Health

Compared with nonpoor children, poor children in the United States experience diminished physical health as measured by a number of indicators of health status and outcomes (see Table 1). In the 1988 National Health Interview Survey; parents reported that poor children were only two-thirds as likely to be in excellent health and almost twice as likely to be in fair or poor health as nonpoor children. These large differences in health status between poor and nonpoor children do not reflect adjustment for potentially confounding factors (factors, other than income, that may be associated with living in poverty nor do they distinguish between long- or short-term poverty or the timing of poverty. This section reviews research on the relationship of poverty to several key measures of child health, low birth weight and infant mortality, growth stunting, and lead poisoning. For the most part, the focus is on research that attempts to adjust for important confounding factors and/or to address the effect of the duration of poverty on child health outcomes.

Birth Outcomes

Low birth weight (2,500 grams or less) and infant mortality are important indicators of child health. Low birth weight is associated with an increased

---

Poverty status had a statistically significant effect on both low birth weight and the neonatal morality rate for whites but not for blacks.

---

likelihood of subsequent physical health and cognitive and emotional problems that can persist through childhood and adolescence. Serious physical disabilities, grade repetition, and learning disabilities are more prevalent among children who were low birth weight as infants, as are lower levels of intelligence and of math and reading achievement. Low birth weight is also the key risk factor for infant mortality (especially death within the first 28 days of life), which is a widely accepted indicator of the health and well-being of children.[13]

Estimating the effects of poverty alone on birth outcomes is complicated by the fact that adverse birth outcomes are more prevalent for unmarried women, those with low levels of education, and black mothers—all groups with high poverty rates. One study that used data from the NLSY to examine the relationship between family income and low birth weight did find, however, that among whites, women with family income below the federal poverty level in the year of birth were 80% more likely to have a low birth weight baby as compared with women whose family incomes were above the poverty level (this study statistically controlled for mothers' age, education, marital status, and smoking status). Further analysis also showed that the duration of poverty had an important effect; if a white woman was poor both at the time when she entered the longitudinal NLSY sample and at the time of her pregnancy (5 to 10 years later), she was more than three times more likely to deliver a low birth weight infant than a white woman who was not poor at both times. For black women in this sample, although the odds of having a low birth weight baby were twice the odds for white mothers, the probability of having a low birth weight baby was not related to family poverty status.[14]

Table 1
Selected Population-Based Indicators of Well-Being for Poor and Nonpoor Children in the United States

Indicator	Percentage of Poor Children (unless noted)	Percentage of Nonpoor Children (unless noted)	Ratio of poor to Nonpoor Children
Physical Health Outcomes (for children between 0 and 17 years unless noted)			
Reported to be in excellent health[a]	37.4	55.2	0.7
Reported to be in fair to poor health[a]	11.7	6.5	1.8
Experienced an accident, poisoning, or injury in the past year that required medical attention[a]	11.8	14.7	0.8
Chronic asthma[a]	4.4	4.3	1.0
Low birth weight (less than 2,500 grams)[b]	1.0	0.6	1.7
Lead poisoning (blood lead levels 10u/dl or greater)[c]	16.3	4.7	3.5
Infant mortality[b]	1.4 deaths per 100 live births	0.8 death per 100 live births	1.7
Deaths During Childhood (0 to 14 years)[d]	1.2	0.8	1.5
Stunting (being in the fifth percentile for height for age for 2 to 17 years)[e]	10.0	5.0	2.0
Number of days spent in bed in past year[a]	5.3 days	3.8 days	1.4
Number of short-stay hospital episodes in past year per 1,000 children[a]	81.3 stays	41.2 stays	2.0
Cognitive Outcomes			
Developmental delay (includes both limited and long-term developmental deficits) (0 to 17 years)[a]	5.0	3.8	1.3
Learning disability (defined as having exceptional difficulty in learning to read, write, and do arithmetic) (3 to 17 years)[a]	8.3	6.1	1.4
School Achievement Outcomes (5 to 17 years)			
Grade repetition (reported to have ever repeated a grade)[a]	28.8	14.1	2.0
Ever expelled or suspended[a]	11.9	6.1	2.0
High school dropout (percentage 16- to 24-year olds who were not in school or did not finish high school in 1994)[f]	21.0	9.6	2.2
Emotional or Behavioral Outcomes (3 to 17 years unless noted)			
Parent reports child has ever had an emotional or behavioral problem that lasted three months or more[g]	16.4	12.7	1.3
Parent reports child ever being treated for an emotional problem or behavioral problem[a]	2.5	4.5	0.6
Parent reports child has experienced one or more of a list of typical child behavioral problems in the last three months[h] (5 to 17 years)	57.4	57.3	1.0
Other			
Female teens who had an out-of-wedlock birth[i]	11.0	3.6	3.1
Economically inactive at age 24 (not employed or in school)[j]	15.9	8.3	1.9
Experienced hunger (food insufficiency) at least once in past year[k]	15.9	1.6	9.9
Reported cases of child abuse and neglect[l]	5.4	0.8	6.8
Violent crimes (experienced by poor families and nonpoor families)[m]	5.4	2.6	2.1

Other studies that used county level data to examine the effects of income or poverty status and a number of pregnancy-related health services on birth outcomes for white and black women also found that income or poverty status had a statistically significant effect on both low birth weight and the neonatal mortality rate for whites but not for blacks.[15,16]

Growth Stunting

Although overt malnutrition and starvation are rare among poor children in the United States, deficits in children's nutritional status are associated with poverty. As described more fully in the Child Indicators article in this journal issue, stunting (low height for age), a measure of nutritional status, is more prevalent among poor than nonpoor chil-

Indicator	Percentage of Poor Children (unless noted)	Percentage of Nonpoor Children (unless noted)	Ratio of poor to Nonpoor Children
Afraid to go out (percentage of family heads in poor and nonpoor families who report they are afraid to go out in their neighborhood)[n]	19.5	8.7	2.2

Note: This list of child outcomes reflects findings from large, nationally representative surveys that collect data on child outcomes and family income. While most data comes from the 1988 National Health Interview Survey Child Health Supplement, data from other nationally representative surveys are included. The rates presented are from simple cross-tabulations. In most cases, the data do not reflect factors that might be important to child outcomes other than poverty status at the time of data collection. The ratios reflect rounding.

[a] Data from the 1988 National Health Interview Survey Child Health Supplement (NHS-CHS), a nationwide household interview survey. Children's health status was reported by the adult household member who knew the most about the sample child's health, usually the child's mother. Figures calculated from Dawson, D.A. *Family structure and children's health: United States, 1988.* Vital Health and Statistics, Series 10, n0. 178. Hyattsville, MD: U.S. Department of Health and Human Services, Public Health Service, June 1991; and Coiro, M.J., Zill, n., and Bloom, B. *Health of our nation's children.* Vital Health and Statistics, Series 10, n0. 191. Hyattsville, MD: U.S. department of Health and Human sErvices, Public Health Service, December 1994.

[b] Data from the National Maternal and Infant Health Survey, data collected in 1989 and 1990, with 1988 as the reference period. Percentages were calculated from the number of deaths and number of low birth weight births per 1,000 live births as reported in Federman, M., Garner, T., Short, K., et al. What does it mean to be poor in America? *Monthly Labor Review* (May 1996) 119, 5:10.

[c] Data from the NHANES III, 1988–1991. Poor children who lived in families with incomes less than 130% of the poverty threshold are classified as poor. All other children are classified as nonpoor.

[d] Percentages include only black and white youths. Percentages calculated from Table 7 in Rogot, E. *A mortality study of 1.3 million persons by demographic, social and economic factors: 1979–1985 follow-up.* Rockville, MD: National Institutes of Health, July 1992.

[e] Data from NHANES II, 1976–1980. For more discussion, see the Child Indicators article in this journal issue.

[f] National Center for Education Statistics. *Dropout rates in the United States: 1994.* Table 7, Status dropout rate, ages 16–24, by income and race ethnicity: October 1994. Available online at: http://www.ed.gov/NCES/pubs/r9410†07.html.

[g] Data from the NHIS-CHS. The question was meant to identify children with common psychological disorders such as attention deficit disorder or depression, as well as more severe problems such as autism.

[h] Data from the NHIS-CHS. Parents responded "sometimes true," "often true,", or "not true" to a list of 32 statements typical of children's behaviors. Each statement corresponded to one of six individual behavior problems—antisocial behavior, anxiety, peer conflict/social withdrawal, dependency, hyperactivity, and headstrong behavior. Statements included behaviors such as cheating or lying, being disobedient in the home, being secretive, and demanding a lot of attention. For a more complete description, see Section P-11 of the NHIS-CHS questionnaire.

[i] Data from the Panel Study of Income Dynamics (PSID). Based on 1,705 children ages 0 to 6 in 1968; outcomes measured at ages 21 to 27. Haveman, R., and Wolfe, B. Succeeding generations: On the effect of investments in children. New York: Russel Sage Foundation, 1994, p. 108, Table 4, 10c.

[j] Data from the PSID. Based on 1,705 children ages 0 to 6 in 1968; outcomes measured at ages 21 to 27. In Succeeding generations: On the effect of investments in children. Haveman, R., and Wolfe, B. New York: Russel Sage Foundation, 1994, p. 108, Table 4, 10d. Economically inactive is defined as not being a full-time student, working 1,000 hours or more per year; attending school part time and working 500 hours; a mother of an infant or mother of two or more children less than five years old; a part-time student and the mother of a child less than five years old.

[k] Data from NHANES III, 1988–1991. Figures reflect food insufficiency, the term used in government hunger-related survey questions. For a more in-depth discussion, see Lewit, E.M., and Kerrebrock, N. Child indicators: Childhood hunger. *The Future of Children* (Spring 1997), 7, 1:128–37.

[l] Data from Study of National Incidence and Prevalence of Child Abuse and Neglect: 1988. In *Wasting America's future.* Children's Defense Fund. Boston: Beacon Press, 1994, pp. 5–29, 87, Tables 5–6. Poor families are those with annual incomes below $15,000.

[m] Data from the National Crime Victimization Interview Survey. Results are for households or persons living in households. Data were collected between January 1992 and June 1993 with 1992 as the reference period. Percentages are calculated from number of violent crimes per 1,000 people per year. Reported in Federman, M., Garner, T., Short, K., et al. What does it mean to be poor in America? *Monthly Labor Review.* (May 1996) 119,5:9.

[n] Data from the Survey of Income and Program Participation. Participation data collection and reference periods are September through December 1992. Reported in Federman, M., Garner, T., Short, K., et al. What does it mean to be poor in America? *Monthly Labor Review* (May 1996) 119,5:9.

dren. Studies using data from the NLSY show that differentials in height for age between poor and nonpoor children are greater when long-term rather than single-year measures of poverty are used in models to predict stunting. These differentials by poverty status are large even in models that statistically control for many other family and child characteristics associated with poverty.[17]

Lead Poisoning

Harmful effects of lead have been documented even at low levels of exposure. Health problems vary with length of exposure, intensity of lead in the environment, and the developmental stage of the child—with risks beginning prior to birth. At very young ages, lead exposure is linked to stunted growth,[18] hearing loss,[19] vitamin D metabolism damage, impaired blood production, and toxic effects on the kidneys.[20] Additionally, even a small increase in blood lead above the Centers for Disease Control and Prevention (CDC) current intervention threshold (10 μg/dL) is associated with a decrease in intelligence quotient (IQ).[21]

Today, deteriorating lead-based house paint remains the primary source of lead for young children. Infants and toddlers in old housing eat the sweet-tasting paint chips and breathe the lead dust from deteriorating paint. Four to five million children reside in homes with lead levels exceeding the accepted threshold for safety,[22] and more than 1.5 million children under six years of age have elevated blood lead levels.[23]

> *The effects of long-term poverty on measures of children's cognitive ability were significantly greater than the effects of short-term poverty.*

Using data from NHANES III (1988–1991), one study found that children's blood lead levels declined as family income increased.[23] All other things being equal, mean blood lead levels were 9% lower for one- to five-year-olds in families with incomes twice the poverty level than for those who were poor. Overall blood levels were highest among one to five-year-olds who were non-Hispanic blacks from low-income families in large central cities. The mean blood lead level for this group, 9.7 μg/dL, was just under the CDC's threshold for intervention and almost three times the mean for all one- to five-year-olds.

Cognitive Abilities

As reported in Table 1, children living below the poverty threshold are 1.3 times as likely as non-poor children to experience learning disabilities and developmental delays. Reliable measures of cognitive ability and school achievement for young children in the Children of the NLSY and IHDP data sets have been used in a number of studies to examine the relationship between cognitive ability and poverty in detail.[6,24–26] This article reports on several studies that control for a number of potentially important family characteristics and attempts to distinguish between the effects of long- and short-term poverty.

A recent study using data from the Children of the NLSY and the IHDP compared children in families with incomes less than half of the poverty threshold to children in families with incomes between 1.5 and twice the poverty threshold. The poorer children scored between 6 and 13 points lower on various standardized tests of IQ, verbal ability; and achievement.[25] These differences are very large from an educational perspective and were present even after controlling for maternal age, marital status, education, and ethnicity. A 6- to 13-point difference might mean, for example, the difference between being placed in a special education class or not. Children in families with incomes closer to, but still below, the poverty line also did worse than children in higher-income families, but the differences were smaller. The smallest differences appeared for the earliest (age two) measure of cognitive ability; however, the sizes of the effects were similar for children from three to eight. These findings suggest that the effects of poverty on children's cognitive development occur early.

The study also found that duration of poverty was an important factor in the lower scores of poor children on measures of cognitive ability. Children who lived in persistently poor families (defined in this study as poor over a four-year span) had scores on the various assessments six to nine points lower than children who were never poor.[25] Another analysis of the NLSY that controlled for a number of important maternal and child health characteristics showed that the effects of long-term poverty (based on family income averaged over 13 years prior to testing of the child) on measures of children's cognitive ability were significantly greater than the effects of short-term poverty (measured by income in the year of observation).[26]

A few studies link long-term family income to cognitive ability and achievement measured during the school years. Research on children's test scores at ages seven and eight found that the effects of income on these scores were similar in size to those reported for three-year-olds.[25] But research relating family income measured during adolescence on cognitive ability finds relatively smaller effects.[27] As summarized in the next section, these modest effects of income on cognitive ability are consistent with literature showing modest effects of income on schooling attainment, but both sets of studies may be biased by the fact that their measurement of parental income is restricted to the child's adolescent years. It is not yet possible to make conclusive statements regarding the size of the effects of poverty on children's long-term cognitive development.

School Achievement Outcomes

Educational attainment is well recognized as a powerful predictor of experiences in later life. A comprehensive review of the relationship between parental income and school attainment, published in 1994, concluded that poverty limited school achievement but that the effect of income on the number of school years completed was small.[28] In general, the studies suggested that a 10% increase in family income is associated with a 0.2% to 2% increase in the number of school years completed.[28]

Several more recent studies using different longitudinal data sets (the PSID, the NLSY and Children of the NLSY) also find that poverty status has a small negative impact on high school graduation and years of schooling obtained. Much of the observed relationship between income and schooling appears to be related to a number of confounding factors such as parental education, family structure, and neighborhood characteristics.[28-30] Some of these studies suggest that the components of income (for example, AFDC) and the way income is measured (number of years in poverty versus annual family income or the ratio of income to the poverty threshold) may lead to somewhat different conclusions. But all the studies suggest that, after controlling for many appropriate confounding variables, the effects of poverty per se on school achievement are likely to be statistically significant, yet small. Based on the results of one study, the authors estimated that, if poverty were eliminated for all children, mean years of schooling for all children would increase by only 0.3% (less than half a month).[30]

Why do not the apparently strong effects of parental income on cognitive abilities and school achievement in the early childhood years translate into larger effects on completed schooling? One possible reason is that extrafamilial environments (for example, schools and neighborhoods) begin to matter as much or more for children than family conditions once children reach school age. A second possible reason is that school-related achievement depends on both ability and behavior. As is discussed in the Emotional and Behavioral Outcomes section, children's behavioral problems, measured either before or after the transition into school, are not very sensitive to parental income differences.

A third, and potentially crucial, reason concerns the timing of economic deprivation. Few studies measure income from early childhood to adolescence, so there is no way to know whether poverty early in childhood has noteworthy effects on later outcomes such as school completion. Because family income varies over time,[31] income measured during adolescence, or even middle childhood, may not reflect income in early childhood. A recent study that attempted to evaluate how the timing of income might affect completed schooling found that family income averaged

---

For low-income children, a $10,000 increase in mean family income between birth and age 5 was associated with nearly a full-year increase in completed schooling.

---

from birth to age 5 had a much more powerful effect on the number of school years a child completes than does family income measured either between ages 5 and 10 or between ages 11 and 15.[7] For low-income children, a $10,000 increase in mean family income between birth and age 5 was associated with nearly a full-year increase in completed schooling. Similar increments to family income later in childhood had no significant impact, suggesting that income may indeed be an important determinant of completed schooling but that only income during the early childhood years matters.

Emotional and Behavioral Outcomes

Poor children suffer from emotional and behavioral problems more frequently than do nonpoor children (see Table 1). Emotional outcomes are often grouped along two dimensions: externalizing behaviors including aggression, fighting, and acting out, and internalizing behaviors such as anxiety, social withdrawal, and depression. Data regarding emotional outcomes are based on parental and teacher reports. This section reviews studies that distingnish between the effects of long- and short-term poverty on emotional outcomes of children at different ages.

One study of low birth weight five-year-olds using the IHDP data set found that children in persistently poor families had more internalizing and externalizing behavior problems than children who had never been poor. The analysis controlled for maternal education and family structure and defined long-term poverty as income below the poverty threshold for each of four consecutive years. Short-term poverty (defined as poor in at least one of four years) was also associated with more behavioral problems, though the effects were not as large as those for persistent poverty.[6]

Two different studies using the NLSY report findings consistent with those of the IHDP study. Both found persistent poverty to be a significant predictor of some behavioral problems.[26,32] One study used data from the 1986 NLSY and found that for four- to eight-year-olds persistent poverty (defined as a specific percentage of years of life

---

Problematic emotional outcomes are associated with family poverty; however, the effects of poverty on emotional outcomes are not as large as its effects on cognitive outcomes.

---

during which the child lived below the poverty level) was positively related to the presence of internalizing symptoms (such as dependence, anxiety, and unhappiness) even after controlling for current poverty status, mother's age, education, and marital status. In contrast, current poverty (defined by current family income below the poverty line) but not persistent poverty was associated with more externalizing problems (such as hyperactivity, peer conflict, and headstrong behavior).[32]

The second study used NLSY data from 1978–1991 and analyzed children ages 3 to 11. On average children living in long-term poverty (defined by the ratio of family income to the poverty level averaged over 13 years) ranked three to seven percentile points higher (indicating more problems) on a behavior problem index than children with incomes above the poverty line. After controlling for a range of factors including mother's characteristics, nutrition, and infant health behaviors, the difference remained though it dropped in magnitude. This study also found that children who experienced one year of poverty had more behavioral problems than children who had lived in long-term poverty.[26]

The above studies demonstrate that problematic emotional outcomes are associated with family poverty. However, it is important to note that the effects of poverty on emotional outcomes are not as large as those found in cognitive outcomes. Also these studies do not show that children in long-term poverty experience emotional problems with greater frequency or of the same type as children who experience only short-term poverty. These studies analyzed data for young children. Few

studies have examined the link between emotional outcomes and poverty for adolescents. One small study of 7th- to 10th-graders in the rural Midwest did not find a statistically significant relationship between poverty and emotional problems, either internalizing or externalizing.[33] Self-reporting by the adolescents rather than maternal reporting, as used in the data sets on younger children, may account for the differences found in the effects of income on emotional outcomes in this study as compared with the previously reviewed research. It may also be that younger children are more affected by poverty than older children.

These findings point to the need for further research to improve understanding of the link between income and children's emotional outcomes.

Teenage Out-of-Wedlock Childbearing

The negative consequences for both mothers and children associated with births to unwed teen mothers make it a source of policy concern.[34] Although the rate of out-of-wedlock births among poor teens is almost three times as high as the rate among those from nonpoor families (see Table 1), the literature on linkages between family income and out-of-wedlock childbearing is not conclusive. A recent review of the evidence put it this way: "[P]arental income is negative and usually, but not always, significant. . . . The few reports of the quantitative effects of simulated changes in variables suggest that decreases in parental income . . . will lead to small increases in the probability that teen girls will experience a nonmarital birth."[28]

A recent study, which used data from the PSID to investigate factors in teen out-of-wedlock births, found that variations in income around the poverty threshold were not predictive of a teenage birth but that the probability of a teenager's having an out-of-wedlock birth declined significantly at family income levels above twice the poverty threshold.[35] The duration and timing of poverty had no effect on the probability of a teen out-of-wedlock birth. These findings are somewhat different from those reported for cognitive outcomes and school achievement. In the case of cognitive outcomes for young children, the variation in income mattered most to children at very low levels of income; for school achievement, the timing and duration of poverty seemed to have important differential effects on outcomes.

Why should poverty status matter more for schooling than for childbearing? This difference is consistent with the more general result that parental income appears more strongly linked with ability and achievement than with behavior. The factors influencing teenage out-of-wedlock childbearing are less well understood than the factors influencing schooling completion: interventions have generally been much less successful in altering teen birthrates than in keeping teens in school.[36,37]

Pathways Through Which Poverty Operates

The research reviewed thus far suggests that living in poverty exacts a heavy toll on children. However, it does not shed light on the pathways or mechanisms by which low income exerts its effects on children. As the term is used in this discussion, a "pathway" is a mechanism through which poverty or income can influence a child outcome. By implication, this definition implies that a pathway should be causally related to both income and at least one child outcome. Exploration of these pathways is important for a more complete understanding of the effects of poverty on children; moreover, exploration of pathways can lead to the identification of leverage points that may be amenable to policy intervention and remediation in the absence of a change in family income.

Research on the size and strength of the pathways through which income might influence child health and development is still scanty. In this section, five potential pathways are discussed: (1) health and nutrition, (2) the home environment, (3) parental interactions with children, (4) parental mental health, and (5) neighborhood conditions. Space limitations preclude a discussion of other potential pathways such as access to and use of prenatal care, access to pediatric

care, exposure to environmental toxins, household stability, provision of learning experiences outside the home, quality of school attended, and peer groups. Further, few studies have tested pathway models using these variables.

A child's home environment accounts for a substantial portion of the effects of family income on cognitive outcomes in young children.

Health and Nutrition

Although health is itself an outcome, it can also be viewed as a pathway by which poverty influences other child outcomes, such as cognitive ability and school achievement. As discussed previously poor children experience increased rates of low birth weight and elevated blood lead levels when compared with nonpoor children. These conditions have, in turn, been associated with reduced IQ and other measures of cognitive functioning in young children and, in the case of low birth weight, with increased rates of learning disabilities, grade retention, and school dropout in older children and youths.

A 1990 analysis indicated that the poverty-related health factors such as low birth weight, ele-

© Steven Rubin

vated blood lead levels, anemia,[38] and recurrent ear infections and hearing loss contributed to the differential in IQ scores between poor and nonpoor four-year-olds.[39] The findings suggest that the cumulative health disadvantage experienced by poor children on these four health measures may have accounted for as much as 13% to 20% of the difference in IQ between the poor and nonpoor four-year-olds during the 1970s and 1980s.[39]

Parents who are poor are likely to be less healthy, both emotionally and physically, than those who are not poor.

As discussed in the Child Indicators article in this journal issue, malnutrition in childhood (as measured by anthropometric indicators) is associated with lower scores on tests of cognitive development. Deficits in these anthropometric measures are associated with poverty among children in the United States, and the effects can be substantial. One recent study found that the effect of stunting on short-term memory was equivalent to the difference in short-term memory between children in families that had experienced poverty for 13 years and children in families with incomes at least three times the poverty level.[26]

Home Environment
A number of studies have found that a child's home environment—opportunities for learning, warmth of mother-child interactions, and the physical condition of the home—account for a substantial portion of the effects of family income on cognitive outcomes in young children. Some large longitudinal data sets use the HOME scale as a measure of the home environment. The HOME scale is made up of items that measure household resources, such as reading materials and toys, and parental practices, such as discipline methods. The HOME scale has been shown to be correlated with family income and poverty, with higher levels of income associated with improved home environments as measured by the scale.[7,40]

Several studies have found that differences in the home environment of higher-and lower-income children, as measured by the HOME scale, account for a substantial portion of the effect of income on the cognitive development of preschool children and on the achievement scores of

elementary school children.[6,26,37] In one study, differences in the home environment also seemed to account for some of the effects of poverty status on behavioral problems. In addition, the provisions of learning experiences in the home (measured by specific subscales of the HOME scale) have been shown to account for up to half of the effect of poverty status on the IQ scores of five-year-olds.[37,41]

Parental Interactions with Children
A number of studies have attempted to go beyond documentation of activities and materials in the home to capture the effects of parent-child interactions on child outcomes. Much of the work is based on small and/or community-based samples. That work suggests that child adjustment and achievement are facilitated by certain parental practices. There is also some evidence that poverty is linked to lower-quality parent-child interaction and to increased use of harsh punishment. This research suggests that parental practices may be an important pathway between economic resources and child outcomes.

Evidence of such a parental-practice pathway from research using large national data sets of the kind reviewed in this article is less consistent. One NLSY-based study found that currently poor mothers spanked their children more often than nonpoor mothers and that this harsh behavior was an important component of the effect of poverty on children's mental health.[32] Mothers' parenting behavior was not, however, found to be an important pathway by which persistent poverty affected children's mental health. A more recent study using the National Survey of Families and Households found that the level of household income was only weakly related to effective parenting and that differences in parent practices did not account for much of the association between poverty and child well-being.[42]

Among adolescents, family economic pressure may lead to conflict with parents, resulting in lower school grades, reduced emotional health, and impaired social relationships.[33,43] Other work suggests that it may be income loss or economic uncertainty due to unemployment, underemployment, and unstable work conditions, rather than poverty or low income per se, that is a source for conflict between parents and teens leading to emotional and school problems.[33,44]

Parental Mental Health
Parents who are poor are likely to be less healthy, both emotionally and physically, than those who are not poor.[45] And parental irritability and depressive symptoms are associated with more con-

flicted interactions with adolescents, leading to less satisfactory emotional, social, and cognitive development.[43,46,47] Some studies have established that parental mental health accounts for some of the effect of economic circumstances on child health and behavior. Additionally, poor parental mental health is associated with impaired parent-child interactions and less provision of learning experiences in the home.[33,41,48]

Neighborhood Conditions

Another possible pathway through which family income operates has to do with the neighborhoods in which poor families reside. Poor parents are constrained in their choice of neighborhoods and schools. Low income may lead to residence in extremely poor neighborhoods characterized by social disorganization (crime, many unemployed adults, neighbors not monitoring the behavior of adolescents) and few resources for child development (playgrounds, child care, health care facilities, parks, after-school programs).[49,50] The affluence of neighborhoods is associated with child and adolescent outcomes (intelligence test scores at ages 3 and 5 and high school graduation rates by age 20) over and above family poverty.[37,51] Neighborhood residence also seems to be associated with parenting practices, over and above family income and education.[52] Neighborhood effects on intelligence scores are in part mediated by the learning environment in the home.[52,53] Living in neighborhoods with high concentrations of poor people is associated with less provision of learning experiences in the homes of preschoolers, over and above the links seen between family income and learning experiences.

A key issue that has not been fully explored is the extent to which neighborhood effects may be overestimated because neighborhood characteristics also reflect the choices of neighborhood residents. One study that examined the effects of peer groups (as measured by the socioeconomic status of students in a respondent's school) on teenage pregnancy and school dropout behavior found that while student body socioeconomic status seemed to be an important predictor of both dropout and teen pregnancy rates, it did not appear to be related to those outcomes in statistical models that treated this peer characteristic as a matter of family choice.[54]

How Much Does Income Cause Child Outcomes?

It may seem odd to raise this question after summarizing evidence indicating that family income does matter—across the childhood and adolescent years and for a number of indicators of well-being. However, these associations have been demonstrated when a relatively small set of family characteristics are controlled through statistical analyses. It is possible, therefore, that other important family characteristics have not been controlled for and that, as a result of this

---

Low income may lead to residence in extremely poor neighborhoods characterized by social disorganization and few resources for child development.

---

omission, the effects of income are estimated incorrectly. . . . Distinguishing between the effects on children of poverty and its related events and conditions is crucial for public policy formulation. Programs that alter family income may not have intended benefits for children if the importance of family income has been mismeasured.

Despite the evidence reviewed in this article and elsewhere, there is an important segment of the population who believes that income per se may not appreciably affect child outcomes. This viewpoint sees parental income mainly as a proxy for other charateristics such as character (a strong work ethic) or genetic endowment that influence both children and parents. A recent book by Susan Mayer, *What Money Can't Buy: The Effect of Parental Income on Children's Outcomes,*[55] presents a series of tests to examine explicitly the effects of income on a set of child outcomes. In one test, measures of income *after* the occurrence of an outcome are added to statistical models of the effects of income and other characteristics on a child outcome. The idea behind this test is that unanticipated future income can capture unmeasured parental characteristics but cannot have caused the child outcome. The inclusion of future income frequently produced a large reduction in the estimated impact of prior parent income. Mayer also tries to estimate the effects on children of components of income (for example, asset income) that are independent of the actions of the family. Although these tests provide some support for the hypothesis that family income may not matter much for child outcomes, even Mayer admits that these statistical procedures are not without their problems. For example, prior income and future income are highly correlated, and if parents take reasonable expectations of future income into consideration in making decisions regarding the well-being of children, then the assumption that child outcomes are independent of future income, which underlies the first test, is violated.

A second approach to the problem that omitted variables may bias the estimation of the effects of income and poverty on children looks at siblings within families. Siblings reared in the same family share many of the same unmeasured family characteristics. Thus, comparing children at the same age within families makes it possible to look at the income of the family at different time points (for example, if a firstborn was five years of age in 1985 and the second child was five years of age in 1988, it is possible to look at their achievement levels at this age and the average family income between 1980 and 1985 for the firstborn and between 1983 and 1988 for the second child). One study that used this approach found that sibling differences in income were associated with sibling differences in completed schooling, which gave support to the notion that family income matters.[7]

Perhaps the most convincing demonstration of the effects of income is to provide poor families with income in the context of a randomized trial. In four Income Maintenance/Negative Income Tax Experiments in the 1960s and 1970s, experimental treatment families received a guaranteed minimum income. (These experiments are discussed in more detail in the article by Janet Currie in this journal issue.) Substantial benefits resulting from increased income effects were found for child nutrition, early school achievement, and high school completion in some sites but not in others. These results might be viewed as inconclusive; however, since the site with the largest effects for younger children (North Carolina) was also the poorest, one interpretation of the results is that income effects are most important for the very poorest families.[56,57]

Conclusion

The evidence reviewed in this article supports the conclusion that family income can substantially influence child and adolescent well-being. However, the associations between income and child outcomes are more complex and varied than suggested by the simple associations presented in Table 1. Family income seems to be more strongly related to children's ability and achievement-related outcomes than to emotional outcomes. In addition, the effects are particularly pronounced for children who live below the poverty line for multiple years and for children who live in extreme poverty (that is, 50% or less of the poverty threshold). These income effects are probably not due to some unmeasured characteristics of low-income families: family income, in and of itself, does appear to matter.

The timing of poverty is also important, although this conclusion is based on only a small number of studies. Low income during the preschool and early school years exhibits the strongest correlation with low rates of high school completion, as compared with low income during the childhood and adolescent years.[7,58] Poor-quality schooling, which is correlated with high neighborhood poverty, may exacerbate this effect.[59] These findings suggest that early childhood interventions may be critical in reducing the impact of low income on children's lives.

The pathways through which low income influences children also suggest some general recommendations. Nutrition programs, especially if they target the most undernourished poor, may have beneficial effects on both physical and cognitive outcomes. Lead abatement and parental education programs may improve cognitive outcomes in poor children residing in inner-city neighborhoods where lead is still an important hazard.

Because about one-half of the effect of family income on cognitive ability is mediated by the home environment, including learning experiences in the home, interventions might profitably focus on working with parents. An example is the Learningames curriculum in which parents are provided instruction, materials, and role playing in learning experiences.[60] Other effective learning-oriented programs might also be pursued.[61–63]

Finally, income policies (as discussed by Robert Plotnick in this journal issue) and in-kind support programs (as discussed by Devaney, Ellwood, and Love in this journal issue) can have immediate impact on the number or children living in poverty and on the circumstances in which they live. Most important, based on this review, would be efforts to eliminate deep and persistent poverty especially during a child's early years. Support to families with older children may be desirable on other grounds, but the available research suggests that it will probably not have the same impact on child outcomes as programs focused on younger children.

The authors would like to thank the National Institute of Child Health and Human Development Research Network on Child and Family Well-being for supporting the writing of this article. The Russell Sage Foundation's contribution is also appreciated as is that of the William T. Grant Foundation, and the Canadian Institute for Advanced Research. The authors are also grateful for the feedback provided by Linda Baker, Pamela K. Klebanov, and Judith Smith and would like to thank Phyllis Gyamfi for her editorial assistance.

1. Hernandez, D.J. *America's children: Resources from family government and the economy.* New York: Russell Sage Foundation, 1993.
2. Duncan, G.J., and Brooks-Gunn, J., eds. *Consequences of growing up poor.* New York: Russell Sage Foundation, 1997.
3. Duncan, G.J., and Rodgers, W.L. Longitudinal aspects of childhood poverty. *Journal of Marriage and the Family* (November 1988) 50,4:1007–21.
4. Chase-Lansdale, P.L., and Brooks-Gunn, J., eds. *Escape from poverty: What makes a difference for children?* New York: Cambridge University Press, 1995.
5. Children's Defense Fund. *Wasting America's future.* Boston: Beacon Press, 1994; Klerman, L. *Alive and well?* New York: National Center for Children in Poverty, Columbia University, 1991.
6. Duncan, G.J., Brooks-Gunn, J., and Klebanov, P.K. Economic deprivation and early-childhood development. *Child Development* (1994) 65,2:296–318.
7. Duncan, G.J., Yeung, W., Brooks-Gunn, J., and Smith, J.R. How much does childhood poverty affect the life chances of children? *American Sociological Review,* in press.
8. Hauser R., Brown, B., and Prosser W. *Indicators of children's well-being.* New York: Russell Sage Foundation, in press.
9. Brooks-Gunn,J., Guo, G., and Furstenberg, F.F.Jr. Who drops out of and who continues beyond high school?: A 20-year study of black youth. *Journal of Research in Adolescence* (1993) 37,3:271–94.
10. Graber, J.A., and Brooks-Gunn, J. Transitions and turning points: Navigating the passage from childhood through adolescence. *Developmental Psychology* (1996) 32,4:768–76.
11. Rutter, M. Beyond longitudinal data: Causes, consequences, changes and continuity. *Journal of Counseling and Clinical Psychology* (1994) 62,5:928–90.
12. Guo, G., Brooks-Gunn, J., and Harris, K.M. Parents' labor-force attachment and grade retention among urban black children. *Sociology of Education* (1996) 69,3:217–36.
13. For a review of the causes and consequences of low birth weight in the United States, see Shiono, P., ed. Low Birth Weight. *The Future of Children* (Spring 1995) 5,1:4–231.
14. Starfield, B., Shapiro, S., Weiss, J., et al. Race, family income, and low birth weight. *American Journal of Epidemiology* (1991) 134,10:1167–74.
15. Corman, H., and Grossman, M. Determinants of neonatal mortality rates in the U.S.: A reduced form model. *Journal of Health Economics* (1985) 4,3:213–36.
16. Frank, R., Strobino, D., Salkever, D., and Jackson, C. Updated estimates of the impact of prenatal care on birthweight outcomes by race. *Journal of Human Resources* (1992) 27,4:629–42.
17. Miller, J., and Korenman, S. Poverty and children's nutritional status in the United States. *American Journal of Epidemiology* (1994) 140,3:233–43.
18. Schwartz, J., Angle, C., and Pitcher, H. Relationship between childhood blood lead levels and stature. *Pediatrics* (1986) 77,3:281–88.
19. Schwartz, J., and Otto, D. Lead and minor hearing impairment. *Archives of Environmental Health* (1991) 46,5:300–05.
20. Agency for Toxic Substances and Disease Registry. *The nature and extent of lead poisoning in the US.: A report to Congress.* Washington, DC: U.S. Department of Health and Human Services, 1988, Section II, p. 7.
21. Schwartz, J. Low level lead exposure and children's IQ: A meta-analysis and search for threshold. *Environmental Research* (1994) 65,1:42–55.
22. Ronald Morony, Deputy Director, U.S. Department of Housing and Urban Development, Office of Lead Based Paint Abatement and Poisoning Prevention, Washington, DC. Personal communication, November 20, 1996.
23. Brody, D.J., Pirkle, L., Kramer, R., et al. Blood lead levels in the U.S. population. *Journal of the American Medical Association* (1994) 272,4:277–81.
24. Brooks-Gunn, J., McCarton, C.M., Casey, P.H., et al. Early intervention in low birth weight premature infants: Results through age 5 years from the Infant Health and Development Program. *Journal of the American Medical Association* (1994) 272,16:1257–62.
25. Smith, J.R., Brooks-Gunn, J., and Klebanov, P. The consequences of living in poverty for young children's cognitive and verbal ability and early school achievement. In *Consequences of growing up poor.* G.J. Duncan and J. Brooks-Gunn, eds. New York: Russell Sage Foundation, 1997.
26. Korenman, S., Miller, J.E., and Sjaastad,J.E. Long-term poverty and child development in the United States: Results from the National Longitudinal Survey of Youth. *Children and Youth Services Review* (1995)17,1/2:127–51.
27. Peters. E., and Mullis, N. The role of the family and source of income in adolescent achievement. In *Consequences of growing up poor:* G. Duncan and J. Brooks-Gunn, eds. New York: Russell Sage Foundation, 1997.
28. Haveman, R., and Wolfe, B. The determinants of children's attainments: A review of methods and findings. *Journal of Economic Literature* (1995) 33,3:1829–78.
29. Teachman,J., Paasch, K.M., Day, R., and Carver, K.P Poverty during adolescence and subsequent educational attainment. In *Consequences of growing*

up poor: G. Duncan and J. Brooks-Gunn, eds. New York: Russell Sage Foundation, 1997.

30. Haveman, R., and Wolfe, B. *Succeeding generations: On the effect of investments in children.* New York: Russell Sage Foundation, 1994.

31. Duncan, G.J. Volatility of family income over the life course. In *Life-span development and behavior.* Vol. 9. P. Baltes, D. Featherman, and R.M. Lerner, eds. Hillsdale, NJ: Erlbaum, 1988, pp. 317–58.

32. McLeod, J.D., and Shanahan, M.J. Poverty, parenting and children's mental health. *American Sociological Review* (June 1993) 58,3:351–66.

33. Conger, R.D., Conger, K.J., and Elder, G.H. Family economic hardship and adolescent adjustment: Mediating and moderating processes. In *Consequences of growing up poor:* G. Duncan and J. Brooks-Gunn, eds. New York: Russell Sage Foundation, 1997.

34. Hotz, V.J., McElroy, S.W., and Sanders, S.G. Costs and consequences of teenage childbearing. *Chicago Policy Review.* Internet: http://www.spc.uchicago.edu/cpr/Teenage_Child.htm.

35. Haveman, R., Wolfe, B., and Wilson, K. Childhood poverty and adolescent schooling and fertility outcomes: Reduced form and structural estimates. In *Consequences of growing up poor.* G.J. Duncan and J. Brooks-Gunn, eds. New York: Russell Sage Foundation, 1997.

36. U.S. Department of Health and Human Services. *Report to Congress on out-of-wedlock childbearing.* PHS-95–1257. Hyattsville, MD: DHHS, September 1995.

37. Brooks-Gunn, J., Duncan, G.J., Klebanov, P.K., and Sealand, N. Do neighborhoods influence child and adolescent behavior? *American Journal of Sociology* (1993) 99,2:335–95.

38. Iron-deficiency anemia is an important health problem that was traditionally identified with child poverty. Iron-deficiency anemia has been associated with impaired exercise capacity, increased susceptibility to lead absorption, and developmental and behavioral problems; see Oski, F. Iron deficiency in infancy and childhood. *The New England Journal of Medicine.* (July 15, 1993) 329,3:190–93. The importance of iron-deficiency anemia and its sequelae among poor children in the United States today is unclear. Increased use of iron-fortified foods and infant formulas along with their provision through public nutrition programs such as the Special Supplemental Food Program for Women, Infants, and Children (see the article by Devaney, Ellwood, and Love in this journal issue) have contributed to a dramatic decline in anemia; see Yip, R., Binkin, N.J., Fleshood, L., and Trowbridge, F.L. Declining prevalence of anemia among low-income children in the U.S. *Journal of American Medical Association* (1987) 258,12:1623. Between 1980 and 1991, the prevalence of anemia among infants and children through age five declined from 7% to 3%. Still, low-income children participating in public health programs have a higher-than-average prevalence of anemia; see Yip, R., Parvanta, I., Scanlon, K., et al. Pediatric Nutrition Surveillance System—United States, 1980–1991. *Morbidity and Mortality Weekly Report* (November 1992) 41,SS-7:1–24.

In part, this is because risk of anemia is a criterion for enrollment in these programs and also because these low-income children have low iron levels.

39. Goldstein, N. *Explaining socioeconomic differences in children's cognitive test scores.* Working Paper No. H-90-1. Cambridge, MA: Malcolm Wiener Center for Social Policy, John F. Kennedy School of Government, Harvard University, 1990.

40. Garrett, P., Ng'andu, N., and Ferron, J. Poverty experience of young children and the quality of their home environments. *Child Development* (1994) 65,2:331–45.

41. Bradley, R.H. Home environment and parenting. In *Handbook of parenting:* M. Bornstein, ed. Hillsdale, NJ: Erlbaum, 1995.

42. Hanson, T., McLanahan, S., and Thomson, E. Economic resources, parental practices, and child well-being. In *Consequences of growing up poor:* G.J. Duncan and J. Brooks-Gunn, eds. New York: Russell Sage Foundation, 1997.

43. Conger, R.D., Ge, S., Elder, G.H., Jr., et al. Economic stress, coercive family process and developmental problems of adolescents. *Child Development* (1994) 65,2:541–61.

44. McLoyd, V.C. The impact of economic hardship on black families and children: Psychological distress, parenting, and socioemotional development. *Child Development* (1990) 61,2:311–46.

45. Adler, N.E., Boyce, T., Chesney, M.A., et al. Socioeconomic inequalities in health: No easy solution. *Journal of the American Medical Association* (1993) 269:3140–45.

46. Liaw, F.R., and Brooks-Gunn, J. Cumulative familial risks and low birth weight children's cognitive and behavioral development. *Journal of Clinical Child Psychology* (1995) 23,4:360–72.

47. McLoyd, V.C., Jayaratne, T.E., Ceballo, R., and Borquez, J. Unemployment and work interruption among African American single mothers. Effects on parenting and adolescent socioemotional functioning. *Child Development* (1994) 65,2:562–89.

48. Brooks-Gunn, J., Klebanov, P.K., and Liaw, F. The learning, physical, and emotional environment of the home in the context of poverty: The Infant Health and Development Program. *Children and Youth Services Review* (1995)17,1/2.251–76.

49. Wilson, W.J. *The truly disadvantaged. The inner city, the underclass, and public policy.* Chicago. University of Chicago Press, 1987.

50. Sampson, R., and Morenoff, J. Ecological perspectives on the neighborhood context of urban poverty: Past and present. In *Neighborhood poverty: Conceptual, methodological, and policy approaches to studying neighborhoods.* Vol. 2. J. Brooks-Gunn, G. Duncan, and J.L. Aber, eds. New York: Russell Sage Foundation, in press.

51. Brooks-Gunn, J., Duncan, G.J., and Aber, J.L., eds. *Neighborhood poverty: Context and consequences for children.* Vol. 1. New York: Russell Sage Foundation, in press.

52. Klebanov, P.K., Brooks-Gunn, J., and Duncan, G.J. Does neighborhood and family poverty affect mother's parenting, mental health and social support? *Journal of Marriage and Family* (1994) 56,2:441–55.

53. Klebanov, P.K., Brooks-Gunn, J., Chase-Lansdale, L., and Gordon, R. The intersection of the neigh-

borhood and home environment and its influence on young children. In *Neighborhood poverty: Context and consequences for children.* Vol. 1. J. Brooks-Gunn, G.J. Duncan, and J.L. Aber, eds. New York: Russell Sage Foundation, in press.

54. Evans, W.N.. Oates, W.E., and Schwab, R.M. Measuring peer group effects: A study of teenage behavior. *Journal of Practical Economy* (1992) 100,5:966–91.

55. Mayer S.E. *What money can't buy: The effect of parental income on children's outcomes.* Cambridge, MA: Harvard University Press, 1997.

56. Kershwa, D., and Fair, J. *The New Jersey income maintenance experiment.* Vol. I. New York: Academic Press, 1976.

57. Salkind, N.J., and Haskins, R. Negative income tax: The impact on children from low-income families. *Journal of Family Issues* (1982) 3,2:165–80.

58. Baydar, N., Brooks-Gunn, J., and Furstenberg, E.F., Jr. Early warning signs of functional illiteracy: Predictors in childhood and adolescence. *Child Development* (1993) 64,3:815–29.

59. Alexander, K.L., and Entwisle, D.R. Achievement in the first 2 years of school: Patterns and processes. *Monographs of the Society for Research in Child Development* (1988) 53,2:1–153.

60. Sparling, J.J., and Lewis, J. *Partner for learning.* Lewisville, NC: Kaplan, 1984.

61. Olds, D.L., and Kitzman, H. Review of research on home visiting for pregnant women and parents of young children. *The Future of Children* (Winter 1993) 3,3:53–92.

62. Brooks-Gunn, J., Denner, J., and Klebanov, P.K. Families and neighborhoods as contexts for education. In *Changing populations, changing schools: Ninety-fourth yearbook of the National Society for the Study of Education, Part II.* E. Flaxman and A. H. Passow, eds. Chicago, IL: National Society for the Study of Education, 1995, pp. 233–52.

63. Brooks-Gunn, J. Strategies for altering the outcomes of poor children and their families. In *Escape from poverty: What makes a difference for children?* P.L. Chase-Lansdale and J. Brooks-Gunn, eds. New York: Cambridge University Press, 1996.

TV VIOLENCE
Myth and Reality

MARY A. HEPBURN

Mary A. Hepburn is professor of social science education and head of the Citizen Education Division at the Carl Vinson Institute of Government, University of Georgia, Athens.

With an average national TV viewing time of 7¼ hours daily, the prevalence of violence in broadcasts is a serious concern. Television programming in the United States is considered the most violent in advanced industrialized nations. Violence is common in TV entertainment—the dramas that portray stories about crime, psychotic murderers, police cases, emergency services, international terrorism, and war. The dramas are played out in highly realistic scenes of violent attacks accompanied by music and other sounds that churn up emotions.

As the realism and gore in the screen images of TV entertainment have intensified, local news cameras have also increasingly focused directly on the bloody violence done to individuals in drive-by shootings, gang attacks, and domestic beatings. Why must these visual details be presented in the news? Why does a typical television evening include so many beatings, shootings, stabbings, and rapes in dramas designed for "entertainment"?

Producers of programming ascertain that scenes of violent action with accompanying fear-striking music can be counted on to hold viewers' attention, keep them awake and watching, and make them less likely to switch channels. The purpose is to gain and maintain a large number of viewers—the factor that appeals to advertisers. The generations of younger adults who have grown up with daily viewing of violence in entertainment are considered to be "hooked." A program has more com- mercial value if it can hold more viewers, and programmers attempt to ensure high viewer attention with doses of violent action in the program. How does all of this violence affect young people?

The Results of Research

Several decades ago, a few psychologists hypothesized that viewing violence in the unreal television world would have a cathartic effect and thus reduce the chances of violent behavior in the real world. But other psychologists began to doubt this notion when their research with children revealed that much action on the TV screen is perceived as real by children. Huesmann and Eron (1986), who studied the effects of media violence on 758 youngsters in grades 1 through 3, found that children's behavior was influenced by television, especially if the youngsters were heavy viewers of violent programming. Television violence, according to the researchers, provided a script for the children to act out aggressive behavior in relationships with others. The most aggressive youngsters strongly identified with aggressive characters in the TV story, had aggressive fantasies, and expressed the attitude that violent programs portrayed life as it is. These children were also likely to perform poorly in school and often were unpopular with their peers.

Huesmann and Eron state that television is not the *only* variable involved, but their many years of research have left them with no doubt that heavy exposure to media violence is a highly influential factor in children and later in their adult lives (see also Institute for Social Research 1994 and medical research by Zuckerman and Zuckerman 1985 and by Holroyd 1985).

Research in the field of public communications also supports the conclusion that exposure to television violence contributes to increased rates of aggression and violent behavior. Centerwall (1989, 1993) analyzed crime data in areas of the world with and without television and, in addition, made comparisons in areas before and after the introduction of TV. His studies determined that homicide rates doubled in ten to fifteen years after TV was introduced for the first time into specified areas of the United States and Canada. Observing that violent television programming exerts its aggressive effects primarily on children, Centerwall noted that the ten- to fifteen-year lag time can be expected before homicide rates increase. Acknowledging that other factors besides TV do have some influence on the quantity of violent crimes, Centerwall's careful statistical analysis indicated, nevertheless, that when the negative effects of TV were removed, quantitative evidence showed "there would be 10,000 fewer homicides, 70,000 fewer rapes, and 700,000 fewer injurious assaults" (1993, 64).

Centerwall (1993) has also brought to light important research literature that has been little known among social scientists and educators concerned about television violence. In the late sixties, as a result of public hearings and a national report implying that exposure to TV increases physical aggression, the large television networks decided to commission their own research projects. NBC appointed a team of four researchers, three of whom were NBC employees, to observe more than two thousand school children up to three years to determine if watching television programs increased their physical aggressiveness. NBC reported no effect. Centerwall points out, however, that every inde-

From *Social Education*, September 1995, pp. 309–311. © 1995 by the National Council for the Social Studies. Reprinted by Permission.

pendent researcher who has analyzed the same data finds an increase in levels of physical aggression.

In the study commissioned by the ABC network, a team at Temple University surveyed young male felons who had been imprisoned for violent crimes. Results of these interviews showed that 22 to 34 percent of the young felons, especially those who were the most violent, said they had consciously imitated crime techniques learned from television programs. It was learned that, as children, felons in the study had watched an average of six hours of TV per day, about twice as much as children in the general population at that time. Research results were published privately by ABC and not released to the general public or to scientists (Centerwall 1993, 65).

CBS commissioned a study to be conducted in London and ultimately published in England (Belson 1978). In the study, 1,565 teenaged boys were studied for behavioral effects of viewing violent television programs, many of which were imported from the United States. The study (Belson 1978) revealed that those who watched above average hours of TV violence before adolescence committed a 49 percent higher rate of serious acts of violence than did boys who had viewed below average quantities of violence. The final report was "very strongly supportive of the hypothesis that high exposure to television violence increases the degree to which boys engage in serious violence" (Belson 1978, 15).

Five types of TV programming were most powerful in triggering violent behavior in the boys in the London study: (1) TV plays or films in which violence is demonstrated in close personal relationships; (2) programs where violence

---

Student Activities to Develop Critical Media Skills

1. Our Favorite Programs. Take a poll of students in your class to find out what their favorite weekday prime time (8–11 p.m.) programs are, and also their favorite programs on Saturday and Sunday. Favorite programs can be summarized by type (e.g., movies, cartoons, police dramas) on a poster for a later study of contents. If each student has a notebook for the study of mass media, the results of this poll could be the first entry.

2. What's on the Air? Assign each student a different TV channel (include local, regular network, public TV, and pay cable network channels), and ask each to use TV listings in newspapers or magazines to determine how many minutes on a specified day are designated for (1) young children's entertainment, (2) special programs for teenagers, (3) public affairs information and discussion programs, (4) adult entertainment programs (dramas, sitcoms, quiz shows, science fiction, detective series, love stories), (5) religious programs, and (6) cooking and household repair programs.

3. What Are the Rules and Obligations? The airwaves are publicly owned. Licensing and oversight of the use of the airwaves is conducted by the Federal Communications Commission (FCC). To obtain guidelines and legal explanation of the responsibilities of all broadcasters to consider community needs and interests in their programming, write or call the FCC, 1919 M Street, NW, Washington, DC 10554; phone 202–418–0200. Reference books and government books in the school library will help clarify the legal framework for radio and television broadcasting.

4. How Much Violence Is in Our Entertainment? Discuss the kinds of violent acts and language in television programs and movies to prepare students to monitor "violence" in TV programs. From the list of "favorite programs" (no. 1 above), prepare slips of paper with program titles, so students can randomly draw a program title and plan to monitor the program for violent action, language, or threats. Students should take notes on the name, time, station, and advertisers for each program, and describe the violence discussed or shown in the program. This monitoring activity can be extended to other programs over a weekend or over several evenings. Students can invite their parents to join them in noting how much violence is depicted, suggested, or threatened.

Following a period of collecting data, student groups can share their findings: Which programs contained the most violence? Is violence common in prime time programs and/or at other times? On cable? On regular network channels? On public channels? Which advertisers support programs with heavy violence? Finally, prepare a class summary listing of the most violent and least violent programs.

5. How Does TV Violence Affect Us? Discussion: Using notes from program monitoring and recollections or videotape of violent scenes, analyze the images, sounds, and dialogue that hold the viewer's attention. Which are the most frightening, hard to forget, or likely to give people nightmares? Why are some viewers fascinated by scenes of beating, killing, and hurting people? Would these scenes and sounds encourage similar behavior by young viewers? Why or why not?

6. How Do Music and Sounds Affect Our Emotions? To further analyze the contents and affects of violent programming, have students return to a selected program that is usually violent and scary. Have them experiment with turning down the sound in dramatic scenes without dialogue. Ask them to observe how pulsating, eerie, pounding music and sounds of howling wind, roaring cars, squealing cats, and other noises can arouse excitement or fear. In turn, they can observe programs where soothing music, laughing children, and cheerful sounds help to make the viewer feel at ease.

7. Why Would Advertisers Select Programs with Violence? Discuss with students the fascination that violence and fast action have for some viewer groups, including youngsters, uncritical adults, and less educated individuals. Discuss how people can be mesmerized and fascinated by images of violent conflict, especially if they watch violence daily and begin to see it as a way of life. (References to writings by psychologists and sociologists in the article above will lead you to books and readings about the appeal of violent scenes and the high vulnerability of certain groups of people.) Students can reflect on how advertisers look for programs with large numbers of viewers. In turn, discuss how critical viewers might influence advertisers to select better quality programs for their ads.

8. TV Consumer Power. Discuss the power potential of viewers to select quality programs. Students can learn about "market share" and Nielsen ratings from magazines and newspapers. A local TV station or radio station manager can explain how "market share" affects program selection.

was not necessary to the plot but just added for its own sake; (3) fictional violence of a very realistic kind; (4) violent "Westerns"; and (5) programs that present violence as being for a good cause. In summarizing the implications of the study, the research director made it clear that the results also applied to boys in U.S. cities with the same kind of violence in TV programming (ibid. 528).

For about fifteen years, these studies have received little attention. Each was either filed away or distributed to a very limited audience—not to the general public, the research community, or the press. Today, that seems eerily similar to the fate of tobacco company research on the ill effects of smoking, the results of which were also disseminated only to a small select group. The Commission on Violence and Youth of the American Psychological Association recently communicated the above-mentioned and other supporting research to its members. It concluded that evidence clearly reveals that viewing and hearing high levels of violence on television, day after day, were correlated with increased acceptance of aggression and more aggressive behavior. The commission noted that the highest level of consumption of television violence is by those most vulnerable to the effects, those who receive no moderating or mediating of what is seen on the screen. (Slaby 1994, Institute for Social Research 1994; see also Holroyd 1985; Zuckerman and Zuckerman 1985).

This information is of great significance to social studies educators. Yet it is only in the last two years that the network-funded studies of the seventies and eighties have been gaining some attention in journals that reach educational professionals. In January 1994, an article in the *Chronicle of Higher Education* pointed up the huge "education gap" that exists between the effects of television violence that have been conclusively documented by psychological and medical researchers and what the general public knows. According to the article, "Until recently, researchers' voices have been drowned out in the din of denial and disinformation coming from executives of the television and movie industries, whose self-serving defense of violent programming has prevailed" (Slaby 1994).

TV industry spokespersons argue that violent programs are a mere reflection of the society, and that any effort to modify programming would interfere with First Amendment guarantees of freedom of the press. Others claim to be giving the public "what they want" and take no responsibility for the effects on viewers. Another response from the networks is that parents or families must take the responsibility for preventing viewing of violent programs. In none of these defenses are the networks willing to recognize research information that shows that an appetite for violence has been stimulated by the glorification of violence and a daily diet of violent programs broadcast into every home in America.

History and Social Science Content

The issue of the influence of electronic media on the American life-style is of direct concern to social studies (Hepburn 1990). The curriculum must include study of the influence of the media. Students should be aware of how persistent viewing of violent acts and violent language and music can motivate violent behavior. A number of suggestions for media-related student activities accompany this article.

Although readings about the influence of media are hard to find in school textbooks, at last, magazines, newspapers, public television, and CNN have begun to examine the role of the mass media in the decline of civility and the loss of community. Commercial television networks have been compared with individuals who seek only their own profit, lack respect for others, and feel no sense of public trust. Are these fair conclusions? Social studies can pick up the debate.

Could a media-literate public demand and get better news presentation and more depth in the discussion of alternative social and economic policies? Is there a parallel between the decades in which the public lacked information about the lethal effects of cigarette smoking and the two decades in which the public has been unaware of the effects of heavy doses of television violence on youngsters? Can the reduction of violence in mass media be accomplished by means of increased citizen knowledge and action? Are First Amendment rights of the broadcast industry threatened by public pressures? Will television and radio respond to public discourse and a changed percep-tion of the public market? These are social studies issues of interest to students.

From many passive hours in front of television, what life roles are instilled in viewers, especially more impressionable young viewers? From TV and radio, what values and visions of family life, leadership, friendship, personal relationships, heroism, and public responsibility are absorbed from the images and voices they see and hear? A discussion of role models, of both the norms and realities, can greatly stimulate the awareness and interest of young citizens. This is the stuff of social studies.

Sources

Belson, W. A. *Television Violence and the Adolescent Boy.* Westmead, England: Saxon House, 1978.

Bowen, Wally. "Media Violence." *Education Week* (March 16, 1994): 60ff.

Centerwall, B. S. "Exposure to Television as a Cause of Violence." In *Public Communication and Behavior.* volume 2, edited by G. Comstock. San Diego: Academic Press, 1989.

——. "Television and Violent Crime." *The Public Interest* 3 (1993): 56–71.

Gamson, W. A., D. Croteau, W. Hoynes, and T. Sasson. "Media Images and the Social Construction of Reality." *Annual Review of Sociology* 18 (1992): 373–393.

Hepburn, M. A. "Americans Glued to the Tube: Mass Media, Information, and Social Studies." *Social Education* 54, no. 4 (April/May 1990): 233–237.

Holroyd, H. J. "Children, Adolescents, and Television." *American Journal of Diseases in Children* 139, no. 6 (1985): 549–550.

Huesmann, L. R., and L. D. Eron. "The Development of Aggression in American Children as a Consequence of Television Violence Viewing." In *Television and the Aggressive Child: A Cross-National Comparison,* edited by L. R. Huesmann and L. D. Eron. Hillsdale, New Jersey: Erlbaum Associates, 1986.

Institute for Social Research. "Televised Violence and Kids: A Public Health Problem?" *ISR Newsletter* 18 (1994): 1.

National Association of Broadcasters. *America's Watching—Public Attitudes Toward Television 1993.* New York: The Network Television Association and the National Association of Broadcasters.

Nielson Media Research. *1992–1993 Report on Television.* New York: A. C. Nielson Co., 1993.

Postman, N. *The Disappearance of Childhood.* New York: Delacorte Press, 1982.

Roper Organization. *Public Attitudes Toward Television and Other Media in a Time of Change.* New York: Television Information Office, 1985.

Slaby, R. G. "Combating Television Violence." *The Chronicle of Higher Education* 40, no. 18 (January 5, 1994): B1–2.

Zuckerman, D. M., and B. S. Zuckerman. "Television's Impact on Children." *Pediatrics* 75, no. 2 (1985): 233–240.

The biology of soul murder

Fear can harm a child's brain. Is it reversible?

By their appearances, the three little girls sitting quietly in molded plastic chairs in the psychiatric clinic of Texas Children's Hospital in Houston betray nothing of the mayhem they have experienced. No one would know that the night before, two armed men broke into their apartment in a drug-ravaged part of the city. That the children were tied up and the youngest, only 3, was threatened with a gun. Or that the men shot the girls' teenage sister in the head before leaving (she survived).

Yet however calm the girls' appearances, their physiology tells a different story. Their hearts are still racing at more than 100 beats per minute, their blood pressure remains high and, inside their heads, the biological chemicals of fear are changing their brains. "People look at kids who seem so normal after these experiences and say, 'All they need is a little love,' " says Bruce Perry, a child psychiatrist at Children's Hospital and at Baylor College of Medicine. But as Perry and other researchers are finding, trauma, neglect, and physical and sexual abuse can have severe effects on a child's developing brain.

Tangled chemistry. Once viewed as genetically programmed, the brain is now known to be plastic, an organ molded by both genes and experience throughout life. A single traumatic experience can alter an adult's brain: A horrifying battle, for instance, may induce the flashbacks, depression and hair-trigger response of post-traumatic stress disorder (PTSD). And researchers are finding that abuse and neglect early

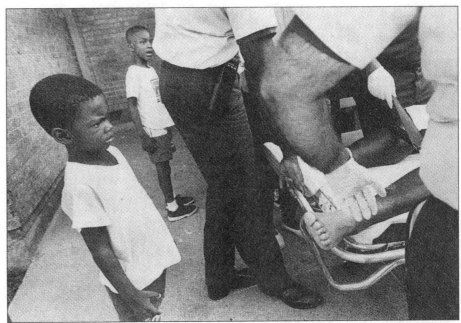

STEPHEN SHAMES—MATRIX

WORLD WITHOUT COMFORT. Living with fear puts children at high risk for problems later in life. Above, two boys watch as medics treat the victim of a gunshot in Houston.

in life can have even more devastating consequences, tangling both the chemistry and the architecture of children's brains and leaving them at risk for drug abuse, teen pregnancy and psychiatric problems later in life.

Yet the brain's plasticity also holds out the chance that positive experiences—psychotherapy, mentoring, loving relationships—might ameliorate some of the damage. Much remains unknown. But if scientists can understand exactly how trauma harms the brain, they may also learn much about healing broken lives.

Trauma's toll on a child's brain begins with fear. Faced with a threat, the body embarks on a cascade of physiological reactions. Adrenalin surges, setting the heart pounding and blood pressure soaring and readying the muscles for action, a response called "fight or flight." At the same time, a more subtle set of changes, called the stress response, releases the hormone cortisol, which also helps the body respond to danger.

Increasing evidence suggests that in abused or neglected children, this system somehow goes awry, causing a

From *U.S. News & World Report*, November 11, 1996, pp. 71-73. © 1996 by U.S. News & World Report. Reprinted by permission.

harmful imbalance of cortisol in the brain. In a study of children in Romanian orphanages, for example, Megan Gunnar, a University of Minnesota developmental psychobiologist, is finding that cognitive and developmental delays correlate with irregular cortisol levels.

Gunnar and others believe that excess cortisol leads to damage in a brain region known as the hippocampus, causing memory lapses, anxiety and an inability to control emotional outbursts. Cortisol and other brain chemicals also can alter brain centers that regulate attention, affecting a child's capacity to attend to words on the blackboard instead of a jackhammer banging outside.

Many of the brain abnormalities seen in abused and neglected children are localized in the brain's left hemisphere, where language and logical thought are processed. Martin Teicher, a psychiatrist at McLean Hospital in Belmont, Mass., compared recordings of brain electrical activity in abused and normal children. His finding: In abused kids, the left hemisphere has fewer nerve-cell connections between different areas. The electrical traces also revealed that tiny seizures, similar to those of epileptics, crackled through various sectors of abused children's brains. Children with the most abnormal recordings were the most likely to be self-destructive or aggressive.

Scanning for danger. Abused children also show a variety of other disturbances in physiology, thinking and behavior. Many have elevated resting heart rates, temperature and blood pressure. Hypervigilance is common. Abused kids continually scan their surroundings for danger and overinterpret the actions of others: An innocent playground bump may be seen as a direct threat. And as many as half of children from some violent neighborhoods show symptoms of

Attention Deficit Hyperactivity Disorder (ADHD), compared with about 6 percent of the general population.

"Children who are aroused [from fear] can't take in cognitive information," says Perry. "They're too busy watching the teacher for threatening gestures, and not listening to what she's saying." Such behavior makes sense, given the constant threats in the child's world. His brain has become exquisitely tuned to emotional and physical cues from other people. At the same time, he may be failing to develop problem solving and language skills. Perry has found that in a group of neglected children, the cortex, or thinking part of the brain, is 20 percent smaller on average than in a control group.

Studies now indicate that abused and neglected children run a high risk of developing mental illnesses. Since 1987, National Institute of Mental Health child psychiatrist Frank Putnam has tracked 90 sexually abused girls, comparing them to a control group who were not abused. The abused girls were more likely to evidence depression and suicide attempts, and many showed the beginnings of PTSD, including anxiety attacks and abnormal levels of cortisol, which are also seen in combat veterans. Putnam also found a decline in the abused girls' IQ over time. Saddest of all, the abused girls are rated by their teachers as not very likable. "That's tragic," says Putnam, "because the one place where they might find some support is at school."

Indeed, for some children, a loving adult can serve as a powerful antidote to abuse and neglect. Infants and young children normally learn from a comforting caretaker how to soothe themselves, thereby regulating their stress response and cortisol levels. Researchers now believe loving relationships also can help

older children reset their response to stress when it has been derailed by abuse. Says Gunnar: "We don't know when the door to the brain's plasticity closes."

Unfortunately, loving damaged children can be tough. One minute they are hostile, the next withdrawn. In class, they escape their feelings by daydreaming. When the teacher confronts them, they retreat even further. Then, says Perry, "the teacher touches the kid. When you touch them, that's incredibly threatening, and the child has a tantrum."

The growing understanding of what's going on in an abused and neglected child's brain has begun to yield new treatments. In addition to psychotherapy, Perry gives some of his young patients clonidine, a drug that helps check the fight-or-flight response. Clonidine, and other drugs that interfere with the release of cortisol, may decrease the chances a child will go on to develop PTSD. Perry also hands out devices that allow teachers and foster parents to monitor a child's heart rate from a distance, so they can refrain from making demands on him when he's frightened.

For every child who finds help at a clinic like Perry's, there are dozens who fall through the cracks. Only a fraction of the millions of children who are mistreated each year receive the kind of help that can reverse the underlying physiological changes they suffer. Ultimately, says McLean's Teicher, failing these kids may be shortsighted. They are less likely to live up to their economic potential, and more likely to wind up in prison, on drugs or in psychiatric units, he says. "The cost on society of having a child who has gone through abuse is enormous."

BY SHANNON BROWNLEE

THE COST OF CHILDREN

Of course they're cute. But have you any idea how much one will set you back? A hardheaded inquiry

BY PHILLIP J. LONGMAN

To examine in coldly economic terms a parent's decision to have children is widely thought to be in bad taste. A child, after all, isn't precisely akin to a consumer product such as a dishwasher, a house, a car, or a personal computer–any one of which, of course, is cheaper to acquire and usually easier to return. A child is a font of love, hope for the future, continuation of one's bloodline, and various other intangible pleasures, and it is these sentimental considerations (along with some earthier imperatives) that prevail when parents bring a child into this world.

But let's face it: Children don't come free. Indeed, their cost is rising. According to one government calculation, the direct cost of raising a child to age 18 has risen by 20 percent since 1960 (adjusted for inflation and changes in family size). And this calculation doesn't take into account the forgone wages that result from a parent taking time off to raise children–an economic cost that has skyrocketed during the last generation as women have entered the work force in unprecedented numbers. "It's become much more expensive to raise children while the economic returns to parents have diminished," notes feminist economist Shirley Burggraf. "The family can't survive on romance."

Knowing the real cost of children is critical to a host of financial questions, such as how much house one can afford, how much one should be saving for college tuition, and how much one must earn to have a larger family. To help answer such questions, *U.S. News* has

undertaken to identify and add up as best it can all the costs of raising a child from birth to college graduation. (For the purposes of this calculation, we're assuming these children will pay for any advanced degrees they may want out of their own pockets.)

Our starting point is data from the United States Department of Agriculture, which every year publishes estimates of how much families in different income brackets spend on raising children to age 18. To these calculations we have added the cost of a college education and wages forgone because of the rigors of child-rearing. (There's plenty we haven't counted: soccer camp, cello lessons, SAT prep., and other extra-cost options.) What we've found is that the typical child in a middle-income family requires a 22-year investment of just over $1.45 million. That's a pretty steep price tag in a country where the median income for families with children is just $41,000. The child's unit cost rises to $2.78 million for the top-third income bracket and drops to $761,871 for the bottom-third income bracket.

Tut tut, you say. Surely this is another case of newsmagazine hyperbole. All right, then, let's take it from the top:

■ **Acquisition costs.** In most cases, conceiving a child biologically is gloriously cost free. But not for all: An estimated 6.1 percent of women ages 15–24, and 11.2 percent of women ages 25–34, suffer from what health statisticians refer to as "impaired fecundity." Serving this huge market are some 300 infertility clinics nationwide that performed 59,142 treatment "cycles" in 1995, according to a recently released study by the Centers for Disease Control and Prevention. The cost of treatments–only 19 percent of which actually produced a take-home baby–averaged around $8,000 a try. It's not uncommon for infertile couples to spend $50,000 or more in pursuit of pregnancy. Though most insurance policies will pay for some form of infertility treatment, insurers are cutting back rapidly in the total bills they'll cover. For the purposes of our tally, we'll ignore fertility treatments, but this can be a significant cost.

For most people, the meter starts running with pregnancy. Costs vary dramatically from hospital to hospital, from region to region, and according to how complicated the pregnancy is. Out-of-pocket costs, obviously, will also vary depending on how much health insurance you have. But here's an idea of what your bills might be.

For an uneventful normal pregnancy, 12 prenatal care visits are usually recommended–the cost of which varies according to one's insurance plan. According to HCIA Inc., a Baltimore health care information company, the cost to insured patients of a normal delivery in a hospital averages about $2,800. (Twins are cheaper on a per-head basis: typical total delivery cost: $4,115.)

For parents without insurance, direct costs are clearly much higher. According to a 1994 study, the cost of an uncomplicated "normal" delivery averages $6,400 nationally. Caesarean delivery costs an average of $11,000, and more complicated births may range up to $400,000. Premature babies requiring neonatal intensive care will cost $1,000 to $2,500 for every day they stay in the hospital. Though most people can count on insurance to cover a majority of such costs, there are many people who can't. According to a report issued in March by the U.S. government's Agency for Health Care Policy and Research, 17 percent of Hispanic children, 12.6 percent of black children, and 6 percent of white ones lack any health in-

surance coverage whatsoever, including coverage by Medicaid or other public programs.

An alternative path to acquiring a child is through adoption. Of the roughly 30,000 adoptions of healthy infants in the United States each year, most involve expenses of $10,000 to $15,000. These include the cost of paying for a social worker to perform a "home study" to vouchsafe the adoptive parents' suitability, agency fees, travel expenses (many adoptions these days cross national boundaries), medical and sometimes living expenses for the birth mother, and legal fees. Off-setting these costs for parents who adopt is a new $5,000 federal tax credit. Since most people don't adopt, these costs, too, are excluded from *U.S. News*'s tally.

THREADS.
To clothe a child to age 18 costs **$22,063.** And yes, girls cost 18 percent more than boys.

■ **Child care.** The Department of Agriculture calculates that the middle-class parents of a 3-to-5-year-old spend just over $1,260 a year on average for child care. (According to the Census Bureau, fully 56 percent of American families with children use paid child care.) Wealthier families are more likely to opt for the pricier nanny. Irish Nanny Services of Dublin advertises Irish nannies "with good moral standards" who are "renowned for their expertise with children." The price for U.S. parents begins at $250 per week; plus 1.5 paid holidays for every month

worked; plus a nonrefundable finder's fee equal to 10 percent of the yearly salary payable upfront.

The average cost for all families using child care is $74.15 a week, or about 7.5 percent of average pretax family income, which is roughly equal to most workers' employee-contribution rate for Social Security. The rate is much steeper, of course, at the low end of the income scale; families making less than $1,200 a month who use day care spend an average 25.1 percent of their income on day-care expenses.

■ **Food.** Middle-class families spend an average $990 a year feeding a child under 2. (Breast-feeding helps: One serving of infant formula can cost as much as $3.29.) As kids get bigger, so do their appetites: Feeding a middle-class 15-year-old currently costs $1,920 a year on average. A middle-class only child born in 1997 can be expected to consume a total of $54,795 in food by age 18.

■ **Housing.** The bigger your family, the bigger the house you need. Families with children also often pay a premium to live in safe, leafy neighborhoods with good schools. USDA estimates that the average middle-class, husband-wife family with one child will spend, on a per capita basis, an additional $97,549 to provide the child with shelter.

■ **Transportation.** Priced a minivan lately? The added transportation cost of having one middle-class child totals $46,345, according to the USDA. This does not include the cost of commuting to jobs parents must hold in order to support their children. Predictably, as children get older, the cost of driving them around grows. Parents with teenagers spend over 70 percent more on transportation than families with infants. Just the cost of providing teenage drivers with auto insurance can run into the thousands.

■ **Health care.** Obviously, this cost varies tremendously, depending largely on the health of the child. The lifetime health costs of a child born with cerebral palsy, for instance, average $503,000; with Down's syndrome, $451,000; and with spina bifida,

$294,000, according to the March of Dimes.

Again, out-of-pocket costs for health care will depend largely on whether the parents have good (or any) health insurance. In 1996, nearly 11 million American children, or 15.4 percent of the population under 18, had none. Deductibles, copayments, and specific coverages also vary widely even among those with insurance. Taking all these variables into account, and including the cost of insurance, the USDA estimates that the average cost of keeping a middle-class child born in 1997 healthy to age 18 will be more than $20,757.

■ **Clothing.** Even after allowing for hand-me-downs and gifts from doting grandparents, keeping an only child properly dressed to age 18 will cost an average total of $22,063, according to the USDA. Predictably, in this realm, daughters cost more than sons: According to the Bureau of Labor Statistics, husband-wife families with children spend nearly 18 percent more on girls' clothes than on those for boys.

■ **Primary and secondary education.** Fully 89 percent of all school-age kids in the United States attend public schools. Public education costs American society more than $293 billion per year, but for the purposes of this tally, we'll exclude taxes (which, after all, are paid by parents and non-parents alike) and consider public education to be free.

For the roughly 5 million grade-school students now enrolled in private schools, costs vary widely. About 50 percent of these students attend parochial schools, where tuition averaged $1,934 in 1993–94, the last school year for which data are available. By contrast, parents earning over $125,000 a year who send a child to the elite Deerfield Academy in Deerfield, Mass., and who manage to qualify for financial aid, are expected to contribute $10,600 a year in tuition. Overall, the U.S. Department of Education reports, private-school tuition in 1993–94 averaged $2,200 a year in elementary schools and $5,500 in secondary schools, with

schools for children who are handicapped or have "special needs" charging an average $15,189. These costs have been rising quickly. Reflecting increasing demand, the average tuition of private schools increased by more than double the overall rate of inflation between 1990 and 1996.

■ **Toys and other miscellaneous expenses.** The USDA doesn't break out spending on toys by income group or the age of children. But for all husband-and-wife families with children, the average amount spent on pets, toys, and playground equipment in 1995 was $485.

> **TUMBLES.**
> Children are usually quite healthy, but they'll still run you **$20,757** to keep fit till age 18.

What do all these bills come to? USDA calculates that a typical middle-class, husband-wife family will spend a total of $301,183 to raise an only child born in 1997 to age 18 (table, "Cost of children born in 1997). More affluent parents (with income over $59,700 a year) will spend an average of $437,869 on an only child. The average figure for lower-income families (with income between $35,500 a year) is $221,750.

Certain economies of scale are available to larger families. As family size increases, food costs per person go down the most. (Just feed everyone stew.) Per capita housing and transportation costs also decrease, but not by as much. All told, for middle-class families, the marginal cost of raising a second child will be approximately 24

percent less than the cost of a single child. The marginal unit cost continues to drop for each successive child.

Now let's consider two costs the USDA calculation leaves out. The first is college. From the start of the 1990s through September of 1997, average tuition at the nation's colleges increased by more than 75 percent, while overall prices in the economy inflated by little more than 26 percent. Common sense would suggest that this rate of tuition inflation cannot possibly sustain itself over the long term, especially if real family income remains flat or grows only slowly. Sooner or later, some combination of new technology and organizational reform will surely render higher education less costly. Still, who would have imagined that the price of a college education would ever have risen to where it is today? With an undergraduate education becoming ever more necessary to guarantee a middle-class lifestyle, perhaps its price will rise even faster in the future. Given these imponderables, we'll assume college costs will continue to rise at the average annual rate of the 1990s, or 7.45 percent, and that the cost of room, board, and books grows at 5 percent, which is the annual inflation rate of the past 20 years.

Now, let's do some illustrative arithmetic. Say you had a child in September 1997. Let's forget straight off about sending him to Harvard or Princeton, or any other private college, and aim for a top state school, the University of Michigan–Ann Arbor. Tuition, fees, plus room and board for in-state students there currently amount to $11,694 a year. Under the inflation assumptions described above, it turns out you'll need a total of $157,831 to see a child born last year through graduation at Ann Arbor (Assuming you are a Michigan resident; tuition is more than three times higher for out-of-state residents).

Ok, now let's figure out how to pay for that tuition. Assuming an average annual 7 percent total return on savings, you'll have put away more than $319 each month, starting on your child's date

Cost of children born in 1997

Higher income (one-child family; 1997 before-tax family income: more than $59,700)

Age	Housing	Food	Transportation	Clothing	Health care	Day care and education	Misc.	College (Princeton)	Forgone wages	Total for year
0	$5,915	$1,624	$1,885	$719	$744	$2,120	$1,860		$44,650	$59,518
1	$6,211	$1,706	$1,979	$755	$781	$2,226	$1,953		$48,669	$64,279
2	$6,521	$1,791	$2,078	$793	$820	$2,338	$2,051		$53,049	$69,440
3	$6,804	$2,124	$2,139	$818	$833	$2,670	$2,168		$57,823	$75,379
4	$7,144	$2,231	$2,246	$859	$874	$2,803	$2,276		$63,027	$81,461
5	$7,501	$2,342	$2,358	$902	$918	$2,944	$2,390		$41,047	$60,402
6	$7,760	$2,974	$2,675	$1,030	$1,097	$2,127	$2,576		$45,847	$66,087
7	$8,148	$3,123	$2,809	$1,082	$1,152	$2,233	$2,704		$52,033	$73,285
8	$8,556	$3,279	$2,950	$1,136	$1,209	$2,345	$2,840		$57,900	$80,214
9	$8,599	$4,001	$3,232	$1,308	$1,366	$1,712	$3,039		$65,315	$88,572
10	$9,029	$4,201	$3,393	$1,373	$1,434	$1,798	$3,191		$72,460	$96,880
11	$9,480	$4,411	$3,563	$1,442	$1,506	$1,888	$3,351		$64,402	$90,042
12	$10,444	$4,855	$3,986	$2,494	$1,581	$1,537	$3,897		$72,230	$101,024
13	$10,966	$5,097	$4,185	$2,619	$1,660	$1,613	$4,092		$82,517	$112,750
14	$11,514	$5,352	$4,395	$2,750	$1,743	$1,694	$4,296		$92,118	$123,863
15	$11,008	$5,929	$5,620	$2,629	$1,933	$3,119	$3,944		$104,460	$138,642
16	$11,558	$6,226	$5,901	$2,761	$2,030	$3,275	$4,141		$116,188	$152,080
17	$12,136	$6,537	$6,196	$2,899	$2,132	$3,439	$4,348		$130,979	$168,665
18								$103,574	$145,257	$248,831
19								$110,831	$140,766	$251,597
20								$118,605	$156,987	$275,592
21								$126,935	$177,732	$304,667
Total	$159,294	$67,805	$61,589	$28,370	$23,813	$41,881	$55,117	$459,945	$1,885,454	$2,783,268

Middle income (one child family; 1997 before-tax family income: $35,500 to $59,700)

Age	Housing	Food	Transportation	Clothing	Health care	Day care and education	Misc.	College (Univ. of Michigan)	Forgone wages	Total for year
0	$3,720	$1,228	$1,352	$546	$645	$1,401	$1,104		$23,600	$33,594
1	$3,906	$1,289	$1,419	$573	$677	$1,471	$1,159		$25,724	$36,218
2	$4,101	$1,353	$1,490	$602	$711	$1,545	$1,217		$28,039	$39,058
3	$4,263	$1,636	$1,522	$617	$718	$1,809	$1,306		$30,563	$42,434
4	$4,476	$1,718	$1,598	$648	$754	$1,899	$1,372		$33,313	$45,778
5	$4,700	$1,804	$1,678	$681	$791	$1,994	$1,440		$21,695	$34,783
6	$4,819	$2,426	$1,961	$798	$947	$1,346	$1,579		$24,233	$38,108
7	$5,060	$2,547	$2,059	$838	$995	$1,413	$1,658		$27,502	$42,072
8	$5,313	$2,675	$2,162	$879	$1,044	$1,484	$1,740		$30,603	$45,901
9	$5,194	$3,289	$2,405	$1,020	$1,193	$1,020	$1,885		$34,523	$50,527

(continued on next page)

of birth, to have enough money on hand to pay for four years of college as each semester's tuition bill comes due. If you wait until the child is in kindergarten to start saving, your monthly savings requirement will jump to $524. If you wait until the child reaches freshman year of high school, the number will jump to $1,957 a month.

Or here's another way to look at the challenge. Take a middle-class fam-

Age	Housing	Food	Transportation	Clothing	Health care	Day care and education	Misc.	College	Forgone wages	Total for year
10	$5,454	$3,454	$2,525	$1,071	$1,252	$1,071	$1,979		$38,299	**$55,104**
11	$5,726	$3,627	$2,651	$1,124	$1,315	$1,124	$2,078		$34,040	**$51,685**
12	$6,502	$3,852	$3,029	$1,982	$1,381	$868	$2,539		$38,178	**$58,331**
13	$6,828	$4,045	$3,180	$2,081	$1,450	$912	$2,666		$43,615	**$64,776**
14	$7,169	$4,247	$3,339	$2,185	$1,522	$957	$2,799		$48,690	**$70,908**
15	$6,445	$4,950	$4,434	$2,037	$1,701	$1,701	$2,372		$55,213	**$78,852**
16	$6,767	$5,197	$4,656	$2,138	$1,786	$1,786	$2,490		$61,412	**$86,233**
17	$7,105	$5,457	$4,888	$2,245	$1,876	$1,876	$2,615		$69,230	**$95,292**
18								$35,821	$76,777	**$112,598**
19								$38,140	$74,402	**$112,543**
20								$40,614	$82,976	**$123,591**
21								$43,255	$93,941	**$137,196**
Total	**$97,549**	**$54,795**	**$46,345**	**$22,063**	**$20,757**	**$25,678**	**$33,996**	**$157,832**	**$996,567**	**$1,455,581**

Lower income (one-child family; 1997 before tax family income: less than $35,500)

Age	Housing	Food	Transportation	Clothing	Health care	Day care and education	Misc.	College (Florida A&M)	Forgone wages	Total for year
0	$2,753	$1,029	$905	$459	$496	$856	$719		$11,050	**$18,267**
1	$2,890	$1,081	$950	$482	$521	$898	$755		$12,045	**$19,622**
2	$3,035	$1,135	$998	$506	$547	$943	$793		$13,129	**$21,085**
3	$3,144	$1,321	$1,005	$517	$545	$1,120	$847		$14,310	**$22,808**
4	$3,301	$1,387	$1,055	$543	$573	$1,176	$889		$15,598	**$24,521**
5	$3,466	$1,456	$1,108	$570	$601	$1,234	$934		$10,158	**$19,527**
6	$3,523	$1,977	$1,363	$681	$731	$764	$1,047		$11,346	**$21,433**
7	$3,699	$2,076	$1,431	$715	$768	$803	$1,099		$12,877	**$23,468**
8	$3,884	$2,180	$1,502	$751	$806	$843	$1,154		$14,329	**$25,450**
9	$3,674	$2,732	$1,712	$866	$923	$539	$1,270		$16,164	**$27,879**
10	$3,858	$2,868	$1,798	$909	$970	$566	$1,333		$17,932	**$30,233**
11	$4,051	$3,012	$1,888	$954	$1,018	$594	$1,400		$15,938	**$28,854**
12	$4,743	$3,318	$2,227	$1,692	$1,069	$445	$1,826		$17,876	**$33,196**
13	$4,980	$3,484	$2,338	$1,777	$1,122	$468	$1,917		$20,421	**$36,508**
14	$5,229	$3,658	$2,455	$1,866	$1,178	$491	$2,013		$22,797	**$39,689**
15	$4,434	$4,150	$3,480	$1,727	$1,315	$851	$1,547		$25,852	**$43,355**
16	$4,656	$4,358	$3,654	$1,814	$1,380	$893	$1,624		$28,754	**$47,133**
17	$4,888	$4,576	$3,837	$1,904	$1,449	$938	$1,705		$32,415	**$51,713**
18								$16,783	$35,948	**$52,731**
19								$17,802	$34,837	**$52,639**
20								$18,886	$38,851	**$57,737**
21								$20,038	$43,985	**$64,023**
Total	**$70,208**	**$45,797**	**$33,705**	**$18,732**	**$61,013**	**$14,421**	**$22,873**	**$73,508**	**$466,613**	**$761,871**

Note: Numbers may not add up because of rounding

ily earning, say, $47,200 in 1998. Assume that inflation will average 5 percent over the next 18 years and that this family's income will grow 4 per- cent above inflation. Assume finally that this family will earn a 7 percent annual average return on its savings. Now suppose this family had a new child last year, and the parents want to prefund the likely cost of sending this child to a top-rank state school. What percent of family income do they need to put away each year toward the child's college expenses? Answer: about 4 percent.

So far, this accounting puts the cost of raising and educating a middle-class, only child at roughly $459,014 ($301,183 in direct expenditures to age 18 plus $157,831 for college costs). Now suppose you're considering having a child and want to have enough money in the bank by the day the child is born to be able to cover all of his or her direct future costs to you. No one actually does this, of course, but as any chief financial officer knows, this is a useful way to calculate the real burden of long-term liabilities. Assume you can earn 7 percent on your investments after your child is born. In that case, you'll need to build a nest egg of $204,470 by delivery day. Assuming you want to raise your child with a middle-class standard of living, this is the approximate present value of your liabilities for future expenses related to that child.

Or, suppose you want to have a child 10 years from now and want to start a regular savings plan that will allow you just enough money by the child's date of birth to cover all future child-related expenses as they occur. What you need to start saving today is $1,181 a month. Again, nobody actually does this, but amortizing the cost of children in this way provides a useful benchmark in figuring how "affordable" children are. Could you "afford" to pay an extra $1,181 every month for the next 10 years servicing your credit-card debt? Failing to prefund future liabilities, such as the future cost of a child, is financially equivalent to borrowing. If your family income goes up substantially in the future, you may be able to afford your child-related "unfunded liabilities," but if it remains stagnant or grows only slowly, as real family income has for decades, then these unfunded liabilities will hurt.

A final expenditure to add to our tally is a bit more abstract but no less real: forgone family income. People who have children tend to have less time on their hands to make money.

Consider first the forgone income for an unwed teenage mother who rears her child alone. Researchers at the University of Michigan have compared the earning power, over 20 years, of women who did and did not have children out of wedlock as teenagers. Interestingly, at ages 19 and 20, women who had given birth to illegitimate children actually had slightly higher incomes on average than women who remained childless during their teenage years; this presumably reflected the effect of welfare payments, which can boost short-term income above what the average childless full-time student earns. But by age 21, unmarried women who refrained from having become pregnant as teenagers, or who had abortions, began to pull well ahead of those who did not. By age 29, women who did not have the burden of raising a child alone as teenagers could expect to have earned a total of $72,191 more than women who did carry this burden.

What does it cost a married woman to have children? The answer depends crucially on her opportunities. Obviously, a woman who gives up a career as a nurse's aide to have a baby does not forgo as much income as a woman who gives up a law partnership. But for both there is an "opportunity cost," which can be roughly estimated. As economist Burggraf points out in her recent book, *The Feminine Economy and Economic Man,* people tend to take marriage partners of similar educational backgrounds and aspirations (social scientists label this "assortive mating"). For example, college-educated men are 15 times more likely to marry college-educated women than are men who never completed high school. This means that the opportunity cost of either spouse taking time off to raise a child is often 50 percent of a family's potential income.

That's exactly the trade-off faced by Colette Hochstein and her husband, Michael Lingenfelter. Both are librarians who work extensively with computer-information retrieval systems. Her position is with the National Institutes of Health in Bethesda,

Md.; he works in the White House library. Together, they spend more money on day care for their 2-year-old daughter, Miranda—about 17 percent of their household income—than on any other expense except their mortgage. Yet since they both earn roughly the same salary, the only way to avoid paying for day care would be to sacrifice half their household income. If either of them were to quit work to take care of Miranda full time, says Hochstein, the economic cost would extend beyond Miranda's childhood years: "In this rapidly changing, high-tech time, there are few professions in which one could take even a year's leave of absence without falling seriously behind."

Given the career opportunities now available to women, virtually all parents face some opportunity cost in having children, and it usually adds up to serious money. Consider this hypothetical middle-class, husband-wife family. They met in college and soon after married. Two years into their marriage, they each were earning $23,600, but then came Junior. She immediately quit her job to stay home with the baby, causing their family income to fall by half. After their child reaches kindergarten, she hopes to begin working half time; by the time the child reaches age 11, she hopes to be able to boost her work hours to 30 a week. But remembering her own escapades while home alone during high school, she does not plan to return to full-time work until the child goes off to college.

What's the opportunity cost of these life choices? Assume, as the USDA does, that inflation averages 5 percent over her working life. Further assume that, because of her "mommy track," her average annual real wage increases come to 2 percent instead of a possible 4 percent she could have earned as a childless and fully committed full-time professional. In that event, she'll sacrifice $996,567 in forgone income over just the next 21 years. Adjusting for inflation, that's equal in today's dollars to roughly $548,563.

Where does this leave the total bill? Combine $996,567 in forgone wages with the USDA's estimates of a typical middle-class family's direct child-related expenses for an only child ($301,183); add in the likely cost of sending a child born last year to a first-rank, in-state public university ($157,831), and the total cost of one typical middle-class child born in 1997 comes in at $1,445,581. Even after adjusting for inflation, the cost of a middle-class child born last year is still $799,913 in today's dollars.

To be sure, parents also receive some direct subsidies for their child-care costs. Being able to claim a dependent is worth $2,650 in federal taxes due this year, for example. And under current law, families are eligible to take a tax credit for child-care expenses, with a maximum credit of $720 for one child in a low-income family and up to $1,440 for two or more children. President Clinton recently proposed making this credit more generous, so that a family of four making $35,000 and saddled with high child-care bills would no longer owe any federal income taxes. But even if Clinton's plan is approved, parents who stay home with their kids will continue to receive no compensation for their lost income, and even those taking the credits will find themselves far worse off financially, in most cases, than if they had decided to remain childless.

Given current economic incentives, it is hardly surprising that the "smartest" people in our society end up being those least likely to have children. Middle-aged women with graduate degrees are more than three times more likely to be childless than those who dropped out of high school. Similarly, two-income married-couple families earning over $75,000 are 70 percent more likely to be childless than those earning between $10,000 and $19,999. You don't have to be an economic materialist to see the financial reality behind these numbers. Highly educated, high-income people have a higher opportunity

cost, in the form of lost income, if they decide to have children.

Government policy makers are forever talking about the need for society to "invest" in today's youth, if for no other reason than to pay for the huge, largely socialized cost of supporting the growing ranks of the elderly. It's a noble goal, but at the individual family level, a child, financially speaking, looks more like a high-priced consumer item with no warranty. It's the decision to remain childless that offers the real investment opportunity.

TUMMIES.
Feeding a middle-class 15-year-old costs **$1,920** a year on average. Hide the Cheez-Its!

Imagine a middle-class, college-age, sexually active woman who is contemplating whether to spend $5,000 to have her tubes tied so she'll never have to worry about getting pregnant. We've already seen how the cost of giving birth to just one child could easily exceed $1.4 million over the next 22 years. Even though many of those costs could be well down the road, a typical middle-class young woman paying $5,000 for such an operation could expect that "investment" to compound at a rate of fully 680 percent over the next 22 years alone. (The return on a vasectomy, which is even cheaper, would be much high-

er.) It will be a long time before anyone finds a deal that lucrative on Wall Street.

But wait a minute. Isn't this an absurd conclusion? Children aren't just a bundle of liabilities. If they were, the way for society to become richer would be for everyone to stop having kids, but of course that wouldn't work. Without a rising new generation of workers, there will be nobody around to assume our debts, and before long, even the store shelves will be empty. So why does our accounting suggest the opposite?

Because society's economic interests and those of parents as individuals don't perfectly coincide. The financial sacrifice a parent makes to have and raise children creates enormous wealth for society as a whole. But the modern reality is that everyone shares in much of that wealth regardless of what role he or she played in creating it. If, for example, you don't choose to have children, or you treat your children badly, you still won't have to give up any of your Social Security pension.

Historically, support in old age did depend, almost entirely, on how many children you had, and on how well your investment in them turned out. Even before parents grew old, they could usually count on their children to perform economically useful tasks around the farm or shop. This made children economic assets—from the point of view of both society at large and parents.

Now the economic returns of parenting mostly bypass parents, and a proper accounting has to reflect that. For economic man in the late 20th century, child-rearing has become a crummy financial bargain. Fortunately, as Mom always said, there's more to life than money.

Amy Graham contributed to this article.

Unit 5

Unit Selections

Key Points to Consider

❖ Why is adolescence going on and on and on?

❖ Why is adolescence difficult for both parents and kids?

❖ Describe some cultural differences in what is considered "bad" behavior?

❖ What factors have contributed to the recent spate of school shootings?

❖ Are there biological as well as environmental reasons for gender differences in intimacy?

❖ Who stole fertility?

 **Links** | **www.dushkin.com/online/**

26. **AMA - Adolescent Health On Line**
http://www.ama-assn.org/adolhlth/adolhlth.htm
27. **American Academy of Child and Adolescent Psychiatry**
http://www.aacap.org/web/aacap/
28. **Ask NOAH About: Mental Health**
http://www.noah.cuny.edu/illness/mentalhealth/mental.html
29. **Biological Changes in Adolescence**
http://www.personal.psu.edu/faculty/n/x/nxd10/biologic2.htm

These sites are annotated on pages 4 and 5.

The amount of time people spend in the limbo between childhood and adulthood is collectively known as adolescence. This term was coined in 1904 by G. Stanley Hall, one of the world's first psychologists. He saw adolescence as a discrete stage of life that bridges the gap between sexual maturity (puberty) and socioemotional and cognitive maturity. At the turn of the twentieth century, it was typical for young men to begin working in middle childhood (there were no child labor laws) and for young women to become wives and mothers as soon as they were fertile and/or spoken for. The beginning of adolescence today is often marked by the desire to be independent of parental control as much as by the beginning of sexual maturation. The end of adolescence, which at the turn of the century coincided with the age of legal maturity (usually 16 or 18 depending on local laws), has now been extended upwards. Although legal maturity is now usually age 18 (voting, enlisting in the armed services, owning property, marrying without permission are all possible), the social norm is to consider persons in their late teens as adolescents, not as adults. Often the twenty-first birthday is viewed as a rite-of-passage into adulthood in the United States because it signals the legal right to buy and drink alcoholic beverages. Most students who accept financial help from their parents for their education are not considered "mature" until they have reached their final or desired educational attainments. "Maturity" is usually reserved for those who have achieved full economic as well as socioemotional independence as adults.

The first article in the adolescence section speaks about the phenomena of extending the period of limbo between childhood and adulthood through the early twenties or beyond. Cynthia Crossen reviews the milestones of the history of adolescence with a pictorial time line. She presents reasons for the lengthening of time it takes to "grow up" in a technologically complicated and affluent society.

Adolescence, by anyone's description, is a time of accelerated growth and change. A child becomes an adult through a series of profound physical changes, including becoming capable of sexual reproduction. Accompanying the physical and physiological alterations in the child's body are stupendous changes in emotions, in cognitions, and in a desire for social freedoms.

The second article included in this section is an excellent description of some of the repercussions of the transformation from child to adult. Virginia Rutter asks and answers the question "Whose Hell Is It?" She provides several quotes from teenagers about their worries: parents, school, peers, guns, gangs, drugs, AIDS. She advises parents to continue parenting through these turbulent years.

The third article in the adolescent section looks at cross-cultural views of adolescent behaviors. The behaviors most frequently associated with a "bad kid" were lack of self-control (American), acts against society (Chinese), and disruptions of interpersonal harmony (Japanese). Do these responses reflect different cultural values?

The fourth article in the adolescent section is an effort to reconcile the research data exploring the origins and antecedents of adolescent violence with the facts as known about the recent number of teenagers who have perpetrated homicidal acts against their teachers, peers, family, and friends. The recent school shootings are puzzling because some of the variables that are usually correlated with antisocial aggressive acts have been absent and other variables have emerged as more significant.

As adolescence has been extended, so too has young adulthood. Later marriages and delayed childbearing have redefined the line between young adulthood and middle age. Erik Erikson, the personal/social personality theorist, marked the passage from adolescence to young adulthood by a change in the nuclear conflicts of the two life stages. Adolescents struggle to answer the question "Who am I?" Young adults struggle to answer questions about their commitments to partnerships and intimate relationships. They struggle to find a place within the existing social order where they can feel propinquity rather than isolation. In the 1960s, Erikson wrote that some females resolve both their conflicts of identity and of intimacy by living vicariously through their husbands. He did not comment, however, on whether or not some males resolve their conflicts of identity and intimacy by living vicariously through their wives. He felt that true intimacy was difficult to achieve if the person seeking it had not first become a trusting, autonomous, self-initiating, industrious, and self-knowledgeable human being. Role confusion and isolation were what Erikson predicted for adolescents and young adults who remain immature.

The first article in the young adulthood section of this unit addresses the Eriksonian nuclear conflict of achieving intimacy. The author, Robert Nadeau, has an alternate to Erikson's belief that women achieve intimacy by living vicariously through their husbands. He reviews research that suggests that the human female brain may biologically evoke more emotional responsivity than the male brain. Women's brains may make them more aware of nuances, hidden meanings, and/or sensory clues to meaning. Women use language to achieve consensus and intimacy. Men use physical presence and physical movement. The second article about young adulthood asks "Who Stole Fertility?" Virginia Rutter considers the impact of reproductive technology on the lives of young couples.

Growing Up Goes On and On and On

By CYNTHIA CROSSEN

Staff Reporter of THE WALL STREET JOURNAL

THERE'S GOOD NEWS and bad news about adolescence, and it's the same: The amount of time Americans spend in limbo between childhood and adulthood is the longest it has ever been—and getting longer.

On the early side, puberty, the physical changes that kick off adolescence, now begins for girls a good two years earlier than it did in the early part of this century. That means the precursors of puberty, the secondary sex characteristics, now appear in girls as young as eight or nine. At the late end, the age of separating from parents—the last and most important task of adolescence—has steadily risen from 16 to 18 to 21 and now often well beyond.

"Alligators drop their eggs, the egg is ready to roll," says David Murray, an anthropologist by training and now director of a statistical research center in Washington, D.C. "We hold on to youth more than any other species."

If you think of adolescents as hormones with feet, as some do, this is troubling news. The baby boom's children are marching toward their teen years; when they arrive, there will be more teenagers than in two decades. Adolescence means drugs, violence and unwed pregnancies, not to mention bad haircuts, big clothes, loud music and pierced everything. Surges of hormones make adolescents emotionally unsteady, and creating their own identities is a mandate to annoy adults, especially their parents. "I think some adults are scared because the bad teenagers are getting 'badder,' " says 14-year-old Sylvia Indyk of Fairway, Kan. Indeed, some experts believe the fact that guns have replaced fists and knives as the weapon of choice among some teens is the single most significant change in adolescence today.

But today's powerful adolescent culture adds zest to a society that is otherwise getting creakier. With the extraordinary increase in life expectancy in this century, every stage of life is longer, and the baby boom will soon begin a very long old age. "Adolescents are delightfully fun, creative and unconstrained people," says Susan Mackey, a clinical psychologist at the Family Institute at Northwestern University. "There's nothing funnier than their sense of humor. They can laugh hysterically for a half hour over one phrase."

Fortunately, youth isn't always wasted on the young. "I enjoy being a teenager," says 16-year-old Jeannie Gardiner of Dayville, Conn. "I get to hang out with my friends, and I don't have to think about major expenses and bills, like house payments and children."

That does sound like a good deal. Which is why a long adolescence is a luxury enjoyed only by societies with money and leisure. In the earliest cultures, where boys and girls could do most adult tasks by their early teens, adolescence was a brief rite of passage: A boy would go away for a few weeks and return a man; girls simply found a mate and began bearing children. Even in early, rural America, few farm families could afford to give their children much in the way of adolescence. In 1879, Henry Ford left his family's farm at the age of 15 to start apprenticing in Detroit machine shops.

In fact, it wasn't until 1904 that adolescence became a recognized and discrete stage of life, instead of simply a brief transition between child and adult. That year G. Stanley Hall, a psychologist and the president of Clark University, declared that youths' minds were too tender to be exposed to the real world's severity—the so-called early ripe, early rot philosophy. Many scholars note the coincidence between Dr. Hall's widely accepted theories and the fact that the industrial economy couldn't absorb as many workers as the rural economy.

The problem of warehousing these able-bodied but impressionable young people was solved by state laws making education compulsory to the age of 16 or 17. In 1900, only 11% of America's high-school age youth were in high school. Today, that figure is over 90%. Some people believe high schools exacerbate the problems of adolescents, confining them to an overcharged world where they are permitted to do far less than they could.

"We now so believe teenagers are ... irresponsible, incapable, can't be trusted, can't be left alone that trying to think about what they might do that's productive is really hard," says Nancy Lesko, an associate professor of education at Indiana University.

That's exactly how many teenagers feel. "I feel like I'm mature enough to have more privileges," says Tara Conte, 15, of Haverhill, Mass. Such as? "Like being able to work part time and drive, but I have to wait until the law says I can do these things. And I think I'm mature enough to make most decisions on my own, but my parents have a difference of opinion."

Others say with the world becoming more technological and complicated, it takes longer to train children for adult responsibilities. "The age at which you are truly established and can support yourself keeps lengthening," says Joseph P. Allen, associate professor of clinical and development psychology at the University of Virginia. "I have graduate students who are in their late 20s and are still a ways away from being able to support themselves." Bob Enright, a professor at the University of Wisconsin with a specialty in adolescent psychology, agrees that "part of the reason we have adolescence is to educate people for an increasingly complex society." But, he adds, "there's also only so much room in a work force that is being downsized."

For many people, the lengthening of adolescence today is less worrisome than the fact that it is starting so early for girls. Earlier menstruation is associated with heavier body weight, so girls may not only be sexual before their minds and hearts are ready, but also out of step with the culture of leanness. Meanwhile, puberty is accelerating the growth process at a time when most of the boys are still shrimps. "For a boy, getting taller and larger is good," says Joan Jacobs Brumberg, a historian and author of the forthcoming "The Body Project: An Intimate History of American Girls." "For girls, it's problematic."

Psychologists who work with teenagers say there is no question that girls are

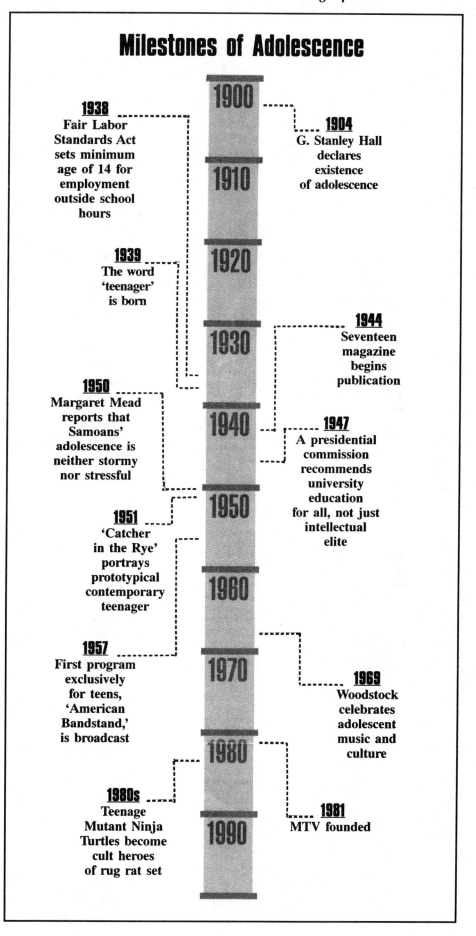

Milestones of Adolescence

1900

1904 G. Stanley Hall declares existence of adolescence

1938 Fair Labor Standards Act sets minimum age of 14 for employment outside school hours

1910

1920

1939 The word 'teenager' is born

1930

1944 Seventeen magazine begins publication

1950 Margaret Mead reports that Samoans' adolescence is neither stormy nor stressful

1940

1947 A presidential commission recommends university education for all, not just intellectual elite

1951 'Catcher in the Rye' portrays prototypical contemporary teenager

1950

1960

1957 First program exclusively for teens, 'American Bandstand,' is broadcast

1970

1969 Woodstock celebrates adolescent music and culture

1980

1980s Teenage Mutant Ninja Turtles become cult heroes of rug rat set

1981 MTV founded

1990

having sex earlier, usually with older males. "Kids have sex a lot younger than they used to, and they're really very young to be doing something that can have the consequences it has," says Anthony E. Wolf, a clinical psychologist in Longmeadow, Mass., and author of "Get Out of My Life, But First Could You Drive Me and Cheryl to the Mall?" "They just don't have the emotional maturity."

The Family Institute's Dr. Mackey cites research showing that the earlier girls hit puberty, the more likely they are to have poor body images, more problems in school, more depression and more drug use; they are also more likely to become sexually active earlier.

Furthermore, early development can exact a psychological price from a girl at home, where some parents back off, both physically and emotionally, from this new sexual person living in such close quarters. Psychologists say this is particularly true of fathers and daughters. "We can maintain the fiction of nonerotic children, but when girls develop breasts and boys get facial hair, we can't do that anymore," says Dr. Lesko. "They're right in our face. That's a trigger of major discomfort." When parents stop hugging their children or holding them on their laps, "the kid thinks, 'Now that I'm a sexual person, the only kind of physical contact I can have is sexual,' " says Dr. Mackey.

Linda Bips, a psychologist who runs the counseling center at Muhlenberg College in Allentown, Pa., says the biggest change she sees among adolescents is the increased intensity of their psychological problems. "In the '80s you'd see kids who had a kind of mild, everyday depression that rattled them; it was supportive therapy," she says. "Today they don't get out of bed. They end up eventually needing medication. I almost never used to refer out to medication. Now it's become more of a necessity."

Despite all this, many teenagers say the 1990s are a great time to be an adolescent. "We've got the Internet, the greatest thing to happen to education in a long time," says Daniel Snow, 18, of Tulsa, Okla. And they've always got their hormones. "Some days you can feel on top of the world, and on other days you feel hopeless, you wonder why you're here," says Mr. Snow. "Our emotions go to extremes, so when we have hope, we can do great things."

Adolescence
Whose Hell Is It?

The image of teenagers as menacing and rebellious is a big fiction that's boomeranging on kids. We've mythologized adolescence to conceal a startling fact: It is indeed a difficult and turbulent time—for parents. The trouble is, kids look like adults much sooner than ever before. Kids wind up feeling abandoned—and angry at the loss of their safety net. If we haven't got adolescence exactly figured out yet, there's some consolation in the fact that it's a brand-new phenomenon in human history.

Virginia Rutter

I recently spent the weekend with a friend's 13-year-old son. In contrast to the tiny tots most of my friends have, Matthew seemed much more like an adult. The time spent with him wasn't so much like baby-sitting; it was like having company. It was impressive to see how self-sufficient he was. Simple matters struck me: he didn't need someone to go to the bathroom with him at the movies; he could help himself to ice cream; he was actually interested in following the O. J. Simpson story, and we discussed it.

He was polite, thoughtful, and interesting. While the intensive caretaking necessary for smaller children has its own rewards (I suppose), Matthew's contrasting autonomy was pleasant to me. And so I imagined it would be for parents of adolescents. But then, I am not a parent. And most parents report not feeling pleasant about their adolescents.

The weekend reminded me of how easy it is to think of these youngsters as adults. Compared to an eight-year-old, an adolescent is a lot like an adult. Can't reason like an adult, but doesn't think like a child anymore, either. Some parents are tempted to

cut 'em loose rather than adjust to the new status of their teenager. Others fail to observe their adolescent's new adultlike status, and continue monitoring them as

---

A couple of teachers are my heroes. My history teacher is great because he listens to what everybody has to say and never judges.
—Chelsea, 14, Bakersfield, California

---

closely as a child. But it's obvious that adolescents aren't miniature adults. They are individuals on their way to adulthood; their brains and bodies—to say nothing of

their sexuality—stretching uneasily toward maturity.

Yet the sight of kids reaching for some form of adult status commonly evokes contempt rather than curiosity. Negative feelings about teenagers have a strong grip on American culture in general, and on surprising numbers of parents in particular. It's not uncommon for parents to anticipate their child's adolescence with fear and trepidation even before they've gotten out of diapers. They expect a war at home.

"It becomes a self-fulfilling prophesy that adolescence is seen as this bizarre, otherworldly period of development, complete with a battleground set for World War III," says Tina Wagers, Psy.D., a psychologist who treats teens and their families at Kaiser Permanente Medical Center in Denver.

We were all once 13, but it seems we can no longer imagine what kind of parenting a 13-year-old needs. Perhaps it's gotten worse with all the outside opportunities for trouble kids have—gangs, guns, drugs. Families used to extend their turf into their children's schools, friends, and athletic activities. But kids now inhabit unknown territory, and it is scary for parents. "I think this fear and lack of understanding makes some parents more likely to back off and neglect teenagers," reports Wagers. "There is an expectation that you can't influence them anyhow."

This skeptical, sometimes hostile view of teens, however, was countered by my experience with Matthew. I found him hardly a "teenager from hell." Like most teens, Matthew prefers to be with his own friends more than with family or other grown-ups. He's not good with time, and music, basketball, and girls are more central to him than achievement, responsibility, and family. (Despite his tastes, he does very well in school.) At home there is more conflict than there has been in the past, though not less love and commitment to his mom, with whom he lives in eastern Washington.

The story of Matthew falls in line with new research on adolescents, and it's causing psychologists to totally revise conventional wisdom on the subject. According to psychologist Laurence Steinberg, Ph.D., of Temple University, the majority of adolescents are not contentious, unpleasant, heartless creatures. They do not hate their parents—although they do fight with them (but not as much as you might think). "In scrutinizing interviews with adolescents and their families, I reaffirmed that adolescence is a relatively peaceful time in the house." Kids report continued high levels of respect for their parents, whether single, divorced, or together, and regardless of economic background.

When fighting does occur, it's in families with younger teenagers, and it has to do at least in part with their burgeoning cognitive abilities. Newly able to grasp abstract ideas, they can become absorbed in pursuing hypocrisy or questioning authority. In time, they learn to deploy relativistic and critical thinking more selectively.

NOT A DISEASE

If adolescents aren't the incorrigibles we think—then what to make of the endless stream of news reports of teen sexism, harassment, drug abuse, depression, delinquency, gangs, guns, and suicide?

Any way you measure it, teens today are in deep trouble. They face increasing rates of depression (now at 20 percent), suicide (12 percent have considered it, 5 percent attempted), substance abuse (20 percent of high school seniors), delinquency (1.5 million juvenile arrests—about 1 percent of teens—in 1992), early sexual activity (29 percent have had sexual relations by age 15), and even an increased rate of health problems (20 percent have conditions that will hamper their health as adults). And kids' problems appear to be getting worse.

How to reconcile the two parts of the story: adolescents aren't so bad, but a grow-

ing number are jeopardizing their future through destructive behavior? Though we look upon teenagers as time bombs set to self-destruct at puberty, in fact the problems teens face are not encoded in their genes. Their natural development, including a surge of hormonal activity during the first few years of adolescence, may make them a little more depressed or aggressive—but how we treat them has much more to do with teenagers' lives today. From the look of it, we aren't treating them very well.

A CRISIS OF ADULTS

If what goes on in adolescence happens largely in the kids, what goes wrong with adolescence happens primarily in the parents. "It wasn't until I turned to the parents' interviews that I really got a sense that something unusual was going on," reports Steinberg of his ongoing studies of over 200 adolescents and their families. As he details in his recent book, *Crossing Paths: How Your Child's Adolescence Triggers Your Own Crisis* (Simon & Schuster), Steinberg finds that adolescence sets off a crisis for parents.

Teenagers say that parents are not understanding and I don't think it is always that way.
—Gabriel, 16, Alburquerque, New Mexico

Parents do not have positive feelings during the time their kids go through adolescence, and it isn't simply because they expect their kids to be bad (although that's part of it). Scientists have studied the behavior and emotions of parents as well as their adolescent children, and found that when children reach puberty, parents experience tremendous changes in themselves. What's more, they shift their attitudes toward their children. It isn't just the kids who are distressed. Parents are too. Consider the following:

- Marital satisfaction, which typically declines over the course of marriage, reaches its all-time low when the oldest child reaches adolescence. Married parents of adolescents have an average of seven minutes alone with each other

every day. For the marriages that don't pass the point of no return during their kids' teen years, there is actually an increase in satisfaction after the kids complete adolescence.
- Happily married parents have more positive interactions with their kids than unhappy parents. In single-parent families, parental happiness also influences their response to adolescence.

Adults want kids to learn to take care of themselves. Kids need guides and advice. That is how you help people mature—not by leaving them alone.
—Michelle, 16, Clackamas, Oregon

- In a surprising finding, the marital satisfaction of fathers is directly affected by how actively their adolescents are dating. Especially when sons are busy dating, fathers report a marked decline in interest in their wives. Dads aren't lusting for the girls Johnny brings home, they just miss what now seem like their own good old days.
- In family discussions, parents become increasingly negative toward their adolescents—there's more criticism, whining, frustration, anger, and defensiveness expressed verbally or in grimaces. While the kids are always more negative than their parents (it comes with increasing cognitive ability, in part), the parents are actually increasing the amount of negativity toward their children at a higher rate.
- Working mothers don't spend less time at home with their teenagers than non-working moms do, but they do risk higher levels of burnout, because they continue to cover the lioness' share of work at home. On the other hand, a mother's employment makes her less vulnerable to the ups and downs of parenting an adolescent. Maternal employment also benefits kids, especially teen daughters, who report higher levels of self-esteem.
- Despite their fulfillment, mothers' self-esteem is actually lower while they are with their adolescents than when they are not. After all, a mother's authority is constantly being challenged, and she

is being shunted to the margins of her child's universe.

- Teenagers turn increasingly to their friends, a distancing maneuver that feels like an emotional divorce to parents. Since mothers are generally more emotionally engaged with their children than are fathers, the separation can feel most painful to them. In fact, mothers typically report looking forward to the departure of their kids after high school. After the kids leave, mothers' emotional state improves.
- Fathers' emotional states follow a different course. Fathers have more difficulty launching their adolescents, mostly because they feel regret about the time they didn't spend with them. Fathers have more difficulty dealing with their kids growing into adolescence and adulthood; they can't get used to the idea that they no longer have a little playmate who is going to do what daddy wants to do.

Add it all up and you get a bona fide midlife crisis in some parents, according to Steinberg. All along we've thought that a midlife crisis happens to some adults around the age of 40. But it turns out that midlife crisis has nothing to do with the age of the adult—and everything to do with the age of the oldest child in a family. It is set off by the entry of a family's first-born into adolescence.

Once the oldest child hits adolescence, parents are catapulted into a process of life review. "Where have I been, where am I now, where am I going?" These questions gnaw at parents who observe their children at the brink of adulthood.

It hits hardest the parent who is the same sex as the adolescent. Mothers and daughters actually have more difficulty than fathers and sons. In either case, the children tend to serve as a mirror of their younger lost selves, and bear the brunt of parents' regrets as parents distance themselves.

Steinberg tracks the psychological unrest associated with midlife crisis in parents:

- The onset of puberty is unavoidable evidence that their child is growing up.
- Along with puberty comes a child's burgeoning sexuality. For parents, this can raise doubts about their own attractiveness, their current sex life, as well as regrets or nostalgia for their teenage sexual experiences.
- The kids' new independence can make parents feel powerless. For fathers in particular this can remind them of the powerlessness they feel in the office if their careers have hit a plateau.
- Teens also become less concerned with their parents' approval. Their peer group approval becomes more impor-

tant. This hits mothers of daughters quite hard, especially single mothers, whose relationship to their daughters most resembles a friendship.
- Finally, de-idealization—kids' often blunt criticism of their parents—is a strong predictor of decline in parental mental health. Parents who used to be the ultimate expert to their kids are now reduced to debating partner for kids who have developed a new cognitive skill called relativism.

A clear picture begins to emerge: parents of a teenager feel depressed about their own life or their own marriage; feel the loss of their child; feel jealous, rejected, and confused about their child's new sexually mature looks, bad moods, withdrawal into privacy at home, and increasing involvement with friends. The kid is tied up in her (or his) own problems and wonders what planet mom and dad are on.

EMOTIONAL DIVORCE

The sad consequence is that parents who experience a midlife crisis begin avoiding their adolescent. Although a small proportion of parents are holding on to their teens too closely—usually they come from traditional families and have fundamentalist religious beliefs—more parents are backing off. The catch is that these teenagers want their parents' guidance. But more and more they just aren't getting it.

Adults need to understand that it is very difficult to be a teenager nowadays. It takes a lot of understanding with so many problems like guns, drugs, AIDS, and gangs.
—Melissa, 14, Dallas, Texas

Some parents back away not out of their own inner confusion but because they think it's hip to do so. Either way, letting go causes confusion in the kids, not help in making their way into adulthood. Even if they are irritating or irritable, or just more withdrawn than they used to be, teens are seeking guidance.

"I have this image of a kid groping through adolescence, kind of by himself,"

confides therapist Wagers, who sees a lot of parents out of touch with their kids. "The parents swarm around him, but don't actually talk to him, only to other people about him."

The mantra of therapists who work with adolescents and their families is "balance." Parents have to hold on, but not too tightly. They need to stay involved, even when their kids are ignoring them. Roland Montemayor, Ph.D., professor of psychology at Ohio State, finds it is not so different from learning how to deal with a two-year-old. You must stay within earshot, and be available whenever they falter or get themselves into trouble.

With a two-year-old, trouble means experimenting with mud pies or bopping a playmate; with a 14-year-old, it means experimenting with your car keys or sex. The task is the same—keep track of them and let them know what the rules are. Parents unfortunately taken up with their own midlife concerns may not embrace the task. God knows, it isn't easy. But it is vital.

Among parents who have gone through a real divorce, the emotional divorce that occurs between adolescents and their parents can heighten difficulty. It may re-awaken feelings of sadness. Parents who don't have many interests outside the family are also vulnerable. Their kids are telling them to "Get a life!"—and that is exactly what they need to do.

DROPOUT PARENTS

As an adolescent reaches age 13, the time she is spending with parents is typically half that before age 10. "Teens come home and go into their bedrooms. They start to feel more comfortable by themselves than with siblings or parents around. They talk on the phone with friends, and their biggest worry usually has to do with a romantic interest," explains Reed Larson, Ph.D., who studies families and adolescents at the University of Illinois, Champaign-Urbana. Larson, coauthor of the recent book, *Divergent Realities: The Emotional Lives of Mothers, Fathers, and Adolescents,* studied 55 families who recorded their feelings and activities for one week, whenever prompted at random intervals by a beeper. He surveyed another 483 adolescents with the beeper method.

The families' reports revealed that a mutual withdrawal occurs. "When kids withdraw, parents get the message. They even feel intimidated. As a result they don't put in the extra effort to maintain contact with their kids," observes Larson. The kids feel abandoned, even though they're the ones retreating to their bedroom. The parents, in effect, cut their kids loose, just when they dip their toes in the waters of autonomy.

Separation is natural among humans as well as in the animal kingdom, Larson notes. Yet humans also need special care during this life transition—and suffer from reduced contact with parents and other adults. They still need to be taught how to do things, how to think about things, but above all they need to know that there is a safety net, a sense that their parents are paying attention and are going to jump in when things go wrong. The kids don't need the direct supervision they received at age two or eight, but they benefit emotionally and intellectually from positive contact with their parents.

> *I don't think adults understand how complicated kids' minds are today, how much they think; they don't just accept something but wonder why it is.*
>
> *—Adam, 14, Bethesda, Maryland*

Despite the tensions in family life, studies continue to confirm that the family remains one of the most effective vehicles to promote values, school success, even confidence in peer relationships. When it works, family functions as what Larson calls a "comfort zone," a place or a relationship that serves as a home base out of which to operate. Kids feel more secure, calm, and confident than those without a comfort zone. Similarly, Steinberg finds, the one common link among the many successful adolescents in his studies is that they all have positive relationships with their parents. Without positive relationships, the kids are subject to depression and likely to do poorly in school.

Parental withdrawal is a prime characteristic of families where adolescents get into trouble. It often catapults families into therapy. Wagers tells the story of a single parent who wasn't simply withdrawn, her head was in the sand: "I was seeing a mother and her 12-year-old son, who had depression and behavior problems. The mother called me up one time to say she had found all this marijuana paraphernalia in her son's room, in his pocket. She said she wasn't sure what it means. When I said 'it means that he's smoking pot,' she was very reluctant to agree. She didn't want to talk to her son about why he was getting into trouble or smoking pot. She wanted me to fix him." (Eventually, in therapy, the mother learned how to give her son a curfew and other rules, and to enforce them. He's doing much better.)

Marital problems also enter into the distancing equation. Although the marital decline among teens' parents is part of the normal course of marriage, the adolescent can exacerbate the problem. "Here is a new person challenging you in ways that might make you irritable or insecure," explains Steinberg. "That can spill over into the marriage. The standard scenario involves the adolescent and the mother who have been home squabbling all afternoon. Well, the mom isn't exactly going to be in a terrific mood to greet her husband. It resembles the marital problems that occur when a couple first has a new baby." Trouble is, when the parents' marriage declines, so does the quality of the parenting—at a time when more parental energy is needed.

> *Teenagers know what is happening around them in school but adults hide things. Parents should shield their kids from some things but not so much that kids are afraid to go out into the world.*
>
> *—Sarah, 17, Hanover, NH*

As if there are not enough psychological forces reducing contact between parents and adolescents today, social trends add to the problem, contends Roland Montemayor. Intensified work schedules, increased divorce and single parenthood, and poverty—often a result of divorce and single parenthood—decrease parent-child contact. A fourth of all teenagers live with one parent, usually their mother. Families have fewer ties to the community, so there are fewer other adults with whom teens have nurturing ties. The negative images of teenagers as violent delinquents may even intimidate parents.

ALONE AND ANGRY

Whatever the source, parental distancing doesn't make for happy kids. "The kids I work with at Ohio State are remarkably in-dependent, yet they are resentful of it," says Montemayor. "There is a sense of not being connected somehow." Kids are angry about being left to themselves, being given independence without the kind of mentoring from their parents to learn how to use their independence.

Adult contact seems to be on teenagers' minds more than ever before. Sociologist Dale Blythe, Ph.D., is an adolescence researcher who directs Minneapolis' noted Search Institute, which specializes in studies of youth policy issues. He has surveyed teens in 30 communities across the country, and found that when you ask teens, they say that family is not the most important thing in their lives—peers and social activities are. Nevertheless a large proportion of them say that they want more time with adults—they want their attention and leadership. They want more respect from adults and more cues on how to make it in the adult world. What a shift from 25 years ago, when the watchword was "never trust anyone over 30"!

So it's up to parents to seek more contact with their kids—despite the conflict they'll encounter. "The role of parents is to socialize children, to help them become responsible adults, to teach them to do the right thing. Conflict is an inevitable part of it," says Montemayor. He notes that one of the biggest sources of conflict between parents and teens is time management. Teens have trouble committing to plans in advance. They want to keep their options wide open all the time. The only surefire way to reduce conflict is to withdraw from teenagers—an equally surefire way to harm them.

> *I am insecure about my future. The main view toward people in my generation is that we are all slackers and it's kind of disturbing. We are actually trying to make something of ourselves.*
>
> *—Jasmine, 16, Brooklyn, New York*

"In other countries parents don't shy away from conflict. In the United States we have this idea that things are going to be hunky-dory and that we are going to go

The Invention of Adolescence

Are Romeo and Juliet the Quintessential adolescents? On the yes side, they were rebelling against family traditions, in the throes of first love, prone to melodrama, and engaged in violent and risky behavior. But the truth is that there was no such thing as adolescence in Shakespeare's time (the 16th century). Young people the ages of Romeo and Juliet (around 13) were adults in the eyes of society—even though they were probably prepubescent.

Paradoxically, puberty came later in eras past while departure from parental supervision came earlier than it does today. Romeo and Juliet carried the weight of the world on their shoulders—although it was a far smaller world than today's teens inhabit.

Another way to look at it is that in centuries past, a sexually mature person was never treated as a "growing child." Today sexually mature folk spend perhaps six years—ages 12 to 18—living under the authority of their parents.

Since the mid-1800s, puberty—the advent of sexual maturation and the starting point of adolescence—has inched back one year for every 25 years elapsed. It now occurs on average six years earlier than it did in 1850—age 11 or 12 for girls; age 12 or 13 for boys. Today adolescents make up 17 percent of the U.S. population and about a third of them belong to racial or ethnic minorities.

It's still not clear exactly what triggers puberty, confides Jeanne Brooks-Gunn, Ph.D., of Columbia University Teachers College, an expert on adolescent development. "The onset of puberty has fallen probably due to better nutrition in the prenatal period as well as throughout childhood. Pubertal age—for girls, when their first period occurs—has been lower in the affluent than the nonaffluent classes throughout recorded history. Differences are still found in countries where starvation and malnutrition are common among the poor. In Western countries, no social-class differences are found." Although adolescence is a new phenomenon in the history of our species, thanks to a stable and abundant food supply, we've already hit its limits—it's not likely puberty onset will drop much below the age of 12.

If kids look like adults sooner than ever before, that doesn't mean they are. The brain begins to change when the body does, but it doesn't become a grown-up thinking organ as quickly as other systems of the body mature. The clash between physical maturity and mental immaturity not only throws parents a curve—they forget how to do their job, or even what it is—it catapults teens into some silly situations. They become intensely interested in romance, for example, only their idea of romance is absurdly simple, culminating in notes passed across the classroom: "Do you like me? Check yes or no."

Puberty isn't the only marker of adolescence. There's a slowly increasing capacity for abstract reasoning and relative thinking. Their new capacity for abstraction allows teens to think about big things—Death, Destruction, Nuclear War—subjects that depress them, especially since they lack the capacity to ameliorate them.

The idea that everything is relative suddenly makes every rule subject to debate. As time passes, teens attain the ability to make finer abstract distinctions. Which is to say, they become better at choosing their fights.

Teens also move toward autonomy. They want to be alone, they say, because they have a lot on their minds. Yet much of the autonomy hinges on the growing importance of social relationships. Evaluating the ups and downs of social situations indeed requires time alone. Family ties, however, remain more important than you might expect as teens increase identification with their peers.

Whatever else turns teens into the moody creatures they are, hormones have been given far too much credit, contends Brooks-Gunn. In fact, she points out, the flow of hormones that eventually shapes their bodies actually starts around age seven or eight. "Certain emotional states and problems increase between ages 11 and 14, at the time puberty takes place. These changes are probably due to the increased social and school demands, the multiple new events that youth confront, their own responses to puberty, and to a much lesser extent hormonal changes themselves."

The nutritional abundance that underlies a long adolescence also prompted the extension of education, which has created a problem entirely novel in the animal kingdom—physically mature creatures living with their parents, and for more years than sexually mature offspring ever have in the past. College-bound kids typically depend on their parents until at least age 21, a decade or more after hitting puberty.

Historically, children never lived at home during the teen years, points out Temple University's Laurence Steinberg. Either they were shipped out to apprenticeships or off to other relatives.

Among lower primates, physically mature beasts simply are not welcome in the family den; sexual competition makes cohabiting untenable. But for animals, physical maturity coincides with mental acuity, so their departure is not a rejection.

The formal study of adolescence began in the 1940s, just before James Dean changed our perception of it forever. There is a long-standing tradition of professional observers looking at adolescence as a pathology—and this one really did start with Freud. It continues still.

A 1988 study reported that although the under-18 population actually declined from 1980 to 1984, adolescent admissions to private psychiatric hospitals increased—450 percent! The study suggests a staggering cultural taste for applying mental health care to any problem life presents. It also hints at the negative feelings Americans have toward adolescence—we consider it a disease.

The study of adolescence has come with a context—a culture of, by, and for youth, arising in the postwar boom of the 1950s and epitomized by James Dean. Once the original badass depressive teenager from hell, Dean seems quaintly tame by today's standards. But the fear and loathing he set in motion among adults is a powerful legacy today's teens are still struggling to live down.—V.R.

Many times teenagers are thought of as a problem that no one really wants to deal with. People are sometimes intimidated and become hostile because teenagers are willing to challenge their authority. It is looked at as being disrespectful. Teenagers are, many times, not treated like an asset and as innovative thinkers who will be the leaders of tomorrow. Adults have the power to teach the younger generation about the world and allow them to feel they have a voice in it.—Zula, 16, Brooklyn, NY

A postpubescent child introduces a third sexually mature person into the household, where once sex was a strictly private domain restricted to the older generation. It's difficult for everyone to get used to.

No matter how you slice it, sex can be an awkward topic. For parents, there's not only the feeling of powerlessness, there's discomfort. Most parents of adolescents aren't experiencing much sexual activity—neither the mechanics of sex nor its poetry—in this stage of the marriage (though this eventually improves).

The fact that fathers' marital satisfaction decreases when their kids start to date suggests the power of kids' sexuality, no matter how silenced, to distort parental behavior. Sex and marital therapist David Schnarch, Ph.D., points out that families, and the my-

I think Al Gore is a super environmentalist. With no ozone layer, the world is just going to melt. It's hard not to worry. The environment is really messed up and with no environment there will be no economy, no education, nothing. I hate it when people throw six-pack rings in the lake. We need to think about the environment because we need to get on with the rest of our lives. I don't think adults generally look to kids for opinions.—Sam, 13, New York City

bowling and have fun together. Most people in the world would find that a pretty fanciful idea. There is an inevitable tension between parents and adolescents, and there's nothing wrong with that."

SILENCED SEX

Who can talk about teens without talking about sex? The topic of teenage sexuality, however, heightens parents' sense of powerlessness. Adults hesitate to acknowledge their own sexual experience in addressing the issue. They resolve the matter by pretending sex doesn't exist.

Doing the right thing and being good at what you're doing is important to me.

As teenagers we have a lot of things on our back, a lot of people are looking for us to do many great things. We also take in a lot of things and we know a lot of things. I care about the environment because it's a place that we all have to live in, not just us but our families and children. Even though I'm 15, I still have to keep those things in mind because it's serious. As for my own future, I've had a good upbringing and I see all open doors.—Semu, 15, New York City

we teach a biological model of sexuality, we imply to the kids 'we know you can't delay. We think these are the best years of your life.' "

Parents can help their children by letting them know that they understand sex and have valuable experience about decisions related to sex; that they know it isn't just a mechanical act; that they recognize that teens are going to figure things out on their own with or without guidance from their parents; and that they are willing to talk about it. But often, the experience or meaning of sex gets lost.

I think there is going to be a lot of destruction and violence. There are all these peace treaties, but I don't think they are going to work out.

—Julia, 12, Albuquerque, NM

Sexuality was conspicuous by its absence in all the family interviews Steinberg, Montemayor, or Larson observed. Calling sex a hidden issue in adolescence verges on an oxymoron. Sprouting pubic hair and expanding busts aren't particularly subtle phenomena. But adolescent sexuality is only heightened by the silence.

thology of the culture, worship teen sexuality, mistakenly believing adolescence is the peak of human sexuality. Boys have more hard-ons than their dads, while the girls have less cellulite than their moms.

These kids may have the biological equipment, says Schnarch, but they don't yet know how to make love. Sex isn't just about orgasms, it is about intimacy. "All of our sex education is designed to raise kids to be healthy, normal adults. But we are confused about what we believe is sexually normal. Textbooks say that boys reach their sexual peak in late adolescence; girls, five to 10 years later. The adolescent believes it, parents believe it, schools believe it. In the hierarchy dictated by this narrow biological model of sexuality, the person with the best sex is the adolescent. On the one hand we are telling kids, 'we would like you to delay sexual involvement.' But when

The future sounds alright. It is probably going to be more modern and really scientific. Things will be run by computers and computers will do more for people. —Emily, 13, New York City

I asked a woman whose parents had handed her birth control pills at age 15 how she felt about it now, at age 30. "I wish sex had been a little more taboo than it was. I got into a lot more sexual acting out before I was 20, and that didn't go very well for me. Even though my parents talked about the health consequences of sex, they did not mention other consequences. Like what it does to your self-esteem when you get involved in a series of one-night stands. So I guess I wish they had been more holistic in their approach to sex. Not just to tell me about the pill when I was 15, but to understand the different issues I was struggling with. In every other aspect of my life, they were my best resource. But it turns out sex is a lot more complicated than I thought it was when I was 15. At 30, sex is a lot better than it was when I was a teenager."

The distortions parents create about teen sexuality lead directly to events like the "Spur Posse," the gang of teenage football stars in Southern California who systematically harassed and raped girls, terrorizing the community in the late 80s. The boys' fathers actually appeared on talk shows—to brag about their sons' conquests. "The fathers were reinforcing the boys' behavior. It was as if it were a reflection on their own sexuality," observes Schnarch.

By closing their eyes to teen sexual behavior, parents don't just disengage from

---

I don't feel any pressure about sex. It's a frequent topic of conversation, but we talk about other things, too—when I'm going to get my history paper done, movies, music. I listen to classical music a lot. I think about my maturity a lot, because I have recently had losses in my immediate family and it feels like I am maturing so fast. But then sometimes I feel so young compared to everything out there. I think adults have always felt that teens were more reckless.—**Amanda, 16, New York City**

Teenagers, like adults, are all different. One has a job that is hard, another has more money and more education, and one just gets by. It is unfair to look at all teens the same way. You have maturity in you, but you just don't want to show it because it's no fun. We've got problems, but not really big ones like my uncle who came over from China when he was 16, or going to war when you're 18. If teenagers make it through this era, adults will just bash the next generation of teenagers.—**Mike, 14, Brooklyn, New York**

---

their kids. They leave them high and dry about understanding anything more than the cold mechanics of sex. Kids raised this

---

Jackie Joyner-Kersee, the Olympic track star, is my hero because she has accomplished so much and she is one of the main female athletes.
—Kristy, 12, Woodbridge, New Jersey

---

way report feeling very alone when it gets down to making intimate decisions for the first time. They feel like they haven't been given any help in what turns out to be the bigger part of sex—the relationship part of it.

Returning to the authoritarian, insular family of Ward, June, Wally, and the Beaver

---

My hero is Queen Latifah. She is herself and doesn't try to be somebody else. My mother is also my hero because she raises me as well as she can and she is a single parent.
—Maria, 15, Bronx, New York

---

is not the solution for teenagers any more than it is for their parents. But teenagers do need parents and other responsible adults actively involved in their lives, just as younger children do. Only when it comes to teenagers, the grown-ups have to tolerate a lot more ambiguity—about authority, safety, responsibility, and closeness—to sustain the connection. If they can learn to do that, a lot of young people will be able to avoid a whole lot of trouble.

What Is a Bad Kid? Answers of Adolescents and Their Mothers in Three Cultures

**David S. Crystal and
Harold W. Stevenson**

University of Michigan

This study examined the behaviors and personality traits attributed to a "bad kid" by a cross-national sample of 204 American high-school students and 204 American mothers, 237 Chinese students and 224 Chinese mothers, and 157 Japanese students and 167 Japanese mothers. Correlates of students' responses were also examined, including the degree of valuing academics, level of academic achievement, level of psychological adjustment, and quality of social relationships. The behaviors most frequently associated with a bad kid were lack of self-control (American), acts against society (Chinese), and disruptions of interpersonal harmony (Japanese). In addition, American students mentioned substance abuse as a feature of a bad kid more often than did their Chinese and Japanese peers. Disturbances in inter-personal harmony received the highest frequency of response from Chinese and Japanese students and second highest frequency of response from American students. Adolescents and their mothers differed significantly in the frequency with which they mentioned the types of conduct attributed to a bad kid. Few associations were found between students' own characteristics and their descriptions of a bad kid.

Requests for reprints should be sent to David S. Crystal, Center for Human Growth and Development, 300 North Ingalls, 10th Level, University of Michigan, Ann Arbor, MI 48109-0406.

Over the past 30 years, due, in large part, to the influence of the labelling theorists (e.g., Becker, 1964; Scheff, 1974), a growing number of social scientists have come to view deviance not as an objective quality but, rather, as a subjective definition made by a particular audience. From this perspective, a behavior is bad, wrong, or abnormal because it is defined that way by members of a particular society (Newman, 1976). Based on this premise, there is an increasing interest among psychologists and sociologists in identifying cross-cultural differences in perceptions of deviance and in understanding how these perceptions reflect the characteristics of the society or culture from which they derive.

One way of understanding the process by which cultural characteristics come to express themselves through perceptions of deviance may be seen in a paradigm put forth by LeVine (1973). According to the paradigm, the environment influences child rearing practices which, in turn, affect the nature of child and adult personality, as well as important facets of group life, including perceptions of good and bad. These latter products of culture may be seen as reflected in what Robin and Spires (1983) called the individual's "projective system" (p. 109) that guides a person's social and moral behavior. Because children and adults are socialized to be able to function within the existing cultural environment, looking at certain aspects of the projective system of children and adults, such as perceptions of deviance, may tell us important

From the *Journal of Research on Adolescence*, Vol. 5, No. 1, 1995, pp. 71–91. © 1995 by Lawrence Erlbaum Associates, Inc. Reprinted by permission.

things about how adaptation within a specific culture takes place.

Cross-cultural studies on perceptions of deviance fall into two basic categories: those that examine expressions of psychological deviance such as mental illness (e.g., Hardy, Cull, & Campbell, 1987; Wilson & Young, 1988) and those that examine expressions of social deviance such as crime and juvenile delinquency (e.g., Newman, 1976; Rivers, Sarata, & Anagnostopulos, 1986). Although the literature contains numerous studies on perceptions of psychological deviance, we found relatively few investigations that examined cultural variations in the perception of social deviance and, of these, none that focused on adolescents.

This gap in the literature is surprising given that adolescents, who are in transition to adult society, should be a particularly rich source of information about perceptions of deviance. Some theories suggest that discrepancies that exist between the definitions of deviance of adolescent peer groups and those of adult society may explain, in part, the increase in antisocial behavior that occurs during the adolescent period (e.g., Sutherland, 1947). Even so, we have found no studies in which adolescents were directly asked what they consider to be deviant and none in which comparisons were made of the responses of adolescents and their parents or other adults.

We responded to this gap by exploring the concept of a "bad kid" among samples of high school students and their mothers in three cultures: American, Chinese, and Japanese. Our goals were threefold:

First, we wished to examine cross-cultural differences in perceptions of deviance as expressed in the image of a bad kid. As mentioned earlier, notions of *good* and *bad* represent fundamental aspects of culture that may be reflected in various projective systems. For example, Funkhouser (1991) studied stereotypes of good and evil by asking college students in five countries to complete a questionnaire while imag-

ining themselves to be, first, a very good person and, then, a very bad person. Ekstrand and Ekstrand (1986) had 9- to 13-year-old Swedish and Indian children and their parents describe what they regarded as good and bad behavior and the sanctions they expected for the latter. None of these studies focused primarily on adolescents and none of them directly compared American respondents with those from East Asian cultures.

We purposefully selected two East Asian cultures for comparison because of their widely diverse histories and cultural traditions and because other investigators have described distinctive attributes of what members of an East Asian society (i.e., Japan) considered a good child (White & LeVine, 1986). Because perceptions of deviance, like perceptions of normalcy, are assumed to be influenced by social values, the description of a bad kid was anticipated to be very different in Japan, Taiwan, and the United States. For example, the high value that Asian cultures traditionally place on education and academic achievement suggests that members of Japanese and Chinese societies would be likely to define a bad kid as someone who disrupts schoolwork and learning. The emphasis on group participation and social cooperation in Japan (e.g., Kojima, 1989; Reischauer, 1977) may also lead Japanese individuals to express more concern about disturbances in interpersonal and other social relationships than would their peers from an individualistic society such as the United States. Similarly given the overriding importance that Asian cultures, especially the Chinese, place on maintaining order in society and in the family, individuals from these cultures would, to a greater degree than Americans, be expected to associate a bad kid with behavior that disrupts the social order or damages family ties. Finally the strongly individualistic nature of American culture (Bellah, Madsen, Sullivan, Swidler, & Tipton, 1985), in

addition to the high incidence of aggressive and externalizing problem behaviors among adolescents in the United States (Weisz, Suwanlert, Chaiyasit, & Walter, 1987), implies that Americans may define a bad kid in terms of individual psychological characteristics, such as lack of self-control.

A second goal was to examine variables other than culture that might affect definitions of deviance. Perceptions of a bad kid are influenced not only by social values but also by the characteristics of the individuals themselves. We were interested in looking at three characteristics of heightened importance during the adolescent years: success in school, general adjustment, and social skills. For example, students within each culture who value academics or are successful in school may be more disturbed by a peer who disrupts activities at school than would students for whom school plays a less important role. Second, students who report good psychological adjustment may be more likely to consider behaviors related to lack of self-control as being characteristic of a bad kid than students who have less satisfactory adjustment. Third, adolescents who get along well with their peers may be more likely than those who are less adept at social relationships to see disturbances in interpersonal harmony as features of a bad kid.

A final goal was to gain a better understanding of the process by which cultural values and behavioral standards regarding deviance are transmitted to children in the different societies. To do this, we compared adolescents' ideas of a bad kid with those of their mothers. Given the emphasis on individualism in the United States, in contrast to the collectivistic orientation of East Asian cultures (e.g., Triandis, 1987) and the fact that parent-adolescent conflict appears to be less extreme and more subtle in Asian than in American families (Rohlen, 1983; White, 1993), we expected to find a greater degree of concordance in perceptions of deviance among Japanese and Chinese adolescents and mothers than among their American counterparts.

METHOD

Subjects

Data were collected in 1990 and 1991 in three large metropolitan areas: Minneapolis; Taipei, Taiwan; and Sendai, Japan. Respondents included 204 American eleventh-grade students and 204 American mothers, 237 Chinese students and 224 Chinese mothers, and 157 Japanese students and 167 Japanese mothers. Although the intent was to interview both students and their mothers, there were some cases in which students were interviewed but their mothers could not be interviewed and vice versa. In addition, some students and some mothers did not respond to the question about the bad kid. The students, who were selected to constitute a representative sample of children in each city, were part of a longitudinal study that was begun in 1980, when they were in first grade (see Stevenson, Stigler, & Lee, 1986, for a detailed description of sampling procedures and subject selection). The percentages of girls from Minneapolis, Taipei, and Sendai in the present samples were 55%, 49%, and 49%, respectively.

In Minneapolis, consent to participate in the study was obtained directly from the students themselves. In Taipei and Sendai, school authorities were responsible for giving consent. We first obtained permission from the school principal and then sought the cooperation of the teachers. After each teacher's permission was granted, participation from the students was obligatory and universal. Such procedures to obtain consent were those approved by the sponsoring agencies and the relevant authorities in each city.

The families represented the full range of socioeconomic levels existing in each metropolitan area; how-ever, the occupational and educational status of the families differed. Skilled workers in Japan (51%) and Taiwan (38%) accounted for the largest percentage of fathers' occupations. In the United States, semiprofessional (40%) was the most frequently indicated level of occupation among fathers. The fathers' average number of years in school was 15 in Minneapolis, 11 in Taipei, and 13 in Sendai. Occupational level of the mothers who worked was similar to that of their husbands, but their average number of years of education was lower: 14 in Minneapolis, 9 in Taipei, and 13 in Sendai.

Measures

We took great care in constructing the measures to ensure that the wording of the questions conveyed the same meaning in each language. Members of our research group included bilingual native speakers of Chinese, Japanese, and English. In contrast to the common procedure of translation and back translation, we devised all the items simultaneously in the three languages. Consensus on item selection and wording of the instruments was arrived at through further discussion with bilingual and trilingual colleagues in the United States, Taiwan, and Japan. We believe this process of simultaneous construction of the questions considerably reduced the inconsistencies in nuance that often arise when items are initially written in English and then translated into unrelated languages, such as Chinese and Japanese. Rather than trying to find appropriate words and questions in a second language after the questions have been constructed, simultaneous composition allows discussion of terms by psychologists familiar with the languages before items are selected.

The items regarding a "bad kid" were part of a questionnaire that was given to students in all three locations.

Bad kid. In line with prior studies defining a good child (e.g., White & LeVine, 1986), we asked both students and their mothers the following question about a bad child: "Think of someone your (child's) age who you would consider to be a 'bad kid.' Describe what kind of person that would be." We also asked whether respondents were thinking of a boy girl, or someone of no specific gender in answering the question about a bad kid.

It is not difficult to find equivalents for the phrase *bad kid* in Japanese and Chinese. We used the term *warui ko* in the Japanese version of the question, and *huai haizi* in the Chinese. The phrases are simple and straightforward and have approximately the same connotations in each language. For example, in a standard Japanese-English dictionary examples of the word *warui* (bad) were given in sentences such as "He is a very bad boy—always up to mischief" (Kondo & Takano, 1986, p. 1897). Similarly, the Chinese word for *bad—huai*—was illustrated in a Chinese-English dictionary in the following way: "Bad elements held sway while good people were pushed around" (*Modern Chinese-English Dictionary*, 1988, p. 376).

We developed the coding scheme for the open-ended questions based on an analysis of the answers from subsamples of respondents in each culture. We were able to sort responses into 12 domains of behavior. We have concentrated our attention on the five major domains that appeared to us to be most likely to yield cross-cultural differences: *society, family, school, interpersonal harmony,* and *self-control.* In addition, two more major domains emerged in the analysis of the results: *substance abuse* and *crime.* (Examples of statements included in each domain are given later.) The seven major domains, including substance abuse and crime, accounted for 81% of American, 67% of Chinese, and 89% of Japanese students' responses. The remaining five domains dealt with *religion, sexual behavior, physical appearance, self-destructive behavior* and *physical aggression.* None of these do-

degree to which they valued academics, their social relationships, and their psychological adjustment (see Table 1).

RESULTS

Students' Responses

There was little concordance between the responses of the American and the Japanese or Chinese students or between the Chinese and Japanese students (see Table 2). Whereas interpersonal harmony predominated in the responses of the Japanese students, the responses of the American and Chinese students were much more evenly distributed across the five domains (see Figure 1). Consistent with the importance to adolescents of having satisfactory relations with their peers, the highest frequency of response of Chinese and Japanese students and the second highest of American students was interpersonal harmony. More than one third of the American students, however, also mentioned behaviors related to self-control, and more than one third of the Chinese students mentioned school and society. Additionally, American students noted substance abuse more frequently than Chinese and Japanese students, but Japanese students noted crime more frequently than did students in the other two groups. Cross-cultural differences in the percentages of students who mentioned a particular behavioral domain were evaluated by computing chi-square values. When they were found to be significant, a series of pairwise comparisons was conducted to identify possible sources of difference. Alpha levels for these pairwise tests were lowered to $p <$ .016, according to the Bonferroni Correction (Neter, Wasserman, & Kutner, 1985).

Society-related behavior. Nearly one and a half times as many Chinese as American adolescents and three times as many Chinese as Japanese adolescents mentioned so-

TABLE 1

Means and Standard Deviations of Measurements of Students' Personal Characteristics

Measure	USA[e] M	USA[e] SD	Taiwan[f] M	Taiwan[f] SD	Japan[g] M	Japan[g] SD
Value of academics[a]	6.2	1.0	5.5	1.2	5.2	1.3
How important is it to you: (a) that you go to college? (b) that you get good grades? (c) to study hard to go to college? (d) to study hard to get good grades?						
Social relationships[b]	5.5	0.8	4.9	1.0	4.6	1.0
How would you rate yourself in comparison to other persons your age: (a) in getting along with other young people? (b) in working out everyday problems on your own? (c) in caring about others?						
Psychological adjustment[c]						
Stress: How often do you feel stressed (under pressure)?	3.7	1.0	3.4	1.2	2.9	1.3
Depression: How often do you feel depressed?	3.0	1.0	3.3	1.1	2.8	1.2
Aggression: In the past month, how often have you: (a) felt like hitting someone? (b) felt like destroying something (c) gotten into serious arguments or fights with other students? (d) felt angry at your teacher?	2.1	0.8	1.8	0.8	1.8	0.7
Achievement[d]	12.1	7.6	21.8	10.4	20.1	6.6

Note. All $dfs = (2,557–572)$, $Fs = 6.93–75.10$, $ps < .001$.
[a]Answers ranged from *not at all important* (1) to *very important* (7). Cronbach alphas ranged from .67 to .71. [b]Questions used 7-point scales ranging from *much below average* (1) to *much above average* (7). Cronback alphas ranged from .65 to .74. [c]Students rated the frequency with which they experienced these feelings on 5-point scales ranging from *never* (a) to *almost every day* (5). Cromback alphas for the aggression ratings ranged from .72 to .77. [d]The test of mathematics achievement (Stevenson, Chen, & Lee, 1993) contained 47 open-ended items covering a broad range of mathematical topics. The Cronback alphas ranged from .92 to .95. [e]$n = 190–199$. [f]$n = 221–228$. [g] $n = 147–154$.

mains encompassed as many as 10% of the students' responses in each culture and yielded no significant cross-cultural differences. Five percent of American, 4% of Chinese, and 6% of Japanese students' responses were idiosyncratic and could not be categorized under one of the 12 domains.

The domains of behavior were coded according to a common scheme for the three languages and cultures. Responses were coded independently by two native speakers of each language. Each pair resolved any disagreements in coding through discussion between themselves and, if necessary through group discussion among the coders from all three locations. The percentage of agreement

among coders before resolution was 87% (United States), 87% (Taiwan), and 84% (Japan).

Respondents were allowed to give as many characteristics of a bad kid as they wished; however, we coded only the first six responses from each subject. Within the six responses, only one mention of each domain was counted, regardless of the number of examples given by a subject for a particular domain. Thus, we sought to determine the number of respondents in each culture who mentioned each domain, rather than the number of responses given by subjects within each of the domains.

Students also rated themselves on a number of variables, including the

ciety-related conduct (i.e., "rebels against society" "makes trouble for society" and "is a member of a street gang") as characteristic of a bad kid. Because of the importance placed in Japan on identifying with the social world, we had anticipated that many more Japanese students would mention society-related behavior.

Family-related behavior. The family-related domain contained responses that referred to behavior such as being disrespectful of or disobedient toward one's parents, running away from home, or physically attacking family members. Contrary to our expectation, Chinese students were no more likely than American students to cite family-related behaviors as being a feature of their image of a bad kid. Both groups mentioned family-related behaviors more frequently than their Japanese peers.

School. Chinese and Japanese students were not more likely, as we had initially posited, than American students to mention behaviors related to school. In fact, nearly three times as many American as Japanese students mentioned misconduct dealing with school as characteristic of a bad kid.

Four major categories of response fell within the domain of school-related behaviors. Two—"skips school" and "having low motivation"—

yielded no significant differences. The other two categories were "breaks rules" and teacher-related responses ("disrespectful to the teacher," "scolded by the teacher," and "badmouthing the teacher"). Among the 82 American, 92 Chinese, and 25 Japanese students giving school-related responses, more Japanese (28%) students mentioned breaking rules than did their Chinese (4%) or American (11%) peers, $\chi^2(1, N = 117) = 12.91, p < .05$ and $\chi^2(1, N = 107) = 4.37, p < .05$, respectively. Chinese (25%) and Japanese (12%) students were more likely, in turn, than American (2%) students to perceive disrespect for teachers as indicative of a bad kid, $\chi^2(1\ N = 174) = 17.94\ p < .05$ and $\chi^2(1, N = 107) = 3.93, p < .05$, respectively.

Interpersonal harmony. As anticipated, Japanese students were much more likely than American or Chinese students to view behaviors disruptive of interpersonal harmony ("hurting other people's feelings," "being argumentative and starting fights," "speaking badly of other people," and "not caring about others") as features of a bad kid.

Self-control. Responses that described a bad kid as "weak-willed," "goes to extremes," "childish," or "immature" were included in the domain of self-control. As anticipated, more American than Chinese or Japa-

nese students associated a bad kid with problems in self-control.

Substance abuse. The domain of substance abuse primarily contained references to the use of drugs and alcohol. In the United States, the major type of substance abuse mentioned was drugs (81%), whereas in Taiwan and Japan it was alcohol (76% and 80%, respectively). American students were more likely than Chinese students, who, in turn were more likely than Japanese students, to perceive substance abuse as characterizing a bad kid.

Crime. Responses coded in the crime domain mentioned acts ranging from milder crimes, such as stealing and destruction of property, to serious crimes, such as rape and murder. Japanese students noted crime as a feature of a bad kid significantly more often than did Chinese students. There were no significant differences in the percentages of American and Asian students who mentioned crime.

To determine whether disparities within each culture in the socioeconomic status of the families might have had a significant effect on cross-cultural differences in adolescents' perceptions of a bad kid, log linear analyses were performed on the data. Each behavioral domain served as the dependent variable, with location and occupational level comprising the independent variables. No significant interactive or main effects of occupational level were found for any behavioral domain mentioned by the students in analyses involving either mothers' or fathers' occupation.

In summary, relative to their peers in the other two locations, American students emphasized problems with self-control, Chinese students emphasized disturbances of the social order, and Japanese students emphasized disruptions in interpersonal harmony in their descriptions of a bad kid. Students in the United States were as likely as Chinese and more likely than Japanese students to mention school-related responses. In addition, American students noted substance abuse

TABLE 2
Percentages and Chi-Square Values for United States, Taiwan, and Japan for Analysis of Students' Responses Falling in Various Behavioral Domains

Domain	Percentage of Students			χ^2			
	U	T	J	U-T-J[ae]	U-T[bf]	U-J[cf]	T-J[df]
Society	29	40	14	29.63	7.28*	8.58	28.91
Family	17	24	5	25.01	ns	11.99	25.11
School	43	42	17	32.79	ns	28.77	25.92
Interpersonal harmony	53	50	84	53.19	ns	39.47	48.31
Self-control	38	24	24	13.00	9.44	9.00	ns
Substance abuse	62	40	12	8.90	19.60	89.16	36.54
Crime	10	8	19	10.80	11.5	11.5	9.75*

Note. All $ps < .001$, except where noted. U = United States. T = Taiwan. J = Japan.
[a]$n = 563.$ [b]$n = 411.$ [c]$n = 340.$ [d]$n = 375.$ [e]$df = 2.$ [f]$df = 1.$
*$p < .01.$

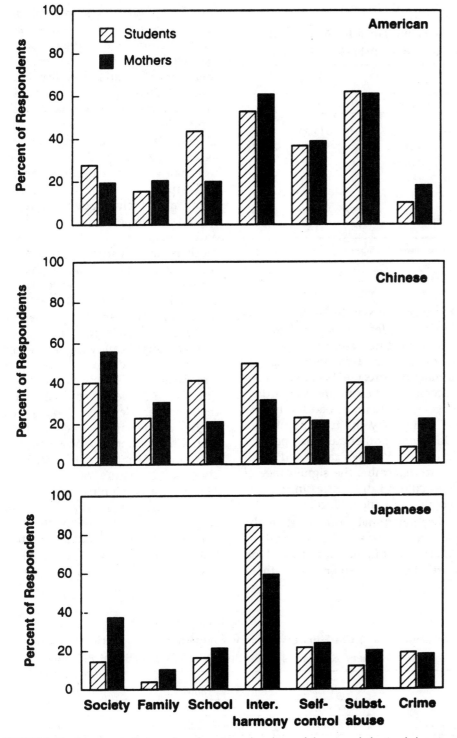

FIGURE 1 Mentions by students and mothers in each culture of the seven behavioral domains

mothers' responses were most frequently related to society. Japanese mothers gave primary emphasis to disruptions in interpersonal harmony. A relatively high proportion of mothers in the United States and Taiwan mentioned substance abuse. References to crime, however, were mentioned with similar frequencies across the three cultures.

Cross-cultural comparisons. With only two exceptions, cross-national differences in mothers' views of a bad kid were similar to those found for their children. First, the mothers in the three cultures displayed a surprising similarity in the low proportion of their responses that were related to school. Second, American mothers were as likely as Japanese, and twice as likely as Chinese mothers, to include disruptions of interpersonal harmony in their descriptions of a bad kid. In line with expectations, American mothers, like their children, tended to perceive lack of self-control as being characteristic of a bad kid more frequently than did their Chinese or Japanese counterparts. Also, Chinese mothers associated a bad kid with behaviors in the domains of society and family. In addition, American mothers were more likely than Chinese mothers, who, in turn, were more likely than Japanese mothers, to mention substance abuse in their descriptions of a bad kid. There were no significant differences in the percentages of mothers in the three cultures who perceived a bad kid as engaging in criminal behavior.

Log linear analyses were conducted to assess the possible influence of socioeconomic status on cross-cultural differences in mothers' perceptions of deviance. Results indicated that neither fathers' nor mothers' occupational level had any significant interactive or main effects on mothers' definitions of a bad kid.

Comparison of Students and Mothers

We next examined the domains in which adolescents' ideas about a

behaviors more frequently than did students in the other two locations. Japanese students mentioned crime significantly more often than Chinese students. For the most part, these emphases were in accord with the cultural orientations in each location.

Mothers' Responses

We next examined the mothers' impressions of a bad kid (see Figure 1 and Table 3). The most frequent responses of American mothers fell into the domain of interpersonal harmony and self-control. Chinese

TABLE 3

Chi-Square Values for United States, Taiwan, and Japan for Analysis of Frequency of Mothers' Responses Falling in Various Behavioral Domains

Domain	Percentage of Mothers			χ^2			
	U	T	J	U-T-J[ae]	U-T[bf]	U-J[cf]	T-J[df]
Society	19	56	37	57.46	57.38	14.33	12.01
Family	20	31	10	21.79	ns	6.61*	21.24
School	20	21	21	ns	ns	ns	ns
Interpersonal harmony	61	32	59	42.64	34.79	ns	27.82
Self-control	39	21	24	17.33	14.75	8.93*	ns
Substance abuse	61	40	20	61.37	17.78	60.50	16.86
Crime	18	22	18	ns	ns	ns	ns

Note. All $ps < .001$, except where noted. U = United States. T = Taiwan. J = Japan.
[a]$n = 562$. [b]$n = 407$. [c]$n = 356$. [d]$n = 361$. [e]$df = 2$. [f]$df = 1$.
*$p < .016$ (Bonferroni correction).

bad kid differed from those of the mothers. As can be seen in Table 4, culture played a major role in determining the nature of the differences. Among the three cultures, American students and mothers evidenced the highest degree of similarity in their perceptions of a bad kid. Only in the school-related domain did the frequency of responses differ between American mothers and students. Adolescents, more than mothers, viewed a bad kid as someone who disrupts activities in school. Chinese students were more likely than Chinese mothers to perceive a bad kid as disturbing school-related activities and interpersonal harmony. Chinese mothers, however, were more likely than students to cite behaviors related to society. Like their Chinese peers, adolescents in Japan referred to interpersonal harmony more often than did the mothers. In contrast, more Japanese mothers than students gave responses that fell in the domains of society and family. There were no significant differences in any of the three cultures in the percentages of responses of students and mothers that referred to substance abuse. Chinese mothers were, however, more likely than Chinese students to include the commission of crimes in their descriptions of a bad kid.

In addition to cross-generational group differences, we also compared the degree of within-family concordance in ideas about a bad kid across the three cultures (see Table 5). *Concordance* was defined as the number of agreements between adolescents and their mothers regarding a specific domain of bad kid behavior divided by the total number of adolescent-mother pairs in a particular culture. We then calculated T values to determine the significance of cross-cultural differences in the percentages of concordance.

Cross-national differences in the pattern of within-family concordance regarding notions of a bad kid were less consistent than those found in the cross-generational group comparisons. American and Chinese students and their mothers exhibited higher concordance in their view of a bad kid as disrupting school-related activities than did their Japanese counterparts. Adolescents and their mothers in the United States were more likely to agree that a bad kid lacked self-control than were their peers in Taiwan and Japan. Similarly, Chinese students and their mothers were in greater agreement than American and Japanese students and their mothers that disruptive behaviors related to family and society characterized a bad kid. In perceiving a bad kid as someone who disturbs interpersonal harmony, Japanese students and their mothers demonstrated a significantly higher degree of concordance than did their American and Chinese peers. Additionally, American students and their mothers demonstrated a much higher degree of concordance than their Chinese and Japanese counterparts in their mention of substance abuse as a feature of a bad kid. There were no significant cross-cultural differences in the degree of concordance with which students and their mothers described a bad kid as someone who commits a crime.

TABLE 4

Percentages and Chi-Square Values for Evaluating the Similarity of Students' and Mothers' Responses Regarding Domains of Bad Kid Behavior

Domain	USA[a]			Taiwan[b]			Japan[c]		
	Percentage			Percentage			Percentage		
	Students	Mothers	χ^2	Students	Mothers	χ^2	Students	Mothers	χ^2
Society	28	19	ns	40	56	9.66*	15	37	19.80
Family	15	20	ns	23	31	ns	4	10	ns
School	44	20	24.29	41	21	19.69	16	21	ns
Interpersonal harmony	53	61	ns	50	32	13.95	85	59	23.52
Self-control	37	39	ns	23	21	ns	22	24	ns
Substance abuse	62	61	ns	40	40	ns	12	20	ns
Crime	10	18	ns	8	22	17.06	19	18	ns

Note. All $ps < .001$, except where noted.
[a]$n = 389$. [b]$n = 429$. [c]$n = 307$.
*$p < .01$.

In general, adolescents and mothers differed significantly in the frequency with which they mentioned behaviors falling under the five major behavioral domains, but within-family comparisons yielded even less concordance between students and their mothers. The domains in which significant discrepancies emerged were those that apparently were the most crucial to students in each of the cultures: school-related behavior in the United States and interpersonal harmony and society-related behavior in Taiwan and Japan. The direction of these differences—students emphasizing school and interpersonal harmony, mothers emphasizing society—suggests the broader, more conventional perspective of the mothers, in contrast to the more personal viewpoint of the students.

In terms of within-family concordance, American students and their mothers were in greater agreement that a bad kid lacked self-control, Chinese students and their mothers that a bad kid disrupted society and family, and Japanese students and their mothers that a bad kid disturbed interpersonal harmony, than were their counterparts in the other two cultures. In addition, American adolescents and their mothers exhibited a much greater degree of concordance regarding the mention of

substance abuse than did their Chinese and Japanese peers. Generally, the domains in which cross-national differences in within-family concordance were the greatest appeared to conform to the social values that are emphasized in each of the cultures.

Correlates of Student Mentions of Bad-Kid Behaviors

Finally, we sought to determine whether the personal characteristics of the adolescents themselves were related to ones they associated with a bad kid. To evaluate whether these characteristics were related to the likelihood that a student would mention behavior in a specific domain, we formed high and low groups on each of the six measures described in Table 1. Students were included in a high group if their ratings on the measures or mathematics test scores fell within the upper third of the students in their respective cultures. Students in the lower third constituted the low group.

We performed log linear analyses using location and one of the student characteristics as the independent variables and each behavioral domain as the dependent variable. To test for significant effects, factors in the model were systematically omitted over successive analyses, and differences in

the -2 log likelihood statistics, which are distributed as chi-square values, were examined. We report these chi-square values in describing main and interaction effects.

There was little relation between the characteristics of the students and their descriptions of a bad kid. Only one main effect was significant. Students who held a high value for academics mentioned deviant behavior in school as characterizing a bad kid more often than did students who did not value academics (44% vs. 25%), $\chi^2(1, N = 384) = 8.36$, $p < .01$.

Gender Differences

Log linear analyses were also used to assess the effects of gender on the likelihood that students in different cultures would include a certain domain of behavior in their concept of a bad kid. Main effects of gender were found in the domains of school and family $\chi^2(1, N = 563) = 7.59$, $p < .01$ and $\chi^2(1, N = 563) = 8.40$, $p < .01$. Girls were more likely than boys to view a bad kid as someone who disrupted school activities (41% vs. 29%) and damaged family ties (19% vs. 11%). No significant gender × country interactions emerged.

When asked whether they were thinking of a boy, girl, or someone of no specific gender in answering the question about the bad kid, the majority of students in all three countries reported that they were thinking of someone of no specific gender (see Figure 2). Furthermore, there were significantly more students in the United States and Taiwan who said they thought of a boy than those who said they thought of a girl, $\chi^2(1, N = 347)$ 22.82, $= p < .01$ and $\chi^2(1, N = 396) = 9.46$, $p < .01$, respectively. In contrast, Japanese students were far more likely than their American and Chinese peers to think of a girl, $\chi^2(1, N = 347) = 21.42$, $p < .001$ and $\chi^2(1, N = 396) = 22.40$, $p < .001$, respectively. Boys in all three countries more often thought of a bad kid as someone of their own gender than did girls (United States:

TABLE 5

Correlations of Mothers' and Their Children's Conceptions of Bad Kid Behavior (Percentage of Pairs in Which Both Mother and Child Mentioned Some Item Falling Within Each Domain)

| Domain | Country | | | t | | |
	U^a	T^b	J^c	U-T	U-J	T-J
Society	.03	.21	.07	5.81	ns	4.06
Family	.04	.09	.01	2.11*	ns	4.82
School	.12	.11	.03	ns	3.23	3.10
Interpersonal harmony	.35	.17	.51	6.32	3.74	6.95
Self-control	.18	.04	.03	4.67	5.00	ns
Substance abuse	.41	.02	.02	10.26	10.26	ns
Crime	.02	.01	.03	ns	ns	ns

Note. U = United States. T = Taiwan. J = Japan. All *ps* < .001, except where noted.
$^a n = 182.$ $^b n = 204.$ $^c n = 146.$
*p < .05.

56% versus 35%, $\chi^2[1, N = 190] = 8.71$, $p < .01$; Taiwan: 49% versus 20%, $\chi^2[1, N = 239] = 22.08$, $p < .001$; Japan: 34% versus 7%, $\chi^2[1, N = 157] = 17.36$, $p < .001$). American (9% vs. 0%) and Japanese (33% vs. 8%), but not Chinese (9% vs 2%), girls thought of a girl significantly more often than did their male peers (United States: $\chi^2[1, N = 190] = 7.98$, $p < .01$; Japan, $\chi^2[1, N = 157] = 15.28$, $p < .001$).

DISCUSSION

When we began this study, we focused on five domains of behavior that we believed would lead to different definitions of a bad kid in American, Chinese, and Japanese cultures. Although our analyses yielded 12 different domains of behavior, 7 were sufficient to encompass the vast majority of the behaviors mentioned. Although there were differences in the degree to which these broad domains were represented among the three cultures, we also found commonalities across the cultures. For example, *disruptions in interpersonal harmony* was a dominant response in all three locations, reflecting the common pattern of adapting to the peer group and to the cultural demands faced by adolescents in all societies.

Interesting cross-cultural differences did emerge. Adolescents and mothers differed significantly in the frequency with which they mentioned behaviors falling under the five major behavioral domains. Students seemed to conceive of deviance from a more personal, circumscribed perspective, in contrast to the mothers, whose descriptions of a bad kid more consistently suggested broader conventional concerns, a finding that agrees with that of Smetana (1988). In other words, students' perceptions of a bad kid tended to deviate more from expected cultural values than did those of the mothers, apparently reflecting the transitional nature of the socialization process that characterizes the adolescent period in the

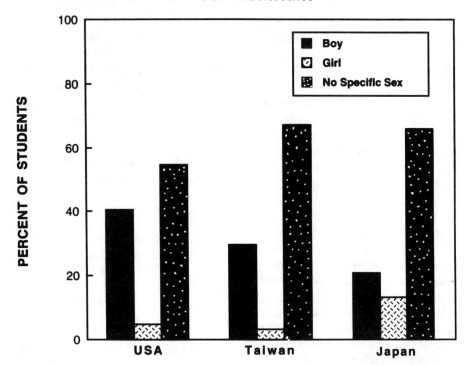

FIGURE 2 Percentages of students thinking of a boy, girl, or someone of no specific gender when describing a bad kid.

three societies (e.g., Chang, 1989; White, 1993).

Cross-cultural differences in the degree of within-family concordance in perceptions of a bad kid were generally found in those domains that appear to represent the most prominent social values in each culture. American adolescents and their mothers exhibited higher concordance in the domain of self-control; Chinese adolescents and their mothers showed a greater level of agreement in the domains of society and family; and Japanese adolescents and their mothers were most likely to agree about the domain of interpersonal harmony. These results suggest that the nature of the socialization process by which perceptions of deviance are transmitted from mothers to children is basically similar in the three cultures. That is, in all three locations, the criteria that mothers deemed as being most important in defining an individual as bad were generally reflected in the responses of their adolescent children.

The concept of a bad kid found among American, Chinese, and Japanese high school students and their mothers, although generally

consistent with the social values espoused in the three cultures, did not necessarily accord with the actual prevalence of deviant behavior in each of the cultures. For example, a higher percentage of Chinese than American students mentioned society-related behavior, despite the fact that Taiwan has a much lower incidence of antisocial behavior than does the United States (Federal Bureau of Investigation, 1990; Ministry of the Interior, Republic of China, 1989). Similarly, a much larger percentage of Japanese than American students cited disruptions in interpersonal harmony in their descriptions of a bad kid, even though interstudent conflict in Japan is not more pervasive or serious than it is in the United States (Federal Bureau of Investigation, 1990; Headquarters of the Youth and Children Program, General Affairs Division, 1989).

The tendency of American students to define a bad kid in terms of lack of self-control is consonant with the work of Tropman (1986) who pointed out the fundamental conflict between control and permissiveness in American culture. A focus on self-control is also compatible with the greater tendency toward an internal locus of control orientation that has been found among American, relative to Chinese and Japanese, individuals (e.g., Chiu, 1986; Evans, 1981). In addition, American adolescents' descriptions of a bad kid as someone lacking in self-control concur with the higher frequency of externalizing and aggressive problem behaviors among adolescents in the United States compared to those in Asian countries (Weisz et al., 1987).

The remarkably high frequency with which Japanese adolescents mentioned behaviors in the domain of interpersonal harmony is in line with the writings of various authors who emphasize the central importance Japanese give to interpersonal consensus and cooperation (e.g., Kojima, 1989; Reischauer, 1977).

The importance of maintaining order and tranquility in the society and in family relationships is a cornerstone of Confucian philosophy upon which much of Chinese culture is based. This traditional emphasis is reflected in the frequent mention of society- and family-related behaviors among the Chinese respondents in our study. (The Chinese culture in Taiwan, it should be noted, tends to be more traditional in terms of customs and values than that in Hong Kong or Mainland China.)

In some cases, the students' responses departed greatly from what we expected on the basis of presumed cultural values. For example, students in the United States mentioned disruptive behaviors at school as characteristic of a bad kid more frequently than did students in Japan. One explanation is that American students place a higher value on school and academic achievement than do their counterparts in Japan, where education and learning are thought to be held in especially high esteem. In support of this explanation, we found that American adolescents indicated significantly higher ratings than did their Japanese peers on our measure assessing the value students gave to academic achievement.

Of special interest was the high frequency of substance abuse, particularly drug-related, mentions in the United States. In Taiwan and Japan, possession of drugs is considered to be a serious felony punishable by imprisonment; the consequences in the United States are less severe. The use of alcohol, which is not considered a serious crime, was the form of substance more frequently mentioned in the Asian countries.

The students' view of what defined a bad kid was not predominantly gender-specific: Over 50% of the students in each country said that they were thinking of neither a boy nor a girl when they answered the question about the bad kid. Nevertheless, when students did reply that they were thinking of a person of a specific gender, boys more than girls said that they were thinking of someone of their own gender. These findings are consistent with statistics showing that adolescent boys are more likely to engage in deviant behavior than are adolescent girls (Federal Bureau of Investigation, 1990).

Just as efforts to describe a good kid (White & Levine, 1986) have yielded interesting insights into cultural differences, this exploratory study of the definitions of a bad kid given by adolescents and their mothers adds to our understanding of the socialization of cultural values in American and East Asian societies. These high school students' responses differed according to culture, as did those of their mothers; but adolescents and mothers were not always in agreement as to which behaviors defined a bad kid.

ACKNOWLEDGMENTS

This study was supported by National Science Foundation Grant MDR 89564683 to Harold W. Stevenson. The collection of the data in Taiwan was supported by National Science Council of R.O.C. Grants No. NSC 79-80-81-0301-H-006-08Y to Chen-Chin Hsu and Huei-Chen Ko.

We thank our colleagues, Shin Ying Lee and Kazuo Kato, and all the other people who have participated in this study. We are indebted to Yann-Yann Shieh, Kathy Kolb, Susan Fust, Heidi Schweingruber, and Etsuko Horikawa, to our research coordinators, and to the teachers and students for their cooperation. We also thank Chuansheng Chen for his helpful comments on the manuscript.

REFERENCES

Becker, H. (1964). *Outsiders.* Glencoe, IL: Free Press.

Bellah, R. N., Madsen, R., Sullivan, W. M., Swidler, A., & Tipton, S. M. (1985). *Habits of the heart: Individualism and commitment in American life.* Berkeley: University of California Press.

Chang, C. (1989). The growing generation in a changing Chinese society: Youth problems and strategies. *Bulletin of Educational Psychology, 22,* 243–254.

Chiu, L.-H. (1986). Locus of control in intellectual situations in American and Chinese schoolchildren. *International Journal of Psychology, 21,* 167–176.

Evans, H. M. (1981). Internal-external locus of control and work association: Research with Japanese and American students. *Journal of Cross-Cultural Psychology, 12,* 372–382.

Ekstrand, G., & Ekstrand, L. H. (1986). How children perceive parental norms and sanctions in two different cultures. *Educational and Psychological Interactions, 88,* p. 28.

Federal Bureau of Investigation. (1990). *Uniform crime reports for the United States.* Washington, DC: United States Government Printing Office.

Funkhouser, G. R. (1991). Cross-cultural similarities and differences in stereotypes of good and evil: A pilot study. *Journal of Social Psychology, 131,* 859–874.

Hardy, R. E., Cull, J. G., & Campbell, M. E. (1987). Perception of selected disabilities in the United States and Portugal: A cross-cultural comparison. *Journal of Human Behavior and Learning 4,* 1–12.

Headquarters of the Youth and Children Program, General Affairs Division (1989) Seishonen hakusho, heisei gannenpan [Adolescent white paper, 1989]. Tokyo, Japan: Okurasho.

Kondo, I., & Takano, F. (Eds.). (1986). *Progressive Japanese-English dictionary.* Tokyo: Shogakkan.

Kojima, H. (1989). *Kosodate no dento o tazunete* [Inquiring into the tradition of childrearing]. Tokyo, Japan: Shinyosha.

LeVine, R. A. (1973). *Culture, behavior and personality.* Chicago: Aldine.

Modern Chinese-English Dictionary. (1988). Beijing, People's Republic of China: Foreign Language and Teaching Research Press.

Ministry of the Interior, Republic of China (1989). *Crime statistics.* Taipei, Taiwan: Ministry of the Interior.

Neter, J., Wasserman, W., & Kutner, M. (1985). *Applied linear statistical models.* Homewood, IL: Irwin.

Newman, G. (1976). *Comparative deviance: Perception and law in six cultures.* New York: Elsevier.

Reischauer, E. O. (1977). *The Japanese.* Cambridge, MA: Harvard University Press.

Rivers, P. C., Sarata, B. P., & Anagnostopulos, M. (1986). Perceptions of deviant stereotypes by alcoholism, mental health, and school personnel in New Zealand and the United States. *International Journal of the Addictions, 21,* 123–129.

Robin, M. W., & Spires, R. (1983). Drawing the line: Deviance in cross-cultural perspective. *International Journal of Group Tensions, 13,* 106–131.

Rohlen, T. (1983). *Japanese high schools.* Berkeley: University of California Press.

Scheff, T. S. (1974). The labelling theory of mental illness. *American Sociological Review, 39,* 444–452.

Smetana, J. G. (1988). Adolescents' and parents' conceptions of parental authority. *Child Development, 59,* 321–335.

Stevenson, H. W, Chen, C., & Lee, S. Y (1993). Mathematics achievement. Chinese, Japanese, and American children: Ten years later. *Science, 259,* 53–58.

Stevenson, H. W., Lee, S. Y., & Stigler, J. W. (1986). Mathematics achievement of Chinese, Japanese, and American children. *Science, 231,* 693–699.

Sutherland, E. (1947). *Principles of criminology.* Philadelphia, PA: Lippincott.

Triandis, H. C. (1987). Collectivism vs. individualism: A reconceptualization of a basic concept in cross-cultural social psychology. In C. Bagley & G. K. Verma (Eds.), *Personality, cognition and values: Cross-cultural perspectives of childhood and adolescence.* London: MacMillan.

Tropman, J. E. (1986). *Conflict in culture: Permissions versus controls and alcohol use in American society.* Lanham, MD: University Press of America.

Weisz, J. R., Suwanlert, S., Chaiyasit, W., & Walter, B. R. (1987). Over- and undercontrolled referral problems among children and adolescents from Thailand and the United States: The *wat* and *wai* of cultural differences. *Journal of Consulting and Clinical Psychology, 55,* 719–726.

White, M. (1993). *The material child: Coming of age in Japan and America.* New York: Free Press.

White, M. I., & LeVine, R. A. (1986). What is an *ii ko* (good child)? In H. Stevenson, H. Azuma, & K. Hakuta (Eds.), *Child development and education in Japan.* New York: Freeman.

Wilson, L. G., & Young, D. (1988). Diagnosis of severely ill inpatients in China: A collaborative project using the Structured Clinical Interview for DSM-III (SCID). *Journal of Nervous and Mental Disease, 176,* 585–592.

Received August 14, 1993
Revision received June 14, 1993
Accepted November 18, 1993

Experts scrambling on school shootings

The recent youth homicides in rural schools represent a violence puzzling to psychologists.

By Scott Sleek
Monitor staff

Like the bubonic plague of medieval Europe, homicidal youth violence has moved from America's impoverished inner-city neighborhoods to rural and suburban areas.

James Garbarino, PhD, uses that analogy to characterize the outbreak of bizarre, fatal shootings that occurred in schools across the country this past year—in communities more reminiscent of Hope, Ark., than South Central Los Angeles.

"What typically happens with epidemics is they first take hold in the most vulnerable parts of the population, and then move out to the more general population," says Garbarino, a Cornell University professor who is interviewing boys jailed for murder and other violent acts as part of a study that will result in a book on violent adolescents. "It's quite possible that this surge of school-based shootings in small towns, in rural and suburban areas, is a kind of second stage of epidemic violence among our youth," he says.

As summer break closes and children and teachers return to the classroom, psychologists like Garbarino fear the eerily similar tragedies in Jonesboro, Ark., Springfield, Ore., and other small towns are not just coincidental anomalies but will continue to occur—perhaps with greater frequency.

In fact, they worry that the recent shootings could represent a new strain of the violence virus—one they know little about. While youth homicide rates in major urban areas have dropped in recent years, rates in rural and suburban areas are constant or even rising, says W. Rodney Hammond, PhD, a psychologist who heads violence-prevention efforts for the Center for Disease Control and Prevention (CDC) in Atlanta.

These incidents have caught behavioral scientists off guard, psychologists posit. After years of study, behavioral scientists have developed a fairly reliable profile of urban juvenile murderers, who are driven by such risk factors as poverty, the crack trade and a thriving black market for handguns. But those scientists understand far less about the rising number of homicidal boys from seemingly sleepy towns like Pearl, Miss., and Edinboro, Pa.

"Little is known about the characteristics that these rural youth share with juvenile murderers in urban areas or about what distinguishes them from those urban children," Hammond says. "It's one of the most serious challenges that lies ahead for behavioral science and psychology."

Distinguishing characteristics

Few psychologists reject the idea that the risk factors that plague inner-city youth have seeped into the suburbs and beyond. Youth are exposed to a growing amount of violent images on television, in movies, in video games and in popular music. Guns are more widely available than they were a generation ago. Drug abuse remains a problem among teenagers everywhere. And street gangs even have satellite chapters in the suburbs and rural areas.

"These are kids who feel very isolated in their emotional pain and use aggressive behavior in an attempt to let people know how distressed they are."

Jeremy Shapiro
Cleveland psychologist

Although they have minimal empirical data to go on, psychologists have noticed some distinguishing characteristics among the rural youth murderers who have made headlines in recent months. These adolescents tend to:

• **Kill and injure multiple victims in a single incident.** The perpetrators don't target only an individual as part of some interpersonal dispute (although sometimes an ex-girlfriend is among those killed), but seem to launch a shooting spree that results in many deaths and injuries.

• **Have no secondary criminal motive, such as robbery.** The primary goal is to kill or harm others.

• **Be younger.** Statistically, most youth murderers are 15 or older. But

Could the recent series of bizarre school murders have been prevented? Is it possible to predict which children might become killers?

Psychologists Robert Zagar, PhD, a Chicago forensic psychologist, Jack Arbit, PhD, of the Northwestern University Medical School, and their colleagues say they can predict with a high degree of accuracy the teens who are most likely to commit murder. They base that claim on studies that compared adolescent murderers with nonviolent delinquents and control subjects matched by age, gender, race and socioeconomic status.

They say children's odds of committing murder are doubled when they:
• Come from criminally violent families.
• Have a history of being abused.
• Belong to gangs.
• Abuse alcohol or drugs.

Their chances of killing are tripled when, along with the above factors, they:
• Use weapons or have prior arrests.
• Have neurological disorders, including epilepsy, mental retardation and hyperactivity.
• Skip school and have other school-related problems.

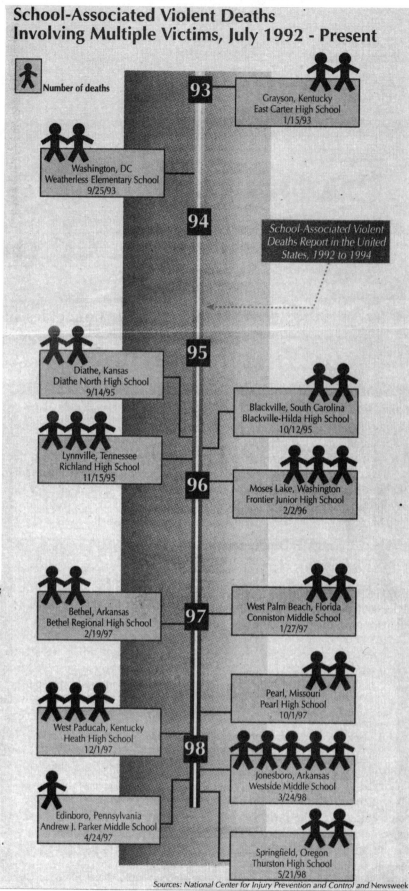

School-Associated Violent Deaths Involving Multiple Victims, July 1992 - Present

Number of deaths

93 Grayson, Kentucky
East Carter High School
1/15/93

Washington, DC
Weatherless Elementary School
9/25/93

94 *School-Associated Violent Deaths Report in the United States, 1992 to 1994*

Diathe, Kansas
Diathe North High School
9/14/95

95 Blackville, South Carolina
Blackville-Hilda High School
10/12/95

Lynnville, Tennessee
Richland High School
11/15/95

96 Moses Lake, Washington
Frontier Junior High School
2/2/96

Bethel, Arkansas
Bethel Regional High School
2/19/97

97 West Palm Beach, Florida
Conniston Middle School
1/27/97

Pearl, Missouri
Pearl High School
10/1/97

West Paducah, Kentucky
Heath High School
12/1/97

98 Jonesboro, Arkansas
Westside Middle School
3/24/98

Edinboro, Pennsylvania
Andrew J. Parker Middle School
4/24/97

Springfield, Oregon
Thurston High School
5/21/98

Sources: National Center for Injury Prevention and Control and Newsweek

Angela E. Terry

"Many scientists believe that if you try, based on our present knowledge, to invent a screening tool to identify who's at risk for engaging in a homicidal act, you would probably identify a lot of kids who engage in antisocial behavior but who may not kill."

W. Rodney Hammond Centers for Disease Control and Prevention

the last six incidents involving shootings at smalltown schools have involved youths no older than 14 according to Kathleen Heide, PhD, a University of South Florida criminologist and APA member who will chronicle her studies of more than 90 youth murderers in a book published this summer.

• **Have a history of social problems.** "We do know that the phenomenon of rejection contributes to their increased aggressiveness over time," says Duke University psychologist John Coie, PhD, who is helping pilot a violence-prevention curriculum called Fast Track. "So, they're more inclined to think that people are out to get them. And it's that kind of reactivity that makes them more at risk for doing this."

Other psychologists believe extreme narcissism, rather than despair or self-loathing, may make youth more violent. In a newly published study that involved 540 college students, psychologists Brad Bushman, PhD, of Iowa State University, and Roy Baumeister of Case Western Reserve University, found that those who exhibited a strong degree of narcissism desperately want to maintain a high opinion of themselves and showed more aggression in a competitive game when someone challenged their self-concept by insulting them.

"Narcissists mainly want to punish or defeat someone who has threatened their highly favorable views of themselves," the authors write in the July issue of the *Journal of Personality and Social Psychology* (Vol. 75, No. 1, p. 219–229).

The youths also seem to be driven by an intense need for attention, psychologists say. While urban youth tend to carry and use guns to wage power, to seek revenge on a rival or to simply protect themselves on the vicious streets, the murderers in these recent, rural incidents seem to be more interested in gaining national notoriety. In fact, many psychologists agree that the intense media attention devoted to these incidents creates a "copycat" effect.

"These are kids who feel very isolated in their emotional pain and use aggressive behavior in an attempt to let people know how distressed they are," says Jeremy Shapiro, PhD, a Cleveland psychologist who studies youth's attitudes toward guns. "When they see the kind of attention that comes to people who commit these crimes, they think. 'Oh my God, that's what I'm looking for.' And robust findings in the psychology literature show that troubled youth find negative attention better than no attention at all."

A wake-up call

Psychologists also believe that the recent school shootings reflect a complacency among rural and suburban school officials compared with their city-dwelling counterparts. Urban school officials and law enforcers have taken concrete steps to stamp out violence. Students have to pass through metal detectors when they enter the school, for example. And in cities like Boston, police and civic activists have beefed up community

policing and antiviolence education programs in recent years and have dramatically reduced the rate of juvenile crime. "But the rural and suburban schools just aren't savvy about this," says Robert Zagar, PhD, a former school psychologist who conducts evaluations of juvenile offenders for the Cook County Circuit Court in Illinois. "I had one principal tell me there's no violence in his school. I just rolled my eyes. It's there. He just doesn't see it."

Yet if schools become too vigilant about tightening security, they can lead more students to feel mistrusted and alienated—which can lead to more violence, says Gary Melton, PhD, a University of South Carolina professor and director of the university's Institute for Families in Society.

"You may get circumstances in which people are more wary of each other and aren't watching out for each other," says Melton, who sat on a panel of youth violence experts that convened to help the U.S. Justice Department gain insight on the school shootings. "As a result, there's a significant change in the perceptions of what the real level of danger is. The more reason kids think that they have to be afraid, and the more disconnected they are, the higher the delinquency rate."

Stemming the tide

Some of the unique aspects of these cases require a closer look, Hammond testified in April before a congressional panel investigating the shootings. In fact, the CDC is stepping up its monitoring of school-associated deaths to document whether these recent multiple-murder incidents represent a trend.

But studying the phenomenon is onerous for several reasons, he says. They include:

• **Legal interference.** Researchers will have difficulty interviewing these children when they're in the midst of legal proceedings and protected by their attorneys. And they may also have trouble identifying causal factors that are untainted by the child's postarrest experiences. For example, they may have trouble discerning whether some of the disturbances a child exhibits prompted them to commit the crime or stem more from the trauma of being jailed.

• **Few cases.** Although the rural school shootings seem to be escalating, the phenomenon is still rare. Scientists simply lack enough cases to draw strong scientific conclusions, Hammond says. (For now, descriptive research may be helpful, he adds.)

• **The risk of overextending.** Is it at all possible to predict which children are potential murderers, and to intervene before they kill? Some psychologists say such an effort may be the equivalent of casting a fishing net too widely.

"Many scientists believe that if you try, based on our present knowledge, to invent a screening tool to identify who's at risk for engaging in a homicidal act, you would probably identify a lot of kids who engage in antisocial behavior but who may not kill," Hammond says. "For instance, all the kids in these murders had access to a firearm. But does that mean we should argue that any kid with access to a gun is a potential killer?"

Still, behavioral scientists know enough about youth violence in general to begin making some efforts to prevent school murders, he says. Plenty of violence-prevention programs have shown promise in the inner cities. Such programs, many of them being used in elementary schools, teach children to praise others, avoid insults, resolve conflicts peacefully, manage their anger and speak about hurt feelings. Many of them also provide parenting training programs for high-risk families.

Although it's not yet clear whether those prevention strategies are applicable in suburban and rural regions, where demographic factors are significantly different, schools and community leaders have no reason not to try them, Hammond says.

"In this kind of situation," he says, "we can't afford to not act on preventing the suggested risk factors, even if the scientific information isn't complete."

Further reading

• American Psychological Association, American Academy of Pediatrics. *Raising Children to Resist Violence: What Can You Do?* (1995).
• Garbarino, J. "Raising Children in a Socially Toxic Environment" (Jossey-Bass, 1995).

• Heide, K.M. "Young Killers: The Challenge of Juvenile Homicide (Sage, 1998).
• Zagar, R. *Adolescent Killers: Are There More Medical Risks?* In Alan Schwartzberg (Ed.), "Adolescents in Turmoil" (Greenwood Publishing, 1998).

BRAIN SEX AND THE LANGUAGE OF LOVE

Robert L. Nadeau

If we can believe the experts, the standard for healthy intimacy in love relationships between men and women is female, and maleness is a disease in desperate need of a cure. Men, say social scientists, have a "trained incapacity to share" and have learned to overvalue in-

dependence and to fear emotional involvement. Female friendships, claim the intimacy experts, are based on emotional bonding and mutual support, and male friendships on competition, emotional inhibition, and aggression.[1] Social scientists have also pathologized maleness because men typically view love as action, or doing things for another, while women view love as talking and acknowledging feelings.

In fairness to the intimacy experts, what they say about differences in the behavior of men and

women has been well documented. Numerous studies have shown that men feel close to other men when working or playing side by side, while women feel close to other women when talking face to face.[2] Male group behavior is characterized by an emphasis on space, privacy, and autonomy, and female group behavior by a need to feel included, connected, and attached.[3] Male conversation tends to center around activities (sports, politics, work), and personal matters are discussed in terms of strengths and achievements. Female conversation,

[1] Mirra Komarovsky, *Blue-collar Marriage* (New York: Vintage, 1964).

[2] D. Goleman, "Two Views of Marriage Explored: His and Hers," *New York Times*, 1 Apr. 1989.

[3] C. Gilligan, *In a Different Voice* (Cambridge, Mass.: Harvard University Press, 1982).

This article originally appeared in *The World & I*, November 1997, pp. 330-339. Reprinted by permission of *The World & I*, a publication of the Washington Times Corporation. © 1997.

The human brain, like the human body, is sexed, and differences in the sex-specific human brain condition a wide range of behaviors that we typically associate with maleness or femaleness.

in contrast, is more likely to center around feelings and relationships, and there is considerably less reluctance to reveal fears and weaknesses.

Men and women also appear to experience intimacy in disparate ways. In men's relationships with other men, the index of intimacy is the degree of comfort and relaxation felt when engaged in activities, such as helping a friend move furniture or repair cars. Even when men comfort one another in crisis situations, like the loss of a family member or a spouse, it is physical presence, rather than intimate talk, that tends to be most valued.[4]

The index for intimacy among women is the extent to which personal feelings can be shared in a climate of mutual support and trust. What tends to be most valued in these interactions is confirmation of feelings as opposed to constructive criticism and advice. When women are asked to describe the benefits of such conversations with other women, they typically mention relief from anxiety and stress, feeling better, and a more enhanced sense of self-worth. Although women also express intimacy by doing things for other

women, the doing is typically viewed as an occasion for verbal intimacy.[5]

The response of males to depression also favors action, or a tendency to "run" when overcome with sadness, anxiety, or dread. And when men talk about their depression in therapy, they typically "rush through" an account of their emotions and describe depression with action metaphors, such as "running in place," "running wide open," and "pushing the edge."[6] When women are clinically depressed, they are more willing to talk about their feelings, to find opportunities to do so with other women, and to seek help in talk therapy. Women also typically disclose the sources of depression in detailed narratives that represent and analyze experience. And while men tend to respond to clinical depression by running or moving, women tend to respond with sedentary activities like uncontrollable crying, staying in bed, and compulsive eating.

The sex-specific patterns that lie beneath the diversity of these behaviors reduce to a male orientation toward action and a female orientation toward talking. Why is this the case? According to the intimacy experts, it is entirely a product of learning and one of the primary sources of male pathology. As psychologist Carol Tavris puts it, "The doing-versus-talking distinction in the emotional styles of males and females begins in childhood, when boys begin to develop what psychologists call 'side by side' relationships, in which intimacy means sharing the same activity—sports, games, watching a

movie or a sports event together." Girls, in contrast, "tend to prefer 'face to face' relationships, in which intimacy means revealing ideas and emotions in a heart-to-heart exchange."[7]

The problem is not, as a best-selling book would have us believe, that women are from Venus and men from Mars. It is that we have only recently come to realize something about the legacy of the evolution of our species on planet Earth. Throughout virtually all of our evolutionary history, men and women lived in small tribes of hunter-gatherers where the terms for survival were not the same. We have long recognized that the different terms for survival, along with mate selection, account for sexual differences in the human body. But only in the last few decades have we discovered that the legacy of our evolutionary past is also apparent in the human brain. The human brain, like the human body, is sexed, and differences in the sex-specific human brain condition a wide range of behaviors that we typically associate with maleness or femaleness.

THE LEGACY OF THE HUNTER-GATHERERS

The family album containing the record of our hunter-gatherer evolutionary past is DNA, and the legacy of that past begins to unfold following the union of sperm and ovum. Normal females have two long X chromosomes, contrib-

[4.] Scott Swain, "Covert Intimacy: Closeness in Men's Friendship," in B. J. Reisman and P. Schwartz, eds., *Gender in Intimate Relations* (Belmont, Calif.: Wadsworth, 1989).

[5.] Robin Lakoff, *Talking Power: The Politics of Language* (New York: Basic Books, 1990).

[6.] Catherine Riessman, *Divorce Talk: Women and Men Make Sense of Personal Relationships* (New Brunswick, N.J.: Rutgers University Press, 1990).

[7.] Carol Tavris, *The Mismeasure of Women* (New York: Simon & Schuster, 1992), 251–52.

While males talk about their status in terms of simple descriptions of individual skills and achievements, Tannen says, females do so with complicated descriptions of overall character.

uted by each biological parent, that closely resemble one another. Normal males have a long X chromosome, contributed by the mother, and a short Y chromosome, contributed by the father. Although each sperm and ovum contributes half of the full complement of forty-six chromosomes, the ovum provides all of the cytoplasmic DNA.

A fetus will develop with a female brain unless a gene on the Y chromosome, known as SRY, is expressed about the sixth week of pregnancy and triggers the release of testosterone in the gonads. The testosterone transforms the developing fetus into a male by interacting with genes that regulate or are regulated by the expression of SRY. The result is a kind of chain reaction in which genes involved in the determination of maleness are activated in a large number of cells. But since the levels of hormones vary across individual brains, the response of brain regions to the presence of hormones is highly variable.

Many of the sex-specific differences in the human brain are located in more primitive brain regions, and they condition male and female copulatory behavior, sexual orientation, and cyclic biological processes like menstruation. Sex-specific differences also exist, however, in the more recently evolved neocortex or in the higher brain regions. The neocortex looks like a redundantly folded sheet and contains 70 percent of the neurons in the central nervous system. It is divided into two hemispheres that process different kinds of information fairly independently, and each communicates with the other via a 200-million-fiber network called the corpus callosum. While the symmetry is not exact, structures in one hemisphere are mirrored in the other. Thus we have two parietal lobes, two occipital lobes, and so on.

In people with normal hemispheric dominance, the left hemisphere has executive control. This hemisphere manages linguistic analysis and expression, as well as sequential motor responses or body movements. The right hemisphere is responsible for perception of spatial relationships, faces, emotional stimuli, and prosody (vocal intonations that modify the literal meaning of a word).[8] The two frontal lobes of each hemisphere, located behind the forehead, integrate inputs from other brain regions and are closely associated with conscious decision making. This portion of our brain, which occupies 29 percent of the cortex, has undergone the most recent evolutionary expansion.

One piece of evidence that suggests why the brains of women and men tend to process information differently involves the corpus callosum, or the network of fibers connecting the two hemispheres. A subregion of this network, the splenium, is significantly larger in women than in men and more bulbous in shape.[9] More connections between the hemispheres in female brains could be a partial explanation for another significant discovery—both hemispheres are normally more active in the brains of females.

Computer-based imaging systems, such as positron emission tomography (PET) and magnetic resonance imaging (MRI), allow scientists to assess which areas of the brains of conscious subjects are active. All of these systems use advanced computers to construct three-dimensional images of brains as they process various kinds of information. Studies based on advanced imaging systems have revealed that cognitive tasks in the female brain tend to be localized in both hemispheres,[10] and that the same tasks in the male brain tend to be localized in one hemisphere.[11] Other recent studies using this technology have revealed sex-specific differences in the brain regions used to process language and sex-specific differences in feedback from more-primitive brain regions.[12] What this research suggests is that differences in the

8. S. F. Wietelson, "Neural Sexual Mosaicism: Sexual Differentiation of the Human Temporo-Parietal Region for Functional Asymmetry," *Psychoneuroendochrinology* 16:1–3 (1991): 131–55.

9. Wietelson, "Neural Sexual Mosaicism," 137–38.

10. I. Jibiki, H. Matsuda, et al., "Quantitative Assessment of Regional Blood Flow with 123I–IMP in Normal Adult Subjects," *Acta-Neurol-Napoli* 15:1 (1993): 7–15, and F. Okada, Y. Tokumitsu, et al., "Gender and Handedness-Related Differences of Forebrain Oxygenation and Hemodynamics," *Brain Research* 601:1–2 (1993): 337–47.

11. S. P. Springer and G. Deutsch, *Left Brain, Right Brain* (San Francisco: W. H. Friedman Co., 1985).

12. Ruben Gur, quoted in Gina Kolata, "Men's World, Women's World? Brain Studies Point to Differences," *New York Times*, 28 Feb. 1995, C1.

communication styles of men and women are not simply the product of learning.[13] They are also conditioned by differences in the sex-specific human brain.[14]

YOU JUST DON'T UNDERSTAND ME

While none of the intimacy experts, to my knowledge, attribute differences in the conversation styles of men and women to the sex-specific human brain, there is a growing consensus that it is extremely difficult to eliminate these differences. In the best-seller *You Just Don't Understand: Women and Men in Conversation*, Deborah Tannen claims that while men use conversation "to preserve their independence and negotiate and maintain status in a hierarchical social order," women use conversation as "a way of establishing connections and negotiating relationships."[15] Based on this assumption, Tannen makes the case that there are some large differences in the languages of men and women.

Men, she says, are more comfortable with public speaking, or "report talk," and women are more comfortable with private or "rapport talk." Men use language that is abstract and categorical, or communicate in "messages," and women use language that conveys subtle nuances and hidden meanings, or communicate in "metamessages." Similarly, men respond to problems with concrete solutions and suggestions, and women respond with empathy and an emphasis on community.

Competitive males, claims Tannen, favor "commands," or statements that indicate what should be done without qualification, while consensus-building females favor "conditional propositions," or statements prefaced with words like "let's," "we could," and "maybe." And while males talk about their status in terms of simple descriptions of individual skills and achievements, Tannen says, females do so with complicated descriptions of overall character.

This sparse theoretical framework, however, does not account for the enormous popularity of Tannen's book. What most impresses readers are the conversations that Tannen uses to illustrate the distinctive character of the languages used by men and women. The following exchange occurs when a husband indicates that he did not get enough sleep:

He: I'm really tired. I didn't sleep well last night.
She: I didn't sleep well either. I never do.
He: Why are you trying to belittle me?
She: I'm not! I'm just trying to show you I understand!

"This woman," says Tannen, "was not only hurt by her husband's reaction; she was mystified by it. How could he think she was belittling him? By 'belittle me,' he meant 'belittle my experience.' He was filtering her attempts to establish connection through his concern with preserving independence and avoiding being put down."[16]

In a discussion of the differences between messages and metamessages, Tannen quotes from Anne Tyler's novel *The Accidental Tourist*. At this point in the narrative the character Macon has left his wife and moved in with a woman named Muriel. The conversation begins when Macon makes an observation about Muriel's son:

"I don't think Alexander's getting a proper education," he said to her one evening.
"Oh, he's okay."
"I asked him to figure what change they'd give back when we bought the milk today, and he didn't have the faintest idea. He didn't even know he'd have to subtract."
"Well, he's only in second grade," Muriel said.
"I think he ought to go to private school."
"Private schools cost money."
"So? I'll pay."
She stopped flipping the bacon and looked over at him. "What are you saying?" she said.
"Pardon?"
"What are you saying, Macon? Are you saying you're committed?"

Muriel then tells Macon that he must decide whether he wants to divorce his wife and marry her, and that she will not put her son in a new school when he could be forced to leave if Macon returns to his wife. Confused and frustrated by Muriel's attack, Macon responds, "But I just want him to learn to subtract." The problem, writes Tannen, is that "Macon is concerned with the message, the simple matter of Alexander's learning math. But Muriel is concerned with the metamessage. What would it say about the relationship if he began paying for her son's education?"[17]

Some reviewers of Tannen's book have rightly complained that these differences are made to appear too categorical. But they also concede, along with the majority of other reviewers, that Tannen has disclosed some actual disparities in the languages used by men and women. How, then, does Tannen account for these remarkable differences in the manner in which men and women linguistically construct reality? She claims that younger children "learn" these languages from older children in single-sex groups on the playground.

13. Melissa Hines, "Gonadal Hormones and Human Cognitive Development," in Jacques Balthazart, ed., *Hormones, Brain and Behavior in Vertebrates* (Basel, Switz.: Karger, 1990), 51–63.

14. Susan Phillips, Susan Steele, and Christine Tanz, eds., *Language, Gender and Sex in Comparative Perspective* (Cambridge, Eng.: Cambridge University Press, 1987); and David Martin and H. D. Hoover, "Sex Differences in Educational Achievement: A Longitudinal Study," *Journal of Early Adolescence* 7 (1987): 65–83.

15. Deborah Tannen, *You Just Don't Understand: Women and Men in Conversation* (New York: Ballantine Books, 1990), 77.

16. Tannen, *You Just Don't Understand*, 51.

17. Quoted in Tannen, *You Just Don't Understand*, 175.

WHY MEN CAN'T ALWAYS TALK LIKE WOMEN

When we examine what Tannen says about differences in the languages used by men and women in the light of what we know about the sex-specific human brain, it seems clear the differences are not simply learned. Report talk and messages may reflect the orientation toward action associated with higher reliance on the primitive region of the limbic system in the male brain and with an orientation toward linear movement in abstract map space in the neocortex.

Although the usual biological explanation for the male tendency to give commands is higher levels of aggression, this linguistic habit also seems consistent with the manner in which reality tends to be constructed in the male brain. Commands may reflect the bias toward action and the organization of particulars in terms of movement between points in map space. All of which suggests that men may perceive commands, as opposed to requests, as more consistent with their sense of the real and as a more expedient way to solve problems.

The relationship between the two hemispheres in the female brain tends to be more symmetric, and there is a greater degree of interaction between these hemispheres. Since linguistic reality in the brains of women seems to invoke a wider range of right-brain cognitive functions, this may enhance awareness of emotionally relevant details, visual clues, verbal nuances, and hidden meanings. This suggests that the female brain tends to construct linguistic reality in terms of more extensive and interrelated cognitive and emotional contexts. If this is the case, all aspects of experience may appear more interdependent and interconnected, and this could contribute to the tendency to perceive people and events in a complex web of relation. Perhaps this is why the language of women tends to feature a more profound sense of identification with others, or why this language seems more "consensual."

Rapport talk may reflect this sense of identification and satisfy the need to feel interconnected. And metamessages, which allow analysis of single events to be extended through a complex web of relation, also seem consistent with the manner in which the female brain tends to construct reality. Since this reality seems more consensual, women may be more inclined to regard decision making as consensual and to prefer "us" instead of "I." Higher reliance in the female brain on the portion of the limbic system associated with symbolic action could also contribute to these tendencies.

Since the male brain tends to construct reality in terms of abstract solutions and sequential movements in map space, men probably perceive action as more commensurate with their sense of the real. If action in the reality of males seems more "actual" than talking, this could explain, in part at least, why men are more inclined to associate intimacy with shared activities, to respond to depression with action, and to describe feelings with action metaphors.

Neuroscience also suggests why women seem to believe that emotions are conveyed more through talking than action. If reality as it is constructed in the female brain features a more extended network of perceptions, memories, associations, and feelings, then the real could be more closely associated with language. This could also explain why women favor "rapport talk," or conversations about the personal and the private. If this talk is more commensurate with the actual character of reality in the female brain, women more than men might depend on conversation to reinforce their reality.

More emotional content in female constructions of reality could also explain why women are more inclined to equate talking with feeling, and to view caring actions that are not accompanied by verbal expressions of feeling as less than authentic. And if linguistic constructions of reality in the female brain feature a broader range of emotional experience, women may have less difficulty, on average, disclosing, describing, and contextualizing feelings.

A NEW VIEW OF THE LANGUAGE OF LOVE

The use of qualifiers like "on average," "tends," "may," "probably," and "might" in the description of behavior associated with the sex-specific human brain is not a concession to political correctness. It is the only way to fairly characterize the differences. There is nothing in this research that argues for a direct causal connection between sex-specific brains and the behavior of men and women. Every human brain is unique and becomes more so as a result of learning, and there is more variation between same-sex brains than opposite-sex brains. What is most striking in virtually all of the research on the sex-specific human brain is not differences between the emotional and cognitive processes of men and women but the amazing degree of overlap, or sameness. And while nature may play a larger role in conditioning same-sex behavior than we previously realized, nurture, or learning, remains the most vital part of the equation.

Although many of the behaviors in the litany of male pathology are obviously learned and subject to change, the tendencies associated with the sex-specific male brain cannot be erased in the learning process. This means that the assumption that love is not love unless men must think, feel, and behave like women in love relationships is not, in the vast majority of instances, realistic. Consider, for example, the primary reason why women seek a divorce.

When divorced women are asked to explain the failure of a marriage, the common refrain is "lack of communication," or the unwillingness of the ex-husband to talk about or share feelings.[18] In one recent study, over two-thirds of the women surveyed felt that men would never understand them, or that the men in their lives would remain forever clueless about the lives of women.[19] And yet numerous studies have also shown that women view men who deviate from the masculine norm by displaying or talking openly about emotions as "too feminine" and "poorly adjusted."[20]

Recognizing discrepancies in reality as it "tends" to be constructed in the brains of men and women does not frustrate the desire of men and women to communicate better with their partners. In fact, the opposite is true. Awareness of the discrepancies makes it much easier to negotiate differences and to communicate to our partners how they might better satisfy our expectations and desires without recourse to blame and anger. And this could lead to a greater willingness to embrace two additional assumptions about human reality that have been grandly reinforced by brain science—the total reality is that of both men and women, and the overlap or sameness of the realities of men and women is far greater than the differences.

Robert L. Nadeau is a professor at George Mason University. This article is based on his most recent book, S/he Brain: Science, Sexual Politics and the Feminist Movement *(Praeger, 1996).*

---

18. Thomas Wills, Robert Weiss, and Gerald Patterson, "A Behavioral Analysis of the Determinants of Marital Separation," *Journal of Consulting and Clinical Psychology* 42 (1974): 802–11.

19. Survey by Yankelovitch Partners, 1993.

20. See, for example, John Robertson and Louise Fitzgerald, "The (Mis)treatment of Men: Effects of Client Gender Role and Lifestyle on Diagnosis and Attribution of Pathology," *Journal of Counseling Psychology* 37 (1990): 3–9.

Who Stole Fertility?

CONTRARY TO POPULAR BELIEF, THERE IS NO INFERTILITY CRISIS SWEEPING THE NATION. WE'VE JUST LOST ALL CONCEPTION OF WHAT IT TAKES TO CONCEIVE. REPRODUCTIVE TECHNOLOGY HAS MADE US IMPATIENT WITH NATURE. SO FOR INCREASING NUMBERS OF COUPLES THE CREATION OF A NEW HUMAN BEING HAS BECOME A STRANGELY DEHUMANIZING PROCESS.

VIRGINIA RUTTER

My great-aunt Emily and great-uncle Harry never had kids, and nobody in our family talked about it. Growing up, I knew not to ask. It would have been impolite, as crass as asking about their income or their weight. The message was clear: If they didn't have kids, they couldn't have them, and talking about it would only be humiliating.

How times have changed. Today, a couple's reproductive prospects—or lack of them—are not only apt to be a conversation topic at your average dinner party, they're the subject of countless news stories illustrating our nationwide infertility "crisis."

In an infertility cover story last year, *Newsweek* reported that more than 3 million American couples would seek procreative help in 1995. Diagnostic tests, hormone treatments, fertility drugs, and assisted-reproduction techniques with names like in vitro fertilization (IVF), gamete intrafallopian transfers (GIFT), intrauterine insemination (IUI), zygote intrafallopian transfer (ZIFT), intracytoplasmic sperm injection (ICSI)—to name the top five procedures—have become as much a part of the reproductive process as the more poetic aspects of family making. While some of those 3 million-plus couples were legitimate candidates for the host of high-tech options now available to them, most wound up needing only low-tech assistance, such as boxer shorts instead of briefs.

Earlier this year, in a four-part series, the *New York Times* reported on the fertility industry's growth and the increased competition among clinics.

And that's how an infertility crisis is created and perpetuated. For contrary to popular belief, infertility rates are not on the rise. Creighton University sociologist Shirley Scritchfield, Ph.D., says that American infertility rates have not increased during the past three decades: in 1965, the infertility rate for the entire U.S. population was around 13.3 percent; in 1988, it was 13.7 percent. According to the U.S. Office of Technology Assessment, infertility rates for married women have actually *decreased* from 11.2 percent in 1965 to a little less than eight percent in 1988. These rates even include the "subfecund," the term used to describe people who have babies, just not as many as they want as quickly as they want. This means that more than 90 percent of couples have as many babies—or more than as many babies—as they want.

LETTING NATURE TAKE ITS COURSE

Rather than an infertility crisis, what we have is a society that's allowed technology to displace biology in the reproductive process, in effect dehumanizing the most human of events. At the very least, this means stress replaces spontaneity as women become tied to thermometers—constantly checking to see when they're ovulating—while men stand by waiting to give command performances. At the most, it involves women and men subjecting themselves to invasive procedures with high price tags. Whatever happened to love and romance and the idea of letting nature take its course? Instead, we seem to have embraced the idea that science, not sex, provides the best chance for producing biological children. Technicians have stolen human reproduction. And there are some 300 fertility clinics—with annual revenues of $2 billion—to prove it.

Infertility has become big business, one that's virtually exempt from government regulation. And it's not for the faint of heart—or pocketbook (see "Bucks for Babies"). But all the hype has made us lose sight of what it really takes to make a baby. Conception takes time. Infertility is classically defined as the inability to conceive or carry a baby to term after one year of unprotected sex two to three times a week. On average, it takes less time for younger (in their 30s) ones; as couples move through their 30s, experts suggest staying on the course for two years. But even couples in their reproductive prime—mid- to late 20s—need around eight months of sex two to three times a week to make a baby. (Last December, the New England Journal of Medicine reported that healthy women are most fertile, and therefore most likely to conceive, when they have intercourse during the six-day period leading up to ovulation.)

The correlation between how often a couple has sex and the speed with which they succeed in conceiving may seem obvious. But psychologist and University of Rochester Medical School professor Susan McDaniel, Ph.D., says she counseled one infertile couple for six months before discovering they had only been having sex once or twice a month!

Of course, these days the one thing many prospective parents feel they don't have is time. During the baby boom, couples began having children at about age 20. But by 1980—when women were in the workforce in record numbers and putting off motherhood—10.5 percent of first births were to women age 30 and older. By 1990, 18 percent of first births were to women age 30 and up. Because more would-be parents are older and hear their biological clocks ticking, they're more likely to become impatient when they don't conceive instantly. But how much of a factor is age in the conception game? Men have fewer age-related fertility problems than women do. The quality of their sperm may diminish with age; when they reach their 50s, men may experience low sperm motility (slow-moving sperm are less likely to inseminate).

After about age 37, women's eggs tend to show their age and may disintegrate more easily. This makes it increasingly difficult for women to conceive or maintain a pregnancy. That's not to say there's anything unusual about a 40-year-old woman having a baby, however. Older women have been having children for eons—just not

The confidence we have in preventing pregnancies has given us a false sense of control over our fertility.

their first ones. In many cultures, the average age of a last child is around age 40.

Some older women may even be as fertile as their younger sisters. A 40-year-old woman who has been taking birth control pills for a good part of her reproductive life—thus inhibiting the release of an egg each month—may actually benefit from having conserved her eggs, says Monica Jarrett, Ph.D., a professor of nursing at the University of Washington. She may even have a slight edge over a 40-year-old mother with one or two children trying to conceive.

"Focusing on aging as the primary source of infertility is a distraction," says Scritchfield. "Age becomes a factor when women have unknowingly always been infertile. These are women who, even if they'd tried to get pregnant at age 20 or 27, would have had difficulty despite the best technology."

GENDER POLITICS AND INFERTILITY

Some feminists suggest all this talk of infertility is part of a backlash, an effort to

drive women out of the boardroom and back into the nursery. While there may be some truth to this, it's only part of the story. The fertility furor is also a result of increasing expectations of control over nature by ordinary men and women.

Ironically, the growing intolerance for the natural course of conception stems from technological advances in contraception. Birth control is more reliable than ever. The confidence we have in preventing pregnancies has given us a false sense of control over our fertility. "People have the idea that if they can prevent conception, then they should also be able to conceive when they want to," says McDaniel.

This illusory sense of control, says Judith Daniluk, Ph.D., a University of British Columbia psychologist and fertility researcher, weighs most heavily on women. "Women are told that if they miss taking even one birth control pill, they risk becoming pregnant. This translates into feeling extremely responsible when it comes to getting pregnant, too."

If we've let technicians steal fertility from us, perhaps it's because it was up for grabs. Until recently, infertility was considered a woman's problem rather than a couple's problem. In the 1950s, physicians and psychologists believed that women whose infertility couldn't be explained were "suppressing" their true femininity. Of course, in those days men were rarely evaluated; the limited technology available focused mostly on women.

When a couple steps into the infertility arena today, both partners receive full evaluations—in theory. In practice, however, this doesn't always happen because technology is such that even a few sperm from an infertile man are enough for high-tech fertilization. About 40 percent of

Who Is Infertile?

Although infertility rates are not on the rise overall, Creighton University sociologist Shirley Scritchfield, Ph.D., points out that they are rising among some subgroups of the population: all young women between the ages of 20 and 24 and women of color. She says this is due to an increase in sexually transmitted diseases (STDs) among the young. STDs, including chlamydia, gonorrhea, and genital warts, can permanently harm reproductive organs. Pelvic inflammatory disease, which women can develop as a consequence of other STDs, is perhaps most responsible for infertility in young women, in part because it—as well as other STDs—often goes undetected.

With few records having been kept, it's difficult to determine whether male infertility is on the rise. A 1992 study by Norwegian scientists looked at semen quality over the past 50 years by pooling the evidence available from earlier

research. They concluded that, in general, sperm counts had decreased.

Rebecca Sokol, M.D., professor of medicine and obstetrics/gynecology at the University of Southern California, says that while the Norwegian study reports a significant reduction in sperm counts over half a century, the reductions are not "clinically significant." That is, if sperm counts have decreased over time—and many scientists do not agree that they have—they've simply gone from a very high count to moderate levels.

"We're exposed to higher levels of estrogens than ever before; we inject cows and other animals with estrogens and estrogen-like hormones to keep them healthy. There isn't any data that directly proves this alters sperm counts, but we know an increase in estrogens in men is toxic to sperm. The theory is that in some way, this low-grade constant exposure to estrogen is ultimately altering sperm."

infertility is the result of "female factors"—problems with hormones, eggs, or reproductive organs. Another 40 percent is explained by "male factors"—problems with low sperm count or slow-moving sperm. The remaining 20 percent is unexplained or due to factors in both partners. There may be an immune problem, where the sperm and egg are "allergic" to each other. Advances—such as ICSI, a way of injecting a single sperm into an egg during IVF—have been made to get around this immune system clash. Advances have also been made in understanding male infertility, including treatments for low sperm motility that involve extracting sperm directly from the testes. But the bulk of fertility treatments still focus on women.

Women also tend to "carry" the issue for a couple, says McDaniel. "As much as men are invested in having children, they don't have to think about it, or perhaps be as conscious of it—because women are so focused on the problem. It makes sense, then, that when it comes to an infertility workup, men will often be the ones to put on the brakes. If both partners were running headlong onto the conveyor belt of technology, there'd be a mess. So what happens—largely because of sex roles—is women become advocates of the process, and men, who may be more ambivalent, question it and wonder whether it's time to stop."

Women will go so far as to protect their partner from the diagnostic process, as well as treatment, observes Daniluk. She says they'll even shield their partner from blame when he's the infertile one.

COMPELLED TO PRODUCE

Regardless of its cause, infertility is a profound blow to people's sense of self, who they are, and who they think they should be. To understand just how devastating infertility is, it helps to know why we want babies in the first place.

"The most essential thing the human animal does is reproduce," insists anthropologist Helen Fisher, Ph.D., author of *Anatomy of Love*. Citing survival of the spe-

An overestimation of success rates by the technofertility industry hooks couples in.

cies as the reason why our drive to reproduce is so strong, Fisher says it's not surprising that couples will go to great emotional and financial lengths to conceive. "The costs of reproducing have always been great. The time-consuming and costly procedures a modern couple uses to pursue their reproductive ends may never be as costly as it was on the grasslands of Africa, when women regularly died in childbirth."

Fisher says men, too, feel obliged to plant their seed or die out, so they'll work very hard to sire and raise their own kids. They aren't exempt from social pressures either. "Male sexuality has always been tied to potency," says William Doherty, Ph.D., a professor of family social science at the University of Minnesota. "The slang term for male infertility is 'shooting blanks.' After all, what good is a man if he can't reproduce? That's probably why we've blamed women for infertility for millennia. It's too humiliating for men."

Animal instincts may provide the primal motivation for having kids. But notions of masculinity and femininity are another big influence. Infertility taps into our deepest anxieties about what it is to be a man or a woman, a core part of our identity. McDaniel says many of the infertile women she sees speak of feeling incomplete. They also talk about a loss of self-confidence and a sense of helplessness and isolation.

Women still get the message that much of their femaleness is derived from motherhood—more so than men are taught their maleness is tied to fatherhood. Losing the dream of motherhood may fill a woman with such grief that she'll consciously avoid the places kids populate. It's a loss that can be difficult to share because it's the death of something that never was.

Infertile men also experience a loss, says McDaniel. They, too, may insulate themselves from the world of kids. They may be even less likely than women, says Doherty, to talk about their sad feelings. "Men feel if they're not able to pass on their seed, they're not living up to what's expected of them as men," says Andrew McCullough, M.D., director of the Male Sexual Health and Fertility Clinic at New York University Medical Center.

Parental expectations are yet another powerful reason people feel the procreational pull. "When it comes to having kids," says McDaniel, "there can be a lot of familial pressure. If you don't have them, everybody wonders why."

TECHNOFERTILITY TAKES OVER

With all of these pressures to produce, is it any wonder couples get caught up in the technofertility maze? Seduced by well-meaning doctors who hold out hope and the availability of all kinds of treatments, two vulnerable people—alone—are left to decide how much reproductive assistance they will or won't accept. There are no guidelines.

It wasn't until about their seventh year of fertility treatments that a physician finally sat Steve and Lori down and told them that their chances of having a baby were slim, given their ages—37 and 32—and their efforts until that point. Steve had had a varicocele, a twisting of veins in the testicles, and Lori had had various explorations of her ovaries by endoscopy in search of ovarian cysts, plus two failed IVFs.

"It turned out that my wife's gynecologist wasn't really competent to tell us about fertility treatments," Steve says. "It ended

Bucks for Babies

The fertility industry may boast of its dedication to bringing healthy babies into the world, but in reality, it appears to be interested in producing only *wealthy* ones.

A thorough fertility workup to diagnose the source of a couple's problem can take up to two months and cost from $3,000 to $8,000. That's just for starters. For a simple procedure, like hormone shots to stimulate egg production, it's $2,300 per cycle. Expect to pay $10,000 for one round of in vitro fertilization (IVF). About 30,000 women a year attempt pregnancy via IVF.

Intracytoplasmic sperm injection, where doctors inject a single sperm into an egg, adds $1,000 to the price of IVF. A procedure requiring an egg donor (in demand among older mothers) runs from $8,500 to $16,000—per cycle. A varicocelectomy, to correct varicose veins around the testicles, costs $3,500. Few health plans include coverage for fertility treatment. Even when insurance does kick in, it doesn't cover all of the direct costs, to say nothing of the many indirect costs, including lost income from missed work and child care expenses.

How Couples Cope with Infertility

In general, couples without children are more likely to split up than partners with children, reports demographer Diane Lye, Ph.D., a professor of sociology at the University of Washington. What about mates who can't have kids, or who want them but encounter difficulties? Researchers don't know about the ones who don't seek fertility treatment—and who tend to be poor. But Lauri Pasch, Ph.D., a psychologist and fertility researcher at the University of California at San Francisco, did study 50 couples who, on average, had been trying to get pregnant for two years. She says infertile couples going for fertility treatment tend to have higher rates of marital satisfaction than the rest of the population.

"Most couples who seek fertility treatment are committed enough to their relationship that they will go through pain and suffering to have a child together," says Pasch. And if they have the skills to address their problem, their relationships tend to become stronger—even if they never have a baby."

So what kind of skills does a couple comfronting infertility need? Mates with matching coping styles do best, says Pasch, who points out that infertility, like other major stressors, tends to bring out people's natural ways of coping. "Couples who have similar ways of living with problems and relieving their distress are better off than those with different styles," says Pasch. "Both might be support seekers, or both might be private and keep to themselves. So long as they both go about things in the same way."

Pasch finds that spouses who rely on emotional expression can do harm to their relationship. That's because they tend to let their feelings out *at* their partner rather than sharing them *with* him or her. (So much for the old saw that talking things out always makes them better.) "In this destructive communication pattern, one person eventually demands and one withdraws," says Pasch. "One member of the couple pressures for change, while the other one withdraws, refusing to discuss the problem."

Though which partner demands and which one withdraws can shift, typically women are the ones who demand more, and men are the ones who withdraw. In the case of an infertile couple, the woman may get alarmed sooner than her husband about not being able to have children. But they may switch roles, and she may become more resigned to it while he becomes more concerned and wants to start treatment. Either way, the couple is at odds.

Tammy and Dan, the parents of two children—the products of five IVFs and eight years of fertility treatments—were just such a couple. "I was the leader, taking care of everything," says Tammy. Her daily routine included being at the fertility clinic at 6:30 every morning for blood tests, and returning every afternoon for more exams. Once she became pregnant, she had to stay in bed practically from the day she conceived until the day her children were born.

"When you're trying to get pregnant, it becomes your whole focus. Everything you do is planned around it. You are told what to do every day, and you can't do very much. Then, all of a sudden, you realize you have focused your whole life on getting pregnant and not on your relationship. After our second child was born, and we didn't have a crisis to deal with every day, it was difficult being normal."

The emotional climate becomes even more difficult when one partner chooses to withdraw from the entire fertility process. Psychologist Susan McDaniel, Ph.D., of the University of Rochester School of Medicine, saw one couple where the wife underwent extensive tests to see whether she was infertile. Her husband, meanwhile, could never seem to make it to the urologist to be tested. He couldn't tolerate the idea that his sperm count might be low. Of course, his wife was furious. She had gone through painful and stressful—not to mention expensive—workups. When her husband finally went to the urologist, he couldn't produce a sperm sample. When he finally did, it turned out he was the infertile one. Both partners had trouble understanding what the prospect of infertility was like for the other one. Eventually, they decided to get a divorce.

up being like going to the Motor Vehicle Bureau. First, they tell you to take care of one thing, but it turns out you need to take care of something else. Then they tell you to go do a third thing. You wind up moving from place to place with no particular plan. It's rare that you get a doctor who explains in plain English what's going on and helps you evaluate your choices. Instead of talking with Lori and me and asking us what was in our hearts, they were saying, 'Okay, you want a baby, how can we make one for you?'"

Even as they went through test after test, procedure after procedure, it seemed at least semicomical to them: drives at the crack of dawn to a distant clinic, painful shots Steve was obliged to administer to Lori, even a "hamster penetration" test that involved Steve producing a sperm sample to see whether his sperm could penetrate a hamster's egg. All of it was very difficult to resist. "I think it was partly the adventure that kept us going," Steve says. "Once you commit and say you're going to give it a go, you don't want to stop midstream. There's always the chance that it might work. I mean, medicine is fantastic; you take some pills, stick some stuff in you, and maybe you get a baby."

Fertility treatments are so technically focused, says McDaniel, that people's feelings get left behind. She advocates a more human "biopsychosocial" approach. "Couples' emotional needs should dictate the pacing and decision making as they move up the pyramid of technological possibilities. But in some, maybe even most clinics, little or no attention is paid to the process, only the possible product. As a result, the patients suffer."

Even under normal circumstances, conception is immaculate—it tends to clean all else out of the mind. Whenever people begin to plan a family, says McDaniel, their world-view narrows. But with technofertility, a couple's worldview can narrow to the exclusion of all else. Because the outcome is the entire focus, fertility treatments intensify our in-

stincts to give birth and nurture a baby. So the very technology that disregards couples' emotions also heightens their desire to nurture. For women, especially, maternal instincts are intensified by all-consuming fertility treatments that leave little time for anything else and cause women to define themselves solely as mothers.

Indeed, as soon as prospective parents seek help, statistics and biology become the focus. Before long, they're up on the latest research and talking in terms of "control groups," "statistical significance," and "replication." The walls of fertility clinics are plastered with pictures of newborns, and staffers and customers alike speak endlessly about "take-home baby rates," the bottom line when it comes to success. But take-home baby rates are more than numbers. They represent people's hopes for a family.

As a result, couples undergoing intensive fertility treatments lose their wide-angle perspective on life. They may fall behind in their careers and cut themselves off from friends and family, all in the narcissistic pursuit of cloning their genes. Technology may provide us with the illusion that it's helping us control our reproductive fate, but in reality, it just adds to the narcissism. "The higher tech the treatment, the more inwardly focused couples become," says Doherty.

"Biological connections are so strongly emphasized in our culture that it's hard not to become self-absorbed," Steve explains. "You even see it in the adoption process. Couples are often concerned that the kids they adopt have similar characteristics to their own. But the truth is, kids are kids." (Steve and Lori have since adopted a baby.)

An overestimation of success rates by the technofertility industry hooks couples in and fuels the narcissism. Fertility clinics typically report about a 25 percent success rate. But this rate is usually calculated after clinics have screened out the most hopeless cases. The true rate—which counts everyone who has sought reproductive help and which considers live births rather than pregnancies as success—is closer to half, Scritchfield says. "Unfortunately, this isn't what the public hears. If we were really concerned about infertility, we would be working on preventive measures. That's not addressed by biomedical entrepreneurs because they don't deal with people, just body parts."

Yet technofertility can create such stress in a couple that it can come close to undoing their relationship—the raison d'être for baby making. McDaniel remembers one couple who were at complete odds, having come to see her a year after having undergone five years of unsuccessful fertility treatments. The woman still hoped technology could help them, but the man felt his wife had gone too far; the procedures were invasive and the lack of results too painful. Attempting to protect both of them from any more disappointment, he insisted they stop.

The husband questioned why they'd ever gotten involved in the first place, and the wife felt unsupported by his reaction. No one at the fertility clinic had helped them work through any of their reactions. In therapy with McDaniel, they ultimately admitted to themselves—and to each other—what their expectations had been and the anxiety and grief they felt over the loss of an early pregnancy. Then they decided to adopt.

Given the single-mindedness of baby making, adding infertility and technology to the mix creates the perfect recipe for obsession. But it's an obsession only for the rich. Which means having a baby becomes a luxury that many truly infertile couples, who might otherwise make wonderful parents, will never be able to afford.

Unit 6

Unit Selections

Key Points to Consider

❖ Do men's and women's brains function differently? Why?

❖ What can be done to protect and preserve memory in the aging brain?

❖ Is love the best drug for heart disease? How much fat is too much fat for the heart?

❖ Describe the new stage of life created by the rapid increase in longevity.

❖ Can the resourceful older brain show plasticity and compensate for lost neurons by using other neurons to get the job done? Explain.

❖ Should expensive, experimental cures be attempted on terminally ill patients? Why or why not?

❖ How does one plan for a funeral?

❖ Why is there solace to be found in predictable patterns of living and dying?

 **Links** | **www.dushkin.com/online/**

These sites are annotated on pages 4 and 5.

There is a gradual slowing of the rate of mitosis of cells of all the organ systems with age (except the neurons, which do not undergo mitosis after birth). This gradual slowing of mitosis translates into a slowed rate of repair of cells of all the organs. By the 30s, signs of aging can be seen in skin, skeleton, vision, hearing, smell, taste, balance, coordination, heart, blood vessels, lungs, liver, kidneys, digestive tract, immune response, endocrine functioning, and ability to reproduce. To some extent, moderate use of any body part (as opposed to disuse or misuse) helps it retain its strength, stamina, and repairability. However, by middle and late adulthood, persons become increasingly aware of the aging effects of their organ systems on their total physical fitness. A loss of height occurs as spinal disks and connective tissues diminish and settle. Demineralization, especially loss of calcium, causes weakening of bones. Muscles atrophy, and the slowing of cardiovascular and respiratory responses creates a loss of stamina for exercise. All of this may seem cruel, but it occurs very gradually and need not adversely affect one's enjoyment of life.

Healthful aging, at least in part, seems to be genetically preprogrammed. The females of many species, including humans, outlive the males. The sex hormones of females may protect them from some early aging effects. Males experience earlier declines in their cardiovascular systems. Diet and exercise can ward off many of the deleterious effects of aging. A reduction in saturated fat intake coupled with regular aerobic exercise contributes to less bone demineralization, less plaque in the arteries, stronger muscles (including heart and lung muscles), and a general increase in stamina.

Cognitive abilities do not appreciably decline with age in healthy adults. Research suggests that the speed with which the brain carries out problems involving abstract (fluid) reasoning may slow, but not cease. Complex problems may simply require more time to solve with age. On the other hand, research suggests that the memory banks of older people may have more crystallized (accumulated and stored) knowledge. One's ken (range of knowledge) and practical skills (common sense) grow with age and experience. Older human beings become more expert at the tasks they frequently do.

The first article included in the middle adulthood section of this unit examines the speculation about sex differences in the cognitive abilities of adults. Are women better at emotional and linguistic types of reasoning? If so, is their superiority due to brain differences, or does it reflect dissimilar experiences from men? Conversely, men seem to be better at spatial orientating ability. Is this superiority a result of nature or nurture? The research suggests that there are subtle but real differences in adults' cognitive styles related to their sex, which may be due to brain differences.

The second article addresses the question of whether exercise, diet and dietary supplements, seminars, audiotapes and the like can ward off the gradual decline of cognitive processing, especially the decline of abstract (fluid) reasoning processes

that accompany age. America has become obsessed with health foods, vitamins, herbal supplements, and alternate forms of health care. This article reviews many of the potions and practices that the current population of middle-aged adults are using to maintain, restore, or even improve their memories. The authors attempt to sift out the grains of truth from the chaff. They point out that both brain mass and frontal cortical activity decrease as a normal consequence of age. Exercise helps keep neurons strong. Anxiety, stress, depression, lack of sleep, sleeping pills, and alcohol mute neuronal messages. Some diets and dietary supplements boost brain power and the authors chart the pros and cons of using them.

Erik Erikson suggested that the most important psychological conflict of late adulthood is achieving a sense of ego integrity. This is fostered by self-respect, self-esteem, love of others, and a sense that one's life has order and meaning. The articles in the section on late adulthood reflect Erikson's concern with experiencing ego integrity rather than despair.

Jack Rosenthal, in "The Age Boom," describes the phenomena of longer life, better health, and greater security in the late years of adulthood. Many elderly people are living life with dignity and élan. The factors that he weighs as contributors to their longevity and integrity are family, school, and work.

Daniel Goleman, in the second article in this section, describes the aging brain from a new perspective, that of two imaging techniques, positron emission tomography (PET scans) and magnetic resonance imaging (MRI). Data from healthy seniors in their 80s and 90s reveal that loss of brain tissue is modest and largely confined to selective areas. Intellectual functioning can continue to be robust and may even continue to grow in some areas.

The third article in the late adulthood section discusses the controversial question of the right to die. Should a patient with an incurable, terminal illness, who accepts death and is ready to die, be kept alive against his or her will? What moral and ethical concerns need to be addressed in order to answer this question? What degree of acceptance should society embrace? The choice is between doctor-assisted suicide, care and pain relief without cure attempts, or all-out cure attempts to the very end even if extraordinary costs or experimental procedures are involved. The author looks for answers that would help resolve these dilemmas.

The fourth article discusses the funeral industry and its escalating costs to mourners. It presents both the price gouging that occurs in some places and efforts of other people to keep the costs of burying a loved one down. It raises questions about dignity and respect for bereaved individuals.

Robert Sapolsky's essay on the patterns of life ends this section and this anthology. He takes a positive view of dying, death, and bereavement. He finds solace in experiencing the human life span as a cycle complete with predictable stages.

Development during Middle and Late Adulthood

Man's World, Woman's World? Brain Studies Point to Differences

Gina Kolata

Dr. Ronald Munson, a philosopher of science at the University of Missouri, was elated when Good Housekeeping magazine considered publishing an excerpt from the latest of the novels he writes on the side. The magazine eventually decided not to publish the piece, but Dr. Munson was much consoled by a letter from an editor telling him that she liked the book, which is written from a woman's point of view, and could hardly believe a man had written it.

It is a popular notion: that men and women are so intrinsically different that they literally live in different worlds, unable to understand each other's perspectives fully. There is a male brain and a female brain, a male way of thinking and a female way. But only now are scientists in a position to address whether the notion is true.

The question of brain differences between the sexes is a sensitive and controversial field of inquiry. It has been smirched by unjustifiable interpretations of data, including claims that women are less intelligent because their brains are smaller than those of men. It has been sullied by overinterpretations of data, like the claims that women are genetically less able to do everyday mathematics because men, on average, are slightly better at mentally rotating three dimensional objects in space.

But over the years, with a large body of animal studies and studies of humans that include psychological tests, anatomical studies, and increasingly, brain scans, researchers are consistently finding that the brains of the two sexes are subtly but significantly different.

Now researchers have a new non-invasive method, functional magnetic resonance imaging, for studying the live human brain at work. With it, one group recently detected certain apparent differences in the way men's and women's brains function while they are thinking. While stressing extreme caution in draw-

New scanner finds more evidence of how the sexes differ in brain functions.

ing conclusions from the data, scientists say nonetheless that the groundwork was being laid for determining what the differences really mean.

"What it means is that we finally have the tools at hand to begin answering these questions," said Dr. Sally Shaywitz, a behavioral scientist at the Yale University School of

Medicine. But she cautioned: "We have to be very very careful. It behooves us to understand that we've just begun."

The most striking evidence that the brains of men and women function differently came from a recent study by Dr. Shaywitz and her husband, Dr. Bennett A. Shaywitz, a neurologist, who is also at the Yale medical school. The Shaywitzes and their colleagues used functional magnetic resonance imaging to watch brains in action as 19 men and 19 women read nonsense words and determined whether they rhymed.

In a paper, published in the Feb. 16 issue of Nature, the Shaywitzes reported that the subjects did equally well at the task, but the men and women used different areas of their brains. The men used just a small area on the left side of the brain, next to Broca's area, which is near the temple. Broca's area has long been thought to be associated with speech. The women used this area as well as an area on the right side of the brain. This was the first dear evidence that men and women can use their brains differently while they are thinking.

Men have larger brains; women have more neurons.

Another recent study by Dr. Ruben C. Gur, the director of the brain behavior laboratory at the University of Pennsylvania School of Medicine, and his colleagues, used magnetic resonance imaging to look at the metabolic activity of the brains of 37 young men and 24 young women when they were at rest, not consciously thinking of anything.

In the study published in the Jan. 27 issue of the journal Science, the investigators found that for the most part, the brains of men and women at rest were indistinguishable from each other. But there was one difference, found in a brain structure called the limbic system that regulates emotions. Men, on average, had higher brain activity in the more ancient and primitive regions of the limbic system, the parts that are more involved with action. Women, on average, had more activity in the newer and more complex parts of the limbic system, which are involved in symbolic actions.

Dr. Gur explained the distinction: "If a dog is angry and jumps and bites, that's an action. If he is angry and bares his fangs and growls, that's more symbolic."

Dr. Sandra Witelson, a neuroscientist at McMaster University in Hamilton, Ontario, has focused on brain anatomy, studying people with terminal cancers that do not involve the brain. The patients have agreed to participate in neurological and psychological tests and then to allow Dr. Witelson and her colleagues to examine their brains after they die, to look for relationships between brain structures and functions. So far she has studied 90 brains.

Several years ago, Dr. Witelson reported that women have a larger corpus callosum, the tangle of fibers that run down the center of the brain and enable the two hemispheres to communicate. In addition, she said, she found that a region in the right side of the brain that corresponds to the region women used in the reading study by the Shaywitzes was larger in women than in men.

Most recently Dr. Witelson discovered, by painstakingly counting brain cells, that although men have larger brains than women, women have about 11 percent more neurons. These extra nerve cells are densely packed in two of the six layers of the cerebral cortex, the outer shell of the brain, in areas at the level of the temple, behind the eye. These are regions used for understanding language and for recognizing melodies and the tones in speech. Although the sample was small, five men and four women, "the results are very very clear," Dr. Witelson said.

Going along with the studies of brain anatomy and activity are a large body of psychological studies showing that men and women have different mental abilities. Psychologists have consistently shown that men, on average, are slightly better than women at spatial tasks, like visualizing figures rotated in three dimensions, and women, on average, are slightly better at verbal tasks.

Dr. Gur and his colleagues recently looked at how well men and women can distinguish emotions on someone else's face. Both men and women were equally adept at noticing when someone else was happy, Dr. Gur found. And women had no trouble telling if a man or a woman was sad. But men were different. They were as sensitive as women in deciding if a man's face was sad—giving correct responses 90 percent of the time. But they were correct about 70 percent of the time in deciding if women were sad; the women were correct 90 percent of the time.

"A woman's face had to be really sad for men to see it," Dr. Gur said. "The subtle expressions went right by them."

Studies in laboratory animals also find differences between male and female brains. In rats, for example, male brains are three to seven times larger than female brains in a specific area, the preoptic nucleus, and this difference is controlled by sex hormones that bathe rats when they are fetuses.

"The potential existence of structural sex differences in human brains is almost predicted from the work in other animals," said Dr. Roger Gorski, a professor of anatomy and cell biology at the University of California in Los Angeles. "I think it's a really fundamental concept and I'm sure, without proof, that it applies to our brains."

But the question is, if there are these differences, what do they mean?

Dr. Gorski and others are wary about drawing conclusions. "What happens is that people overinterpret these things," Dr. Gorski said. "The brain is very complicated, and even in animals that we've studied for many years, we don't really know the function of many brain areas."

This is exemplified, Dr. Gorski said, in his own work on differences in rat brains. Fifteen years ago, he and his colleagues discovered that males have a comparatively huge preoptic nucleus and that the area in females is tiny. But Dr. Gorski added: "We've been studying this nucleus for 15 years, and we still don't know what it does. The most likely explanation is that it has to do with sexual behavior, but it is very very difficult to study. These regions are very small and they are interconnected with other things." Moreover, he said, "nothing like it has been shown in humans."

And, with the exception of the work by the Shaywitzes, all other findings of differences in the brains or mental abilities of men and women have also found that there is an amazing degree of overlap. "There is so much overlap that if you take any individual man and woman, they might show differences in the opposite direction" from the statistical findings, Dr. Gorski said.

Dr. Munson, the philosopher of science, said that with the findings so far, "we still can't tell whether the experiences are different" when men and women think. "All we can tell is that the brain processes are different," he said, adding that "there is no Archimedean point on which you can stand, outside of experience, and say the two are the same. It reminds me of the people who show what the world looks like through a multiplicity of lenses and say 'This is what the fly sees.' "But, Dr. Munson added, "We don't know what the fly sees." All we know he explained, is what we see looking through those lenses.

Some researchers, however, say that the science is at least showing the way to answering the ancient mind-body problem, as applied to the cognitive worlds of men and women.

Dr. Norman Krasnegor, who directs the human learning and behavior branch at the National Institute of Child Health and Human Development, said the difference that science made was that when philosophers talked about mind, they "always were saying, 'We've got this black box.' " But now he said, "we don't have a black box; now we are beginning to get to its operations."

Dr. Gur said science was the best hope for discovering whether men and women inhabited different worlds. It is not possible to answer that question simply by asking people to describe what they perceive, Dr. Gur said, because "when you talk and ask questions, you are talking to the very small portion of the brain that is capable of talking." If investigators ask people to tell them what they are thinking, "that may or may not be closely related to what was taking place" in the brain, Dr. Gur said.

On the other hand, he said, scientists have discovered that what primates perceived depends on how their brains function. Some neurons fire only in response to lines that are oriented at particular angles, while others seem to recognize faces. The world may well be what the philosopher Descartes said it was, an embodiment of the workings of the human mind, Dr. Gur said. "Descartes said that we are creating our world," he said. "But there is a world out there that we can't know."

Dr. Gur said that at this point he would hesitate to boldly proclaim that men and women inhabit different worlds. "I'd say that science might be leading us in that direction," he said, but before he commits himself he would like to see more definite differences in the way men's and women's brains function and to know more about what the differences mean.

Dr. Witelson cautioned that "at this point, it is a very big leap to go from any of the structural or organizational differences that were demonstrated to the cognitive differences that were demonstrated." She explained that "all you have is two sets of differences, and whether one is the basis of the other has not been shown." But she added, "One can speculate."

Dr. Witelson emphasized that in speculating she was "making a very big leap," but she noted that "we all live in our different worlds and our worlds depend on our brains.

"And," she said, "if these sex differences in the brain, with 'if' in big capital letters, do have cognitive consequences, and it would be hard to believe there would be none, then it is possible that there is a genuine difference in the kinds of things that men and women perceive and how these things are integrated. To that extent it may be possible that in some respects there is less of an easy cognitive or emotional communication between the sexes as a group because our brains may be wired differently."

The Shaywitzes said they were reluctant even to speculate from the data at hand. But, they said, they think that the deep philosophical questions about the perceptual worlds of men and women can eventually be resolved by science.

"It is a truism that men and women are different," Dr. Bennett Shaywitz said. "What I think we can do now is to take what is essentially folklore and place it in the context of science. There is a real scientific method available to answer some of these questions."

Dr. Sally Shaywitz added: "I think we've taken a qualitative leap forward in our ability to ask questions." But, she said, "the field is simply too young to have provided more than a very intriguing appetizer."

MEMORY

Forgetfulness is America's latest health obsession. How much is normal? Can we do anything about it? An explosion of new research offers reassuring insights.
BY GEOFFREY COWLEY AND ANNE UNDERWOOD

STAN FIELD KNOWS WHAT AGE can do to a person's memory, and he's not taking any chances with his. He chooses his food carefully and gets plenty of vigorous exercise. He also avoids stress, soda pop and cigarette smoke. But that's just for starters. At breakfast each morning, the 69-year-old chemical engineer downs a plateful of pills in the hope of boosting his brainpower.

He starts with deprenyl and piracetam—drugs that are normally used to treat diseases like Parkinson's but that casual users can get from overseas sources—and moves on to a series of amino acids (glutamine, phenylalarine, tyrosine). Then he takes several multivitamins, some ginkgo biloba (a plant extract), 1,000 units of vitamin E and, for good measure, a stiff shot of cod-liver oil.

Michelle Arnove is less than half Field's age, but no less concerned about her memory. While working round the clock to finish a degree in film studies, the 33-year-old New Yorker had the alarming sensation that she had stopped retaining anything. "I couldn't even remember names," she says. "I thought, 'Oh no, I'm over 30. It's all downhill from here'." Besides loading up on supplements (she favors ginseng, choline and St. John's wort), Arnove signed up for a memory-enhancement course at New York's Mount Sinai Medical Center. And when she got there, she found herself sur-

Tested Your Memory Lately?

When it comes to our memories we are our harshest critics, focusing not on countless facts recalled every day, but on the forgotten few. This quiz offers a rough guide to how your memory stacks up against the norm. Now, where did you put that pen?

1 point	**Not within the last six months**
2 points	**Once or twice in the last six months**
3 points	**About once a month**
4 points	**About once a week**
5 points	**Daily**
6 points	**More than once a day**

☐ How often do you fail to recognize places you've been before?

☐ How often do you forget whether you did something, such as lock the door or turn off the lights or the oven?

☐ How often do you forget when something happened—wondering whether it was yesterday or last week?

☐ How often do you forget where you put items like house keys or wallet?

☐ How often do you forget something you were told recently and had to be reminded of it?

☐ How often are you unable to remember a word or name, even though it's "on the tip of your tongue"?

☐ In conversation, how often do you forget what you were just talking about?

☐ **Total points**

Score: 7–14 = better than average memory; 15–25 = average; 26 or higher = below average

ADAPTED FROM: "MEMORY," BY DR. BARRY GORDON AND FROM A. SUNDERLAND, ET AL. (1983 AND 1986).

rounded by people who were just as worried as she was.

For millions of Americans, and especially for baby boomers, the demands of the Information Age are colliding with a sense of waning vigor. "When boomers were in their 30s and 40s, they launched the fitness boom," says Cynthia Green, the psychologist who teaches Mount Sinai's memory class. "Now we have the mental-fitness boom. Memory is the boomers' new life-crisis issue." And, of course, a major marketing opportunity. The demand for books and seminars has never been greater, says Jack Lannom, a Baptist minister and longtime memory trainer whose weekly TV show, "Mind Unlimited," goes out to 33 million homes on the Christian Network. Anxious consumers are rushing to buy do-it-yourself programs like Kevin Trudeau's "Mega Memory," a series of audiotapes that sells for $49.97. And supplement makers are touting everything but sawdust as a brain booster.

But before you get out your checkbook, a few questions are in order. Does everyday forgetfulness signal flagging brain function? Is "megamemory" a realistic goal for normal people? And if you could have a perfect memory, would you really want it? Until recently, no one could address those issues with much authority, but our knowledge of memory is exploding. New imaging techniques are revealing how different parts of the brain interact to preserve meaningful experiences. Biologists are decoding the underlying chemical processes—and neuroscientists are discovering how age, stress and other factors can disrupt them. No one is close to finding the secret to flawless recall, but as you'll see, that may be just as well.

To scientists who study the brain, the wonder is that we retain as much as we do. As Harvard psychologist Daniel Schacter observes in his 1996 book, "Searching for Memory," the simple act of meeting a friend for lunch requires a vast store of memory—a compendium of words, sounds and grammatical rules; a record of the friend's appearance and manner; a catalog of restaurants; a mental map to get you to one, and so on.

How do we manage so much information? Brains are different from computers, but the analogy can be helpful. Like the PC on your desk, your mind is equipped with two basic types of memory: "working memory" for juggling information in the present moment, and long-term memory for storing it over extended periods. Contrary to popular wisdom, our brains don't record everything that happens to us and then bury it until a

Connections Matter

Our brains aren't designed to retain random bits of information. We remember things by linking them to what we already know. The process is called 'elaborative encoding.'

Why We Forget

I'm Carol

❶ A name is easy to forget when its only point of reference is a face. Lacking links to other memories, it fades within seconds.

CAROL

❷ As you learn facts about a person, such as her profession, her name gets embedded in a web of thoughts and impressions. If you don't know her, random associations have a similar effect.

Norma? Doris? Lisa? Karen?

❸ As the web of associations grows, so does the number of paths leading back to the name. Well-encoded memories last a lifetime.

How We Remember

I'm Joanne

JOE — FRIEND
JOANNE   COFFEE
'FRASIER' — SEATTLE
PSYCHOLOGIST

Joanne!

DIAGRAM BY CHRISTOPH BLUMRICH—NEWSWEEK

hypnotist or a therapist helps us dredge it up. Most of what we perceive hovers briefly in working memory, a mental play space akin to a computer's RAM (or random-access memory), then simply evaporates. Working memory enables you to perform simple calculations in your head or retain phone numbers long enough to dial them. And like RAM, it lets you analyze and invent things without creating a lasting record.

Long-term memory acts more like a hard drive, physically recording past experiences in the brain region known as the cerebral cortex. The cortex, or outer layer of the brain, houses a thicket of 10 billion vinelike nerve cells, which communicate by relaying chemical and electrical impulses. Every time we perceive something—a sight, a sound, an idea—a unique subset of these neurons gets activated. And they don't always return to their original state. Instead, they may strengthen their connections to one another, becoming more densely intertwined. Once that happens, anything that activates the network will bring back the original perception as a memory. "What we think of as memories are ultimately patterns of connection among nerve cells," says Dr. Barry

Gordon, head of the memory-disorders clinic at the Johns Hopkins School of Medicine. A newly encoded memory may involve thousands of neurons spanning the entire cortex. If it doesn't get used, it will quickly fade. But if we activate it repeatedly, the pattern of connection gets more and more deeply embedded in our tissue.

We can will things into long-term memory simply by rehearsing them. But the decision to store or discard a piece of information rarely involves any conscious thought. It's usually handled automatically by the hippocampus, a small, two-winged structure nestled deep in the center of the brain. Like the keyboard on your computer, the hippocampus serves as a kind of switching station. As neurons out in the cortex receive sensory information, they relay it to the hippocampus. If the hippocampus responds, the sensory neurons start forming a durable network. But without that act of consent, the experience vanishes forever.

The hippocampal verdict seems to hinge on two questions. First, does the information have any emotional significance? The name of a potential lover is more likely to get a rise out of the hippocampus than that of Warren Harding's Agriculture secretary. Like Saul Steinberg's cartoon map of America (showing the Midwest as a sliver between Manhattan and the West Coast), the brain constructs the world according to its own parochial interests. And it's more attuned to the sensational than the mundane. In a 1994 experiment, researchers at the University of California, Irvine, told volunteers alternate versions of a story, then quizzed them on the details. In one version, a boy and his mom pass a guard on their way to visit his father. In the other version, the boy is hit by a car. You can guess which one had more staying power.

The second question the hippocampus asks is whether the information entering the brain relates to things we already know. Unlike a computer, which stores related facts separately, the brain strives constantly to make associations. If you have already devoted a lot of neural circuitry to American political history, the name of Harding's Agriculture secretary may actually hold some interest. And if the hippocampus marks the name for storage, it will lodge easily among the related bits of information already linked together in the cortex. In short, we use the nets woven by past experience to capture new information. And because our backgrounds vary, we often retain very different aspects of similar experiences.

Sophie Calle, a French artist, illustrated the point nicely by removing Magritte's "The

Menaced Assassin" from its usual place at New York's Museum of Modern Art and asking museum staffers to describe the painting. One respondent (the janitor?) remembered only "men in dark suits" and some "dashes of red blood." Another (the conservator?) remembered little about the style or content of the painting but readily described the dimensions of the canvas, the condition of the paint and the quality of the frame. Still another respondent (the curator?) held forth on the painting's film noir atmosphere, describing how each figure in the eerie tableau helps convey a sense of mystery.

By storing only the information we're most likely to use, our brains make the world manageable. As Columbia University neuroscientist Eric Kandel puts it, "You want to keep the junk of everyday life out of the way so you can focus on what matters." Perfect retention may sound like a godsend, but when the hippocampus gets overly permissive, the results can be devastating. Neurologists sometimes encounter people with superhuman memories. These savants can recite colossal strings of facts, words and numbers. But most are incapable of abstract thought. Lacking a filter on their experience, they're powerless to make sense of it.

At the other end of the spectrum stands H.M., a Connecticut factory worker who made medical history in 1953. He was 27 at the time, and suffering from intractable epilepsy. In a desperate bid to stop his seizures, surgeons removed his hippocampus. The operation made his condition manageable without disrupting his existing memories. But H.M. lost the ability to form new ones. To this day, he can't tell you what he had for breakfast, let alone make a new acquaintance. "Nearly 40 years after his surgery," Boston University researchers wrote in 1993, "H.M. does not know his age or the current date [or] where he is living."

It doesn't take brain surgery to disrupt the hippocampus. Alzheimer's disease gradually destroys the organ, and the ability to form new memories (sidebar). Normal aging can cause subtle impairments, too. Autopsy studies suggest that our overall brain mass declines by 5 to 10 percent per decade during our 60s and 70s. And imaging tests show that both the hip-

---

Alzheimer's: Losing More Than Memory

Researchers have no good weapons against this devasting disease—but there is hope

CAR KEYS ARE MISPLACED, A NAME resists moving past the tip of the tongue. Often, we respond with humor: "I must be getting Alzheimer's." But the memory loss that age can bring differs greatly from the dementia of Alzheimer's. Slowly, fatally, Alzheimer's erodes memory, personality and self-awareness. As many as 4 million Americans have it—one in 10 people over 65 and half of those over 85.

It has no cure, and few effective treatments. But in the last decade scientists have started to understand the biochemistry behind Alzheimer's. Today at least 17 drugs are in development. "We don't have the penicillin for Alzheimer's yet," says Roger Rosenberg, director of the Alzheimer's Disease Center at the University of Texas Southwestern Medical Center. "But it's coming." And some of what researchers learn about how this illness rots memory might even help those folks who mislaid their keys.

Today's treatments only ease symptoms. One of Alzheimer's main effects is the destruction of brain cells that produce the neurotransmitter acetylcholine, a chemical essential to learning and memory. Neither of the drugs used most widely for Alzheimer's, Cognex and Aricept, slow the death of those cells. Instead, the drugs slow the deterioration by inhibiting the action of acetylcholinesterase, an enzyme that breaks acetylcholine down. "[The drugs] help make the best use of what you have left," says Rudy Tanzi, a neurogeneticist at Harvard. Yet the drugs have limitations: Cognex only works for a few patients and can cause liver problems. Aricept spares the liver, but its benefits are mod-est. At least three improved acetylcholinesterase inhibitors are on deck; the first could be out by fall.

Future treatments will have to attack the disease more directly. Scientists hope to control the physical changes in the brain that cause the dementia, such as plaques made of a protein called beta amyloid that gum up neurons. Amyloid is found throughout the body but has an abnormal form toxic to neurons in the brain. For reasons no one is sure of, an enzyme can divide a larger protein improperly, creating the dangerous amyloid beta. Some chemicals appear to block the cleaving enzyme; they may someday lead to new usable drugs.

The body's defense against plaques may make matters worse. The rogue form of amyloid beta triggers an immune response, leading to inflammation that cuts off nutrients and oxygen and further damages the Alzheimer's brain. Nonsteroidal anti-inflammatory drugs, such as aspirin and ibuprofen, may protect against Alzheimer's, and a 1997 study suggested the drugs also slowed the disease's progress. Other anti-inflammatories called cyclooxygenase (COX-2) inhibitors, developed to treat arthritis, are in clinical trials for use in Alzheimer's patients. And a new class of anti-inflammatories that targets the brain, without harming the stomach, liver and kidneys like current NSAIDS, could be only two years away.

The hormone estrogen might also help. Several studies have suggested that post-menopausal women on hormone replacement therapy (HRT) were less likely to get Alzheimer's. Pharmaceutical giant Wyeth-Ayerst is now test-ing HRT on 8,000 healthy women and will monitor them for Alzheimer's. In women who don't have dementia, the hormone seems to enhance memory, and it may prevent damage to cells in the brain. Alzheimer's experts would love to have a drug that acts like estrogen in the brain, but not in the breasts or uterus, where it may cause cancer. The current danger "is that people will go and self-medicate because of early positive reports," says Zaven Khachaturian, director of the Ronald and Nancy Reagan Research Institute of the Alzheimer's Association.

Other long-shot approaches could have even bigger payoffs. Last week three labs identified the gene responsible for the formation of the abnormal protein tau, the main component of tangled neurons in the Alzheimer's brain. Suppressing "apoptosis," the process by which the body kills its own cells, including neurons damaged by Alzheimer's, might work—if it doesn't spark tumors kept in check by apoptotic machinery. And a company called NeoTherapeutics is touting AIT-082, a chemical it says induces brain cells to reproduce and grow new neurons. Meanwhile, nonprescription remedies like ginkgo biloba or vitamin E might one day be shown to help Alzheimer's, as well as normal memory loss. We may always try to laugh off our fears of the disease, but as research continues, humor need no longer be the best medicine.

KAREN SPRINGEN and ADAM ROGERS
with THOMAS HAYDEN

pocampus and the frontal cortex become less active. As you would expect, young people generally outperform the elderly on tests that gauge encoding and retrieval ability.

Fortunately, the differences are minor. Experts now agree that unless you develop a particular condition, such as Alzheimer's or vascular disease, age alone won't ruin your memory. At worst, it will make you a little slower and less precise. "We continue to encode the general features of our experiences," says Schacter, "but we leave off more details." For example, Schacter has found that young adults are usually better than old folks at remembering the details of a picture. But the oldsters quickly catch up when coached to pay more attention. And not everyone needs coaching. Though *average* scores decline with age, some octogenarians remain sharper and quicker than college kids.

Whatever their age, people vary widely in recall ability. "Bill Clinton will probably always remember more names than you will," says Gordon. "Unless he has to testify." But that's not to say our abilities are completely fixed. Researchers have identified various influences that can keep the brain from working at full capacity. High blood pressure can impair mental function, even if it doesn't cause a stroke. One study found that over a 25-year period, men with hypertension lost twice as much cognitive ability as those with normal blood pressure. Too little sleep (or too many sleeping pills) can disrupt the formation of new memories. So can too much alcohol, or a dysfunctional thyroid gland. Other memory busters include depression, anxiety and a simple lack of stimulation—all of which keep us from paying full attention to our surroundings.

And then there's information overload. "You used to have time to reflect and think" Gordon observes. "Now you're just a conduit for a constant stream of information." It comes at us with terrifying speed—via fax, phone and e-mail, over scores of cable channels, even at the newsstand. And when information bombards us faster than we can assimilate it, we miss out on more than the surplus. As Michelle Arnove (remember her?) discovered, an overwhelmed mind has trouble absorbing anything.

The problem often boils down to stress. Besides leaving us sleepless, distractible and more likely to drink, chronic stress can directly affect our brain chemistry. Like a strong cup of coffee, a stressful experience can energize our brains in the short run. It triggers the release of adrenaline and other glucocorticoid hormones, which boost circulation and unleash the energy stored in our tissues as glucose. The stress response is nicely tailored to the environments we evolved in—where surprise encounters with hungry predators were more common than looming deadlines and gridlocked calendars. But this fight-or-flight mechanism causes

Can Supplements Boost Brain Power?

Enthusiasts have embraced a wide range of herbs, vitamins and hormones as mental elixirs. Unfortunately, few of them have been shown to sharpen recall in healthy people, and some have dangerous side effects.

Ginkgo Biloba: The most popular purported memory aid comes from the leaves of an ornamental tree. Ginkgo may help increase oxygen flow to the brain, while acting as an antioxidant. One preliminary study suggests it may help relieve mild dementia.

Vitamin E: This antioxidant helps prevent heart disease and boost immune function. Preliminary studies suggest it may also slow the progression of Alzheimer's. But no one has shown it can improve memory in healthy people.

DHEA: After the age of 30, the adrenal glands produce less and less of this hormone. Mice given DHEA supplements excel on learning tasks. It's not clear whether people do.

Aspirin: Regular use of nonsteroidal anti-inflammatories such as aspirin and ibuprofen may delay the onset of Alzheimer's. These drugs can cause gastrointestinal damage, but new versions may not.

Estrogen: Besides lowering the risk of Alzheimer's disease in postmenopausal women, estrogen helps support normal brain function. Studies suggest that estrogen-replacement therapy helps maintain both verbal and visual memory.

DHA: This omega-3 fatty acid, abundant in breast milk, is critical for babies' brain development. No one has shown that it enhances cognition later in life, but supplements are popular.

harm if it's turned on all the time. After about 30 minutes, says Stanford neuroscientist Robert Sapolsky, stress hormones start to knock out the molecules that transport glucose into the hippocampus—leaving the brain *low* on energy. And over longer periods, stress hormones can act like so much battery acid, severing connections among neurons and literally shrinking the hippocampus. "This atrophy is reversible if the stress is short-lived," says Bruce McEwen, a neuroscientist at Rockefeller University.

"But stress lasting months or years can kill hippocampal neurons."

What, then, are the best ways to protect your memory? Obviously, anyone concerned about staying sharp should make a point of sleeping enough and managing stress. And because the brain is at the mercy of the circulatory system, a heart-healthy lifestyle may have cognitive benefits as well. In a 1997 survey of older adults, researchers in Madrid found an association between high mental-test scores and high intake of fruits, vegetables and fiber. An earlier study, conducted at the University of Southern California, found that people in their 70s were less likely to slip mentally during a three-year period if they stayed physically active. Besides protecting our arteries, exercise may boost the body's production of brain-derived nerve growth factor (BDNF), a molecule that helps keep neurons strong.

What about all those seminars and supplements? Can they help, too? The techniques that memory coaches teach can be powerful, but there's nothing magical about them. They work mainly by inspiring us to pay attention, to repeat what's worth remembering and to link what we're trying to remember to things we already know. To remember a new name, says Green of Mount Sinai, listen intently. Then spell it to yourself and make a mental comment about it. Popping vitamins and herbs is easier, but it's no substitute. Preliminary studies suggest that nutritional supplements such as vitamin E and ginkgo biloba may help preserve brain function (chart). But no one has shown convincingly that over-the-counter remedies improve recall in healthy adults.

Estrogen is a different story. While the hormone may not supercharge your memory, it clearly supports brain function. Barbara Sherwin, codirector of the McGill University Menopause Clinic, revealed estrogen's importance two years ago, by testing verbal memory in young women before and after they underwent treatment for uterine tumors. The women's estrogen levels plummeted after 12 weeks of chemotherapy—as did their scores on tests of reading retention. But when half of the women added estrogen to their treatment regimen, their performance promptly rebounded. Researchers at the National Institute on Aging have since found that estrogen may affect visual as well as verbal memory (though not as strongly). And other studies suggest that women who take estrogen may lower their risk of Alzheimer's disease. The reasons are still unclear, but the hormone seems to fuel the development of hippocampal neurons and boost the production of acetylcholine, a chemical that helps brain cells communicate. Unfortunately estrogen has risks as well as benefits, especially for women predisposed to breast cancer. For now, few experts recommend it as a memory aid.

Estrogen is just one of many compounds that pharmaceutical companies are now eying as potential brain savers. "There are so many drugs under study that I have to believe one or more will make it," says James McGaugh, a neuroscientist at the University of California, Irvine. Most are being developed as treatments for Alzheimer's disease, but researchers foresee a day when people will treat even the minor lapses that come with age. "We want to optimize the opportunity to live a free and independent life," says Columbia's Kandel. "It would be nice to have a little red pill that would take care of it."

Kandel has formed a company called Memory Pharmaceuticals to exploit his seminal findings about memory. You'll recall that the brain stores information by strengthening the connections among stimulated neurons. To lock in a memory, the neurons inquestion actually sprout new branches, creating more avenues for the exchange of chemical signals. Kandel has identified a pair of genes—CREB1 and CREB2—that help regulate that process. CREB1 initiates the growth process, while CREB2 holds it in check. Together, they act as a kind of thermostat. Kandel hopes that by selectively inhibiting one gene or the other, we may be able to change the setting on that thermostat. Partially disabling CREB2 might help anyone retain things more easily, without becoming an indiscriminate sponge. And a drug that *activated* CREB2 (or hogtied CREB1) might help trauma victims avoid having painful experiences seared so vividly into their brains.

It's a thrilling enterprise, but fraught with possible pitfalls. New treatments create new expectations, and not just for the infirm. "Suppose the drug raises your score on a job test," says McGaugh. "Who gets hired? Does the other guy file suit? Can the employer fire you if you stop taking the drug?" And suppose parents start feeding the drug to their school-age kids. Others would have to take it just to keep up. Those worries may be vastly premature. Our memory systems have evolved over several million years. If a slight modification made them far more efficient, chances are it would have cropped up naturally by now. The fact is, "maximal memory" and "optimal memory" are not synonymous, says Cesare Mondadori, chief of research for nervous-system drugs at Hoechst Marion Roussel. As any savant can tell you, forgetting is as important as remembering. So be careful what you wish for.

With KAREN SPRINGEN *and*
T. TRENT GEGAX

The Age Boom

America discovers a new stage of life as many more people live much longer—and better. By Jack Rosenthal

When my father died at 67, leaving my mother alone in Portland, Ore., I thought almost automatically that she should come home with me to New York. Considering her heavy Lithuanian accent and how she shrank from dealing with authority, I thought she'd surely need help getting along. "Are you kidding?" she exclaimed. Managing her affairs became her work and her pride, and it soon occurred to me that this was the first time that she, traditional wife, had ever experienced autonomy. Every few days she would make her rounds to the bank, the doctor, the class in calligraphy. Then, in her personal brand of English, she would make her telephone rounds. She would complain that waiting for her pension check was "like sitting on pins and noodles" or entreat her granddaughter to stop spending money "like a drunken driver." Proudly, stubbornly, she managed on her own for 18 years. And even then, at 83, frustrated by strokes and angry at the very thought of a nursing home, she refused to eat. In days, she made herself die.

Reflecting on those last days, I realize that the striking thing was not her death but those 18 years of later life. For almost all that time, she had the health and the modest income to live on her own terms. She could travel if she chose, or send birthday checks to family members, or buy yet another pair of shoes. A woman who had been swept by the waves of two world wars from continent to continent to continent—who had experienced some of this century's worst aspects—came finally to typify one of its best. I began to understand what people around America are coming to understand: the transformation of old age. We are discovering the emergence of a new stage of life.

The transformation begins with longer life. Increased longevity is one of the striking developments of the century; it has grown more in the last 100 years than in the prior 5,000, since the Bronze Age. But it's easy to misconstrue. What's new is not the number of years people live; it's the number of people who live them. Science hasn't lengthened life, says Dr. Robert Butler, a pioneering authority on aging. It has enabled many more people to reach very old age. And at this moment in history, even to say "many more people" is an understatement. The baby boom generation is about to turn into an age boom.

Still, there's an even larger story rumbling here, and longevity and boomers tell only part of it. The enduring anguish of many elders lays continuing claim on our conscience. But as my mother's last 18 years attest, older adults are not only living longer; generally speaking, they're living better—in reasonably good health and with enough money to escape the anxiety and poverty long associated with aging.

Shakespeare perceived seven ages of man—mewling infant, whining schoolboy, sighing lover, quarrelsome soldier, bearded justice, spectacled wheezer and finally second childhood, "sans teeth, sans eyes, sans taste, sans everything." This special issue of the Magazine examines the emerging new state, a warm autumn that's already altering the climate of life for millions of older adults, for their children, indeed for all society.

Longer Life

In 1900, life expectancy at birth in America was 49. Today, it is 76, and people who have reached 55 can expect to live into their 80's. Improved nutrition and modern medical miracles sound like obvious explanations. But a noted demographer, Samuel Preston of the University of Pennsylvania, has just published a paper in which he contends that, at least until mid-century, the principal reason was neither. It as what he calls the "germ theory of disease" that generated personal health reforms like washing hands, protecting food from flies, isolating sick children, boiling bottles and milk and ventilating rooms.

Jack Rosenthal is the editor of The New York Times Magazine.

Since 1950, he argues likewise, the continuing longevity gains derive less from Big Medicine than from changes in personal behavior, like stopping smoking.

The rapid increase in longevity is now about to be magnified. The baby boom generation born between 1946 and 1964 has always bulged out—population peristalsis—like a pig in a python. Twice as many Americans were born in 1955 as in 1935. Between now and the year 2030, the proportion of people over 65 will almost double. In short, more old people. And there's a parallel fact now starting to reverberate around the world: fewer young people. An aging population inescapably results when younger couples bear fewer children—which is what they are doing almost everywhere.

The fertility news is particularly striking in developed countries. To maintain a stable population size, the necessary replacement rate is 2.1 children per couple. The United States figure is barely 2.0, and it has been below the replacement rate for 30 years. The figure in China is 1.8. Couples in Japan are typically having 1.5 children, in Germany 1.3 and in Italy and Spain, 1.2.

To some people, these are alarming portents of national decline and call for pronatalist policies. That smacks of coarse chauvinism. The challenge is not to dilute the number of older people by promoting more births. It is to improve the quality of life at all ages, and a good place to start is to conquer misconceptions about later life.

Better Health

"This," Gloria Steinem once said famously, "is what 40 looks like." And this, many older adults now say, is what 60, 70, and even 80 look like. Health and vitality are constantly improving, as a result of more exercise, better medicine and much better prevention. I can't imagine my late father in a sweatsuit, let alone on a Stairmaster, but when I look into the mirrored halls of a health-club gym on upper Broadway I see, among the intent young women in black leotards, white-haired men who are every bit as earnest, climbing, climbing, climbing.

Consider the glow that radiates from the faces on today's cover, or contemplate the standards maintained by people like Bob Cousy, Max Roach, Ruth Bernhard and others who speak out in the following pages.

That people are living healthier lives is evident from the work of Kenneth G. Manton and his colleagues at Duke's Center for Demographic Studies. The National Long-Term Care Survey they started in 1982 shows a steady decline in disability, a 15 percent drop in 12 years. Some of this progress derives from advances in medicine. For instance, estrogen supplements substantially relieve bone weakness in older women—and now seem effective also against other dis-

I go out and play 18 holes in the morning and then three sets in the afternoon.
Bob Cousy, 68

Sports Commentator

I still thrive on competition, and when I feel those competitive juices flowing, I've got to find an outlet. Of course, at 68, it's not going to be playing basketball. Basketball's not a sport you grow old with. Sure, I can manage a few from the free-throw line, but being in shape for basketball's something you lose three months after you retire. I stay in shape by doing as little as possible. I play mediocre golf and terrible tennis. My wife calls it my doubleheader days, when I go out and play 18 holes in the morning and then three sets in the afternoon. Now I'm working in broadcasting and schmoozing the corporates. I'm a commentator for the Celtics' away games. I like it because I'm controlling my own destiny. Everything I've done since I graduated from Holy Cross in 1950 has been sports-related, and it's all because I learned to throw a little ball into a hole. A playground director taught me how to play when I was 13. To me it'll always be child's game.

After 10 weeks of leg-extension exercises, the participants, some as old as 98, typically doubled the strength of the quadriceps, the major thigh muscle. For many, that meant they could walk. Consider what this single change—the ability among other things to go to the bathroom alone—means to the quality and dignity of their lives.

eases. But much of the progress may also derive from advances in perception.

When Clare Friedman, the mother of a New York lawyer, observed her 80th birthday, she said to her son, "You know, Steve, I'm not middle-aged anymore." It's no joke. Manton recalls survey research in which people over 50 are asked when old age begins. Typically, they, too, say "80." Traditionally, spirited older adults have been urged to act their age. But what age is that in this era of 80-year-old marathoners and 90-year-old ice skaters? As Manton says, "We no longer need to accept loss of physical function as an inevitable consequence of aging." To act younger is, in a very real sense, to be younger.

Stirring evidence of that comes from a 1994 research project in which high-resistance strength training was given to 100 frail nursing-home residents in Boston, median age 87 and some as old as 98. Dr. Maria Fiatarone of Tufts University and her fellow researchers found that after 10 weeks of leg-extension exercises, participants typically doubled the strength of the quadriceps, the major thigh muscle. For many, that meant they could walk, or walk without shuffling; the implications for reduced falls are obvious. Consider what this single change—enabling many, for instance, to go to the bathroom alone—means to the quality and dignity of their lives.

Just as old does not necessarily mean feeble, older does not necessarily mean sicker. Harry Moody, executive director of Hunter College's Brookdale Canter on Aging, makes a telling distinction between the "wellderly" and the "illderly." Yes, one of every three people over 65 needs some kind of hospital care in any given year. But only one in 20 needs nursing-home care at any given time. That is, 95 percent of people over 65 continue to live in the community.

Greater Security

The very words "poor" and "old" glide easily together, just as "poverty" and "age" have kept sad company through history. But suddenly that's changing. In the mid-1960's, when Medicare began, the poverty rate among elders was 29 percent, nearly three times the rate of the rest of the population. Now it is 11 percent, if anything a little below the rate for everyone else. That still leaves five million old people struggling below the poverty line, many of them women. And not many of the other 30 million elders are free of anxiety or free to indulge themselves in luxury. Yet most are, literally, socially secure, able to taste pleasures like travel and education that they may have denied themselves during decades of work. Indeed, many find this to be the time of their lives.

Elderhostel offers a striking illustration. This program, begun in 1975, combines inexpensive travel with courses in an array of subjects and cultures. It started as a summer program with 220 participants at six New Hampshire colleges. Last year, it enrolled 323,000 participants at sites in every state and in 70 foreign countries. Older Americans already exercise formidable electoral force, given how many of them vote. With the age boom bearing down, that influence is growing. As a result, minutemen like the investment banker Peter G. Peterson are sounding alarms about the impending explosion in Social Security and Medicare costs. Others regard such alarms as merely alarmist; either way a result is a spirited public debate, joined by Max Frankel in his column* and by the economist Paul Krugman in his appraisal of the future of Medicare and medical costs.**

Politicians respect the electoral power of the senior vote; why is the economic power of older adults not understood? Television networks and advertisers remain oddly blind to this market, says Vicki Thomas of Thomas & Partners, a Westport, Conn., firm specializing in the "mature market." One reason is probably the youth of copywriters and media buyers. Another is advertisers' desire to identify with imagery that is young, hip, cool. Yet she cites a stream of survey data showing that householders 45 and over buy half

*See page 30, *New York Times Magazine,* March 9, 1997.
**See page 58, *New York Times Magazine,* March 9, 1997.

of all new cars and trucks, that those 55 and over buy almost a third of the total and that people over 50 take 163 million trips a year and a third of all overseas packaged tours.

How much silver there is in this "silver market" is Jerry Della Femina's subject.*** It is also evident from Modern Maturity magazine, published by the American Association of Retired Persons. Its bimonthly circulation is more than 20 million; a full-page ad costs $244,000.

All this spending by older adults may not please everyone. Andrew Hacker, the Queens College political scientist, observes that the longer the parents live, the less they're likely to leave to the children—and the longer the wait. He reports spotting a bumper sticker to that effect, on a passing Winnebago: "I'm Spending My Kids' Inheritance!" Even so, the net effect of generational income transfers remains highly favorable to the next generation. For one thing, every dollar the public spends to support older adults is a dollar that their children won't be called on to spend. For another, older adults sooner or late engage in some pretty sizable income transfers of their own. As Hacker observes, the baby boomers' children may have to wait for their legacies, but their ultimate inheritances will constitute the largest income transfer to any generation ever.

Longer years, better health, comparative security: this new stage of life emerges more clearly every day. What's less clear is how older adults will spend it. The other stages of life are bounded by expectations and institutions. We start life in the institution called family. That's soon augmented for 15 or 20 years by school, tightly organized by age, subject and social webs. Then follows the still-more-structured world of work, for 40 or 50 years. And then—fanfare!—what? What institutions then give shape and meaning to everyday life?

Some people are satisfied, as my mother was, by managing their finances, by tending to family relationships and by prayer, worship and hobbies. Others, more restless, will invent new institutions, just as they did in Cleveland in the 1950's with Golden Age Clubs, or in the 1970's with Elderhostel. For the moment, the institutions that figure most heavily for older adults are precisely those that govern the other stages of life—family, school and work.

FAMILY: The focus on family often arises out of necessity. In a world of divorce and working parents, grandparents are raising 3.4 million children; six million families depend on grandparents for primary child care. And that's only one of the intensified relationships arising among the generations. Children have many more years to relate to their parents as adults, as equals, as friends—a

***See page 70, *New York Times Magazine,* March 9, 1997.

Sure, someone's probably saying: 'Oh, my God! What's this old bag doing in that suit?'

Ann Cole

Age: "Between 59 and Forest Lawn"
Swimsuit Designer

Everyone has certain features that they hate, and that doesn't change much as you get older—it just gets closer to the ground, as Gypsy Rose Lee once said. So you do just grin and bear it, unless you want to sit indoors and grump about it. I get a lot of women who come in and say, "You wouldn't wear that." And I say, "Why, yes I would." I haven't become more comfortable with my body. I've just taken an attitude that it's easier not to care or worry. Just do it. Sure, someone's probably saying: "Oh, my God! What's this old bag doing in that suit?" I've always been a great advocate of people not listening to their children. There used to be a lot of children who weren't happy unless their mother wore a skirted suit down to her knees. They'd say. "Oh, Mom, you can't wear that." I tried to get people over that in the 60's and 70's, because what do they know? You can't be worried about every bump and lump.

fact demonstrated firsthand by the Kotlowitz-to-Kotlowitz letters. ****

SCHOOL: Increasingly, many elders go back to school, to get the education they've always longed for, or to learn new skills—or for the sheer joy of learning. Nearly half a million people over 50 have gone back to school at the college level, giving a senior cast to junior colleges; adults over age 40 now account for about 15 percent of all college students. The 92d Street Y in New York has sponsored activities for seniors since 1874. Suddenly, it finds, many "New Age Seniors" want to do more than play cards or float in the pool. They are signing up by the score for classes on, for instance, Greece and Rome. At a senior center in Westport, Conn., older adults, far from being averse to technology, flock to computer classes and find satisfaction in managing their finances online and traversing the Internet.

****See page 46, *New York Times Magazine*, March 9, 1997.

WORK: American attitudes toward retirement have never been simple. The justifications include a humane belief that retirees have earned their rest; or a bottom-line argument that employers need cheaper workers; or a theoretical contention that a healthy economy needs to make room for younger workers. In any case, scholars find a notable trend toward early retirement, arguably in response to pension and Social Security incentives. Two out of three men on Social Security retire before age 65. One explanation is that they are likely to have spent their lives on a boring assembly line or in debilitating service jobs. Others, typically from more fulfilling professional work, retire gradually, continuing to work part time or to find engagement in serious volunteer effort. In Florida, many schools, hospitals and local governments have come to depend on elders who volunteer their skills and time.

FAMILY, SCHOOL, WORK—AND INSTITUTIONS yet to come: these are the framework for the evolving new stage of later life. But even if happy and healthy, it only precedes and does not replace the last of Shakespeare's age of mankind. One need not be 80 or 90 to understand that there comes a time to be tired, or sick, or caught up by the deeply rooted desire to reflect on the meaning of one's life. For many people, there comes a moment when the proud desire for independence turns into frank, mutual acknowledgment of dependence. As the Boston University sociologist Alan Wolfe wrote in The New Republic in 1995, "We owe [our elders] the courage to acknowledge their dependence on us. Only then will we be able, when we are like them, to ask for help."

That time will come, as it always has, for each of us—as children and then as parents. But it will come later. The new challenge is to explore the broad terrain of longer, fuller life with intelligence and respect. One such explorer, a woman named Florida Scott-Maxwell, reported her findings in "The Measure of My Days," a diary she began in her 80's. "Age puzzles me," she wrote, expressing sentiments that my mother personified. "I thought it was a quiet time. My 70's were interesting and fairly serene, but my 80's are passionate. I grow more intense as I age. To my surprise I burst out with hot conviction. . . . I must calm down."

Studies Suggest Older Minds Are Stronger Than Expected

DANIEL GOLEMAN

The conventional image of the aging brain is that people lose neurons the way balding men lose hair. Brain cells are supposed to start falling away around the age of 20, with everything downhill from there. Some people go bald, or senile, early. Some lucky and unusual ones keep their hair, or their wits, about them into their 90's and beyond.

Science has precious little good news about hair loss, but new findings on the death of brain cells suggest that minoxidil for the mind is unnecessary. Data from men and women who continue to flourish into their 80's and 90's show that in a healthy brain, any loss of brain cells is relatively modest and largely confined to specific areas, leaving others robust. In fact, about 1 of every 10 people continues to increase in mental abilities like vocabulary through those decades.

New imaging techniques, like the PET scan and magnetic resonance imaging, or M.R.I., have shown that the brain does gradually shrink in life's later decades, just not as much as had been thought. Furthermore, the shrinkage of a healthy brain does not seem to result in any great loss of mental ability.

"We used to think that you lost brain cells every day of your life everywhere in the brain," said Dr. Marilyn Albert, a psychologist at Massachusetts General Hospital in Boston. "That's just not so—you do have some loss with healthy aging, but not so dramatic, and in very selective brain areas."

The new imaging techniques have also enabled neuroscientists to discover a flaw in many earlier studies of the aging brain: they included findings from people in the early stages of Alzheimer's disease. Now, both by scanning the brain and by more carefully screening to measure cognitive function, most people with Alzheimer's are excluded from such studies.

Researchers measure brain shrinkage by keeping track of the fjord-like spaces that crease the wrinkled surface layer of the cerebral cortex, the topmost layer that is critical for thought. These tiny crevasses are called ventricles and sulci, and the amount of space in them gradually increases with age, reflecting a loss in the overall mass of the brain.

From age 20 to 70, the average brain loses about 10 percent of its mass, said Dr. Stanley Rapoport, chief of the neuroscience laboratory at the National Institute on Aging in Bethesda, Md.

But that loss "seems related only to subtle differences in cognitive abilities, Dr. Rapoport said. "We think the brain's integrity is maintained because the massive redundancy of interconnection among neurons means that even if you lose some, the brain can often compensate."

Compensation is precisely what studies of the "successful" elderly show. When neuroscientists weed out people with cognitive decline that is a sure sign of illness, the shrinkage is still there, but performance on mental tests is good. And what analyses of healthy old brains show is that old people may use different parts of the brain from young people to accomplish the same task. In some ways a healthy old brain is like a pitcher whose fastball has faded but who can still strike a batter out with other pitches.

Some of the data come from autopsies of 25 men and women from 71 to 95 years old who had volunteered to be part of a control group in a 16-year study of Alzheimer's disease. Dr. John Morris, a neurologist at Washington University in St. Louis who did the study, said the brains of the mentally alert group showed some of the tangles that, more than shrinkage, seem to be the main problem in Alzheimer's disease. But these tangles were in the hippocampus, a structure involved in memory, rather than the centrally important cerebral cortex.

Dr. Morris said his data, which will be published next month in the journal Neurology, suggest "there may be a pool of people who not only have no important cognitive declines, but no brain changes of consequence for mental function, even into their 80's and 90's." Changes in the hippocampus may only slow the rate of retrieval from memory, he said, but not diminish its accuracy.

Similar findings have been made by Dr. Brad Hyman of Massachusetts General Hospital. "We've found no appreciable neuronal loss in people from their 60's to 90's who had retained their mental clarity until they died," said Dr. Hyman, who studied two specific regions of the cortex. "The dire picture we've had of huge cell losses is wrong for a healthy person whose brain remains structurally intact into old age."

Apart from a reduction in the number of brain cells, another aspect of aging in the healthy brain seems to be a drop in the connections between them. Dr. Albert at Massachusetts General said her studies of brain tissue had uncovered specific structures deep in the brain that did show more neuronal loss, even with healthy aging. These include areas important for memory like the basal forebrain.

But, Dr. Albert said, "It's important for mental abilities that most of the neurons in the cortex are retained—they store information once you've learned it."

Some of the most intriguing evidence for the resourcefulness of the aging brain comes from PET scans of the brain at rest and while engaged in mental tasks. In one study using PET scans that compared people in their 20's with those 60 to 75, Dr. Cheryl L. Grady, a neuroscientist at the National Institute on Aging, found that the younger people were indeed quicker and more accurate in recognizing faces, and used more diverse areas of their brains during the task, than did the older people.

But in similar studies at the institute comparing people from 20 to 40 with those 55 and older, the older group was able to recognize the faces with about the same accuracy, though they needed more time to do so than the younger group, Dr. Rapoport said. Images of the brains of the older group showed less activity in visual areas of the brain, but more activity in the prefrontal cortex, suggesting increased mental effort.

Dr. Rapoport said that in older people there seemed to be some loss of circuits involved in visual memory. "So the brain has to recruit other circuits to get the task done," he said.

But recruit it does. The prefrontal cortex, which is the brain's executive area for intellectual activity, appears especially crucial in compensating for areas that no longer function so well in mental tasks.

All is not rosy. The number of people who do end up with Alzheimer's disease and fall into senility is still quite large.

"There are three very different groups among the elderly," said Dr. Guy McKhann, director of the Zanville and Krieger Mind Brain Institute at the Johns Hopkins Medical School. "One does remarkably well, aging very successfully into their 80's and 90's. The second group slides a bit, having some problems with memory and recall, but the problems are typically more aggravating than they are real."

Dr. McKhann said that the third group, which largely consists of people with Alzheimer's disease, suffers inexorable losses in mental function leading to senility. That group accounts for about 15 percent of those in their 70's and 30 percent to 40 percent of those in their 80's.

But for those without disease, the brain can withstand aging remarkably well. "Some people stay very good at intellectual tasks all their lives," said Dr. Judith Saxton, a neuropsychologist at the University of Pittsburgh Medical Center, who is analyzing data from a two-year follow-up of more than 700 men and women from 65 to 92.

"Their overall knowledge and vocabulary continues to grow as they age, even though their speed of retrieval slows a bit," Dr. Saxton added. "I'd guess up to 10 percent of people above 70 fall in this range." The question that interests many people who are headed toward 70, as well as some new and unconventional researchers, is how and why one ends up in the 10 percent. Is a person's neurological fate predetermined? Or is their something that can be done to stay healthy and mentally alert?

Cure or Care?

The Future of Medical Ethics

By Robert B. Mellert

Deciding when to live and when to die is an issue that has only recently begun to confront the human species. It is a difficult decision, and we are not yet skilled in making it. Today, doctors and patients are increasingly being forced to make these life and death—and *quality* of life and death—decisions amid rapid technological change, startling new medical discoveries, an aggressively litigious society, and sharply disagreeing medical ethicists.

Discussion on medical ethics now involves two competing theories about the nature of health care. One is the "curing" approach, based upon traditional medical ethical principles that go back as far as the Hippocratic oath. These principles have been neatly formulated into a list of standards that can be found in just about every textbook in medical ethics: the principle of life, the principle of beneficence, the principle of nonmaleficence, and the principle of justice.

The second approach, "caring," focuses on patient autonomy, proper "bedside manners" by health-care

Physicians and patients alike are facing a host of difficult questions, including the ethical dilemma of doctor-assisted suicide.

providers, preparation of living wills, and the hospice movement. The concerns represented by this approach have, of course, always been present in medical assistance, but their emergence as a primary focus of medicine is more recent.

The Curing Tradition

The "curing" approach to medical ethics argues that the role of medicine is to heal. This objective is in harmony with the person's right to life. To subordinate healing to some other function, such as caring, would violate the nature of medicine itself. Caring, of course, is important, but it must only be seen as subservient to the primary task of curing.

Traditional Western religious ethics can be used to support the curing

approach. The sanctity of human life is an important ideal in this morality. Because it is a gift from God, life must be sustained to the extent reasonably possible, and all ordinary measures must be taken to preserve it. This tradition holds that only God's authority can decide the time of death. Even if a dying patient is suffering, the job of the health professional must never include options such as assisted suicide, or even medication that would shorten life.

In the curing approach, physicians are the primary decision makers. What to do in order to preserve life is primarily a medical judgment. As professionals who are knowledgeable about the relevant medical procedures and who are best able to judge their efficacy, physicians can expect patients to trust them and accept their recommendations. The phy-

Originally appeared in the July/August 1997 issue of *The Futurist,* pp. 35-38. Used with permission from the World Future Society, 7910 Woodmont Avenue, Suite 450, Bethesda, MD 20814. Tel. 301/656-8274; fax 301/951-0394; http://www.wfs.org/wfs.

sician explains to the patient why specific procedures are recommended in the given circumstances, and then the patient consents. This model of the doctor-patient relationship is often called the paternalistic model.

An Emphasis on Caring

The second approach to medical ethics, "caring," is more utilitarian or situational. Jeremy Bentham, the nineteenth-century British philosopher, perhaps best expresses the utilitarian standard as "the maximization of pleasure and the minimization of pain." This standard is justified on the grounds that all men seek pleasure and avoid pain and that these constitute the fundamental values of all human existence.

In "caring" medicine, the role of the health-care professional is to minimize pain. Of course, pain or discomfort may sometimes be necessary in order to restore health and thus provide further opportunities for pleasure. But the moral judgment is always made by an analysis of probable outcomes. How much pain will be necessary to permit how much quality of life thereafter? The weighing of alternatives as to their anticipated consequences determines the ethically preferred procedure. It is the subsequent quality of life, not the intrinsic sanctity of life, that provides the basis for moral judgment.

The caring model of medical ethics differs from the curing model in that the *consequences* of the action determines its morality, rather than the action itself. Hence, the focus of ethics changes from the issue of right vs. wrong (saving the patient vs. not saving the patient) to that of doing good vs. avoiding harm (saving the patient vs. relieving the patient's suffering). Furthermore, what constitutes care for one person may not be the same as the care desired by another. What one practitioner does to provide care may be different from what another does. The caring

> "In the 'caring' approach, the physician becomes a medical consultant, not a health-care provider."

approach thus is far more subjective than the curing approach.

The role of the physician changes dramatically in the "caring" approach. Here, the physician becomes a medical consultant, not a health-care provider. The job is to lay out the options as clearly as possible, explaining to the patient possible procedures, the prognosis for each, probable discomforts and side effects, costs, and risks. Once informed, the patient is responsible for making the choice, and based upon that choice, the physician will proceed, even if that choice does not represent the one the physician would have personally preferred.

Unthinkable Scenarios?

Let me give two examples to illustrate the tension between the curing and caring approaches. The first one is familiar to most of us. Jack Kevorkian has become a household name because of his willingness to assist his terminal patients in committing suicide when their pain becomes too much of a burden and they choose death rather than prolonged suffering. Those who are unable to get the help of Kevorkian can try one of the do-it-yourself techniques described in Derek Humphry's best seller *Final Exit* (Penguin, 1991).

The media have portrayed Kevorkian as a lawbreaker, and at least one reviewer referred to Humphry's

book as "ghoulish." But they have forced us into thinking about the unthinkable scenario: I am the one who is terminally ill, facing pain and suffering for the rest of my life, and the cost of prolonging my life is wiping out the money I have saved for my children and grandchildren. What if, on the basis of a utilitarian morality, I conclude that the goal to maximize happiness (for my kin) and minimize pain (for myself) warrants my terminating my life? Then the most caring act that a doctor can offer me is to assist me in suicide. Can I turn to my physician or my nurse to help me carry out my decision, or would such help constitute a breech of their medical ethics?

Here is another scenario: Suppose I, a layman in the field of medicine, am the person to whom such an appeal is made by my mother, wife, or daughter. How shall I respond? "The outlook may be dim," I might say, adopting the curing approach, "but one must never give up hope. A remedy might be around the corner; stronger pain relief may be developed; you may go into remission and even recover." Or will my response be based upon the caring approach? Then, understanding my loved one's dilemma and respecting her autonomy, I may begin to explore with her the option of removing vital life-support mechanisms or even assisting in her suicide. In other words, will I do what is right by the law and by traditional morality, or will I do what is good according to a utilitarian or situational morality?

Today we must think about these two "unthinkable" scenarios. At some point in the future, some of us will almost certainly be called upon to render judgment regarding the dilemma. For a lot of people torn between "curing" and "caring," the judgments will not be made easily.

Doing the Right Thing

In a film entitled *Code Gray*, which I still use in my medical ethics classes, there is a scene in which an elderly woman in a nursing home is gently confronted by a nurse about a decision to restrain her from leaving the wheelchair and walking about on her own.

"If you fall, you may be seriously injured, and none of us would want that to happen," the nurse explains. But for the elderly woman, her ability to stand up and walk is the last vestige of freedom she enjoys in her old age. To be restrained and forced to call for assistance every time she wants to move about seems too high a price to pay for avoiding the risk of a fall. Nevertheless, the nurse urges her at least to try on the restraint and wear it for a while, and in the end the old woman can do nothing but acquiesce.

In this case, the curing model takes on a new dimension. The woman is not sick or injured, but she risks falling and breaking a bone, becoming disabled. So safety and the preservation of health dictate that she be protected from an accident, even if that means protecting her from herself. On the other hand, while one sympathizes with the old woman, one can also understand why caring for her as she would wish to be cared for would impose an unbearable burden upon the nursing facility. Such facilities are responsible for many elderly persons and are generally not staffed adequately to provide constant surveillance for each patient individually. The use of restraints, tranquilizers, and medications as a way of minimizing risk, therefore, ends up sacrificing caring for safety.

The ethical dilemma we confront here involves the choice between doing what is "right"—e.g., making the woman safe from injury—or doing what results in pleasure—e.g., allowing her the freedom to move about on her own. In choosing to keep the woman safe rather than free, the nursing home opted to do what was "right," even though it resulted in displeasure, rather than to do what was "wrong" (not safeguarding the woman from a fall),

even though this would have resulted in the woman's satisfaction.

Tension between Cure and Care

Many of us who are part of the health-care-delivery system, either as providers or as consumers—and we all eventually are consumers—have been troubled by the tension that is sometimes created between these two approaches. Why do we encounter this tension in contemporary society and how might we learn to deal with it?

"*Patients who seek a caring approach had better [be] prepared to insist upon their right to decide.*"

The conscientious physician sees death as a defeat, much as good teachers see their students' failure as their own failure. So physicians attempt to conquer injury and disease with whatever technological weapons are available to them, and there is always the possibility of a lawsuit to consider if they waver in seeking a cure. Malpractice insurance is so costly today that it behooves any physician to order every conceivable test and tube and to attach every available monitor in order to escape a legal challenge that begins with the question, "But why didn't you do 'X'?"

To protect themselves from aggressive medical intervention, consumers have also had to resort to legal instruments. The living will, or advance directive, is simply a formalized way to restore to consumers

some control over their medical situation. By signing such a document, legal in many states, consumers attempt to prevent aggressive procedures by physicians worried about aggressive lawyers representing aggressive district attorneys, patients, or their next of kin.

Nobody is permitted to trust anybody anymore, it seems, and this means that the health practitioner must always go for the cure, even at the expense of care. Consequently, patients who seek a caring approach had better come to the health-care provider or facility prepared to insist upon their right to decide. This is especially true when the cure may employ complicated medical technology that the patient may not be able to afford.

Patients' express desires are often disregarded. A recent study in the *Journal of the American Medical Association* reported that only about half of the terminally ill patients who had requested do-not-resuscitate orders actually had their wishes respected. Seventy percent of the patients surveyed were never asked their preferences at all.

Of course, not every serious illness creates a confrontation. Physician and patient are often of one mind, so there is no tension. Sometimes, patients are unable or unwilling to assume the responsibilities required of them by the caring model, and they surrender their autonomy to the physician. "You're the doctor. You do what you think best." But occasionally there is no meeting of the minds, and what the physician recommends is not what the patient chooses. Second and third opinions are sought, and patients are left struggling with the consequences of their autonomy at a time when they are least capable of the struggle.

Choices for the Future

The tension between curing and caring in medical ethics is likely to continue, raising some important new issues: What are the duties and rights of patients? What are the roles and responsibilities of providers?

Patients will have to learn enough about their medical condition to make necessary choices. This will not be an easy task because the world of medicine changes so rapidly. If the patient chooses to instruct the providers to do everything possible to attempt a cure, including the use of extraordinary or experimental procedures, does that choice become obligatory upon the providers? Does the patient—any patient—have a right to the best medical services available?

Other questions come to mind. If patient autonomy in medical decisions is to be treated as a right, does this imply a new entitlement to medical services? If the patient cannot finance these services, does the cost of this new entitlement get passed along, in one way or another, to the general public? Does anyone in the medical profession get to veto those procedures deemed too marginal or not cost-effective?

Additional concerns relate directly to physicians. What will become of their role if, for some patients, they attempt every possible procedure for a cure, and for other patients, they act to assist their suicide? Are these two roles professionally and psychologically compatible? Are physicians still professionals under these conditions, or do they become mere paid functionaries for their patients? What happens when their own professional or religious opinions are at odds with the choices of their patients?

In this new world of medicine, the physician will struggle with three alternatives: (1) do what the patient wants, (2) do what common practice requires in order to avoid malpractice suits, or (3) follow his or her own best professional judgment. The second option is the safest choice; the first is realistic only if there is written documentation, as with a living will; and the third is the most risky of all.

Looking for Answers

Ultimately, I as patient will have to place my confidence in my physician. But if I am going to be treated in the manner of my own choosing—either with predisposition toward effecting a cure or toward providing care—I must convey to the physician my attitude regarding a number of very fundamental philosophical questions: How do I view my life at this stage and under these conditions? What do I see as the continuing purpose of my existence? Under what conditions do I wish to exercise my right to maintain my life? Are there conditions in which I would not wish to continue? And what do I want my physician to do for me then?

A living will may answer some of these questions, but I am not so sure that it can convey all of the nuances. And I am not sure my physician will be willing to spend the time it takes to listen, especially if that physician is not my primary care provider, but someone to whom I have been referred and whom I do not know. Most significantly, when the time comes, I am not at all sure I will have the answers to those questions. I don't have them now, and I'm not optimistic that somehow they will be revealed to me in my hour of need.

Despite the pile of literature that keeps growing on this subject, medical ethics is troubled today, but it is not the fault of medical ethicists, or even of lawyers, physicians, hospitals, or nursing homes. And it is not the fault of patients. It is merely a reflection of the fact that we are all troubled today by the complexity of technology, by the innumerable options and choices, and by the larger questions about the purpose of being alive. Now, more than ever, we need the wisdom of a Socrates to remind us that, of all our obligations, the primary one is to "know thyself." Attaining that would go a long way toward resolving these dilemmas.

About the Author
Robert B. Mellert is a professor of philosophy and religious studies at Brookdale Community College, 765 Newman Springs Road, Lincroft, New Jersey 07738. He is the author of Seven Ethical Theories (Kendall-Hunt, 1996).

THE DEATHCARE BUSINESS

The Goliaths of the funeral industry are making lots of money off your grief

BY MIRIAM HORN

Father Henry Wasielewski doesn't look like a man who would get threatening phone calls in the middle of the night. An absent-minded, gray-haired little elf, padding about his small apartment in sweatpants and stocking feet—it is hard to imagine him being chased by sheriffs, exiled by his bishop, or warned by gloomy morticians that the next corpse they disposed of would be his. But unlikely as it may seem, this 68-year-old Catholic priest from Tempe, Ariz., has become serious trouble for the nation's morticians and coffin sellers and the new corporate kingpins of the death-care trade—the "lying thieves," as he calls them, "who prey upon the poor and bereaved."

Wasielewski is a connoisseur of the techniques many funeral directors use to take advantage of vulnerable people, from exorbitant markups to deceptive sales practices. But nothing before has distressed the priest as much as the latest twist in the charnel trade. Last September, the Catholic archdiocese of Los Angeles—the nation's largest, home to nearly 4 million Catholics—signed a deal with Stewart Enterprises, a Louisiana-based corporation. The church, worried about losing its market share of burials, agreed to allow Stewart to build mortuaries in its six biggest cemeteries—a valuable endorsement for a death-care provider. In return, the church will get an undisclosed percentage of the proceeds from each funeral Stewart performs at the cemeteries, money that will help Cardinal Roger

Mahony realize his dream of building a $100 million cathedral downtown. "Sinful," Wasielewski calls the deal. "Most Stewart homes charge thousands more than many other mortuaries for the same funeral." A director of the archdiocese's cemeteries responds that Stewart has agreed "to honor the cardinal's request to keep prices reasonable."

The L.A. agreement augurs a new economic reality for church-going Americans, as Stewart's competitors scramble to make similar arrangements with other dioceses and faiths. But its implications are broader still, reflecting a radical change in the way all of America takes care of its dead. Chains are coming to dominate the country's $25 billion funeral business. While there are a number of smaller chains, Service Corp. International (SCI), the Loewen Group, and Stewart ("the Big Three") own 15 percent of the country's 23,000 funeral homes, handle 1 in every 5 funerals, and have established a set of practices others feel pressured to emulate. The casket business is dominated by two companies, York and Batesville, which together handle two thirds of casket and urn sales; Batesville's parent company, Hillenbrand Inc., also owns Forethought, the largest "pre-need" insurance company. Even the Neptune Society, which scatters ashes at sea, is now owned by SCI.

Markups in the funeral industry have always been high. But in the past five years, funeral prices have risen three times faster than the cost of living. Knowing that mourners don't shop

around at their hour of need (a lack of price sensitivity the Loewen Group described in a report to the SEC as one of the "attractive industry fundamentals"), chains often raise prices soon after acquiring an established independent home, sometimes upping fees more than 100 percent. Caskets, which typically make up half a funeral's cost, can be marked up more than five times. Stewart's South Park Cemetery in Pearland, Texas, for instance, charges $3,495 for Batesville's Kensington Green casket, which wholesales for $675. At many mortuaries, two hours of hearse time, which cost about $25 to provide, are billed to the bereaved at $200 or more; flowers, grave vaults, monuments, thank-you cards—all are marked up 300 to 800 percent. With a cemetery plot and marker, the typical American funeral now costs $8,000 or more.

Mortuaries have refined the art of merchandising, a necessity at a time when more than 21 percent of Americans opt for cremation, up from about 4 percent in 1963. At a seminar sponsored by an industry newsletter, one speaker advised funeral directors "how to add $1,400 to each cremation call" by requiring an "identification viewing" of the loved one. "If the family has not opted for an expensive container, make sure you show them Mom's body in the cardboard box. Someone in the family is bound to say, 'Maybe we should get something nicer.'" Consolidators also profit by owning a number of funeral businesses in one place. Cemeteries and mortuaries owned by a chain feed one

From *U.S. News & World Report*, March 23, 1998, pp. 50-58. © 1998 by U.S. News & World Report. Reprinted by permission.

another bodies, and most economies achieved by "clustering"—sharing hearses, embalming facilities, and staff—are passed on to stockholders, not consumers.

The rewards of such strategies are great. Both Stewart and SCI, which is the largest funeral company in the world, had 1997 profit margins on operations of about 25 percent. Since going public in 1991, Stewart's stock price had, by last October, risen 426 percent. Stock analysts predict a still rosier future, as America enters the golden era of the death-care industry. After a century of declining mortality, an aging America will reverse that trend, pushing the present death rate of 8.7 per 1,000 to 13.6 per 1,000 in 2050. The Big Three already are snaring those futures: In 1997, SCI had $3.2 billion in prearranged funerals on the books. Young job hunters are taking note: Top funeral directors can make $100,000 or more a year. Mortuary-school enrollments are up 45 percent since 1990. The National Academy of Mortuary Sciences advertises on the Web (*www.drkloss.com*); the curious can click on an opening casket lid.

Friend to consumers. Wasielewski's ongoing battle with these death-care Goliaths might be utterly quixotic were it not for a relentlessness that can weary even his supporters. Using only an old computer, a few volunteers, and a copy machine at Kinko's, he surveys cities to find both price gougers and fair-priced funeral homes, then makes that information available to consumers by phone or on the Web: Someone in Houston, for instance, can call and learn which funeral home charges $1,495 for essentially the same service and casket that cost $9,910 at a chain-owned home. With his circle of "spies" in the business, the priest has documented such common mortuary practices as selling pricey caskets sealed to protect the loved one's body from the elements, containers that many mausoleum managers say in fact can liquefy the flesh and even explode—sometimes blowing the front right off the crypt. Every corner of his small apartment is stuffed with "evidence": spilling from battered, metal file cabinets, heaped on hard plastic chairs and his single bed. He shows a visitor a sheet of paper in an 80-cent plastic frame. When a widow mentioned that she'd prefer gifts to charity over flowers, the funeral home took the initiative to print the notice, "then charged the lady

> # In the past five years, funeral prices have risen three times faster than the cost of living.

$75 for paper and frame. She's not supposed to be paying attention, you see. She's supposed to be too grieved."

The priest's efforts reflect the belated maturing of a consumer movement first given life 35 years ago by the late Jessica Mitford's hilarious exposé of the funeral industry. *The American Way of Death.* The dogged old priest, whom Mitford in later life admired as "an avenging angel," has been the movement's most persistent crusader, but he is just one of many activists who devote themselves to educating consumers and developing affordable options for care of the dead. A national network of memorial societies now serve as buyers' cooperatives for a half-million members, finding low-priced mortuaries and sometimes negotiating rates for their members; their association, FAMSA (Funeral and Memorial Societies of America), lobbies Washington on consumers' behalf. A network of alternative suppliers has emerged, offering caskets and urns via catalog shopping and the Web. There is even a growing home-funeral movement that helps people bypass funeral directors entirely, teaching them to handle body preparation, paperwork, transport, and arrangements with a cemetery or a crematory themselves (box, "A Home Funeral for Her Husband").

Wasielewski's own crusade on behalf of funeral buyers began 20 years ago, when someone called to say that an old woman in his parish was on the street begging money to bury her husband. When he called on the widow, ill and alone in her small abode, she said the funeral would cost $995, for her an unimaginable sum. Wasielewski then called the mortician, who explained that

the woman had chosen a fancy casket. At the rosary that night, the priest decided to see for himself. "I thumped the casket, and called others up to do the same, and we realized it was the cheapest plywood box you could find." The next morning, he called the mortician and threatened to go to the state attorney general. "He instantly said he'd cut the price in half. I thought, 'If you can cut it just like that, you were ripping her off and knew you were.' "

The priest's concern turned to obsession a few years later when Jack Botimer, a local mortician dismayed at his peers' efforts to squeeze thousands of dollars extra from clients, slipped Wasielewski a list of wholesale casket prices. In the close fraternity of funeral directors, it was a rare betrayal. Botimer also confirmed a practice the priest had seen firsthand: morticians bribing clergy in exchange for a recommendation from the pulpit. Wasielewski, whose personal resources are so modest he frequently makes a meal of the free appetizers at local bars, had himself been offered gifts by a high-priced mortuary. With an *Arizona Republic* reporter, he found morticians boasting of the cases of Scotch and trips to Las Vegas they'd given priests who let them hand out advertising calendars in church. Remembering the mortuary calendar that hung on his own family's wall—and his later realization that they had used that funeral home for every burial and "every time they ripped us off"—Wasielewski would in his poor parishes from that day on cut the ads off the calendars, one by one.

Swing your partner. People who spend their lives around funeral homes—like Edward Chavez, a Phoenix casket distributor who sells his wares for a fraction of what most mortuaries charge—have observed funeral directors cultivating other useful friends. "They'll bring an ICU nurse a big old color TV at Christmas," says Chavez, "and in return, she'll call when a patient is about to die. They show up 10 minutes later and say, 'We've been called to pick up your husband,' and the family doesn't know any better, so they go along."

Wasielewski's criticisms of the clergy have brought him reprimands from his Catholic superiors, and not for the first time. As a young man, he once was expelled from seminary for recording commercial albums of square-dance calls. (Before becoming a priest, he worked as a square-dance caller and hosted a children's TV show.) His record deal was discovered by the seminary, despite a trick he contrived to look at his album covers secretly. "The record company would hide the stuff at night under a big rock at the edge of the seminary. In the morning, we'd do walking prayer; I'd just kind of pray on down toward the rock, slip the stuff under my cassock, and take a look."

When, in 1982, Wasielewski cofounded the Interfaith Funeral Information Committee and began publicizing mortuary prices, he again was called in by his superiors: "We've got a mortician complaining you lost him $70,000 last year." "Well," replied Wasielewski. "He overcharges more than $1,000 a funeral, and did 250 funerals, which means he's ripped our people off for a quarter-million dollars. If I only cost him $70,000, we've got $180,000 to go."

By 1985, his bishop had had enough. For the next six years, he effectively suspended the troublemaking priest, neither assigning him a parish nor allowing him to live in a rectory. Only in 1992, two years before retirement, did Wasielewski get a small rural parish near Phoenix called Queen Creek. He hadn't been there long when he wrote a letter to a local mortuary banning their "body delivery-men" (he refuses to call them funeral directors) from entering the church, "disrupting the congregation with their attempts to imitate Catholic genuflections, and passing out mortuary advertising and prepay-plan leaflets." Again, the mortician complained to the bishop, who ordered Wasielewski to write a letter of apology. He did write a letter—urging the mortuary to refund money to families he believed the mortuary had overcharged.

In the past decade, Wasielewski has focused on the chains that increasingly dominate the industry, and most recently on Stewart's "unholy" alliance with the church in L.A., one region where consolidators' impact has been greatest: The Big Three own 40 percent of all funeral homes and have in some cases bought cemeteries to which they direct bodies from those homes; Loewen, for instance, recently outbid SCI and purchased a stake in Rose Hills Memorial Park, the largest cemetery in North America. The corporations have expanded their dominion virtually unnoticed, since when they buy a home they typically keep the old name and even hire the previous owner, making it appear that the home

is still locally owned. (William Heiligbrodt, president and chief operating officer of SCI, said the company does not put the SCI name on homes it acquires "because we never have. It's in our best interest to do it that way.")

Megamarketing by the conglomerates—heavy on pre-need and packaged deals—has forced independents to change their own sales practices in self-defense. In L.A., for example, the archdiocese found its cemetery plots harder to sell. "We'd had successful penetration into the Catholic market until the chains came in, then our annual interments dropped from 10,000 to 8,000," says

> ## With a cemetery plot and marker, the typical American funeral now costs $8,000 or more.

James Tixier, a director of the archdiocese cemeteries. "Cemeteries are a big revenue generator for the diocese. We call ourselves a ministry, but we must straddle spiritual and temporal needs." Cardinal Mahony, Tixier says, decided to deal with Stewart only after getting a cold call at home from someone selling funeral services and a gravesite. "The cardinal figured we better get in the game and provide the same one-stop shopping offered by the competition."

Stewart's goal is to perform funerals for at least half those buried in archdiocese cemeteries. The church will advertise and provide the company's salesmen with parish lists, Tixier predicts, and stands to gain significantly. Not only will the church receive new income from its share of mortuary proceeds, but Stewart will steer Catholic bodies from its other mortuaries to the church's cemeteries. "To handle the volume,

we're building mausolea," says Tixier, "which can stack 16 caskets in the space of one grave."

McDeath. A similar defensive strategy is visible in Colma, a town near San Francisco that is the nation's largest necropolis, with 17 cemeteries and nearly 2 million graves. When SCI bought Woodlawn Cemetery and began bidding on others, the nearby independent cemeteries decided they had better turn up the heat. Cypress Lawn, for instance, a cemetery where people pay up to $18,000 for a crypt near the Hearsts and de Youngs, jettisoned its upper-crust exclusivity. "The arrival of McDeath," says manager Kenneth Varner, "forced us to create a marketing team to do cold calling and direct-mail sales."

Funeral directors have introduced other innovations in the selling of the American funeral. Consumers often complain that mortuary salesmen ambush them while they are visiting Mother's grave or "borrow" funeral registry books and solicit those who came to pay their respects. SCI counselors are advised to remember "the four S's: Serve the family, sell the family, solicit referrals, sell referrals." Wasielewski describes the industry's widespread use of the "third-unit, target-merchandising system," which capitalizes on the propensity of the bereaved to avoid the two cheapest caskets in the showroom: Homes generally display only midrange to expensive caskets, assuring a higher-end choice. Edward Chavez describes another technique: "For the Mexicans, they glue a $3 picture of the Blessed Mother inside the lid and charge hundreds more." People don't question such charges, says Wasielewski, because they are intimidated by the pseudo-religious atmosphere funeral homes contrive. "You don't sign the papers for a new car with Jesus staring down at you over the salesman's shoulder."

Industry defenders respond that business is business. People associated with death have always been unfairly shunned, they say, and deserve whatever compensation they can get for their gruesome work. Besides, customers should pay more for fancier locations and facilities. Heiligbrodt, for instance, SCI's COO, explains that the company's homes are consistently among the priciest in any market because, "It's like the difference between a Cadillac and a Ford." Asked to be more specific about what extra value a customer gets at an

OPTING OUT
A home funeral for her husband

On a winter's night in March 1981, Vermont housewife Lisa Carlson, mother of two young children, was in terrible straits: Her 31-year-old husband was dead, and funeral homes were asking impossibly high cremation fees. One home charged $750; another said she would have to pay $350 for paperwork, even though she had access to all that was needed; a death certificate and permits for transport and cremation. Finally, Carlson called a crematory herself. To her surprise, they said that to cremate her husband's body would cost only $85, and the coffin could be cardboard or homemade. Carlson bought a cheap box and a friend drove her in his pickup to the crematory. There, with a screwdriver from under the front seat, she pried the lid off the coffin to say goodbye. Only then did she realize what it had meant to her to stay with her husband's body and forgo the embalmer's magic. "When I opened the box, he was very white. If he'd been made to look alive, I would have bargained with God to wake him. To see a body that looked so dead made it easier to let go."

Moved by her experience, Carlson wrote *Caring for Your Own Dead,* a book that launched a home-funeral movement that has taken root around the country. Organizations like the Natural Death Care Project in California inform people of legal requirements, which are few: In most states, no undertaker is required. The groups teach people how to keep a body at home for a few days using ice, saltwater washes, and oils. Since most home funerals are for someone who also died at home, family members are accustomed to washing the body, NDCP Director Jerri Lyons says, and most don't mind the task.

Making it harder. Mourners who opt out of using funeral homes are sometimes bullied. Karen Leonard, head of Redwood Funeral Society in northern California, says the group's members are often refused access to crematoria or forced to pay an extra "nonfuneral-director charge." Jan Berman of Martha's Vineyard wanted a home funeral for her husband, she recently told National Public Radio. She had a burial permit, but when the hospice nurse saw her homemade casket, she called a funeral director and gave him the death certificate, making it impossible for Berman to proceed. (Though hospice and home-funeral movements share a common ethic, many hospices have funeral directors on their boards and do not support alternatives.) The funeral director told Berman, falsely, that it was illegal to bury a body without going through a funeral director and that there had to be a hearse, which alone would cost $1,900. When Berman called the state funeral board, the chairman, who owned 14 funeral homes, threatened to report her, though he wouldn't say to whom.

SCI home, he illustrates with a story about a company he once worked with that made screwdrivers: The same item, of first-rate steel, was 29 cents with a green handle, he says, but with a yellow handle, they sold it for $2.29. "The guy that bought the high-priced one associated the yellow handle with quality, and was satisfied." Funeral retailing, he says, is the same. "If I tried to sell a $1,400 funeral at one of our good properties, like Campbell funeral home on Madison Avenue in New York, nobody would come. Spending $10,000 makes some people feel better."

Here's the bill. Such arguments failed to convince Jessica Mitford, who took a parting shot at SCI's CEO, Robert Waltrip, on the eve of her death in 1996.

Having been repeatedly turned down by him for an interview, she made a last request that, given the fame she'd brought the company, he pay her $562.31 bill for the direct cremation she'd arranged through her buyers' cooperative. It was a huge savings, she noted, over what it would have cost had SCI handled her remains.

With her preference for bargain-priced cremation, Mitford was not, she well knew, the kind of customer the consolidators most desire. In fact, the death industry is increasingly targeting Catholics, Hispanics, African-Americans, and Asians precisely because these groups still hold to traditional rituals and have not participated in the great shift among white Protestants: toward cremation and

bodiless memorials, away from store-bought funeral services with an expensively embalmed body on view in an expensive casket. Twenty-one percent of whites now opt for what the industry scorns as "bake and shake," a figure predicted to double by 2010. Cremation rates among all races are higher still in regions where the population is mobile, says theologian Tom Long, author of a forthcoming history of the Christian funeral: 50 percent in Nevada, "where almost no one has a home church or cemetery," versus 3 percent in Alabama, "the rare part of America where people still have a sense that they're from somewhere." In San Francisco, says Varner, 80 percent of Anglos now opt for cremation.

The funeral industry has made some effort to recover the Anglo market. Pat Hatfield, a white-haired woman who runs the Colma Historical Society, talks eagerly about how modern and cheerful the town's 17 cemeteries have become, showing pictures of their "state of the art ovens" and monuments like the one marking Woodlawn's children's section, of Snow White and the seven dwarfs. They used to have angels, says Hatfield, an acrid whiff of crematory smoke wafting into her office on a passing breeze, but "angels are kind of down." To encourage a "lighter frame of mind," she says, several cemeteries now offer free get-acquainted buffet lunches on the grounds. Elsewhere, the business has taken a similar Disney-like turn: A funeral home in Florida organizes cruises to the Bahamas to help mourners bounce back; another offers drive-by viewing of the deceased behind glass. Still, the crowds that once thronged Colma on Memorial Day and Mother's Day have disappeared. Though Hispanic and Filipino visitors regularly come to place flowers and to picnic on the graves, Anglo visitors, say residents, are invariably tourists—or are headed to visit Fido at the pet cemetery on top of the hill.

A political battle now underway in Colma underscores just how important the ethnic market has become. This town of nearly 2 million dead souls and 1,100 live ones has for two years been arguing over a plan to build a $20 million casino near the Serbian cemetery. The developer charmed local voters with barbecues and birthday cakes and free bus trips to the wine country, and most approvals have been won. But opponents are still hoping to defeat the project with testimony by a master of feng shui—a Chinese technique for assessing the good or bad fortune yielded by arrangements of physical space. His warning of grim prospects, both for the card players and the buried ancestors, has alarmed cemetery owners. They covet Chinese customers, who compose a large part of the Bay Area market and since the 1949 revolution have made a practice of bringing ancestors' bones from the homeland to join them in the New World. Selling one grave, in this case, means selling to past as well as to future generations.

The other highly desirable market for death-care providers is among African-Americans, who often favor grand funerals. The big companies are also attracted by high mortality rates among young blacks. York, for instance, now sells a casket that can be drawn on with magic market. A salesman at the annual National Funeral Directors Association meeting told a reporter that York expects it to be "a big seller in the inner cities, for the teenage market."

The appeal of ethnic markets suggests that chain-church alliances are the wave of the future. In 1995, the National Baptist Convention—the association of black churches—agreed to endorse

> # One chain teaches the four S's: serve the family, sell the family, solicit referrals, sell referrals.

Loewen of British Columbia as its preferred death-care provider and to appoint two members of each congregation for training as funeral counselors. Introduced from the pulpit as the people to see for mortuary services, graves, and tombstones, the counselors received a 10 percent sales commission from Loewen, with the pastor getting an added 6 percent, the convention 5 percent. African-American undertakers—proprietors of one of the oldest black-owned businesses in America and traditional pillars of their communities—protested that the

convention had sold them out, to no avail. (The deal was terminated when convention leader Henry Lyons came under investigation for fraud and extortion, charges on which he was arrested in Florida last month.) Still, the *Funeral Service Insider Newsletter* predicts many more such partnerships: "Given the power that chain-church relations have to pull market share, independent Christian homes, with their long history of helping the poor, will be unable to compete . . . and will sell out to chains, who do not do charity funerals." For L.A.'s Catholic poor, Tixier says, the plot will be free; the Stewart funeral will not. Stewart Vice President Hughes Drumm says the company will consider charity cases on an individual basis.

Bad blood. As the stakes grow higher, the fights among funeral homes, discounters, and consumer activists grow meaner. In 1997, SCI filed a defamation suit against Darryl Roberts, former funeral-home company president and author of *Profits of Death: An Insider Exposes the Death Care Industry.* SCI claimed Roberts falsely quoted CEO Waltrip saying his goal was to make the company "the True Value Hardware of the funeral-service industry." In 1988, soon after Jack Botimer began helping Wasielewski dig up dirty trade secrets,

---

DON'T GET STIFFED
Using tips for a tough time

1. Plan ahead: Contact FAMSA (800-765-0107; *www.funerals.org/famsa*) for lists of low-cost mortuaries and reputable memorial societies. Father Wasielewski (602-253-6814; *www.xroads.com/funerals*) will send information on fair prices. (In most cities, he says, you can find a complete funeral, with metal casket, for under $2,200; cremation for under $550.) A good consumer guide is *The Affordable Funeral: Going in Style, Not in Debt,* by R. E. Markin (to order, call 757-427-0220). The American Association of Retired Persons (601 E St., NW, Washington, DC 20049) also offers a guide.

2. Don't prepay. Each year, more than 1 million people, most over 55, buy pre-need plans to cover future costs of services, casket, gravesite, and monument, believing they are a hedge against inflation and a relief for survivors. But problems are common: Plans are often

nonrefundable or nontransferable, meaning consumers can't switch mortuaries or change their minds. Hidden fees can mean survivors pay much more when the time comes. In the worst cases, the money disappears. In 1995, *Consumer's Digest* found $50 million had been stolen by unscrupulous funeral homes or lost in poor investments. Consumer advocates advise earmarking a certificate of deposit or life insurance policy, or opening a designated savings account jointly with a family member who has right of survivorship so funds are not taxed. Never sign over an insurance policy to the mortuary.

3. Take your time. Leave the body at the hospital or nursing home until you're ready. Phone funeral homes or have them fax you price lists; make decisions out of reach of the mortuary's "grief counselor" and divulge little about your financial means. You'll save

by not buying a casket or urn at the home. Consumer Casket USA (800-611-8778) and Direct Casket (800-732-2753) will ship to the mortuary within 24 hours. Funeral homes cannot refuse or charge to handle caskets bought elsewhere, or demand you be present for delivery.

4. Buy the minimum. Hold visitations at your house or church—this also frees you to use a lower-priced mortuary, even one far from home. Watch for hidden costs: Mortuaries often charge for use of common areas, like restrooms and parking lots. A cemetery may sell you a low-cost marker, then charge hundreds for placement and inspection.

5. Don't be bullied. If a funeral director tells you "the state requires . . . ," he must show you the law to prove it.—*M. H. with Warren Cohen in Chicago*

> # One mortuary organizes cruises to the Bahamas for mourners.

Botimer's mortuary burned down as a result of what investigators believe was arson. His funeral home was also hit with $47,000 in fines by the Arizona State Funeral Board, a board dominated, as in most states, by funeral directors. When Edward Chavez resisted pressure from morticians to quit selling caskets to Botimer, he wound up with sugar in his gas tank and late-night calls advising him he'd "better get one of his caskets ready" for himself. He often has received angry calls from customers demanding their money back: They arrived at the funeral home, they tell him, only to be shown a casket busted at its hinges and propped open by a two-by-four; Chavez had delivered damaged goods, the funeral director told them. Consumer Casket USA, a low-price national distributor, had problems with "funeral director vandalism" so often, says President James St. George, that the company now takes videos as the casket leaves the shop and requires truckers to sign for its condition on delivery. The Federal Trade Commission (FTC) receives regular complaints of boycotts: casket

factories refusing to sell to discounters or to mortuaries that won't sell out to the chains.

Despite lobbying efforts by consumer activists for more stringent government oversight, the FTC has been a weak conscience for the funeral business. Though in 1984 it issued a Funeral Rule, requiring homes to provide an itemized price list to customers without delay, only in recent years, an FTC spokeswoman says, has the commission sent out undercover buyers to find violators, who are usually penalized with no more than a few hours of "offender's education." The rule also works against consumers by permitting homes to charge a "nondeclinable fee" in addition to markups on specific merchandise and services. That means homes that do just a couple of funerals a month—as many do—stay in business by loading all overhead onto a few consumers.

The courts have been somewhat more active. In 1995, independent funeral-home owner Jeremiah O'Keefe sued Loewen for engaging in predatory trade practices. He accepted a $175 million settlement after a rural Mississippi jury awarded $500 million, having heard testimony by former Loewen employees confirming that they were ordered by the company to sharply raise prices at newly acquired homes or face dismissal. The settlement left Loewen open to a hostile takeover bid by SCI, but the company survived and the following year acquired $1 billion worth of new homes.

Wasielewski's latest obsession is the protective-sealer casket. For years, Wasielewski had heard from mausoleum

managers that these expensive coffins—sold by the millions with promises that the elements will be kept at bay—in fact often lead to the body's putrefaction. In the sealed environment, anaerobic bacteria devour soft tissues, producing gas that sometimes bursts the casket with a great spewing of goo. Danell Pepson of Uniontown, Pa., says she discovered the problem when her grandmother's remains began seeping out of a fancy copper casket, leaving a brown, foul-smelling tar in front of the mausoleum; not knowing what it was, Pepson had repeatedly scrubbed away the ooze. When her grandmother was finally disentombed, Pepson says the funeral director offered her a "disaster kit"—a kind of rubber suit to hold liquefied remains within the casket. Pepson eventually won $40,000 settlements both from the undertaker and from the York casket company, though it denied wrongdoing.

Now Wasielewski is busy thinking up new ways to draw attention to the oozing caskets. His latest brainstorm: laying out a dead pig in a sealer casket, along with a video camera to record the process of liquefaction. Meanwhile, his protests against the deal between Stewart and the archdiocese have not quieted. The priest still hopes that Catholic funerals might one day again conform to what he believes are church teachings: "A funeral is a sacred ritual that belongs in church. It should be as simple as the white pall that covers a Catholic casket, signifying every man's equality and humility in death." His battle in Los Angeles may be lost, but the avenger has not given up.

The Solace of Patterns

The strange attractors that define life's stages give shape even to grief

ROBERT M. SAPOLSKY

Robert M. Sapolsky is a MacArthur Fellow and a professor of biological sciences and neuroscience at Stanford University. His most recent book, Why Zebras Don't Get Ulcers: A Guide to Stress, Stress-Related Diseases, and Coping, *is published by W. H. Freeman and Company.*

A SHORT TIME AGO MY FATHER died, having spent far too many of his last years in pain and degeneration. Although I had expected his death and tried to prepare myself for it, when the time came it naturally turned out that you really can't prepare. A week afterward I found myself back at work, bludgeoned by emotions that swirled around a numb core of unreality—a feeling of disconnection from the events that had just taken place on the other side of the continent, of disbelief that it was really him frozen in that nightmare of stillness. The members of my laboratory were solicitous. One, a medical student, asked me how I was doing, and I replied, "Well, today it seems as if I must have imagined it all." "That makes sense," she said. "Don't forget about DABDA."

DABDA. In 1969 the psychiatrist Elisabeth Kübler-Ross published a landmark book, *On Death and Dying.* Drawing on her research with terminally ill people and their families, she described the process whereby people mourn the death of others and, when impending, of themselves. Most of us, she observed, go through a fairly well defined sequence of stages. First we deny the death is happening. Then we become angry at the unfairness of it

all. We pass through a stage of irrational bargaining, with the doctors, with God: *Just let this not be fatal and I will change my ways. Please, just wait until Christmas.* There follows a stage of depression and, if one is fortunate, the final chapter, serene acceptance. The sequence is not ironclad; individuals may skip certain stages, experience them out of order or regress to earlier ones. DABDA, moreover, is generally thought to give a better description of one's own preparation for dying than of one's mourning the demise of someone else. Nevertheless, there is a broadly recognized consistency in the overall pattern of mourning: denial, anger, bargaining, depression, acceptance. I was stuck at stage one, right on schedule.

Brevity is the soul of DABDA. A few years ago I saw that point brilliantly dramatized on television—on, of all programs, *The Simpsons.* It was the episode in which Homer, the father, accidentally eats a poisonous fish and is told he has twenty-four hours to live. There ensues a thirty-second sequence in which the cartoon character races through the death and dying stages, something like this: "No way! I'm not dying." He ponders a second, then grabs the doctor by the neck. "Why you little. . . ." He trembles in fear, then pleads, "Doc, get me outta this! I'll make it worth your while." Finally he composes himself and says, "Well, we all gotta go sometime." I thought it was hilarious. Homer substituted fear for depression and got it on the other side of anger. Even so, here was a cartoon suitable to be watched happily by children, and the writers had sneaked in a parody of Kübler-Ross.

But for sheer conciseness, of course, Homer Simpson's vignette has nothing on DABDA. That's why medical students, my laboratory colleague included, memorize the acronym along with hundreds of other mnemonic devices in preparation for their national board examinations. What strikes me now is the power of those letters to encapsulate human experience. My father, by dint of having been human, was unique; thus was my relationship to him, and thus must be my grieving. And yet I come up with something reducible to a medical school acronym. Poems, paintings, symphonies by the most creative artists who ever lived have been born out of mourning; yet, on some level, they all sprang from the pattern invoked by two pedestrian syllables of pseudo-English. We cry, we rage, we demand that the oceans' waves stop, that the planets halt their movements in the sky, all because the earth will no longer be graced by the one who sang lullabies as no one else could; yet that, too, is reducible to DABDA. Why should grief be so stereotypical?

SCIENTISTS WHO STUDY HUMAN thought and behavior have discerned many stereotyped, structured stages through which all of us move at various times. Some of the sequences are obvious, their logic a quick study. It is no surprise that infants learn to crawl before they take their first tentative steps, and only later learn to run. Other sequences are more subtle. Freudians claim that in normal development the child undergoes the invariant transition from a so-called oral stage to an anal stage to a genital stage, and they attribute various aspects of psychological dysfunction in the adult to an earlier failure to move successfully from one stage to the next.

Similarly, the Swiss psychologist Jean Piaget mapped stages of cognitive development. For example, he noted, there is a stage at which children begin to grasp the concept of object permanence: Before that developmental transition, a toy does not exist once it is removed from the child's sight. Afterward, the toy exists—and the child will look for it— even when it is no longer visible. Only at a reliably later stage do children begin to grasp concepts such as the conservation of volume—that two pitchers of different shapes can hold the same quantity of liquid. The same developmental patterns occur across numerous cultures, and so the sequence seems to describe the universal way that human beings learn to comprehend a cognitively complex world.

The American psychologist Lawrence Kohlberg mapped the stereotyped stages people undergo in developing morally. At one early stage of life, moral decisions are based on rules and on the motivation to avoid punishment: actions considered for their effects on oneself. Only at a later stage are decisions made on the basis of a respect for the community: actions considered for their effects on others. Later still, and far more rarely, some people develop a morality driven by a set of their own internalized standards, derived from a sense of what is right and what is wrong for all possible communities. The pattern is progressive: people who now act out of conscience invariably, at some earlier stage of life, believed that you don't do bad things because you might get caught.

The American psychoanalyst Erik Erikson discerned a sequence of psychosocial development, framing it as crises that a person resolves or fails to resolve at each stage. For infants, the issue is whether one attains a basic attitude of trust toward the world; for adolescents, it is identity versus identity confusion; for young adults, intimacy versus isolation; for adults, generativity versus stagnation; and for the aged, peaceful acceptance and integrity versus despair. Erikson's pioneering insight that one's later years represent a series of transitions that must be successfully negotiated is reflected in a quip by the geriatrician Walter M. Bortz II of Stanford University Medical School. Asked whether he was interested in curing aging, Bortz responded, "No, I'm not interested in arrested development."

MOST COMPLEX PATTERNS collapse into extinction. Only a few combinations beat the odds.

Those are some of the patterns we all are reported or theorized to have in common, across many settings and cultures. I think such conceptualizations are often legitimate, not just artificial structures that scientists impose on inchoate reality. Why should we share such patterning? It is certainly not for lack of alternatives. As living beings, we represent complex, organized systems—an eddy in the random entropy of the universe. When all the possibilities are taken into account, it is supremely unlikely for elements to assemble themselves into molecules, for molecules to form cells, for vast assemblages of cells to form us. How much more unlikely, it seems, that such complex organisms conform to such relatively simple patterns of behavior, of development, of thought.

ONE WAY OF COMING TO GRIPS with the properties of complex systems is through a field of mathematics devoted to the study of so-called cellular automata. The best way of explaining its style of analysis is by example. Imagine a long row of boxes—some black, some white—arranged to form some initial pattern, a starting stage. The row of boxes is to give rise to a second row, just below the first. The way that takes place in a cellular automaton is that each box in the first row is subjected to a set of reproduction rules. For example, one rule might stipulate that a black box in the first row gives rise to a black box immediately below it in the next row, only if exactly one of its two nearest neighbors is black. Other rules might apply to a black box flanked by two white boxes or two black boxes. Once the set of rules is applied to each box in the first row, a second row of black and white boxes is generated; then the rules are applied again to each box in the second row to generate a third row and so on.

Metaphorically, each row represents one generation, one tick of a clock. A properly programmed computer could track any possible combination of colored boxes, following any conceivable set of reproduction rules, down through the generations. In the vast majority of cases, somewhere down the line it would end up with a row of boxes all the same color. After that, the single color would repeat itself forever. In other words, the line would go extinct.

Return now to my earlier question: How can it be, in this entropic world, that we human beings share so many stable patterns—one nose; two eyes; a reliable lag time before we learn object permanence; happier adulthoods if we become confident about our identities as adolescents; a tendency to find it hard to believe in tragedy when it strikes? What keeps us from following an almost infinite number of alternative developmental paths? The studies of cellular automata provide a hint.

Not all complex patterns, it turns out, eventually collapse into extinction. A few combinations of starting states and reproduction rules beat the odds and settle down into mature stable patterns that continue down through the generations forever. In general, it is impossible to predict whether a given starting state will survive, let alone which pattern it will generate after, say, n generations. The only way to tell is to crank it through the computer and see. It has been shown, however, that a surprisingly small number of such mature patterns are possible.

A similar tendency in living systems has long been known to evolutionary biologists. They call it convergence. Among the staggering number of species on this planet, there are only a few handfuls of solutions to the problem of how to locomote, how to conserve fluids in a hot environment, how to store and mobilize energy. And among the staggering variety of humans, it may be a convergent feature of our complexity that there are a small number of ways in which we grow through life or mourn its inevitabilities.

IN AN ENTROPIC WORLD, WE CAN TAKE a common comfort from our common patterns, and there is often consolation in attributing such patterns to forces larger than ourselves. As an atheist, I have long taken an almost religious solace from a story by the Argentine minimalist Jorge Luis Borges. In his famous short story, *The Library of Babel*, Borges describes the world as a library filled with an unimaginably vast number of books, each with the same number of pages and the same number of letters on each page. The library contains a single copy of every possible book, every possible permutation of letters. People spend their lives sorting through this ocean of gibberish for the incalculably rare books whose random arrays of letters form something meaningful, searching above all else for the single book (which must exist) that explains everything. And of course, given the completeness of the library, in addition to that perfect book, there must also be one that convincingly disproves the conclusions put forth in it, and yet another book that refutes the malicious solipsisms of the second book, plus hundreds of thousands of books that differ from any of those three by a single letter or a comma.

The narrator writes in his old age, in an isolation brought about by the suicides of people who have been driven to despair by the futility of wandering through the library. In this parable of the search for meaning amid entropy, Borges concludes:

Those who judge [the library to be finite] postulate that in remote places the corridors and stairways and hexagons can conceivably come to an end—which is absurd. Those who imagine it to be without limit forget that the possible number of books does have such a limit. I venture to suggest this solution to the ancient problem: *The library is unlimited and cyclical.* If an eternal traveler were to cross it in any direction, after centuries he would see that the same volumes were repeated in the same disorder (which, thus repeated, would be an order: the Order). My solitude is gladdened by this elegant hope.

IT APPEARS THAT AMID THE ORDER with which we mature and decline, there is an order to our mourning. And my own recent solitude is glad-dened by that elegant hope, in at least two ways. One is inward-looking. This stereotypy, this ordering, brings the promise of solace in the predicted final stage: if one is fortunate, DABDA ends in A.

Another hope looks outward, to a world whose tragedies are inexorably delivered from its remotest corners to our nightly news. Look at the image of a survivor of some carnage and, knowing nothing of her language, culture, beliefs or circumstances, you can still recognize in the fixed action patterns of her facial muscles the unmistakable lineaments of grief. That instant recognition, the universal predictability of certain aspects of human beings, whether in a facial expression or in the stages of mourning, is an emblem of our kinship and an imperative of empathy.

genital warts, 192
germ theory of disease, 207
ginkgo biloba, memory and, 204
glial cells, 48
glutamate, 53
Goodman, Corey, 49, 51
gonorrhea, 192
goodness of fit, 129
Gordon, Barry, 202, 204
Gorski, Roger, 199–200
grammar, universal, 58–59
grandparents, 208–209
Green, Cynthia, 202–204
Greenough, William, 52, 67, 91
Greenspan, Stanley, 49, 51, 129–130
grief, death and, 222–224
growth, effect of poverty on children's, 134–135
growth cone, 50
guns, school violence and, 181–184

AE Article Review Form

We encourage you to photocopy and use this page as a tool to assess how the articles in **Annual Editions** expand on the information in your textbook. By reflecting on the articles you will gain enhanced text information. You can also access this useful form on a product's book support Web site at **http://www.dushkin.com/online/.**

NAME: _____ DATE: _____

TITLE AND NUMBER OF ARTICLE: _____

BRIEFLY STATE THE MAIN IDEA OF THIS ARTICLE: _____

LIST THREE IMPORTANT FACTS THAT THE AUTHOR USES TO SUPPORT THE MAIN IDEA:

WHAT INFORMATION OR IDEAS DISCUSSED IN THIS ARTICLE ARE ALSO DISCUSSED IN YOUR TEXTBOOK OR OTHER READINGS THAT YOU HAVE DONE? LIST THE TEXTBOOK CHAPTERS AND PAGE NUMBERS:

LIST ANY EXAMPLES OF BIAS OR FAULTY REASONING THAT YOU FOUND IN THE ARTICLE:

LIST ANY NEW TERMS/CONCEPTS THAT WERE DISCUSSED IN THE ARTICLE, AND WRITE A SHORT DEFINITION:

ANNUAL EDITIONS revisions depend on two major opinion sources: one is our Advisory Board, listed in the front of this volume, which works with us in scanning the thousands of articles published in the public press each year; the other is you—the person actually using the book. Please help us and the users of the next edition by completing the prepaid article rating form on this page and returning it to us. Thank you for your help!

ANNUAL EDITIONS: Human Development 99/00

ARTICLE RATING FORM

Here is an opportunity for you to have direct input into the next revision of this volume. We would like you to rate each of the 41 articles listed below, using the following scale:

1. **Excellent: should definitely be retained**
2. **Above average: should probably be retained**
3. **Below average: should probably be deleted**
4. **Poor: should definitely be deleted**

Your ratings will play a vital part in the next revision. So please mail this prepaid form to us just as soon as you complete it. Thanks for your help!

We Want Your Advice

RATING

ARTICLE

1. The Struggle to Decipher Human Genes
2. The World after Cloning
3. Nature's Clones
4. The Role of Lifestyle in Preventing Low Birth Weight
5. Behaviors of a Newborn Can Be Traced to the Fetus
6. Maternal Emotions May Influence Fetal Behaviors
7. Drug-Exposed Infants
8. Sperm under Siege
9. Fertile Minds
10. Temperament and the Reactions to Unfamiliarity
11. Baby Talk
12. Your Child's Brain
13. Defining the Trait That Makes Us Human
14. Parents Speak: Zero to Three's Findings from Research on Parents' Views of Early Childhood Development
15. The Genetics of Cognitive Abilities and Disabilities
16. Basing Teaching on Piaget's Constructivism
17. In Search of a Metatheory for Cognitive Development (or, Piaget Is Dead and I Don't Feel So Good Myself)
18. Bell, Book, and Scandal
19. The Death of Child Nature: Education in the Postmodern World

RATING

ARTICLE

20. Teaching Television to Empower Students
21. School Phobias Hold Many Children Back
22. Fathers' Time
23. Invincible Kids
24. Do Parents Really Matter? Kid Stuff
25. The Effects of Poverty on Children
26. TV Violence: Myth and Reality
27. The Biology of Soul Murder
28. The Cost of Children
29. Growing Up Goes On and On and On
30. Adolescence: Whose Hell Is It?
31. What Is a Bad Kid? Answers of Adolescents and Their Mothers in Three Cultures
32. Experts Scrambling on School Shootings
33. Brain Sex and the Language of Love
34. Who Stole Fertility?
35. Man's World, Woman's World? Brain Studies Point to Differences
36. Memory
37. The Age Boom
38. Studies Suggest Older Minds Are Stronger than Expected
39. Cure or Care? The Future of Medical Ethics
40. The DeathCare Business
41. The Solace of Patterns

(Continued on next page)

BUSINESS REPLY MAIL
FIRST-CLASS MAIL   PERMIT NO. 84   GUILFORD CT

POSTAGE WILL BE PAID BY ADDRESSEE

Dushkin/McGraw-Hill
Sluice Dock
Guilford, CT 06437-9989

NO POSTAGE
NECESSARY
IF MAILED
IN THE
UNITED STATES

ABOUT YOU

Name   Date

Are you a teacher? ☐ A student? ☐
Your school's name

Department

Address   City   State   Zip

School telephone #

YOUR COMMENTS ARE IMPORTANT TO US !

Please fill in the following information:
For which course did you use this book?

Did you use a text with this *ANNUAL EDITION*? ☐ yes ☐ no
What was the title of the text?

What are your general reactions to the *Annual Editions* concept?

Have you read any particular articles recently that you think should be included in the next edition?

Are there any articles you feel should be replaced in the next edition? Why?

Are there any World Wide Web sites you feel should be included in the next edition? Please annotate.

May we contact you for editorial input? ☐ yes ☐ no
May we quote your comments? ☐ yes ☐ no